MW00587962

PSALM 119

PSALM 119

AN EXPOSITION

Charles Bridges

THE BANNER OF TRUTH TRUST

THE BANNER OF TRUTH TRUST

3 *Murrayfield Road, Edinburgh* EH12 6EL
P.O. Box 652, *Carlisle, Pennsylvania* 17013

*

First published 1827
First Banner of Truth Trust edition 1974

ISBN 0 85151 176 7

*

Printed in Great Britain by
Billing & Sons Ltd,
Guildford and London

PREFACE.

A CONSIDERABLE portion of the Sacred Volume (as the Book of Psalms and Canticles in the Old Testament, and a large part of the several Epistles in the New Testament) is occupied with the interesting subject of Christian Experience; and exhibits its character, under different dispensations of religion, and diversified with an endless variety of circumstances, as ever essentially the same. As the same features of countenance and elevation of stature have always marked the human species in the midst of the creation of God; so an identity of feature and "measure of the stature of the fulness of Christ" has, in all ages, and under every shade of outward difference, distinguished the family of God," as the people that should dwell alone, and should not be reckoned among the nations." (Num. xxiii. 9.) This indeed was to have been expected. Human nature has undergone no change since the fall. In its unrenewed state it is still captivated in the same chains of sin; and, when renewed, it is under the influence of the same Spirit of grace. " That which is born of the flesh is flesh; and

that which is born of the Spirit is spirit." (John, iii. 6.)
The modern believer, therefore, when employed in tracing
the records of Patriarchal or Mosaical experience, will
mark in the infirmities of the ancient people of God a
picture of his own heart, " answering, as in water face
answereth to face" (Prov. xxvii. 19); and in comparing
their gracious exercises with his own, he will be ready to
acknowledge,—" All these worketh that one and the self-
same Spirit, dividing to every man severally as he will."
(1 Cor. xii. 11.)

In this view, it is the object of this work to exhibit an
Old Testament believer in a New Testament garb, as one
" walking in the same spirit, and in the same steps" with
ourselves ; and, in bringing his features of character to
the Evangelical standard, it is presumed, that the correspondence will be found to be complete. " Faith which
worketh by love" (Gal. v. 6)—the fundamental distinction of the Gospel—pervades the whole man ; with at
least *an implied* reference to the One way of access to God
(verses 41, 88, 132, 135), and a distinct regard alike to
the promises (verses 25, 32, 49, 74, 169, 170), and to the
precepts (verses 66, 166), of Divine revelation. Nor are
the workings of this principle delineated with less accuracy.
In all the variety of Christian feelings and holy conduct,
we observe its operations leading the soul into communion
with God, and moulding every part into a progressive conformity to his image. When we view the " man after
God's own heart," taking God for his portion (verse 57),
associating with his people (verses 63, 79), and feeding

upon his word (verses 47, 48, 97, 111); when we mark his
zeal for his Master's glory (verse 139); his devotedness
(verse 38) and self-denial (verse 62) in his Master's work ;
when we see him ever ready to confess his name (verses 45,
46, 115, 172), to bear his reproach (verses 23, 69, 87, 141),
and caring only to answer it by a more steady adherence to
his service (verses 51, 78, 157)—do we not in those lineaments of character recognise the picture of one, who in
after times could turn to the churches of Christ, and say
—" Wherefore, I beseech you, be ye followers of me ?" (1
Cor. iv. 16.) Or can we recollect the Psalmist's insight
into the extent and spirituality of the law of God (verse
96), and his continual conflict with indwelling sin (verses
113, 163), awakening in him the spirit of wrestling prayer
(verses 25, 28), and confidence in the God of his salvation
(verses 114, 176); and not be again forcibly reminded of
him, who has left upon record the corresponding history of
his own experience—" I was alive without the law once ;
but when the commandment came, sin revived, and I died.
We know that the law is spiritual ; but I am carnal, sold
under sin. O wretched man that I am ! who shall deliver
me from the body of this death ? I thank God, through
Jesus Christ our Lord!" (Rom. vii. 9, 14, 24, 25.) In
short, let his instancy in prayer (verses 145–149) and praise
(verse 164) be remembered ; his determined (verses 5, 36,
80) and persevering (verses 44, 102, 112) cultivation of
heart-religion (verses 30–32, 59, 60) and practical holiness (verses 106, 167, 168), his hungering and thirsting

after righteousness (verses 20, 40, 131, 174); his jealous
fear (verse 161) and watchful tenderness (verses 11, 37,
133) against sin, and regard for the honour of his God
(verse 39); his yearning compassion over his fellow-sinners
(verses 53, 136, 158); his spiritual taste (verses 103, 140);
his accurate discernment (verses 98–100, 104, 129, 130);
the " simplicity " of his dependence (verses 8, 10, 86, 116,
117), and the " godly sincerity" of his obedience (verses
104, 128); his peace of mind and stability of profession
(verse 165); his sanctified improvement of the cross (verses
67, 71, 75); his victory over the world (verses 14, 36, 72,
127, 162); his acknowledgment of the Lord's mercy (verses
64, 65, 68); his trials of faith and patience (verses 81–83,
107, 123); his heavenly liberty in the ways of God (verses
32, 45); his habitual living in his presence (verse 168), and
under the quickening (verses 50, 93)—restraining (verse
101)—directing (verses 9, 24, 30, 105)—and supporting
(verses 92, 143) influence of his word—let these holy
exercises be considered, either separately, or as forming
one admirable concentration of Christian excellence ; and
what do we desire more to complete the portrait of a finished
servant of God upon the Divine model? Is not this a
visible demonstration of the power of the word, " perfecting
the man of God, and furnishing him throughly unto all
good works ?" (2 Tim. iii. 16, 17.)

Having explained the Evangelical character of this
Psalm, we may notice its peculiar adaptation to Christian
experience. It may be considered as the journal of one,

who was deeply taught in the things of God, long practised in the life and walk of faith. It contains the anatomy of experimental religion, the interior lineaments of the family of God. It is given for the use of believers in all ages, as an excellent touchstone of vital godliness, a touchstone which appears especially needful in this day of profession ; not as warranting our confidence in the Saviour, or as constituting in any measure our ground of acceptance with God : but as exciting us to "give diligence to make our calling and election sure" (2 Pet. i. 10), and quicken our sluggish steps in the path of self-denying obedience. The Writer is free to confess, that his main design in the study of this Psalm was to furnish a correct standard of Evangelical sincerity for the habitual scrutiny of his own heart ; and if in the course of this Exposition, any suggestion should be thrown out, to call the attention of his fellow-Christians to this most important, but, alas ! too much neglected duty, he will have reason to "rejoice in the day of Christ, that he has not run in vain, neither laboured in vain."* Never let it be supposed, that a dili-

* 'I know of no part of the Holy Scriptures,'— remarks a profound divine —' where the nature and evidences of true and sincere godliness are so fully and largely insisted on and delineated as in the 119th Psalm. The Psalmist declares his design in the first verses of the Psalm, keeps his eye on it all along, and pursues it to the end. The excellence of holiness is represented as the immediate object of a spiritual taste and delight. God's law, that grand expression and emanation of the holiness of God's nature, and prescription of holiness to the creature — is all along represented as the great object of the love, the complacence, and the rejoicing of the gracious nature, which prizes God's commandments "above gold,

gent, prayerful, probing examination of the " chambers of
imagery," " gendereth unto bondage." Invariably will it
be found to establish the enjoyment of Scriptural assurance.
"*Hereby* we know that we are of the truth, and shall assure
our hearts before him." (1 John, iii. 19, with 18, 20, 21.)
As therefore the preceptive part of the Gospel thus becomes our guide in the happy path of filial obedience, our
beloved rule of duty, and the standard of our daily progress;
we shall learn in the use of it to depend more entirely upon
the Saviour, fresh energy will be thrown into our prayers;
and the promises of pardon and grace will be doubly precious to our souls.

These views of the Divine life cannot be found un-
friendly to the best happiness of mankind. The Psalm
opens with a most inviting picture of blessedness, and
describes throughout the feelings of one, encompassed indeed with trials superadded to the common lot of men,
but yet evidently in possession of a satisfying portion —
of a " joy, with which a stranger does not intermedle."
(Prov. xiv. 10.) Of those, therefore, who would affix the
stigma of melancholy to evangelical religion, we are constrained to remark, that they " understand neither what
they say, nor whereof they affirm." (1 Tim. i. 7.) The
children of Edom have never tasted the " clusters of
Canaan," and cannot therefore form any just estimate

yea, the finest gold:" and to which they are " sweeter than the
honey and the honeycomb."' EDWARDS *on Religious Affections,*
Part iii. Sect. iii. ' The ordinary and serious breathing of my soul '—
observes a deeply spiritual thinker —' is such as that of the Psalmist throughout the 119th Psalm.'—HALYBURTON'S *Life.*

of that goodly land. They that have spied the land bring a good report of it, and tell — " Surely it floweth with milk and honey, and this is the fruit of it." (Numb. xiii. 27.) " The work of righteousness is peace ; and the effect of righteousness, quietness and assurance for ever." (Isa. xxxii. 17.)

The structure of this Psalm is peculiar. It is divided into twenty-two parts, according to the number of the letters of the Hebrew Alphabet ; each part, and its several verses, beginning with the corresponding letter of the Alphabet.* The whole Psalm is in the form of an ejaculatory address, with the exception of the first three verses, which may almost be considered as a preface to the whole, and one other verse in the course of it, where the man of God rebukes the ungodly from his presence, as if intruding into his " hiding-place," and interrupting his communion with God. (Verse 115, with 113, 114.) It is not always easy to trace the connexion between the several verses ; at least not beyond the several divisions of the Psalm. Probably nothing more was intended, than the record of the exercises of his own heart at different periods, and under different circumstances. If, however, they are not links on the same chain, in continuous and unbroken dependence ; they may at least be considered as pearls upon one string, of equal, though independent, value. The prominent characteristic

---

* 'Intelligimus ideo per literas Hebræorum, Psalmum hunc esse digestum, ut homo noster, tanquam parvulus, et ab infantiâ per literarum elementa formatus, quibus ætas puerilis assuevit, usque ad maturitatem virtutis exerceat.'—AMBROSE.

of the Psalm is a love for the word of God, which is brought
before us under no less than ten different names,* referring
to some latent and distinguishing properties of the Divine
word, whose manifold excellencies and perfections are thus
illustrated with much elegant variety of diction.† In many
instances, however the several terms appear to have been
varied, to adapt themselves to the metre ; while, perhaps,
at other times they may be promiscuously used for the
whole revelation of God,‡ that the view of its inexhaustible fulness might thus conciliate a more attentive regard
to its authority ; and might add fresh strength to the obligation to read, believe, love, and live in it.

If the Writer may be permitted to suggest the method,
in which this Exposition may be best studied to advantage,
he would beg to refer to the advice of the excellent Philip
Henry to his children—that they should ' take a verse of
Psalm cxix. every morning to meditate upon, and so go
over the Psalm twice in a year :' and ' *that*'—said he —
' will bring you to be in love with all the rest of the Scrip-

* Such as way, law, judgments, words, statutes, commandments,
precepts, testimonies, righteousness, truth.
† Rev. T. H. HORNE's Introduction to Scripture, vol. ii. 536.
‡ As a proof of the promiscuous and extended application of
those terms, whose definite sense is restricted to particular parts
of revelation — we may mark the use of the word "law" applied by
our Saviour to quotations from the book of Psalms. Comp. John,
xv. 25; with Ps. xxxv. 16 ; lxix. 4; also John, x. 34; with Ps.
lxxxii. 6. ' Under this word—"law"—Calvin observes —'there is
no doubt but that David comprehended the sum of all the doctrine
which God gave to his church.' Sermons on Ps. cxix. verse 153.
Comp. Ps. xix. 7, margin.

ture.'* The Writer does not presume to suppose, that this superficial sketch will supply food for meditation year after year. Yet he ventures to hope that it may have its use, in directing the attention from time to time to a most precious portion of Holy Writ; which however unfruitful it may have proved to the undiscerning mind, will be found by the serious and intelligent reader to be "profitable for doctrine, for reproof, for correction, for instruction in righteousness."†

* P. HENRY's Life, WILLIAMS's Edition, p. 247. In conformity with this rule, we find his godly daughter writing thus in her diary: —1687-8, 'March 9, Friday morning. I have been of late taking some pains to learn by heart Ps. cxix., and have made some progress therein.' Extracted from Mrs. SAVAGE's MSS. in P. HENRY's Life—Ditto. As an illustration of the view given by this excellent man of the importance of this Psalm, an Index is added to this work of the several matters more or less touched upon; to which, as well as to the texts referred to throughout the work, the reader's attention is invited.

† 2 Tim. iii. 16. Luther professed that he prized this Psalm so highly, that he would not take the whole world in exchange for one leaf of it. Bishop Cowper sweetly calls it—' a holy Alphabet —so plain that children may understand it—so rich and instructive, that the wisest and most experienced may every day learn something from it.' Added to this and other testimonies before given, we give the remarks of a deeply experimental and solid divine :—' I am now'—writes the Rev. H. Venn to one of his correspondents—' upon the point of expounding the 119th Psalm, which I never did go through; yet I know not any part of Scripture much more profit-able. In that Psalm the whole inner man is delineated, and the several changing frames of our poor hearts, and the several blessed motions and inspirations of the Holy Spirit are touched in a very affecting manner. This is the Psalm I have often had recourse to, when I could find no spirit of prayer in my own heart, and at length the fire was kindled, and I could pray. What has been your expe-

The composition of this work has been diversified with
as much variety as the nature of the subject would allow.
The descriptive character of the book will be found to be
interspersed with matter of discussion, personal address,
hints for self-inquiry, and occasional supplication, with the
earnest endeavour to cast the mind into that meditative,
self-scrutinizing, devotional frame, in which the new creature is strengthened, and increases, and goes on to perfection. Such, however, as the work is, the Writer would
commend it to the gracious consideration of the great
Head of the Church ; imploring pardon for what in it may
be his own, and a blessing on what may be traced to a
purer source : and in giving both the pardon and the
blessing, may His holy name be abundantly glorified!*

rience regarding this extraordinary Psalm? I know you do not
read the Scriptures idly, and without self-application. Have you
not found it pleasant and nourishing to your soul, and fastening
upon your mind?'—(Life and Correspondence, p. 410.) Identical
with this representation was the use and blessing which H. Martyn
found in this Psalm:—' Found some devotion in learning some of
119th Psalm.—In the evening grew better by reading Psalm 119,
which generally brings me into a spiritual frame of mind.—My
mind was beginning to sink into discontent at my unprofitableness ; but by reading some of Psalm 119, and prayer, I recovered.'
Again in a fretful frame—' It was not till I learnt some of Psalm
119 that I could return to a proper spirit.' Again—' The 119th Psalm
was very solemnizing.'—See his interesting Journals, vol. i. pp. 75,
114, 118, 175, 193, 194.

    * ' Domine Deus, quæcunque dixi de tuo, agnoscant et tui. Siqua
de meo, et tu ignosce et tui.'—August. Lib. 15, de Trin.

Old Newton Vicarage,
July 20th, 1827.

PREFACE TO THE SIXTEENTH EDITION.

THE Writer gratefully acknowledges the kind indulgence, with which his work has been received by the Church of Christ. Oh! may his God and Saviour have all the glory, while he is humbled in thankfulness for the high privilege of leading his fellow-sinners into the " ways of pleasantness and peace," and ministering to the spiritual blessing of the family of God!

He has carefully revised the work, and trusts that he has been enabled to give increased perspicuity to the style, and a deeper moulding of evangelical statement to the matter. He desired, that every page should be lighted up with the beam of the " Sun of Righteousness," who is the glory of the Revelation of God — the Christian's " All in all." He has endeavoured to illustrate true religion, as the work of the Divine Spirit, grounded on the knowledge of Christ, advancing in communion with Him, and completed in the enjoyment of Him, and of the Father by Him. He has also aimed to elevate the standard of Christian privilege, as flowing immediately from Him : by giving such a Scriptural statement of the doctrine of assurance, as may quicken the slothful to greater diligence in their holy profession, and at the same time encourage the weak and fearful to a clearer apprehension of their present salvation.

The work has been recently translated into German under the kind patronage of her Majesty the Queen Dowager. The Writer requests the prayers of his Readers, that this new channel of usefulness may be abundantly blessed for the grand object of extending the influence of vital religion throughout the churches.

Old Newton Vicarage, October 12, 1842.

PREFACE TO THE TWENTY-SECOND EDITION.

THIS work—once more revised—is now stereotyped, in order to reduce the price, and to open for it a wider circulation. The Writer again commends it to the blessing of God, desiring only that fruit may abound for His glory, and for the edifying of His Church.

Hinton Martell Rectory,
June 4th, 1857.

EXPOSITION OF PSALM CXIX.

PART I.

1. *Blessed are the undefiled in the way, who walk in the law of the Lord.*

THIS most interesting and instructive Psalm, like the Psalter itself, " opens with a Beatitude for our comfort and encouragement, directing us immediately to that happiness, which all mankind in different ways are seeking and inquiring after. All would secure themselves from the incursions of misery ; but all do not consider that misery is the offspring of sin, from which therefore it is necessary to be delivered and preserved, in order to become happy or '*blessed.*'"*

The *undefiled* character described in this verse marks, in an evangelical sense, " an Israelite indeed, in whom is no guile" (John, i. 47. Comp. Acts, xxiv. 16), not one who is without sin, but one who in the sincerity of his heart can say, " That which I do, I allow not." (Rom. vii. 15.) As his *way* is, so is his " *walk*"— " *in the law of the Lord.*" He is " strengthened in the Lord, and he walks up and down in his name" (Zech. x. 12) ; his " ears hearing a

---

* Bishop Horne on Ps. i. 1.

word behind him, saying, This is the way,—walk ye in
it"—when he is "turning to the right hand or to the left."
(Isa. xxx. 21.) And if the pardon of sin, imputation of
righteousness (Ps. xxxii. 1, 2, with Rom. iv. 6–8), the communion of saints, and a sense of acceptance with God
(1 John, i. 7); if protection in providence and grace
(2 Chron. xvi. 9. Job, i. 8, 10) ; and—finally and for
ever, the beatific vision (Matt. v. 8), are the sealed privileges of his upright people, then there can be no doubt,
that "*blessed are the undefiled in the way.*" And if temporal prosperity (Josh. i. 7, 8. 1 Tim. iv. 8. 2 Chron.
xvii. 4, 5), spiritual renovation and fruitfulness (Ps. i. 2,
3), increasing illumination (John, vii. 17), intercourse with
the Saviour (Ib. xiv. 23 ; xv. 14, 15), peace within (Verse
165. Gal. vi. 16. Isa. xxxii. 17), and—throughout eternity—a right to the tree of life (Rev. xxii. 14), are privileges of incalculable value ; then surely "*the walk in the
law of the Lord*" is "the path of pleasantness and peace."
"Truly"—indeed may we say—"God is good to Israel,
even to such as are of a clean heart." (Ps. lxxiii. 1.)

But let each of us ask—What is the "*way*" of my
heart with God? Is it always an "*undefiled way?*" Is
"iniquity" never "regarded in the heart?" Is all that
God hates habitually lamented, abhorred, forsaken? "Search
me, O God, and know my heart : try me, and know my
thoughts ; and see if there be any wicked way in me, and
lead me in the way everlasting." (Ps. cxxxix. 23, 24.)

Again—What is my "*walk?*" Is it from the living
principle of union with Christ? This is the direct—the
only source of spiritual life. We are first quickened in
him. Then we walk in him and after him. Oh! that
this my walk may be steady, consistent, advancing! Oh!
that I may be ever listening to my Father's voice—"I am
the Almighty God ; walk before me, and be thou perfect!"
(Gen. xvii. 1.)

Is there not enough of defilement in the most " *undefiled way*," and enough of inconsistency in the most consistent " *walk*" to endear to us the gracious declaration of the gospel—" If any man sin, we have an advocate with the Father, Jesus Christ the Righteous?" (1 John, ii. 1.)

2. *Blessed are they that keep his testimonies, and that seek him with the whole heart.*

The " testimony," in the singular number, usually denotes the whole canon of the inspired writings—the revelation of the will of God to mankind—the standard of their faith. (Comp. Isa. viii. 20.) " *Testimonies*" appear, chiefly, to mark the preceptive part of Scripture (Verse 138); that part, in which this man of God always found his spiritual delight and perfect freedom. Mark his language : " *I have rejoiced in the way of thy testimonies, as much as in all riches. Thy testimonies have I taken as an heritage for ever ; for they are the rejoicing of my heart.*" (Verses 14, 111.) Not, however, that this blessedness belongs to the mere outward act of obedience ;* but rather to that practical habit of mind, which seeks to know the will of God in order to " *keep*" it. This habit is under the influence of the promise of God, " I will put my Spirit within you, and cause you to walk in my statutes, and ye shall keep my judgments, and do them." (Ezek. xxxvi. 27.) And in thus " *keeping the testimonies of God*," the believer maintains the character of one, that " *seeks him with the whole heart.*"

Oh! how many seek, and seek in vain, for no other reason, than because they do *not* " *seek him with the whole heart!*" The worldling's " heart is divided ; now shall he be found faulty." (Hos. x. 2.) The professor " with his mouth shows much love ; but his heart goeth after his

* " Treasure up his testimonies."—Bp. HORSLEY.

covetousness." (Ezek. xxxiii. 31.) The backslider "*hath not turned unto me with his whole heart*, but feignedly, saith the Lord." (Jer. iii. 10.) The faithful, upright believer alone brings his heart, *his whole heart*, to the Lord : " When thou saidst, Seek ye my face, my heart said unto thee, Thy face, Lord, will I seek." (Ps. xxvii. 8.) For he only has found an object, that attracts and fills his whole heart, and, if he had a thousand hearts, would attract and fill them all. He has found his way to God by faith in Jesus. In that way he continues to *seek*. His whole heart is engaged to know and love more and more. Here alone the blessing is enjoyed, and the promise made good : " Ye shall seek me, and find me, when *ye shall search for me with all your heart*." (Jer. xxix. 13.)

But let me not shrink from the question, Do I "*keep his testimonies*" from constraint, or from love ? Surely when I consider my own natural aversion and enmity to the law of God, and the danger of self-deception in the external service of the Lord, I have much need to pray—"*Incline my heart to thy testimonies. Give me understanding—save me, and I shall keep thy testimonies*." (Verses 36, 125, 146.) And if they are blessed, who seek the Lord *with their whole heart*, how am I seeking him ? Alas ! with how much distraction ! with how little heart-work ! Oh ! let me " seek his strength" in order to " seek his face." (Ps. cv. 4.)

Lord ! search—teach—incline—uphold me. Help me to plead thy gracious promise—" I will give them an heart to know me, that I am the Lord ; and they shall be my people, and I will be their God ; *for they shall return unto me with their whole heart*." (Jer. xxiv. 7.)

3. *They also do no iniquity; they walk in his ways.*

This was not their character from their birth. Once they were *doing* nothing but *iniquity*. It was without mix-

ture, without cessation—from the fountain-head.* Now it
is written of them—" *they do no iniquity.*" Once they
walked, even as others (Eph. ii. 2, 3. Col. i. 21), in the
way of their own hearts—" enemies to God by wicked
works." Now " *they walk in his ways.*" They are " new
creatures in Christ ; old things are passed away ; behold !
all things are become new." (2 Cor. v. 17.) This is their
highly-privileged state—" Sin shall have no dominion over
them : for they are not under the law, but under grace."
(Rom. vi. 14.) They are " born of God, and they cannot
commit sin : for their seed remaineth in them, and they
cannot sin, because they are born of God." (1 John, iii. 9.)
Their hatred and resistance to sin are therefore now as
instinctive, as was their former enmity and opposition to
God. Not, indeed, that the people of God are as " the saints
made perfect," who " *do no iniquity.*" This is a dream of
perfection—unscriptural and self-deluding. (Comp. Eccles.
vii. 20, with Job, ix. 20 ; Philip. iii. 12.) The unceasing
advocacy of their Heavenly Friend evidently supposes the
indwelling power of sin, to the termination of our earthly
pilgrimage. The supplication, also, in the prayer of our
Lord teaches them to ask for daily pardon and deliverance
from " temptation," as for " daily bread." (Matt. vi. 11–
13.) Yes—to our shame be it spoken—we are sinners
still ; yet—praised be God !—not " walking after the
course," not " fulfilling the desires," of sin. The acting

* " Every imagination of the thoughts of the heart is evil—only
evil—continually." And this " God saw"—before whom " all
things are naked and open"—who searcheth the heart, and therefore cannot be mistaken. (Gen. vi. 5.)

But lest we should conceive this to be the picture of some
generation of so peculiarly aggravated a character, that the awful
demonstration of his wrath could be no longer restrained; this
testimony is repeated by the same Omniscient Judge, immediately
subsequent to the flood (Gen. viii. 21), and confirmed by him in
many express declarations. (Jer. xvii. 9, 10. Matt. xv. 19.)

of sin is now like the motion of a stone upward, violent and
unnatural. If it is not cast out, it is dethroned. We are
not, as before, "its willing people," but its reluctant,
struggling captives. It is not "the day of its power."

And here lies the holy liberty of the Gospel—not, as
some have feigned,—a liberty to "continue in sin, that
grace may abound" (Rom. vi. 1, 2); but a deliverance from
the guilt and condemnation *of abhorred, resisted, yet still
indwelling, sin.* When our better will hath cast it off—when
we can say in the sight of an heart-searching God—" *What
we hate, that do we*"—the responsibility is not ours : " It is
not we that do it, but sin that dwelleth in us." (Rom. vii.
15–20.) Still let us inquire, is the promise of deliverance
from sin sweet to us? (Ib. vi. 14.) And does our successful
resistance in the spiritual conflict realize the earnest of its
complete fulfilment? Blessed Jesus! what do we owe to
thy cross for the present redemption from its guilt and
curse, and much more for the blissful prospect of the glorified state, when this hated guest shall be an inmate no
more for ever! (Rev. xxi. 27.) Oh, let us take the very
print of thy death into our souls in the daily crucifixion of
sin. (Rom. vi. 6.) Let us know the "power of thy resurrection," in an habitual "walk in newness of life." (Philip.
iii. 10. Rom. vi. 4, 5.)

4. *Thou hast commanded us to keep thy precepts diligently.*

We have seen the character of the Man of God. Let
us mark the authority of God, *commanding* him to a *diligent*
obedience. The very sight of the *command* is enough for
him. He obeys for the *command's* sake, however contrary
it may be to his own will. But has he any reason to complain of the yoke? Even under the dispensation, which
" gendereth unto bondage" most encouraging were the
obligations to obedience—" *that it may be well* with them,

and with their children for ever." (Deut. v. 24. Comp.
Deut. vi. 17, 18 ; xxviii. 1, 2 ; Jer. vii. 23.) Much more,
then, we, under a dispensation of love, can never want a
motive for obedience ! Let the daily mercies of Providence
stir up the question—" What shall I render unto the
Lord?" (Ps. cxvi. 12.) Let the far richer mercies of grace
produce " a living sacrifice" to be " presented to the Lord."
(Rom. xii. 1.) Let " the love of Christ constrain us."
(2 Cor. v. 14.) Let the recollection of the " price with
which we were bought," remind us of the Lord's property
in us, and of our obligations to " glorify him in our body,
and in our spirit, which are his." (1 Cor. vi. 19, 20.) Let
us only " behold the Lamb of God ; " let us hear his
wrestling supplications, his deserted cry, his expiring
agonies—the price of our redemption ; and then let us ask
ourselves — Can we want a motive ?

But what is the scriptural character of evangelical
obedience? It is the work of the Spirit, enabling us to
" obey the truth." (1 Pet. i. 22.) It is the end of the purpose of God, who " hath chosen us in Christ before the
foundation of the world, *that we should be* holy and without
blame before him in love." (Eph. i. 4.) It is the only
satisfactory test of our profession. (Matt. xii. 33. John,
xiv. 15, 21.)

Then let me begin my morning with the inquiry,
" Lord, what wilt thou have me to do?" " Teach me thy
way, O Lord ; I will walk in thy truth ; unite my heart to
fear thy name." (Acts, ix. 6. Ps. lxxxvi. 11.) Let me
trade with all my talents for thee : ever watchful, that I
may be employed in thy work ; setting a guard upon my
thoughts, my lips, my tempers, my pursuits, that nothing
may hinder, but rather everything may help me, in *keeping
thy precepts diligently.*

But why do I ever find *the precepts* to be " grievous" to
me ? Is it not that some indolence is indulged ; or some

"iniquity regarded in my heart;" or some principle of
unfaithfulness divides my services with two masters, when
I ought to be "following the Lord fully?" Oh! for the
spirit of "simplicity and godly sincerity" in *the precepts* of
God. Oh! for that warm and constant love, which is the
main-spring of devoted diligence in the service of God.
Oh! for a larger supply of that "wisdom which is from
above," and which is "without partiality and without
hypocrisy!" (Jam. iii. 17.)

5. *Oh that my ways were directed to keep thy statutes!*

The Lord has indeed "*commanded us to keep his precepts.*"
But, alas! where is our power? Satan would make the
sense of our weakness an excuse for indolence. The Spirit
of God convinces us of it, as an incitement to prayer, and
an exercise of faith. If, Reader, your heart is perfect with
God, you "consent to the law that it is good;" you "delight
in it after the inner man" (Rom. vii. 16, 22); you would
not have one jot or tittle altered, mitigated, or repealed,
that it might be more conformed to your own will, or allow
you more liberty or self-indulgence in the ways of sin.
But do you not sigh to think, that, when you aim at the
perfect standard of holiness, you should, at your best moments, and in your highest attainments, fall so far below
it; seeing indeed the way before you, but feeling yourself
without ability to walk in it? Then let a sense of your
helplessness for the work of the Lord lead you to the throne
of grace, to pray, and watch, and wait, for the strengthening and refreshing influences of the Spirit of grace. Here
let your faith realize at one and the same view your utter
insufficiency, and your complete All-sufficiency. (2 Cor.
iii. 5.) Here behold Him, who is ever presenting himself
before God as our glorious Head, receiving in himself, according to the good pleasure of the Father (Col. i. 18, 19),

the full supply for this and every successive moment of inexpressible need. Our work is not therefore left upon our own hands, or wrought out at our " own charges." So long as " He hath the residue of the Spirit" (Mal. ii. 15), " grace" will be found " sufficient ; "— Divine " strength will be made perfect in weakness." (2 Cor. xii. 9.) " Without him we can do nothing" (John, xv. 5) ; " through him, all things." (Phil. iv. 13.) Even the " worm Jacob shall thresh the mountains," when the Lord says, " Fear not, I will help thee." (Isa. xli. 14, 15.)

In connecting this verse with the preceding, how accurately is the middle path preserved, equally distant from the idea of self-sufficiency to "keep the Lord's statutes," and self-justification in neglecting them! The first attempt to render spiritual obedience will quickly convince us of our utter helplessness. We might as soon create a world, as create in our hearts one pulse of spiritual life. And yet our inability does not cancel our obligation. Shall God lose his right, because sin has palsied our ability? Is not a drunken servant still under his master's law? and is not the sin which prevents him from performing his duty, not his excuse, but his aggravation? Thus our weakness is that of an heart, which " cannot be subject to the law of God," only because it is carnal, " enmity against God."*
The obligation therefore remains in full force. Our inability is our sin, our guilt, and condemnation.

What then remains for us, but to return the mandate to heaven, accompanied with an earnest prayer, that the Lord would write upon our hearts those *statutes*, to which he requires obedience in his word? —" *Thou hast commanded*

* Rom. viii. 7. Comp. Gen. xxxvii. 4; John, viii. 43; v. 40; 2 Pet. ii. 14,—where the moral inability is clearly traced to the love of sin, or the obstinate unbelief of the heart, and therefore is inexcusable. The case of the heathen is traced to the same wilful source. (Rom. i. 20–28.)

us to keep thy statutes diligently." We acknowledge, Lord,
our obligation ; but we feel our impotency. Lord, help
us : we look unto thee. " *Oh that our ways were directed to
keep thy statutes!*" " Give what thou commandest ; and
then command what thou wilt."* Now, as if to exhibit
the fulness and suitableness of the promises of the gospel,
the commands and prayers are returned back again from
heaven with promises of quickening and directing grace.
Thus does the Lord fully answer his end with us. He did
not issue the commands, expecting that we could turn our
own hearts to them ; but that the conviction of our entire
helplessness might cast us upon him, who loves to be sought,
and never will be thus sought in vain. And indeed this is
a part of the " mystery of godliness," that in proportion as
we depend upon him who is alike, " the Lord our righteousness," and our strength, our desire after holiness will increase, and our prayers become more fervent. He who
commands our duty, perfectly knows our weakness, and he
who feels his own weakness is fully encouraged to depend
upon the power of his Saviour. Faith is then the principle
of evangelical obedience, and the promises of his grace
enable us for duty, at the very time that we are commanded
to it.† In this view are brought together the supreme
authority of the Lawgiver, the total insufficiency of the
creature, the full provisions of the Saviour, and the all-
sufficiency of " the God of grace." We pray for what we
want ; we are thankful for what we have ; we trust for
what is promised. Thus " all is of God." Christ " is the
Alpha and the Omega, the beginning and the end, the first
and the last." (Rev. xxii. 13.) Thus " grace reigns " triumphant. The foundation is laid in grace, and the head-
stone will be brought forth with shoutings, crying, " Grace,

---

* " Da quod jubes, et jube quod vis."—AUGUSTINE.
† " Quod lex imperat, fides impetrat."

grace unto it." (Zech. iv. 7.) The Saviour's work is finished, and Jesus is crowned Lord of all for ever.

6. *Then shall I not be ashamed, when I have respect unto all thy commandments.*

The Lord expects our obedience to be not only " *diligent*," but universal. Willingly to dispense with the least of the *commandments*, proves that we have yet to learn the spirit of acceptable obedience. (Matt. v. 19.) Grace is given and suited for all, no less than for one of them, " that we might walk worthy of the Lord *unto all pleasing.*" (Col. i. 10.) One lust " regarded in the heart " is sufficient to keep possession for the tyrant, however others may be restrained. Even Herod could " do many things ; " and yet his adulterous wife cherished in his bosom, too plainly proved the sovereignty of sin to be undisturbed. (Mark, vi. 11–20.) Saul slew all the Amalekites *but one;* and that single exception to universal obedience marked his unsoundness, cost him the loss of his throne, and brought him under the awful displeasure of his God. (1 Sam. xv. 12–23.) And thus the corrupt unmortified member brings the whole body to hell. (Mark, ix. 43–48.) Reserves are the canker upon godly sincerity. A secret indulgence —" the rolling of the sweet morsel under the tongue,"—" the part of the price kept back " (Acts, v. 1, 2) — stamps our service as a robbery, not as an offering. We may be free, sincere, and earnest in many parts of our prescribed duty ; but this " root of bitterness " renders the whole an abomination.

Sincerity therefore must be the stamp of my Christian profession. Though utterly unable to render perfect obedience to the least of the commandments, yet my desire and purpose will *have respect unto them all.* I shall no more venture to break the least than the greatest of them ; much less shall I ever think of attempting to atone for the breach of one by the performance of the rest. They are indeed

many commandments ; yet — like links in a chain — they
form but one law ; and I know who has said, " Whosoever shall keep the whole law, and yet offend in one point,
he is guilty of all." (Jam. ii. 10, 11.) However the professor may confine his regard to the second table (as if the
first were ceremonial, or obsolete, or the regulation of the
outward man was the utmost extent of the requirement,) I
would fix my eye with equal regard to both ; yet specially
marking any command in either of them ; that may appear
most directly opposed to my besetting corruptions.   Thus
" walking in the fear of the Lord," I may hope to walk " in
the comfort of the Holy Ghost " (Acts, ix. 31) ; and
" hereby shall I know that I am of the truth, and shall
assure my heart before God." (1 John, iii. 19.)

But where, in my strictest walk, is my hope of acceptance, but in him, whose obedience has " fulfilled all righteousness " (Matt. iii. 15) in my stead, and whose death " has
redeemed me from the curse " (Gal. iii. 13) of my unrighteousness, when repentance, prayers, and tears, would have
been of no avail ?   Yet it is only in the path of holiness
that we can realize our acceptance. (1 John, i. 7 ; ii. 5 ;
iii. 21, 24.)   The heart occupied with this world's pleasure
knows nothing of this heavenly joy.   Its brightness is
dimmed — its freshness fades — its life withers — in the
very breath of an unholy world.   A godly assurance of the
present favour of God must be weakened by self-indulgence,
unwatchfulness, allowance of secret sins, or neglect of secret
duties.   " If thou return to the Almighty "— said a wise
man —" thou shalt be built up, *thou shalt put away iniquity*
far from thy tabernacles.   *Then* shalt thou have thy delight
in the Almighty, and *shalt lift up thy face* unto God." (Job,
xxii. 23, 26.)

Let us then carefully examine the character of our
assurance.   Does it rest simply and exclusively upon the
testimony of the Gospel ?   Will it abide the test of the
word of God ?   Is it productive of tenderness of conscience,

watchfulness, and circumspection of conduct? Does it exercise our diligence in adding grace to grace, that we may "make our calling and election sure," and that "an entrance may be ministered to us *abundantly* into the everlasting kingdom of our Lord and Saviour Jesus Christ?" (2 Pet. i. 5–11.) How boldly can we plead our Christian confidence in the path of godliness —" *I have stuck unto thy testimonies; O Lord, put me not to shame. Let my heart be sound in thy statutes, that I be not ashamed.*" (Verses 31, 80.)

7. *I will praise thee with uprightness of heart, when I shall have learned thy righteous judgments.*

The righteous judgments of God include the whole revelation of his word — so called — as the rule by which he judges our present state, and will pronounce our final sentence. (John, xii. 48.) David's attainments here seemed to be as nothing. So much remained unlearned and unknown, that he could only anticipate the time, *when he should have learned* them. " *Thy commandment* "—he exclaims—" is *exceeding broad.*" (Verse 96.) When the Apostle, after twenty years' acquaintance with the gospel, expressed it as the one desire of his heart —" That I may know Christ " (Philip. iii. 10–14); evidently he entertained the same humbling views of his high attainments, and the same exalted apprehensions of the value of treasures yet unexplored, and progressively opening before him. Thus the wisest saints are only students in the Divine School. Yet whatever their *learning* be, it casts them into the mould and spirit of their doctrine. (Rom. vi. 17.) Conceit, however, of knowledge is the greatest enemy to knowledge, and the strongest proof of ignorance ; so that, " if any man think that he knoweth anything, he knoweth nothing yet as he ought to know."—" He deceiveth himself." (1 Cor. viii. 2. Gal. vi. 3.)

But what is the motive, that enlivens the believer in this holy *learning?* Is it that he may live upon the airy breath of human applause? No, rather that he may "*praise his God with uprightness of heart.*" When our mind is dark, our lips are sealed. But when "he opens our understandings" to "*learn his judgments,*" he will next "open our lips, and our mouth shall show forth his praise." (Ps. li. 15; also verses 27, 171.) And this indeed is the end for which "his people are formed" (Isa. xliii. 21); for which they "are called out of darkness into marvellous light." (1 Pet. ii. 9.) This is the daily frame, in which our God will be glorified.* Yet must we live as well as sing his praise. "*The praise of the upright heart* will be shown in the holy walk and conversation." (Ps. cxvi. 12–14.)

But let us watch, that our *praise* really flows "out of the abundance" of what our hearts have "*learned*" of his "*righteous judgments.*" For do we not sometimes speak of our Saviour with a secret lurking after self-exaltation? May we not really be seeking and serving ourselves in the very act of seeming to serve and honour him? Surely the very thought of the selfishness that defiles our holiest earthly praise, may well quicken our longings after that world of praise, where the flame burns active, bright, incessant; where we shall offer our sacrifices without defilement, without intermission, without weariness, without end. (Rev. iv. 8.)

8. *I will keep thy statutes: O forsake me not utterly.*

The resolution to "*keep the Lord's statutes*" is the natural result of having "*learned his righteous judgments.*" But how happily does David combine "simplicity" of dependence with "godly sincerity" of obedience! Firm in his

---

* Ps. l. 23. For an example of the *uprightness of heart* in the service of *praise* here alluded to, see 1 Chron. xxix. 13–18.

purpose, but distrustful of his strength, instantly upon
forming his resolution, he recollects that the performance is
beyond his power ; and therefore the next moment, and
almost the same moment, he follows it up with prayer,
" I will keep thy statutes : O forsake me not utterly. Oh !
beware of self-confidence in the Christian course.   We
stumble or advance, as we lean upon an arm of flesh, or
upon an Almighty Saviour.   Temporary desertion may be
the seasonable chastisement of spiritual wantonness.   When
grace has been given in answer to prayer, it was not duly
prized, or diligently improved.   The " Beloved "— in answer
to solicitation —" is come into his garden :" he knocks at
the door, but the spouse is " asleep."   The answer to prayer
was not expected, not waited for, and therefore not enjoyed ;
and the sleeper awakes too late, and finds herself forsaken
by the object of her desire. (Cant. iv. 16, with v. 1–6.)
Again—when we have given place to temptation (2 Chron.
xxxii. 31) ; when " our mountain stands strong" (Ps. xxx.
6, 7) ; when love for our Saviour " waxes cold," and our
earnestness in seeking him is fainting (Cant. iii. 1–4) ; we
must not be surprised, if we are left for a time to the trial
of a deserted state.

Yet we sometimes speak of the hidings of God's countenance, as if it were a sovereign act, calling for implicit
submission ; when the cause should at least be sought for,
and will generally be found, in some " secret thing " of indulgence, unwatchfulness, or self-dependence. (Job, xv. 11.)
It was while David " kept silence " from the language of
contrition, that he felt the pressure of the heavy hand of
his frowning God (Ps. xxxii. 3, 4) ; and may not the darkness, which has sometimes clouded our path, be the voice
of our God—" Thine own wickedness shall correct thee,
and thy backslidings shall reprove thee ; know therefore
and see, that it is an evil thing and bitter, that thou hast
forsaken the Lord thy God." (Jer. ii. 19.)

But in the engagement of the Lord's everlasting covenant, how clear is the warrant of faith !—how ample the encouragement for prayer—"*Forsake me not utterly!*" David knew and wrote of the Lord's unchangeable faithfulness to his people ; and while he dreaded even a temporary separation from his God more than any worldly affliction, he could plead that gracious declaration—" Nevertheless, my loving-kindness will I not utterly take from him, nor suffer my faithfulness to fail." (Ps. lxxxix. 33.) We would not indeed make the promises of grace an encouragement to carelessness : yet it is indispensable to our spiritual establishment that we receive them in their full, free, and sovereign declaration. How many fainting souls have been refreshed by the assurances—" For a small moment have I forsaken thee ; but with great mercies will I gather thee : with everlasting kindness will I have mercy on thee, saith the Lord thy Redeemer !" " My sheep shall never perish ; neither shall any pluck them out of my hand." (Isa. liv. 7, 8. John, x. 28.) In a lowly, self-abased, and dependent spirit, we shall best, however, learn to " make our boast in the Lord ;" " confident of this very thing, that he which hath begun a good work in us, will perform it until the day of Jesus Christ." (Ps. xxxiv. 2. Philip. i. 6.) And even if awhile destitute of sensible consolation, still our language will be, " I will wait upon the Lord, that hideth his face from the house of Jacob ; and I will look for him." (Isa. viii. 17.)

Great, indeed, is the danger and evil to the soul, if we apprehend the Lord to have *forsaken* us, because we are in darkness ; or that we are out of the way, because we are in perplexity. These are the very hand-posts, that show us that we are in the way of his own promised leading — painful exercise—faithful keeping—eternal salvation : " I will bring the blind by a way that they knew not ; I will lead them in paths that they have not known ; I will make

darkness light before them, and crooked things straight.
These things will I do unto them, *and not forsake them.*"
(Isa. xlii. 16.) Oh! the rest—the satisfaction of placing
an implicit confidence in a covenant-keeping God!
Forsaken we may be—but not *utterly.* David was *for-saken,* not like Saul. (Ps. xxx. 7; with 1 Sam. xxviii. 6,
16.) Peter was *forsaken,* not like Judas (Matt. xxvi. 75;
with xxvii. 3–6), *utterly* and for ever. What foreboding
have you of such desertion? Is your heart willing to for-sake him? Have you no mournings and thirstings for
his return? " If, indeed, you forsake him, he will *forsake*
you." (2 Chron. xv. 2. Comp. 1 Chron. xxviii. 9.) But
can you forsake him? ' Let him do as seemeth him
good (is the language of your heart); I will wait for him,
follow after him, cleave to his word, cling to his cross.'
Mark his dealings with you. Inquire into their reason.
Submit to his dispensation. If he *forsakes,* beg his re-turn: but trust your *forsaking* God. " Though he slay
me, yet will I trust in him." (Job, xiii. 15. Isa. l. 10. Hab.
iii. 17, 18.) Though my comfort is clouded, my hope
remains unchanging, unchangeable—such as I would not
resign for the glory of an earthly crown. What are these
earnest breathings—this abiding confidence, but his own
work in us? And can the Lord " forsake the work of his
own hands?" (Ps. cxxxviii. 8.) Sooner should heaven and
earth pass, than the faithful engagements of the gospel be
thus broken.*

* Augustine's paraphrase of this verse is beautifully illustrative
of the believer's conflict in a state of temporary desertion. " O
Lord, if—lest I should be proud, and should ' say in my prosperity,
I shall never be removed'—it pleaseth thee to tempt me, yet forsake
me not over-long;" that is, if thou hast thus forsaken me, that I
may know how weak I am without thy help, yet *"forsake me not
utterly,"* lest I perish. I know that of thy good-will thou hast given
me strength; and if thou turnest away thy face from me, I shall
forthwith be troubled. " O forsake me not, that I perish not."

PART II.

9. *Wherewithal shall a young man cleanse his way? by taking heed thereto according to thy word.*

W HY is the *young man* so especially called to *cleanse his way?* Because God justly claims the first and the best. And is it not a most affecting proof of the alienation of the heart from God, that the youth of man — the bloom and freshness of his mind — " his first love " — should naturally be devoted to the service of sin? Ever since fallen man " begat a son in his own likeness," " the imagination of man's heart has been evil from his youth." (Gen. v. 3 ; viii. 21.) For " who can bring a clean thing out of an unclean ?" (Job, xiv. 4.) And never does the heart utter the cry, " My Father ! thou art the guide of my youth" (Jer. iii. 4), until the misery of wandering without a guide has been painfully felt. And even when Divine grace has awakened the desire to return homewards, the habit of wandering from God, and the long-cherished pollutions of sin, seem to form an almost invincible barrier to progress.

The fearful power of " youthful lusts," and the madness with which the heart is hurried into forbidden indulgences, give solemn weight to the inquiry, " *Wherewithal shall a young man cleanse his way?*" And the answer is ready. Let him " *take heed thereto according to thy word.*" Thus did Joseph (Gen. xxxix. 9), and Daniel with his young companions (Dan. i. 8–20 ; iii. 12–18), " *cleanse their way*" in the defilement of an heathen atmosphere. It was probably the recollection of this purifying efficacy of *the word*, that induced the venerable Beza to mention in his will, among his chief matters of thankfulness to God, the mercy of having been called to the knowledge of the truth at the age of sixteen ; thus, during a course of more than seventy years' walk with God, " escaping the pollutions of the world through lust." But the " *way can only be cleansed*" by the cleansing of the heart ; for how can a corrupt fountain " send forth" other than " bitter waters ?" (Jam. iii. 11, 12.) " Out of the heart are the issues of life." Hence the urgent need to cry—" Create in me a clean heart, O God, and renew a right spirit within me." (Prov. iv. 23. Ps. li. 10.)

How precious, therefore, is *the word of God*, as the means of this cleansing operation ! When our Saviour had been setting forth himself as " the way, the truth, and the life," and exhibiting the high privilege of union with himself, " Now," he adds, " *ye are clean, through the word which I have spoken unto you.*" (John, xiv. 6 ; xv. 1–3.) This is " the truth," which he pleaded with his Father as the means of our sanctification. (Ib. xvii. 17.) This sets out our purifying hope. (1 John, iii. 3.) Here are the promises, by which we " cleanse ourselves from all filthiness of flesh and spirit, perfecting holiness in the fear of God."* Thus is restored to man that golden " crown "—the stamp of his Maker's holiness — which " fell from his head when he sinned." (Lam. v. 16, with Gen. i. 27 ; Eph. iv. 24.)

But oh ! how does the recollection force itself upon us,

---

* 2 Cor. vii. 1. Comp. 2 Pet. i. 4. Augustine's recorded account of his own conversion furnishes a striking illustration of this subject. Confessions, books, viii., ix. The substance of it may be found in Milner's Church History, vol. ii. 353–356. See Dr. Owen's valuable work on the Spirit for a most instructive use made of it, as throwing light upon the doctrine of conversion. Book iii. chap. vi.

that our way wants daily *cleansing!* so defiled are our actions, our thoughts, our motives,—nay more, our prayers and services.   Let us then " *take heed according to the word of God*"—specially thankful for its heavenly light, which guides us to the " Fountain, that is opened for sin and for uncleanness." (Zech. xiii. 1.)   Let us also, under the same Divine light, seek for the daily sanctifying influence of the Spirit of God.   " *Who can understand his errors?   Cleanse thou me from secret faults.*" (Ps. xix. 12.)   " *Cleanse the thoughts of my heart by the inspiration of thy Holy Spirit.*" (Prayer-Book.)

10. *With my whole heart have I sought thee ; O let me not wander from thy commandments.*

Attention to the word, however important (ver. 9), can never be practically effective without earnest prayer.   Indeed this is the character of the Lord's people, " a generation of *seekers*" (Ps. xxiv. 6); and yet how much do we lose of the comfort of our religion, and obscure the glory of our profession, by neglecting to bring " *our whole heart*" to this work !   When sin is vigorous, and our spiritual affections are dull, and various hindrances combine in prayer, at this crisis strong faith is needed to overcome and to persevere. But here the soul too commonly yields to the difficulty, and contents itself either with heartless complainings, or with just sufficient exertion to quiet the voice of conscience, and produce a delusive peace within.   But the Lord will not be found thus.   His promise is not to such seekers as these ; and if we are satisfied with this state, we must look for a very scanty measure of spiritual success, accompanied with the total absence of spiritual enjoyment.   In a far different spirit David could appeal—" *With my whole heart have I sought thee.*"   And this assurance, instead of producing self-confidence, will, so far as it is genuine, invari-

ably show itself in a prayerful acknowledgment of our
weakness —" *O let me not wander from thy commandments.*"
Yet the feeblest desire and attempt to seek the Lord is
the Spirit's rising beam in the heart, a " day of small
things" not to be " despised." (Zech. iv. 10.) It is distinguished from every other principle by the simplicity of its
object —" This one thing I do. One thing have I desired of the Lord ; that will I seek after." (Philip. iii. 13.
Ps. xxvii. 4.)   My God ! my Saviour ! *with my whole
heart have I sought thee.* "The desire of my soul is to thy
name, and to the remembrance of thee. With my soul
have I desired thee in the night ; yea, with my spirit
within me will I seek thee early." (Isa. xxvi. 8; 9.)

When the soul is thus conscious of " following the
Lord fully," there is a peculiar *dread of wandering.* In a
careless or half-hearted state, wanderings are not watched,
so long as they do not lead to any open declension. Secret
prayer will be hurried over, worldly thoughts unresisted,
waste of time in frivolous pursuits indulged, without much
concern. Not so, when the heart is *fully* in pursuit of its
object. There is a carefulness, lest wandering thoughts
should become habitual. There is a resistance of the first
step, that might lead into a devious path. The soul re-
members the " wormwood and the gall" (Lam. iii. 19),
" the roaring lion," and the devouring wolf ; and in the
recollection of the misery of its former wandering, dreads
any departure from the Shepherd's fold. This blessed
state of mind the flock of Christ should cherish with godly
jealousy. Yet let it be remembered, that daily progress in
the heavenly walk is not maintained by *yesterday's* grace.
Humble and dependent prayer must fetch in a fresh supply
continually —" *O let me not wander from thy commandments.*"
' Lord, I feel my heart so prone to wander. My affections
are often scattered to the ends of the earth. " Unite my
heart to fear thy name." (Ps. lxxxvi. 11.) Concentrate

every thought, every desire, in thyself, as the one object
of attraction.'

11. *Thy word have I hid in my heart, that I might not sin
against thee.*

What an aggregate of guilt and misery is comprehended
in this short word " sin "—the greatest curse that ever
entered the universe of God, and the parent of every other
curse! Its guilt is aggravated beyond the conception of
thought. Injury to a Superior—a Father—a Sovereign!
Its power is misery wherever it extends—in the family—
in the world. In eternity its power is unrestrained. Sometimes the death-bed scene casts a fearful gleam of light
upon " the worm that never dieth, and the fire that never
shall be quenched" (Mark, ix. 44) : but experience only
can develope its full-grown horrors. How supremely important therefore is the object of our preservation from sin!
and how wisely adapted are the means to the end! That
word—which the man of God had just before mentioned
as the guide to the *cleansing of the way* (Verse 9)—he *hides
within his heart*—not for concealment, but for security
(Matt. xxv. 25 ; Ps. xl. 10 ; with Exod. xxv. 21 ; Job,
xxii. 22), that it may be ready for constant use. (Josh. i. 8.)
It is not therefore a mere acquaintance with *the word*, that
will avail us. There must be a cordial assent—a sound
digestion—a constant respect. It must be to us the rule
that we would not transgress—the treasure that we are
afraid to lose. (Matt. xiii. 44.) Often indeed Satan shuts
out its entrance. He " catches away that which was sown."
Too often, again, it is " withered or choked" in the soil. But
" the honest and good heart" " *hides it*, keeps it, and brings
forth fruit with patience, unto perfection." (Luke, viii. 15,
with the whole parable.) Here it " dwells richly in all
wisdom" (Col. iii. 16), the storehouse, as occasion requires;

a principle of holiness ; a covering from sin. In this view
it is recommended by one who had well acquainted himself
with its valuable uses : " My son, let them not " (the
Divine precepts) " depart from thine eyes ; keep sound
wisdom and discretion. So shall they be life unto thy soul,
and grace to thy neck. Then shalt thou walk in thy way
safely, and thy foot shall not stumble." (Prov. iii. 21–24.
Comp. Prov. ii. 10–15.) David also gives us the same
experience : " By the word of thy lips I have kept me
from the paths of the destroyer." (Ps. xvii. 4.) And it
was probably this recollection, combined with a sense of
continual danger, that suggested the prayer—" Order my
steps in thy word ; and let not any iniquity have dominion
over me." (Verse 133.)

The value of *the word* is inestimable, as our means of
walking with God in the hurry, business, and temptation
of the day. The Psalms furnish precious materials for
ejaculatory prayer ; the promises, food for comfort (Verses
50, 92) ; the rules, such light in perplexity (Verse 105.
Prov. iii. 5, 6) ; the instruction, such solid matter for
godly conference (Col. iii. 16)—all operating for one end
—a preservation from sin. Being from *the word*—a manifestation of the Saviour's love—what a keeping of the
heart ! what a quickening motive ! How seasonable in
worldly temptation is the warning of *the word hid* in the
heart, " No man, having put his hand to the plough, and
looking back, is fit for the kingdom of God !" (Luke, ix.
61, 62.) So in the spiritual conflict, let this *word*—" Him
that cometh to me, I will in no wise cast out," be *hid in
the heart*—what a preservation is it against unbelief !
(John, vi. 37.) Take *the word* to the unbelieving believer
(if the expression may be allowed), alarmed by ridicule or
persecution—" If the world hate you, ye know that it hated
me before it hated you." (John, xv. 18.) Fearing that he
shall never hold out to the end ; " I will never leave thee

nor forsake thee." (Heb. xiii. 5.) Trembling lest his sins
should rise up to his condemnation—" The blood of Jesus
Christ the Son of God cleanseth from all sin." (1 John, i.
7.) And then as to duties : Let his Saviour's *word* rebuke
his indolence and unwatchfulness—" What ! could ye not
watch with me one hour ? Watch and pray, that ye enter
not into temptation." (Matt. xxvi. 40, 41.) Hide in the
heart the sorrowful story of his agony in the garden, and
his death on the cross, that " sin may appear yet more
exceeding sinful."

But how is *the word* to gain entrance into hearts like
ours ? How shall it be " *hid*" in so unkindly a soil ? No
power of man surely can plant it there. The Holy Spirit's
Almighty agency must be diligently sought ; for in proportion as we are filled with his gracious influence shall we
be armed, as was our Master, for the effectual resistance of
our spiritual temptations. (Comp. Luke, iv. 1–12.)

Lastly, connected with this subject, mark *the Christian's
character*—" In whose heart is my law." (Isa. li. 7.) *His
security*—" None of his steps shall slide." (Ps. xxxvii. 31.)
His happiness—" O how I love thy law." (Verse 97.)
His victory—" The word of God abideth in him, and he
hath overcome the wicked one." (1 John, ii. 14 ; with Eph.
vi. 17.) All infallibly provided by the covenant promise,
" I will put my law in their inward parts, and write it in
their hearts." (Jer. xxxi. 33.) Oh ! let us not then shrink
from a close contact with *the word*, though the cost may be
the cutting off a right hand for the saving of the life. There
is no better test of our security, than our willingness to
come to the searching light of *the word*. (Comp. John, iii.
20, 21.)

12. *Blessed art thou, O Lord: teach me thy statutes.*

" Praise is comely for the upright." (Ps. xxxiii. 1, 2.)

It is at once their duty and their privilege. But what does its highest exercise amount to, when placed on the ground of its own merit? We clothe our ideas with magnificence of language, and deck them out with all the richness of imagery ; and perhaps we are pleased with our forms of praise. But what are they in his sight beyond the offering of a contemptible worm, spreading before its Maker its own mean and low notions of Divine Majesty? If a worm were to raise its head, and cry—' O sun! thou art the source of light and heat to a widely-extended universe'—it would, in fact, render a higher praise to the sun, than we can ever give to our Maker. Between it and us there is some proportion—between us and God none. Yet, unworthy as the offering confessedly is, he will not despise it. Nay, more, instead of spurning it from his presence, he has revealed himself as "inhabiting the praises of Israel" (Ps. xxii. 3) ; thus intimating to us, that the service of praise is "set forth in his sight as incense ;" and at the same time, that it should be the daily and unceasing exercise of one at his own home.

The true character of praise, however, depends entirely upon the state of the heart. In the contemplative philosopher it is only cheerless, barren admiration : in the believer it becomes a principle of comfort and encouragement. For, can he forget the revelation, which his God has given of himself in the gospel of his dear Son ; how it divests every attribute of its terrors, and shines before us in all the glory of his faithfulness and love? The ascription of praise— "*Blessed art thou, O Lord*," frames itself therefore into the prophet's song—"Who is a God like unto thee, that pardoneth iniquity, and passeth by the transgression of the remnant of his heritage? He retaineth not his anger for ever, because he delighteth in mercy." (Mic. vii. 18.)

Truly then he is "*blessed*" in himself, and delights to communicate his blessedness to his people. Hence we are

emboldened to ask for continual "*teaching in his statutes*,"*
in the truths which he has revealed, and the precepts which
he has enjoined ; that we may " be followers of him, as dear
children," and " walk with him in love." (Eph. v. 1, 2.)
The practical influence, however, of Divine light, constitutes its peculiar privilege. Man's teaching puffeth up
— God's teaching humbleth. Man's teaching may lead us
into error as well as into truth — God's teaching is " the
unction from the Holy One, by which we know all things."
(1 John, ii. 20.) Man's teaching may make us more
learned — God's teaching makes us more holy. It persuades,
while it enlightens. It draws the heart, inclines the will,
and carries out the soul to Christ. (John, vi. 44, 45.) The
tried character of God encourages us to look for his teaching — "*Good and upright* is the Lord ; *therefore* will he
teach sinners in the way." (Ps. xxv. 8.) Our warrant is
especially confirmed in approaching him as our covenant
God — " Lead me in thy truth, and *teach me; for thou art
the God of my salvation.* Teach me to do thy will : *for thou
art my God.*" (Ps. cxliii. 10.)

Reader ! do you desire to praise your God ? Then learn
to frequent the new and living way, " by which alone you
can offer your sacrifice acceptably." (Heb. x. 20 ; xiii. 15.
1 Pet. ii. 5.) And while engaged in this holy service,
inquire, surrounded as you are with the means of instruction, what progress you are making in *his statutes*. Seek to
have a deeper acquaintance with the character of God.
Seek to be the vessels of honour and glory, into which he
is pouring more and more continually, " until they be filled
with all the fulness of God." (Eph. iii. 19.) Value the
unspeakable blessing of Divine teaching, by which you learn
to live the life, and begin the *blessedness of God.*

---

* The same acknowledgment and plea are made in verses 64, 68.

13. *With my lips have I declared all the judgments of thy mouth.*

We have seen the *word hid in the heart:* now we see it poured forth from *the lips.* The *Lord has taught us his statutes;* now we *declare these judgments of his mouth.* But who can *declare* them with unction and power, save those who are *taught of God?* Now we are introduced to the high and honourable privilege of becoming a witness for our Saviour! (Philip. ii. 16.) Our opportunities of service are our talents, and we trade with a large increase ; for " to every one that hath shall be given, and he shall have abundance." (Matt. xxv. 29.) But—" our lips are our own" (Ps. xii. 4)—is the proud language of the world. Blessed be God ; " we know that we are not our own." (1 Cor. vi. 19.) Most gladly do we acknowledge, that he, who fashioned our lips, has the best claim to their service. And when he has added to the claim of creation the right of purchase (1 Cor. vi. 20), what further constraining can we need, to induce the consecration of all that we are, and all that we have, to his glory !

This is a family obligation—*to declare the judgments of God's mouth.* Thus did Abraham obtain a blessing for his children. (Gen. xviii. 19.) Heavenly blessings are the gracious reward of thus honouring our God. (Deut. xi. 18–21.) This also is the material of our general intercourse — fruitful in spiritual results. Thus did Andrew bring Peter (John, i. 40–42), and the women of Samaria her neighbours (John, iv. 29, 30), to Jesus. What might we not do for our fellow-sinners, if our intercourse with them was the overflowing of a heart full of love ; guided by a single desire to glorify our Saviour, and to edify his Church ! Fearful, indeed, is the guilt of sinful silence ; and those, who thus prove their unfaithfulness to God, may well tremble at his awful denunciations. And yet it is possible to be bold in speech for God, when in the closet, the family, or the world, our consciences justly convict us of insincerity : " Thou that teachest another, teachest thou not thyself?" (Rom. ii. 21.) Let us seek, therefore, to have our hearts " filled with the Spirit" (Eph. v. 18, 19); otherwise ours will be " the talk of the lips, which tendeth only to penury." (Prov. xiv. 23 ; with x. 19.)

This subject illustrates the *character* of the Lord's people—" The mouth of the righteous speaketh wisdom, and his tongue talketh of judgment" (Ps. xxxvii. 30) ; *their resolution* —" My mouth shall show forth thy righteousness and thy salvation all the day ; for I know not the numbers thereof" (Ps. lxxi. 15) ; *their prayer*—" O Lord, open thou my lips, and my mouth shall show forth thy praise" (Ps. li. 15) ; *their blessing* —" The lips of the righteous feed many. A wholesome tongue is a tree of life." (Prov. x. 21; xv. 4.) The example of the Saviour, here as everywhere, is our perfect and encouraging pattern : " I have preached righteousness in the great congregation ; Lo ! I have not refrained my lips, O Lord, thou knowest." (Ps. xl. 9, 10 ; with Luke, iv. 16–22.) In this spirit of their Master, the Apostles awed their persecutors into forbearance : " We cannot but speak the things which we have seen and heard." (Acts, iv. 20.)

How sinful is it to employ our lips for any but the Lord! Yet not less sinful is our reluctance to employ them for him ! Surely the day, when perhaps we have been fluent in worldly conversation, and yet have neglected our opportunities of speaking a word for him, must be considered a lost day ! Is there not much cause for watchfulness, prayer, and self-denial ; lest our silence should deny him, whom by every obligation we are bound to confess ? If our inability to bear a testimony for our Lord is not painful to us (Comp. Ps. xxxix. 1, 2 ; Jer. xx. 9), must we not suspect, if not the sincerity, at least the strength, of our attachment to his precious name? and we can do no better than retire into our closets with the prayer of contrition—" Enter not into judgment with thy servant, O Lord." (Ps. cxliii. 2.)

14. *I have rejoiced in the way of thy testimonies, as much as in all riches.*

How natural is it to be speaking of that which is our delight! The man of God was always *declaring the Lord's judgments*, because they were his *rejoicing*. There is indeed a real joy in despising earthly joys. " How sweet"—said Augustine, referring to the period of his conversion—" was it in a moment to be free from those delightful vanities, to lose which had been my dread ; to part with which was now my joy!"* More satisfying is the believer's *rejoicing in the way of God*, than that of the miser in his untold riches. (Verses 72, 127.) Here he may safely say to his soul, " Soul, thou hast much goods laid up for many years ; take thine ease." And these are the only riches within the reach of all. If we are poor in this world, it is the Lord's providence. If we are poor in grace, it is our own fault. It is because we have despised our Lord's " counsel to buy of him gold tried in the fire, that we may be rich." (Rev. iii. 18.) And what is this enriching portion?—" Things

* " Quas amittere metus erat, jam dimittere gaudium fuit."— Aug. Confess. Book ix. Never man in his unregenerate state, by his own confession, more strongly illustrated the truth of our Lord's declaration, "Whosoever committeth sin is the servant of sin." (John, viii. 34 ; with 2 Pet. ii. 19.) He describes himself actually as "wallowing in the mire," with as much delight, as if he were rolling himself in a bed of spices, or perfuming himself with the most precious ointment. ("Volutare in cœno, tanquam cinnamonis et unguentis pretiosis.") Yet when the word pierced his heart, and brought a new bias and taste into his soul, how delightfully was his language changed in the recollection of his past " excess of riot ! " " Quam suave est istis suavitatibus carere ! "

present or things to come" (1 Cor. iii. 22); something
enjoyed, and much more expected : the mercies of eternity
added to the blessings of time ; the riches of both worlds
—all assured to him by the covenant of grace " *in the way
of the Lord's testimonies.*" Is it not then most strange, that,
with such treasure in possession and in prospect, the child
of God should be so careless in increasing his store, and in
confirming his own interest in it? But the *riches of God's
testimonies* have this peculiar property, that they cease to
rejoice the heart, when they are not uppermost there. Have
there not been times, when we have actually rejoiced in the
accession of some worldly good, or the accomplishment of
some worldly desire, more than in this heavenly treasure?
What then do we count our *riches?* To thrive in grace, or
in the world? To be rich towards God, or for our own indulgence ?

But though we would *rejoice in the testimonies,* and would
not, for all this world can afford, lose a verse or a letter of
our Bibles, yet we cannot be satisfied with a general interest.
Many texts—doctrinal, practical, or experimental—have
been specially sealed by the Divine Spirit upon our hearts.*
This or that promise—yea, all the land of promise, as much
as I can set my foot upon—is mine. From these precious
testimonies, shall we not increase our little stock, until we
have apprehended the full enjoyment of the whole ; if indeed the fulness of that which is called " unsearchable "
(Eph. iii. 8) can ever be, in this life at least, completely
enjoyed ?

But it is not so much in the Lord's testimonies, as " *in
the way of them,*" that David rejoiced—the way to God, of
which they testify (John, xiv. 6 ; with v. 39) ; " the way
of holiness " (Isa. xxxv. 8), in which they lead—the narrow
way of the cross—so contrary to our natural desires and

---

* " This is my scripture "— Origen used to say of such texts.

inclinations, that none but the true sheep of Christ can ever enter, or continue in it. Who that walks in these *ways* will fail to find them, in duties no less than in privileges, " paths of pleasantness and peace ?" Our happiness is not withered, but flourishing. " Thus saith the Lord, Stand ye in the ways, and see, and ask for the old paths, where is the good way, and walk therein, and ye shall find rest for your souls." (Jer. vi. 16.)

15. *I will meditate in thy precepts, and have respect unto thy ways.*

Our *rejoicing in the testimonies of God* will naturally flow in an habitual *meditation in them.* (Verse 97. Ps. i. 2.) The thoughts follow the affections. The carnal man can never be brought to this resolution. Having no spiritual taste, he has no ability for spiritual *meditation.* Indeed many sincere Christians, through remaining weakness and depravity, are too often reluctant to it. They are content with indolent reading : and, with scarcely a struggle or a trial, yield themselves up to the persuasion, that they are unable sufficiently to abstract their minds for this blessed employment. But let the trial prove the work. Perseverance will accomplish the victory over mental instability, and the spiritual difficulty will give way to prayer, " Lord ! help me." The fruitfulness of this employment will soon be manifest. Does it not " stir up the gift of God that is in us" (2 Tim. i. 6), and keep the energies of the heart in a wakeful posture of conflict and resistance ? Besides this, it is the digestive faculty of the soul, which converts the word into real and proper nourishment : so that this revolving of a single verse in our minds is often better than the mere reading of whole chapters. " Thy words were found, and *I did eat them;* and thy word was unto me the joy and

the rejoicing of my heart."*   Thus the mind becomes the
instrument of faith and love—of joy and strength.

But this meditation not only includes the stated times
of thought, but the train of holy thoughts, that pass
through the mind during the busy hours of the day.   This
maintains an habitual flow of spiritual desires, and excites
the flame of love within, till at length the Psalmist's resolution becomes the inwrought habit of our minds—" *I will
meditate in thy precepts.*"

Can we want a subject for meditation, if indeed the
salvation of Jesus has been made known to our souls?
While musing upon the glorious theme, does not " the fire
burn" (Ps. xxxix. 3 ; and comp. xlv. 1) within, as if our
hearts were touched with a live coal from the altar of God?
Chide then, believer, thy dull and sluggish spirit, that
suffers the precious manna to lie ungathered upon the
ground, that is slow to entertain these heavenly thoughts,
or rather that heavenly guest, whose peculiar office it is
to " help our infirmities" (Rom. viii. 26), and especially
to " take of Christ's, and show it unto us." (John, xvi.
14, 15.)

The exercise, however, of this, as of every other duty,
may prove a barren form, that imparts neither pleasure nor
profit.†   Let each of us then ask—'What distinct experimental benefit have I received from the word?   Do I en-

---

* Jer. xv. 16. " Meditation is that exercise of mind, whereby it
recalls a known truth, as some kinds of creatures do their food, to be
ruminated upon, until the nutritious parts are extracted, and fitted
for the purposes of life."—BISHOP HORNE on this verse.

+ " If a chapter be read with the eye merely, while the mind
remains inattentive, and the book be shut as soon as the chapter
is finished, and thus, what has been read immediately escape the
memory; what is there to surprise, if, after the whole Bible has
been several times read through, we discover in ourselves no increase of piety and devotion?"—PROFESSOR FRANCKE.

deavour to read it with prayerful meditation, until I find my heart filled with it?

But this communing with the word is not for contemplation, but for practice. (Josh. i. 8.) By *meditating on God's precepts*, we learn to *have respect unto his ways* — carefully "pondering the path of our feet," that we "turn not aside." (Prov. iv. 26, 27.) "*Thy loving-kindness is before mine eyes; and I have walked in thy truth.*" (Ps. xxvi. 3.) " My foot," saith Job, " hath held his steps ; his ways have I kept, and not declined. Neither have I gone back from the commandment of his lips ; *I have esteemed the words of his mouth more than my necessary food.*" (Job, xxiii. 11, 12.)

16. *I will delight myself* * *in thy statutes: I will not forget thy word.*

As *delight* quickens to *meditation* (Verses 14, 15), so does the practical habit of *meditation* strengthen the principle of *delight.* In the enjoyment of this delight, the Christian (however small his attainments may be) would rather live and die, than in the pursuit, and even in the possession, of the most satisfying pleasures of a vain and empty world. But if it be a real "*delight in the Lord's statutes,*" it will be universal — when they probe the secret lurking-places within, and draw out to the full light the hidden indulgences of a heart that is yet carnal (see Rom. vii. 14 ; 1 Cor. iii. 1, 3) ; when they call for the entire crucifixion of every corrupt inclination, and the unreserved surrender of all to the self-denying service of our God. This spirit is very different from the *delight* of the hypocrite, which is rather to " know," than to do, the " ways of his God" (Isa. lviii. 2) ; and, therefore, which is satisfied with

* " I will solace and recreate myself."—AINSWORTH. A beautiful illustration of the refreshment of the word, when the mind is tired out with the toilsome encumbering cares of the world.

outward conformity, with little or no desire to " understand the errors" of his heart, that he might be " cleansed from secret faults." (Ps. xix. 12.) The spring of our obedience will therefore prove its sincerity ; and the reality of our love will be manifested by its fruitfulness and active cheerfulness in our appointed sphere of duty.

We may also observe here an evidence of adoption. Obedience is not a burden, but a *delight*. The servant may *perform* the statutes of God, but it is only the son who " *delights in them*." But what—we may ask—is the spring of adoption? It is " the Spirit of the Son sent into our hearts, whereby we cry, Abba, Father." (Gal. iv. 6.) It is because we are at peace with God through Jesus Christ ; because the *statutes* are the message of reconciliation through him, that they become delightful to those, who are partakers of this great salvation. " The spirit of adoption," therefore, as the principle of delight, is the spring of acceptable obedience in the Lord's service.

And surely those who are serving him in this happy filial walk, are not likely to "*forget his word*." As the eye is continually turned to the object of its affection, so the eye of the soul, that has been fixed with *delight* on the ways of God, will be habitually resting upon them. As one of the wise heathens observed—' I never yet heard of a covetous old man, who had forgotten where he had buried his treasure.'* The reason is abundantly evident. His heart is in it. And this explains the forgetfulness of the ungodly or the formalist. They have no *delight in the statutes*. And who is not glad to *forget* what is distasteful? But if we " have tasted that the Lord is gracious"—if we have found a treasure "in the way of his testimonies"—we cannot *forget* the sweetness of the experience, or where to go to refresh ourselves with the repetition of it.

* " Nec vero quenquam senem audivi oblitum quo loco thesaurum obruisset."— Cicero *de Senectute*. Comp. Matt. vi. 21.

Forgetfulness of the word is, however, to the Christian, a source of continual complaint, and sometimes also of most distressing temptation. Not that there is always a real charge of guilt upon the conscience. For, as Boston somewhat quaintly observes—' Grace makes a good heart-memory, even where there is no good head-memory.' But means must be used, and helps may be suggested. Watchfulness against the influence of the world is of the first importance. How much of the good seed is choked by the springing thorns! (Matt. xiii. 22.) If our hearts are ever refreshed with spiritual delight, we should be as cautious of an uncalled-for advance into the world, as of exposing an invalid's susceptible frame to a damp or an unhealthy atmosphere. Whatever warmth has been kindled in spiritual duties, may be chilled by one moment's unwary rush into an unkindly clime. We would also recommend increasing attention to the word, as the means of its preservation (Heb. ii. 1)—the exercise of " faith," without which it will " not profit" (Ib. iv. 2)—the active habit of love, bringing with it a more habitual interest in the statutes (Verse 15)—all accompanied with unceasing prayer for the gift of the Holy Spirit, made the express subject of promise for this purpose. (John, xiv. 26.) Under his heavenly teaching and recollection, what *delight* will be found *in the statutes!* what blessed remembrance of his word! And what a happy spirit is this *delight and remembrance of the word*—the affections glowing—the memory pondering—the presence and manifestation of truth keeping the heart in close communion with God! " O Lord God, *keep this for ever* in the imagination of the thoughts of the heart of thy people, and prepare their hearts unto thee." (1 Chron. xxix. 18.)

PART III.

17. Deal bountifully with thy servant, that I may live, and keep thy word.

THIS prayer appears to have been much upon David's heart, and in its substance and object it is again repeated. (Verse 77.) Nor does he fail to acknowledge the answer to it. (Verse 65. Comp. Ps. xiii. 6 ; cxvi. 7, 8.) The believer, like David, is a man of large expectations. As regards himself—his own daily provocations and backslidings—he cannot stand upon his own ground. But when he brings with him the name, the blood, the intercession of Jesus ; as soon could God deny his own beloved Son, as resist the supplication of those who present this allprevailing plea. (John, xvi. 23, 24.) Nay—is he not his own gift to his children, as the pledge of every other gift? (Rom. viii. 32.) And what other pledge can they need, to encourage them to draw nigh with the largest desire, and the most heavenly expectation ? We may, indeed, be too bold in our manner of approach to God ;* but we cannot be too bold in our expectations from him. Standing as we do upon such high and sure ground, it is equally dishonourable to him, and impoverishing to ourselves, to ask only a little

---

* A beautiful example of reverential approach, and of the acceptance manifested, is given in Abram's history (Gen. xvii. 3), and is in some degree illustrated by the private records of Luther.—Note on verses 147, 148.

of him. Rather let us, according to his own command, " open our mouths wide ; and he will fill them." (Ps. lxxxi. 10.) Rather let us expect that he will *deal*—not only favourably—but *bountifully with his servants*—that, as " our God, he will supply all our need according to his riches in glory by Christ Jesus." (Philip. iv. 19.)

And, indeed, the most experienced believer cannot forget, that he is in himself still the same poor, weak, empty, helpless creature as at first. Nothing, therefore, short of a *bountiful* supply can answer his emergency. And such a supply is always at hand. The act of prayer increases the power to pray. The throne of grace is a well, which no power or malice of the Philistines can stop up. (Comp. Gen. xxvi. 15.) We need not say, " We have nothing to draw with, and the well is deep." (John, iv. 11.) Faith will enable us " with joy to draw out of this well of salvation." (Isa. xii. 3.) Let us bring our empty vessels, until " there is not a vessel more." (Comp. 2 Kings, iv. 3–6.) Yes—believer—there is indeed a *bountiful* supply of grace—of every kind—suited to every want—grace to pardon—grace to quicken—grace to bless. Oh! see, then, that you come not empty away. Remember—who it is that pleads before the throne. Remember—that the grace you need is in his hand. From eternity he foreknew your case. He laid your portion by. He has kept it for the time of need ; and now he only waits for an empty vessel, into which to pour his supply. He is ready to show you, how infinitely his grace exceeds all thoughts—all prayers—all desires—all praises.

And say—what has been the fruit of your pleading, waiting expectancy at " the throne of grace ?" Have you not returned thence with a fresh spring of devotedness in his service, with every selfish thought forgotten in the desire, that you " *may live, and keep his word* ?" Nothing touched or moved your reluctant heart, but the apprehension of *bountiful* redeeming love. This makes obedience

easy—delightful—natural—in a manner unavoidable. It
" constrains" (2 Cor. v. 14) to it.   The man now *lives*—
not the animal life of appetite—not the sensual life of
vanity and pleasure—but the only life that deserves the
name.   He lives singly, supremely " to him that died for
him, and rose again." (2 Cor. v. 15.)   He " *lives, and keeps
his word.*"   His motto and character now is, " To me to
live is Christ." (Philip. i. 21. Comp. Acts, xiii. 36.)   He
values life only by his opportunities of serving his God.
(Philip. i. 20.)   The first archangel knows not a higher
object of existence.   And how encouraging the reflection,
that in this glorious object the meanest servant in the
household of God is an equal participant with the most
blessed inhabitant of heaven!

18. *Open thou mine eyes, that I may behold wondrous things
out of thy law.*

In order to *keep God's word*, must we not pray to understand it?   What then is the prayer?   Not—give me
a plainer Bible—but *open mine eyes* to know my Bible.
Not—show me some new revelations beside *the law*—but
make me *behold the wonders of the law.*   David had acquired
in the Divine school " more understanding than all his
teachers" (Verses 99, 100) ; yet he ever comes to his God
under a deep sense of his blindness.   Indeed those who
have been best and longest taught, are always the most
ready to " sit at the feet of Jesus" (Luke, x. 39), as if they
had everything to learn.   It is an unspeakable mercy to
know a little, and at the same time to feel that it is only a
little.   We shall then be longing to know more, and yet
anxious to know nothing, except as we are taught of God.
There are indeed in *God's law* things so *wondrous*, that
" the angels desire to look into them." (1 Pet. i. 12.)   The
exhibition of the scheme of redemption is in itself a world

of wonders. The display of justice exercised in the way of mercy, and of mercy glorified in the exercise of justice, is a wonder, that must fill the intelligent universe of God with everlasting astonishment. And yet these "*wondrous things*" are hid from multitudes, who are most deeply interested in the knowledge of them. They are " hid," not only from the ignorant and unconcerned, but " from the wise and prudent ; and revealed" only " to babes " (Matt. xi. 25)— to those who practically acknowledge that important truth, that a man " can receive nothing, except it be given him from heaven." (John, iii. 27.) External knowledge is like the child spelling the letters without any apprehension of the meaning. It is like reading a large and clear print with a thick veil before our eyes. Oh! how needful then is the prayer—' Unveil ;' *—" *Open thou mine eyes :*" let the veil be taken away from the law, that I may understand it ; and from my heart, that I may receive it !

But do not even Christians often find the word of God to be as a sealed book ? They go through their accustomed portion, without gaining any increasing acquaintance with its light, life, and power, and without any distinct application of its contents to their hearts. And thus it must be, whenever reading has been unaccompanied with prayer for Divine influence. For we not only need to have our " *eyes opened to behold*" fresh wonders, but also to give a more spiritual and transforming (2 Cor. iii. 18) perception of those wonders, which we have already beheld.

But are we conscious of our blindness ? Then let us hear the counsel of our Lord, that we " anoint our eyes with eye-salve, that we may see." (Rev. iii. 18.) The recollection of the promises of Divine teaching is fraught with encouragement. The Spirit is freely and abundantly promised in this very character, as " the Spirit of wisdom

* " Revela oculos meos. Velamen detrahe oculis meis."—POLI *Synopsis.* Margin, " Reveal." Comp. 2 Cor. iii. 14–16.

and revelation in the knowledge of God." (Eph. i. 17.) If, therefore, we desire a clearer insight into these "*wondrous things*" of revelation—if we would behold the glorious beauty of our Immanuel—if we would comprehend something more of the immeasurable extent of that love, with which "God so loved the world, as to give his only-begotten Son" (John, iii. 16), and of that equally incomprehensible love, which moved that Son so cheerfully to undertake our cause (Heb. x. 5–7), we must make daily, hourly use of this important petition—"*Open thou mine eyes.*"

19. *I am a stranger in the earth: hide not thy commandments from me.*

Such is the condition of the child of God—*a stranger in the earth!* This confession, however, from a solitary wanderer would have had little comparative meaning. But in the mouth of one, who was probably surrounded with every sort of worldly enjoyment, it shows at once the vanity of "earth's best joys," and the heavenly tendency of the religion of the Bible. This has been ever the character, confession, and glory of the Lord's people.* We "would not live always" (Job, vii. 16); and gladly do we hear the warning voice, that reminds us to "arise and depart, for this is not our rest." (Mic. ii. 10.) And was not this especially the character, not of David only, but of David's Lord? Born at an inn (Luke, ii. 7)—not "having where to lay his head" (Matt. viii. 20)—suffering hunger (Ib. xxi. 18)—subsisting upon alms (Luke, viii. 3)—neglected by his own (John, i. 11)—he "looked for some to take pity, but there was none, and for his comforters, but he found none" (Ps. lxix. 20)—might he not justly take up the confession—"I am *a stranger in the earth?*"

* Abraham, Gen. xxiii. 4. Jacob, Gen. xlvii. 9. David, Ps. xxxix. 12. All, Heb. xi. 13.

This verse exhibits the Christian in many most interesting points of view; distant from his proper home (Heb. xi. 9, 10)—without a fixed residence (1 Chron. xxix. 15)—with no particular interest in the world (Philip. iii. 20)—and submitting to all the inconveniences of a *stranger* on his journey homewards. (Acts, xiv. 22. Heb. x. 34.) Such is his state! And the word of God includes all that he wants—a guide, a guard, a companion—to direct, secure, and cheer his way. " When thou goest, it shall lead thee; when thou sleepest, it shall keep thee; and when thou awakest, it shall talk with thee." (Prov. vi. 22.) Most suitable then is *the stranger's* prayer—*" Hide not thy commandments from me."* Acquaintance with the word of God supplies the place of friends and counsellors. It furnishes light, joy, strength, food, armour, and whatever else he may need on his way homewards.

The pilgrim-spirit is the pulse of the soul. All of us are travelling to eternity. The worldling is at home *in the earth*—a pilgrim only by restraint. His heart would say—" It is good for me to be here. Let God dispose of heaven at his pleasure. I am content to have my " portion in this life." (Ps. xvii. 14. Comp. Luke, vi. 24; xii. 19, 20; xvi. 25.) The child of God is *a stranger in the earth.* Heaven is the country of his birth. (Gal. iv. 26.) His kindred (Eph. iii. 15)—his inheritance (Eph. i. 3, 11, 6. Matt. xxv. 34)—his Saviour (John, xiv. 3. Col. iii. 1)—his hope (Philip. iii. 20)—his home (2 Cor. v. 1–6)—all is there. He is " a citizen of no mean city," of " the heavenly Jerusalem." (Heb. xii. 22.) He is therefore a pilgrim in affection no less than in character. How cheering is the thought, that " here we have no continuing city," if in heart and soul we are " seeking one to come !" (Heb. xiii. 14.)

We know, indeed, that we cannot—we would not—call this world our home, and that it is far better to be without it, than to have our portion in it. But do we

never feel at home *in the earth*, thus forgetting our proper
character, and our eternal prospects? Do we always live,
speak, and act as " *strangers in the earth ;*" in the midst of
earthly enjoyments sitting loose to them, as if our treasure
was in heaven? Does our conversation in the society of
the world savour of the home, whither we profess to be
going? Is the world gaining ascendancy in our affection?
Let the cross of Calvary be the object of our daily contemplation — the ground of our constant " glorying ;" and the
world will then be to us as a " crucified" object. (Gal. vi.
14.) And lastly, let us not forget, that we are looking
forward, and making a progress towards a world, where
none are strangers — where all are children of one family,
dwelling in one eternal home. " *In our Father's house*,"
said our gracious Head, " *are many mansions : I go to prepare a place for you.*" (John, xiv. 2.)

20. *My soul breaketh for the longing that it hath unto thy
judgments at all times.*

This intense desire and affection is the Christian's
answer to his prayers—*Open thou mine eyes*—*Hide not thy
commandments from me.* For who that is conversant with
this blessed revelation but *longs* to be filled with it? In
contrasting this glow with the church of Laodicea, under a
brighter dispensation, " neither cold nor hot" (Rev. iii. 15):
which state, we may ask, most nearly resembles our own?
Observe also, not only the fervour, but the steady uniformity, of this religion. It was not a rapture, but a habit ;
constant and uniform ; " *at all times.*" With us such enjoyments are too often favoured seasons, happy moments ;
alas! only moments — why not days, and months, and
years? The object of our desires is an inexhaustible
spring. *The longing of the soul* can never over-reach its
object. The *cherished desire*, therefore, will become the

established habit—the element in which the child of God lives and thrives.

This uniformity is the most satisfactory test of our profession. Often are *the judgments* prized in affliction, when all other resources fail: or under a pang of conscience when the terror of the Lord is frowning upon the sinner. (Isa. xxvi. 16.) But the excitement wears off, and the heart returns to its hardness. Often also the impulse of novelty gives a strong but temporary impression. (John, v. 35.) This is very different from the Christian, whose study is stretching out its desires *at all times ;* finding *the judgments* a cordial or a discipline, a support or a preservation, as his need may require.

Not less important is this habit, as the test of the soul's prosperity. We are not satisfied with *occasional* intercourse with a beloved friend. His society is the life of our life. We seek him in his own ways, where he is used to resort. We feel the blank of his absence. We look out for his return with joyous anticipation. Now, is this the picture of *our soul's longing* for communion with Jesus ? We may feel his loss, should the stated seasons of prayer fail in bringing him near to us. But do we *long* for him *at all times ?* Do we " wait for him in the way of *his judgments,*" where he is wont to be found ? (Isa. xxvi. 8; lxiv. 5.) And when spiritual exercises are necessarily exchanged for the occupations of the world, do we seize the leisure moment to catch a word — a glimpse — a look ? Is not the heart dumb with shame in the recollection of the cold habit of external or occasional duty ?

But whence this low ebbing of spiritual desire ? Do we live near to the throne of grace ? Have we not neglected prayer for the influence of the Spirit ? Have we not indulged a light, vain, and worldly spirit, than which nothing more tends to wither the growth of vital religion ? Or have not the workings of unbelief been too faintly

resisted ? This of itself will account for much of our
dulness ; since the rule of the kingdom of grace is, " According to your faith be it unto you." (Matt. ix. 29.)
Grace is, indeed, an insatiable principle. Enjoyment, instead of surfeiting, only serves to sharpen the appetite.
Yet if we are content to live at a low rate, there will be no
sensible interest in the consolation of the Gospel. We
know, desire, and are satisfied with little ; and, *therefore*,
we enjoy but little. We live as borderers on the land,
instead of bearing our testimony: " Surely it floweth with
milk and honey; *and this is the fruit of it.*" (Num. xiii. 27.)
This is not the thriving, the cheerfulness, the adorning of
the Gospel. It is rather the obscuring of the glory of our
Christian profession, and of the happiness of its attendant
privileges.

Let not the fervour of desire here expressed be conceived to be out of reach ; nor let it be expected in the
way of some sudden manifestation or excitement. Rather
let us look for it in a patient, humble, and persevering
waiting upon the Lord. We may have still to complain
of coldness and wanderings. Yet strength to wait will be
imperceptibly given : faith will be sustained for the conflict ; and thus " our souls will make their boast in the
Lord," even though an excited flow of enjoyment should
be withheld. One desire will, however, tread upon another,
increasing in fulness, as the grand object is nearer our
grasp.

At all events, let us beware of resting satisfied with
the confession of our lukewarmness to our fellow-creatures,
without " pouring out our heart before the Lord." There
is a fulness of grace in our glorious Head to " strengthen
the things that remain, that are ready to die," as well as
at the beginning to " quicken " us when " dead in trespasses
and sins." Abundant, also, are the promises and encouragements to poor, dry, barren souls,—" I will heal their

backslidings ; I will be as the dew unto Israel : he shall
grow as the lily, and cast forth his roots as Lebanon."
(Hos. xiv. 4–6.) For what purpose are promises such as
these given, but that they may be " arguments," wherewith
to "fill our mouth," when in the contrition of faith we again
venture to " order our cause before God ?" And " will he
plead against us with his great power?" No ; but " he
will put his strength in us" (Job, xxiii. 4–6); and we
shall yet again " run the way of his commandments"
(Verse 32) with an enlarged heart.

21. *Thou hast rebuked the proud that are cursed, which do err
from thy commandments.*

Let the histories of Cain (Gen. iv. 5, 13–16), Pharaoh
(Exod. xiv. 15–31), Haman (Esth. vii. 7–10), Nebuchad-
nezzar (Dan. iv. 29–33), and Herod (Acts, xii. 21–23),
exhibit *the proud under the rebuke and curse* of God. He
abhors their persons (Prov. vi. 16, 17), and their offerings
(Luke, xviii. 11, 12, 14) ; he " knows them afar off" (Ps.
cxxxviii. 6) ; "he resisteth them" (1 Pet. v. 5 ; with
Prov. iii. 34) ; " he scattereth them in the imaginations
of their hearts." (Luke, i. 51.) Especially hateful are they
in his sight, when cloaking themselves under a spiritual
garb ; " They say, Stand by thyself, come not near to me ;
for I am holier than thou : *these are a smoke in my nose, a
fire that burneth all the day.*" (Isa. lxv. 5 ; with Luke, xviii.
11.) Most of all, is this sin an abomination in his own
beloved people. David (2 Sam. xxiv. 1–15) and Hezekiah
(2 Kings, xx. 12–18. 2 Chron. xxxii. 31) are instructive
beacons in the church, that they, least of all, must expect
to escape his rebuke—" Thou wast a God that forgavest
them ; *though thou tookest vengeance on their inventions.*"
(Ps. xcix. 8.) " Now they call *the proud* happy." (Mal.
iii. 15.) But will they be counted so, when they shall be

manifestly under the *curse of God;* when "the day of the Lord shall be upon them to bring them low," yea, to "burn them in the oven" of "his wrath?" (Isa. ii. 12–17. Mal. iv. 1.)

Pride probably influences all, that "*do err from the Lord's commandments;*" yet doubtless "the Righteous Judge" will make an infinite difference between *errors* of infirmity and obstinate wilfulness. (Ps. xix. 12 ; with xcv. 10.) The confession of the man of God, " I have gone astray like a lost sheep " (Verse 176)—is widely different in character from the subjects of this awful *rebuke and curse.* " *Thou hast trodden down all them that err from thy statutes ; for their deceit is falsehood.*" (Verse 118.)

We wonder not at this expression of the mind of God concerning pride. There is no sin more abhorrent to his character. It is as if we were taking the crown from his head, and placing it upon our own. It is man making a god of himself—acting from himself, and for himself. Nor is this principle less destructive to our own happiness. And yet it is not only rooted, but it often rears its head and blossoms, and bears fruit, even in hearts which " hate and abhor " its influence. It is most like its father, the Devil, in serpentine deceitfulness. It is always active—always ready imperceptibly to mix itself up with everything. When it is mortified in one shape, it rises in another. When we have thought that it was gone, in some unexpected moment we find it here still. It can convert everything into nourishment, even God's choicest gifts—yea, the graces of his Spirit. Let no saint, therefore, however near he may be living to God, however favoured with the shinings of his countenance —consider himself beyond the reach of this temptation. Paul was most in danger, when he seemed to be most out of it ; and nothing but an instant miracle of grace and power saved him from the " snare of the Devil." (See 2 Cor. xii. 7.) Indeed, the whole plan of salvation is intended to humble the pride of man, by ex-hibiting his restoration to the Divine favour, as a free gift through the atoning blood of the cross. How hateful, therefore, is *proud* man's resistance to this humbling doc-trine of the cross, and the humbling requisitions of the life of faith flowing from it! This makes the sure "founda-tion" of the believer's hope, "a stone of stumbling" to the unbeliever's ruin. (Rom. ix. 32, 33. 1 Pet. ii. 7, 8.) As regards also the means of salvation—how can pride lift up his head in the view of the Son of God, "taking upon him the form of a servant," that he might bear the curse of man? (Philip. ii. 5–8.) " Behold, the soul that is lifted up is not upright in him." (Hab. ii. 4.)

But can a sinner—can a saint—be *proud?*—one that owes everything to free and sovereign grace —one that has wasted so much time— abused so much mercy— so grieved the Spirit of God—that has a heart so full of atheism— unbelief—selfishness? Nay, the very pride itself should be the matter of the deepest daily humiliation. Thus the remembrance of it may, under Divine grace, prove an effec-tual means of subduing it in our hearts. We shall overcome corruption by its own working, and meet our adversary with his own weapons. And if this cursed principle be not wholly destroyed, yet the very sight of its corruption, deepening our contrition, will be overruled for our spiritual advancement.

O blessed end intended by the Lord's dealings with us! to "humble and to prove us"—" to know," and to make us know " what was in our heart, that he might do us good at the latter end!" (Deut. viii. 2, 16.) Let us not frustrate his gracious intentions, or build again the things which he would have destroyed. May we love to lie low—lower than ever—infinitely low before him! Lord! teach us to remember, that " that which is highly esteemed among men, is abomination in thy sight." (Luke, xvi. 15.) Teach us to bless thee, for even thy sharp and painful discipline which tends to subjugate this hateful pride of our hearts before our Saviour's cross !

22. *Remove from me reproach and contempt; for I have kept thy testimonies.*

The *proud under the rebuke of God* are usually distinguished by their enmity to his people. They delight to pour upon them "*reproach and contempt,*" with no other provocation given, than that their *keeping the testimonies* of God condemns their own neglect. (Heb. xi. 7.) This must, however, be counted as the cost of a decided, separate, and consistent profession. Yet it is such a portion as Moses valued above all the treasures of the world (Heb. xi. 24–26) ; yet it is that *reproach*, which our Master himself "despised," as "reckoning it not worthy to be compared with " "the joy that was set before him." (Heb. xii. 2.) For did he bear his cross only on the way to Calvary ? It was laid for every step in his path ; it met him in every form of suffering, of "*reproach and contempt.*" Look then at him, as taking up his daily cross in breathing the atmosphere of a world of sin, and "enduring the contradiction of sinners against himself." (Heb. xii. 3.) Mark him consummating his course of "*reproach and contempt,*" by suffering "without the gate ;" and can we hesitate to " go forth unto him without the camp, bearing his reproach?" (Heb. xiii. 12, 13.)

The trial, however—especially if cast upon us by those whom we have loved and valued, or by those whom we wish to love and value us—proves most severe ; and the spreading our case, after David's example, before the Lord, is the only preservation from faintness—"*Remove from me reproach and contempt.*"

Perhaps "*contempt*" is more hard to bear than "*reproach.*" Even our enemies think of us so much better than we deserve, that it strikes with peculiar poignancy. Yet when the submissive prayer of deprecation (see verse 134) is sent us; doubtless some answer — and *that* the right answer — will be given ; and whether the " *reproach* " *be removed*, or " grace " vouchsafed " sufficient " to endure it (2 Cor. xii. 8, 9), the issue will prove alike for the glory of God, and the prosperity of our own souls.

But let us beware of that " way of escape " in returning to the world, which the insincere are ever ready to pursue. They dare not act according to the full conviction of their consciences : they dare not confront their friends with the avowal of their full determination to form their conduct by the principles of the word of God. This is hard — this is impossible. They know not the " victory that overcometh the world " (see 1 John, v. 4, 5), and, therefore, cannot bear the mark upon their foreheads —" These are they, which follow the Lamb whithersoever he goeth." (Rev. xiv. 4.) Far better, however, will be the heaviest weight of " *reproach and contempt*," than any such endeavour to *remove it* from ourselves. The desire to escape the cross convicts the heart of unfaithfulness, and makes way for tenfold difficulties in our path. Every worldly compliance against the voice of God is a step into the by-path, which deviates wider and wider from the strait and narrow way, brings discredit upon our professions, proves a stumbling-block in the way of the weak, and will cause us, if not actually to come short, at least to " *seem to come short*, of the promised rest." (Heb. iv. 1.)

But is the weight of the cross really "above that we are able to bear ? " He that bore it for us will surely enable us to endure it for him, and, upheld by him, we cannot sink. It is a sweet exchange, by which the burden of sin is removed, and bound to his cross; and what remains to us is the lighter cross of " *reproach and contempt*,"— the badge of our discipleship. (Matt. xvi. 24.) If, then, we have the testimony of our consciences, that in the midst of the persecuting world we " *have kept his testimonies* " (Verses 61, 69, 87, 95, 110), here is our evidence of adoption, of our Father's special love, of the indwelling, comforting, supporting Spirit. (John, xiv. 15–18, 21–23.) Here, then, is our warrant of hope, that the overwhelming weight will be *removed from us;* and that we shall be able to testify to our Master's praise in the Churches of God, that " his yoke is easy, and his burden is light." (Matt. xi. 30.)

23. *Princes also did sit and speak against me; but thy servant did meditate in thy statutes.*

David might well give his testimony to " the words of the Lord," that they were "tried words" (Ps. xii. 7, Prayer-book translation) ; for perhaps no one had ever tried them more than himself, and certainly no one had more experience of their faithfulness, sweetness, and support. Saul and his " *princes might indeed sit and speak against him ;*" but he had a resource, of which they could never deprive him— " Not as the world giveth, give I unto you." (John, xiv. 27.) As our blessed Master was employed in communion with his Father, and delighting in his work at the time when the " *princes did sit and speak against him* " (John, xi. 47, 54–57) ; so, under similar circumstances of trial, this faithful servant of God, by *meditation in' the Lord's statutes,* extracted spiritual food for his support (comp. Ps. xciv. 19–22) ; and in this strength of his God he was enabled to " suffer according to his will, and to commit the keeping of his soul to him in well-doing, as unto a faithful Creator." (1 Pet. iv. 19.)

The children of Israel in Egypt (Exod. i. 10), Daniel in Babylon (Dan. vi. 4), and the disciples of Christ in the early ages of the Church (Matt. x. 17, 18. Acts, iv. 27–29), have severally found " this same affliction to be accomplished in themselves." God is pleased to permit it, to show "that his kingdom is not of this world" (John, xviii. 36), to wean his people from earthly dependencies, and to bring out before the world a more full testimony of his name. (Matt. x. 18.) One other reason is suggested by this verse—to make his word more precious by the experience of its sustaining consolation in the conflict with the power of the world. Often, indeed, from a want of a present application of the word, young Christians especially are in danger of being put to rebuke by the scorner's sneer. The habit of scriptural *meditation* will realize to them a present God, speaking "words of spirit and life" to their souls. The importance, therefore, of an accurate and well-digested acquaintance with this precious book cannot be too highly estimated. In the Christian's conflict it is "the sword of the Spirit" (Eph. vi. 17), which, if it be kept bright by constant use, will never be wielded without the victory of faith. Such powerful support does it give against fainting under persecution, that the good soldier may ever be ready to thank God, and to take courage. (Acts, xxviii. 15.) Christ has left it, indeed, as the portion of his people— " In the world ye shall have tribulation ;" counterbalanced, however, most abundantly, by the portion which they enjoy in him—" In me ye shall have peace." * If, therefore, the one-half of this portion may seem hard, the whole legacy is such as no servant of Christ can refuse to accept, or indeed will receive without thankfulness.

24. *Thy testimonies also are my delight, and my counsellors.*

What could we want more in a time of difficulty than comfort and direction? David had both these blessings.

* John, xvi. 33. See the beautiful illustration of this *whole declaration*—Acts, xvi. 22–25.

As the fruit of his " *meditation in the Lord's statutes*," in
his distress they were his " *delight;*" in his perplexity they
were his " *counsellors*." He would not have exchanged his
delight for the best joys of earth (Verses 14, 97, 103, 127 ;
with Ps. iv. 7.) And so wisely did his counsellors direct
his course, that, though " *princes sat and spake against him*,"
they " could find none occasion nor fault." (1 Sam. xviii. 14.
Ps. ci. 2 ; with Dan. vi. 4, 5.) The testimonies of God
were truly " *the men of his counsel*." (Margin.) He guided
his own conduct by the rules laid before him in the book
of God, as if he were having recourse to the most experienced counsellors, or rather as if the prophets of his God
were giving the word from his mouth. (Comp. 2 Sam. vii.
4, 5 ; also xvi. 23.) Thus the subject as well as the
sovereign, had his counsel. On one side was Saul and his
counsellors (Verse 23)—on the other side, David and the
testimonies of his God. Which, think we, was better furnished with that " wisdom which is profitable to direct ?"
Subsequently as a king, David was constrained to make
" *the testimonies of his God his counsellors*" (Deut. xvii.
18–20) ; and, probably, to his constant regard to their
voice he owed much of his earthly prosperity.*

In such a dark world as this, beset with temptation at
every turn, we pre-eminently need sound and wise counsel.
But all of us carry an evil *counsellor* within us, and it is
our folly to listen to his voice. (Prov. xxviii. 26.) God
has given us his word as a sure counsellor, and " he that
hearkeneth to its counsel is wise." (Prov. xii. 15.)

Now, do we value the privilege of this heavenly counsel ?
Every improvement must increase our *delight* in it ; a heartless interest shuts out this blessing. But those who make
the word their delight will always find it *their counsellor*.

---

* 2 Sam. viii. 6, 14. Compare also his dying and most encouraging advice to Solomon on this subject, founded, doubtless,
upon the recollection of his own experience. 1 Kings, ii. 3.

Yet a mere cursory reading will never realize to us its holy delight or counsel. It must be brought home to our own experience, and consulted on those trivial occasions of every day, when, unconscious of our need of Divine direction, we are too often inclined to lean to our own counsel. The Christian is a man of faith, every step of his way. And this habitual use and daily familiarity with the testimonies of God will show him the pillar and the cloud (Num. ix. 15–23), in all the dark turns of his heavenly road. The word will be to him as the " Urim and Thummim " (Num. xxvii. 21)—an infallible *counsellor*.

Sometimes, however, perplexity arises from the conflict, not between conscience and sinful indulgence (in which case Christian sincerity would always determine the path), but between duty and duty. When, however, acknowledged obligations seem to interfere with each other, the counsel of the word will mark their relative importance, connexion, and dependence : the present path in providence : the guidance which has been vouchsafed to the Lord's people in similar emergencies ; and the light which the daily life of our Great Exemplar exhibits before us. The great concern, however, is to cultivate the habit of mind, which falls in most naturally with the counsel of the word. " Walking in the fear of the Lord" (see Ps. xxv. 12, 14), in a simple spirit of dependence (Ps. xxv. 4, 5, 9 ; cxliii. 8), and torn away from the idolatry of taking counsel from our own hearts, we cannot *materially* err ; because there is *here a suitableness between the disposition and the promise*—a watchfulness against the impetuous bias of the flesh ; a paramount regard to the glory of God, and a meek submission to his gracious appointment. If the counsel, however, should not prove infallible, the fault is not in the word, but in the indistinctness of our own perception. We want not a clearer rule, or a surer guide, but a more single eye. And if, after all, it may not mark every precise act of duty (for to do this, even the world itself " could not contain the books that should be written"), yet it determines the standard to which the most minute acting of the mind should be brought (1 Cor. x. 31. Col. iii. 17) ; and the disposition, which will reflect the light of the will of God upon our path. (Matt. vi. 22, 23.)

But let it be remembered, that any want of sincerity in the heart (1 Sam. xxviii. 6. Ezek. xiv. 2–4)—any allowance of self-dependence (Prov. iii. 5, 6), will always close the avenues of this Divine light and counsel. We are often unconsciously "walking in the light of our own fire, and in the sparks that we have kindled" (Isa. l. 11.) Perhaps we sought, as we conceived, the guidance of the Lord's counsel, and supposed that we were walking in it. But, in the act of seeking, and as the preparation for seeking, did we subject our motives and inclinations to a strict, cautious, self-suspecting scrutiny? Was the heart schooled to the discipline of the cross? Was " every thought brought into captivity to the obedience of Christ?" (2 Cor. x. 5.) Or was not our heart possessed with the object, before counsel was sought at the mouth of God? (Jer. xlii.) Oh ! how careful should we be to walk warily in those uncertain marks of heavenly counsel, that fall in with the bias of our own inclination ! How many false steps in the record of past experience may be traced to the counsel of our own hearts, sought and followed to the neglect and counsel of God (Josh. ix. 14. Isa. xxx. 1–3) ; while no circumstance of perplexity can befall us in the spirit of humility, simplicity, and sanctity, when the counsel of the Lord will fail !

An undue dependence upon human counsel (Isa. ii. 22), whether of the living or the dead, greatly hinders the full influence of the counsel of the word. However valuable such counsel may be, and however closely it may agree with the word, we must not forget, that it is not the word— that it is fallible, and therefore must never be resorted to in the first place, or followed with that full reliance, which we are warranted to place on the revelation of God. On the other hand, what is it to have God's word as our *" Counsellor?"* Is it not to have himself — " the only wise God?" When our Bibles, in seasons of difficulty, are searched in a humble, prayerful, teachable spirit, we are as much depending upon the Lord himself for counsel, as if we were listening to an immediate revelation from heaven. We want not a new revelation, or a sensible voice from above, for every fresh emergency. It is enough, that our Father has given us this blessed " word as a light to our feet, and a lamp to our path." (Verse 105. Comp. Prov. vi. 23.)

Let me then inquire — What is the counsel of God, that speaks directly to myself? If I am an unawakened sinner, it warns me to turn from sin (Prov. i. 24–31. Ezek. xxxiii. 11) ; it invites me to the Saviour (Isa. lv. 1. John, vii. 37) ; it directs me to wait upon God (Hos. xii. 6). If I am a professor, slumbering in the form of godliness, it shows me my real condition (Rev. iii. 17) ; it instructs me in the all-sufficiency of Christ (Rev. iii. 18), and cautions me of the danger of hypocrisy (Luke, xii. 1). If through grace I am made a child of God, still do I need my Father's counsel to recover me from perpetual backsliding (Jer. iii. 12, 13), to excite me to increased watchfulness (1 Thess. v. 6. Rev. iii. 2), and to strengthen my confidence in the fulness of his grace (Isa. xxvi. 4), and the faithfulness of his love (Heb. xii. 5, 6). Ever shall I have reason for the grateful acknowledgment — " I will bless the Lord, who hath given me counsel." (Ps. xvi. 7.) And every step of my way would I advance, glorifying my God and Father by confiding in his counsel unto the end : " Thou shalt guide me with thy counsel, and afterwards receive me to glory." (Ps. lxxiii. 24.)

PART IV.

25. *My soul cleaveth unto the dust; quicken thou me according*
to thy word.

SIN is no trifle to a child of God. It is his heaviest sorrow. Thus David—thus the Great Apostle found it.
(Ps. xxxviii. 4. Rom. vii. 24.) And where is the believer
who has not full sympathy with their complaints? To
have a *soul cleaving to the dust,* and not to feel the trouble,
is the black mark of a sinner, dead in sins—dead to God.
To " know the plague of our own heart" (1 Kings, viii.
38), to feel our misery, to believe and to apply the remedy
(Rom. vii. 24, 25), is the satisfactory evidence of a child
of God. *Dust* is the portion of the world, and they wish
for no better. But that the soul of the man of God should
continually *cleave to the dust,* is most strange and humbling.
And yet such is the influence of his evil nature—such the
power of self-will and self-indulgence—such the regard to
human praise, and cherishing of self-admiration, that were
it not that he " abhors himself " for the very *dust that
cleaves* to him, he would question the existence of a renewing change. He knows what he ought to be. He has
tasted the blessedness of " mounting upward on eagles'
wings." (Isa. xl. 31.) But every attempt to rise is hindered
by the clogging weight that keeps him down. It is, however, the *cleaving of his soul* that is so painful—not occasional, but constant—not like the bird of the morning that
descends for a moment, and then soars his upward flight;

but it seems as if, like the " serpent — dust was to be his
meat " (Isa. lxv. 25) ; as if the spiritual, heaven-born soul
was to sink and grovel below. And then, as the dust of
the summer-road blinds the eye, and obscures the prospect:
how does this earthliness of soul darken the view of the
Saviour, dim the eye of faith, and hide the glorious prospects which, when beheld in the clear horizon, enliven the
weary pilgrim on his way !

But this complaint is the language of conflict and
humiliation — not of despondency. Mark the believer
carrying it to the Lord —' Here I lie in the *dust*, without
life or power. Oh ! thou Saviour, who " camest that I
might have life, and that I might have it more abundantly"
(John, x. 10)— *Quicken me:* Breathe into me thine own
life, that I may rise from the *dust*, and *cleave* to thee.'
This cry for quickening grace is the exercise of faith. We
have a covenant to plead. Faith is the hand that takes
hold of the promise —" *according to thy word.*" Can this
word fail ? " Sooner shall heaven and earth pass away,
than one jot or one tittle pass " from the engagements of a
covenant-keeping God. " He is faithful that hath promised." (Heb. x. 23 ; with Luke, xxi. 33.) The man who
takes hold of this plea, is " a Prince who has power with
God, and prevails." (Gen. xxxii. 28.)

But how different is the character of the mere professor ! ready probably to make the same confession, yet
without humiliation, without prayer, without faith. Nothing is more common than to hear the complaint—' " *My
soul cleaveth unto the dust.*" The world has such power over
us — we are so cold — so dead to spiritual things :' while,
perhaps, the complaint is never once brought with wrestling
supplication, but rather urged in indolent self-complacency,
as an evidence of the good state of the heart before God.
Yet it is not the complaint of sickness, but an application
to the physician, that advances the recovery of the patient.

We do not usually expect to better our condition, by mourning over its badness, or merely wishing for its improvement. Nor is it the confession of sin, but the application to the Great Physician, that marks genuine contrition before God. That confession which evaporates in heartless complaints, belongs not to the tenderness of a renewed heart. But the utterance of genuine prayer is the voice of God's own " Spirit making intercession for us ; " and then, indeed, how cheering the encouragement, that he " that searcheth the hearts, knoweth what is the mind of the Spirit, because he maketh intercession for the saints according to the will of God!" (Rom. viii. 26, 27.) Some are ready to give up or delay their duty, when they have been unable to bring their heart to it. Thus does " Satan get advantage of us " by our " ignorance of his devices." *Quickening* grace is not the ground or warrant for duty. Indisposition to duty is not our weakness, but our sin — not therefore to be indulged, but resisted. We must mourn over the dulness that hinders us, and diligently wait for the ' help we every moment need.' God keeps the grace in his own hands, and gives it at his pleasure, to exercise our daily dependence upon him. (Philip. ii. 12, 13.) The acting of grace strengthens the habit. Praying helps to pray. If the door is closed, " Knock, and it shall be opened." (Matt. vii. 7, 8.) Assuredly it will not long be shut to him, who has faith and patience to wait until it be opened.

Now let me sift the character of my profession. Is it an habitual, persevering, overcoming conflict with sin ? Do I not sometimes indulge in fruitless bemoanings of my state, when I had far better be exercising myself in vigorous actings of grace ? If I find "*my soul cleaving to the dust,*" am I not sometimes " lying on my face " (Josh. vii. 10), when I ought to be " taking heaven by violence " (Matt. xi. 12), by importunate petitions for *quickening* grace ? Are my prayers invigorated by confidence in the word of God? Oh! let me remember that "they that wait upon the Lord" shall shake off *the dust* to which they have *cleaved* so long, and "shall mount with wings like eagles" (Isa. xl. 31), to take possession of their heavenly home.

O Lord, make me more deeply ashamed, that "*my soul should cleave to the dust*." Breathe upon me fresh influence from thy *quickening* Spirit. Help me to plead thy word of promise; and oh! may every fresh view of my sinfulness, while it prostrates me in self-abasement before thee, be overruled to make the Saviour daily and hourly more precious to my soul. For defiled as I am in myself, in every service of my heart, what but the unceasing application of his blood, and the uninterrupted prevalence of his intercession, give me a moment's confidence before thee, or prevent the very sins that mingle with my prayers from sealing my condemnation? Blessed Saviour! it is nothing but thy everlasting merit, covering my person, and honouring my sacrifice, that satisfies the justice of an offended God, and restrains it from breaking forth as a devouring fire, to consume me upon my very knees.

26. *I have declared my ways, and thou heardest me; teach me thy statutes.*

A beautiful description of the "simplicity and godly sincerity" of the believer's "walk with God!" He spreads his whole case before his God, "*declaring his ways*" of sinfulness (Ps. li. 3), of difficulty (Ps. v. 8; xxvii. 11), and of conduct. (Ps. cxliii. 8, 10; lxix. 5.) And, indeed, it is our privilege to acquaint our Father with all our care and need, that we may be pitied by his love, and guided by his counsel, and confirmed by his strength. Who would not find relief by unbosoming himself to his Father? This

showing of ourselves to God—*declaring our ways* of sin
before him without guile—is the short and sure way of
rest. " *Thou heardest me.*" " *When I kept silence*, my bones
waxed old through my roaring all the day long." (Ps.
xxxii. 3.) While the voice of ingenuous confession was
suppressed, cries and lamentations were disregarded. It
was not the voice of the penitent child ; and, therefore,
" where was the sounding of his father's bowels, and of his
mercies towards him ?" (Isa. lxiii. 15.) But now, on the
first utterance of confession from his lips, or rather on the
first purpose of contrition formed in his heart ; " while he is
yet speaking" (Dan. ix. 20), the full and free pardon, which
had been signed in heaven, comes down with royal parental
love to his soul—" I said, I will confess my transgression
unto the Lord ; and thou forgavest the iniquity of my
sin." (Ps. xxxii. 5. 2 Sam. xii. 13. Comp. Jer. iii. 12, 13.)
Oh ! what cannot he testify of the more than parental
tenderness, with which " his transgression is forgiven, and
his sin covered !" (Comp. Ps. xxxii. 1 ; Luke, xv. 18–22 ;
Prov. xxviii. 13.) And yet, how necessary to the free
declaration of our ways is an acquaintance with the way of
forgiveness ! Had not our great " High Priest passed into
the heavens," how awful would have been the thought, that
all things were naked and opened unto the eyes of him
with whom we have to do !" We could only then have " covered our transgressions as Adam, by hiding our iniquity
in our bosom." (Job, xxxi. 33.) But now, even though
" *our ways*" are so defiled, so crooked that we cannot but
abhor ourselves," on account of them, we are yet encouraged
" boldly" to " *declare*" them all before God, with the assurance of finding present acceptance, and seasonable grace.
(Heb. iv. 13–16.)

And now, having found the happy fruit of this sincere
and child-like spirit, then follows the obligation of walking

worthy of this mercy. (Ps. lxxxv. 8.) Hence our need of
the prayer for continual *teaching*. The same heavenly
guidance, that brought us into the way of return, we need
for every successive step to the end—" Teach me thy way,
O Lord : I will walk in thy truth." (Ps. lxxxvi. 11.) "*I
have declared my*" ignorance, my sinfulness, and my whole
experience before thee, looking for thy pardoning mercy,
thy teaching Spirit, and assisting grace, "*And thou hast
heard me.*" O continue to me what thou hast been, and
teach me more of thyself ?

The hypocrite may pray after his manner. But he
never thus opens his heart, and " *declares his ways*" beneath
his God. And are we sincere in our dealings with him?
How often do we treat our Almighty Friend as if we were
weary of dealing with him! And even when we do " *declare our ways*" before him, are we not often content to
leave the result as a matter of uncertainty? We do not
watch for the answer to our prayer. It will come in the
diligent exercise of faith, but not perhaps in our way. We
may have asked for temporal blessings, and we receive
spiritual. (Matt. ix. 2.) We may have " besought" deliverance from trial, and we receive " grace sufficient" to
bear it. (2 Cor. xii. 8, 9.) But this is the Lord's wise and
gracious answer—*thou heardest me.* And how sweet are
those mercies, which come to us manifestly marked with
this inscription—" Received by prayer!" They are such
encouragement to pray again. (Ps. cxvi. 1, 2.) It is not
our inevitable weakness (Rom. vii. 21), nor our lamented
dulness (Mark, xiv. 38, 40), nor our abhorred wanderings
(Verse 113), nor our opposed distractions (Ps. lxxxvi. 11,
last clause), nor our mistaken unbelief (Mark, ix. 22, 24);
it is not any—no, nor all these—that can shut out prayer.
If " iniquity" is not " regarded in our heart," we may always
hear our Saviour's voice, " Verily, verily, I say unto you,
Whatsoever ye shall ask the Father in my name, he will

give it you.   Hitherto have ye asked nothing in my name.
Ask, and ye shall receive, that your joy may be full."*

27. *Make me to understand the way of thy precepts ; so shall
I talk of thy wondrous works.*

Mark the reiterated cries of the man of God for heavenly light, *Teach me thy statutes—make me to understand
the way of thy precepts.*   The need and the encouragement
for these cries is equally manifest.   Who has ever been
known to *understand the way* of himself ?   And to whom
—walking in a well-ordered conversation—has the Lord
ever failed to show it? (See Ps. l. 23.)   A man, untaught
by the Spirit of God, may be able to criticise, and even
clearly to expound, much of the word of God.   But such
a prayer as this has never ascended from the heart ; the
necessity of it has never been felt.   And, doubtless, from
this neglect of prayer have arisen those floating fancies and
false and unscriptural doctrines, which crude, unexercised
minds have too hastily embraced.   Instead of humbly and
simply asking, " *Make me to understand*"—men too often
" lean to their own understanding," and are " vainly puffed
up " by their fleshly mind, " *not holding the Head.*" (Col. ii.
18, 19.) Such men may obtain loose fragments of spiritual
knowledge ; but they will not be in the faith, " grounded
and settled." (Col. i. 23.)   They never know when they
are upon safe ground ; and being " unlearned and unstable,

* John, xvi. 23, 24.   Every way worthy of that great man,
and a most instructive illustration of Christian sincerity, was the
resolution of President Edwards: ' Resolved to exercise myself in
this all my life long, viz., with the greatest openness to *declare my
ways to God*, and lay open my soul to him—all my sins, temptations, difficulties, sorrows, fears, hopes, desires, and everything, and
every circumstance, according to Dr. Manton's twenty-seventh sermon on the cxix. Psalm.' Resol. 65.   Extracted from his Diary.
Works, vol. i. 16.

they wrest the Scriptures"—except the sovereign grace
of God interpose—"unto their own destruction." (2 Pet.
iii. 16.)

Never must we forget, that teaching from above is
indispensable to a right knowledge of the most simple
truths. Ignorance and prejudice pervert the understanding. "Spiritual things can only be spiritually discerned."
(1 Cor. ii. 14.) Divine doctrines can only be apprehended
by Divine light. (Ps. xxxvi. 9.) But under heavenly
teaching, the deeper and more mysterious truths (so far as
they are needful to be understood) are manifested with the
same clearness, as the more elementary doctrines : " Eye
hath not seen nor ear heard, nor have entered into the
heart of man, the things which God hath prepared for
them that love him. But God hath revealed them to us
by his Spirit. Now we have received—not the spirit of
the world, *but the Spirit which is of God, that we might know
the things that are freely given to us of God.*" (1 Cor. ii. 9,
10, 12.)

Wondrous, indeed, is the spiritual revelation in the
knowledge of himself; including " the hope of his calling ;
— the riches of the glory of his inheritance in his saints ;—
the exceeding greatness of his power" manifested to, and
wrought in, his people ;—no other or less than that " which
he wrought in Christ, when he raised him from the dead."
(Eph. i. 17–20.) In the understanding of the way, we
would be progressing until the new man " grows up into
the measure of the stature of the fulness of Christ." (Eph.
iv. 13.) The smallest attainment in this knowledge is (as
the great day will fully declare) of infinitely greater value
than the highest intelligence in the field of earthly science.

But how important is it to grow in this knowledge!
(2 Pet. iii. 18.) Theoretical attainment is at a stand.
Spiritual and practical knowledge is always advancing.
Little, indeed, comparatively, is necessary for salvation.

But much for comfort and stedfastness—much also for the clear discernment of that narrow way *of the precepts* so difficult to trace, and when traced so difficult to maintain. Not less important is it to keep the object in constant view. Why do I desire to *understand that way?* That I may commend it to others—that I may *talk of thy wondrous works.* Abhorred be the thought of indulging in a self-complacent view of my attainments! But oh! let my God be more admired by me, and glorified in me. (Gal. i. 24. Matt. v. 16.) And may I advance both myself and others in his obedience and praise!

Often do we complain of restraint in religious conversation. But the prayer—*Make me to understand while I talk*—will bring " a live coal to our lips" from the altar of God—" Our mouths will then speak out of the abundance of the heart" (Matt. xii. 34), and " minister grace to the hearers." (Eph. iv. 29.) Humility, teachableness, simplicity, will bring light into the understanding, influence the heart, " open the lips," and unite every member that we have in the service and praise of God.

28. *My soul melteth for heaviness; strengthen thou me according unto thy word.*

Is this David. " whose heart is as the heart of a lion, here utterly *melting?*" (2 Sam. xvii. 10. Comp. Josh. vii. 5; Ps. cvii. 26.) But the sorrows, as the joys of the spiritual man—dealing immediately with the Infinite and Eternal God—are beyond conception. (See Job, xxxiv. 29.) Ordinary courage may support under the trials of this life ; but when " the arrows of the Almighty are within us, the poison thereof drinketh up our spirit." (Job, vi. 4. Comp. Prov. xviii. 14.) How, then, can the Christian's lot be so enviable, when their *souls* thus *melt for heaviness?* But this, be it remembered, is only " for a season." There is a "needs-be" for it, while it remains: and in the end it "will be found unto praise, and honour, and glory." (1 Pet. i. 6, 7. Comp. Ps. xxx. 5.) Never, perhaps, are their graces more lively, or the ground of their assurance more clear, than in these seasons of sorrow. They complain, indeed, of the diversified power of indwelling sin. But their very complaints are the evidence of the mighty working of indwelling grace. For what is it but the principle of faith, that makes unbelief their burden? What but hope, that struggles with their tears? What but love, that makes their coldness a grief? What but humility, that causes them to loathe their pride? What but the secret spring of thankfulness, that shows them their unthankfulness, and shames them for it? And, therefore, the very depth of " that *heaviness* which *melts their souls*" away, is the exhibition of the strength of God's work within, upholding them in perseverance of conflict to the end. Would not the believer then, when eyeing in his heaviest moments the most prosperous condition of the ungodly, say—" Let me not eat of their dainties?" (Ps. cxli. 4.) Far better, and, we may add, far happier, is godly sorrow than worldly joy. In the midst of his misery, the Christian would not exchange his hope in the gospel—though often obscured by unbelief, and clouded by fear—for all " the kingdoms of the world, and the glory of them." " If the heart knoweth his own bitterness, a stranger doth not intermeddle with his joy."* Yet the bitterness is keenly felt. Sin displeases a tender and gracious Father. (Ps. li. 4.) It has " pierced" the heart that loves him (Zech. xii. 10); and shed the blood that saves him. It grieves (Eph. iv.

---

* Prov. xiv. 10. " A good man lying on his bed of sickness, and being asked, Which were the most comfortable days that he ever knew? cried out—O give me my *mourning* days; give me my mourning days again, for they were the joyfullest days that ever I had."—BROOKES, *Works.*

30) the indwelling Comforter of his soul.   God expects to
see him a mourner ; and he feels he has reason enough to
mourn —" *My soul melteth for heaviness.*"

But this cry of distress is sometimes that of the child
under his Father's needful chastisement. The world is
dethroned, but not extirpated, in the heart. Much dross
is yet to be removed. The sources of the too attractive
earthly joy must be embittered : and now it is that the
discipline of the cross forces the cry—" *My soul melteth for
heaviness.*" Yet in the midst of heaviness, the child of God
cannot forget that he is loved — that he is saved ; and the
recollection of this sovereign mercy makes his tears of
godly sorrow, tears of joy.

But this *melting heaviness* has not wrought its work,
until it has bowed us before the throne of grace with the
pleading cry of faith—*Strengthen thou me !* For do we
stand by the strength of our own resolutions or habits of
grace ?   Unless the Lord renew his supply from moment
to moment, all is frail and withering. But what burden
or difficulty is too great for Almighty strength ?   " Fear
not, thou worm Jacob ; thou shalt thresh the mountains,
and beat them small." (Isa. xli. 14, 15.) And especially is
our success assured, when the plea is drawn, as it is repeat-
edly in this Psalm (Verses 25, 41, 58, &c.)—*according to
thy word.* For what does that word assure us?—" As thy
days, so shall thy strength be." (Deut. xxxiii. 25.) "Will
he plead against me"— said Job—" with his great power ?
No ; but he will put strength in me." (Job, xxiii. 6.) Thus
David found it in his own case : " In the day when I cried,
thou answeredst me, and strengthenedst me with strength
in my soul." (Ps. cxxxviii. 3.) Thus also to the Apostle
was the promise given and fulfilled : " My grace is sufficient
for thee ; for my strength is made perfect in weakness."
(2 Cor. xii. 9.) And is not " the God of Israel" still " he
that giveth strength and power unto his people"(Ps.

lxviii. 35)? still the same " faithful God, who will not
suffer them to be tempted above that they are able, but
will with the temptation also make a way to escape, that
they may be able to bear it?" (1 Cor. x. 13.)

When we are most sensible of our utter helplessness,
and most simple in our reliance upon Divine strength,
then it is, that the "*soul melting for heaviness*," is most
especially upheld and established. "*Heaviness* in the heart
of man maketh it stoop ; but a good word maketh it glad."
(Prov. xii. 25.) And how reviving is that "good word"
of the Gospel, which proclaims the Saviour anointed to
" give the garment of praise for the spirit of *heaviness*"
(Isa. lxi. 3), and gifted with " the tongue of the learned,
that he might know how to speak a word in season unto
him that is weary!" (Isa. l. 4.) And no less encouraging
is it to view *Him* " *melting for heaviness*" (Ps. xxii. 14)—
" sore amazed, and very heavy" under the accumulated
weight of imputed guilt ; learning by this bitter discipline,
" in that he himself suffered being tempted, to succour them
that are tempted." (Mark, xiv. 33; with Heb. ii. 18.) Yet
was he, like his faithful servant, *strengthened according to
his Father's word*, in the moment of his bitterest agony, by
the agency of his own creation. (Luke, xxii. 43; with 2 Cor.
xii. 8, 9.) And this faithful support, vouchsafed to the
Head, is the seal and pledge of what every member in
every trouble will most assuredly enjoy. " As the sufferings of Christ abound in his people, so their consolation
also aboundeth by Christ." (2 Cor. i. 5.) The blessed
word will supply all their need—life for their quickening,
light for their direction, comfort for their enjoyment,
strength for their support—" *Strengthen thou me according
unto thy word.*"

Lord, may I ever be kept from despondency—regarding it as sinful in itself, dishonourable to thy name, and
weakening to my soul ; and though I must " needs be

sometime in heaviness through manifold temptations," yet
let the power of faith be in constant exercise, that I may
be able to expostulate with my soul—"Why art thou
cast down, O my soul? and why art thou disquieted
within me? hope thou in God: for I shall yet praise
him, who is the health of my countenance, and my God."
(Ps. xlii. 11.)

29. *Remove from me the way of lying; and grant me thy law
graciously.*

Every deviation in principle and conduct from the strait
and narrow path, is *a way of lying.* Every traveller in *the
way* " feedeth on the ashes" of his own delusion. (Isa. xliv.
20.) Does it seem a marvel, that the man of God should
deprecate so earnestly the influence of gross sin? " The
brand plucked out of the fire" retains a susceptibility of
the fire. The oldest Christian in the family of God might
at any moment of unwatchfulness be captivated by the chain
of his former sins. Might not the recollection of past
compliances with this shameful sin (1 Sam. xxi. 13 ; xxvii.
10) naturally have suggested the prayer—*Remove from me
the way of lying?* But even in the profession of the Gospel,
should we " be removed from him that called us into the
grace of Christ unto another gospel" (Gal. i. 6); should
erroneous doctrines find a place in our system; and—as
the natural consequence of doctrinal errors—should any
inconsistency be marked in our practice ; should there be
any allowed principles of sinful indulgence, self-righteousness, conformity to the world, or shrinking from the daily
cross—then, indeed, will the prayer naturally flow from
our hearts—*Remove from me the way of lying.*

Most justly are ways such as these called " *ways of
lying.*" They promise what it is impossible, in the nature
of things, that they can ever perform : and prove to their

deluded followers, that "they that observe lying vanities, forsake their own mercy." (Jonah, ii. 8.) We can be at no loss to trace these "*ways*," to their proper source;—to him, who, "when he speaketh a lie, speaketh of his own: for he is a liar, and the father of it." (John, viii. 44.) A lie was his first—alas! too successful—instrument of temptation, by which he "beguiled Eve through his subtlety" (Gen. iii. 1–6; with 2 Cor. xi. 3), and still does he pursue the same deadly work throughout the world lying under his sway, beguiling the blinded "children of disobedience" (Rev. xii. 9; with 2 Cor. iv. 4. Eph. ii. 2), into the awful deception of mistaking their God, and into the blind choice of preferring "broken cisterns" to "the fountain of living waters." (Jer. ii. 13.)

The gracious knowledge of the law is the only means of the *removal* of this evil way. David, as a king, had it written by him. (Deut. xvii. 18, 19.) He wished it written on him—not the book only before his eyes, but stamped on the heart. The external knowledge is the common benefit of all. The *gracious* knowledge is the covenant-blessing of the Lord's people (Heb. viii. 10)—the only effective principle of holiness. The law is still what it was—an enemy to the ungodly—forcing a hateful light upon their conscience; but a delight to the servant of God—framing his will, and directing his conduct. Thus truth extirpates *lying*. Christ reigns instead of Belial.

Thus also we are enabled to "keep our hearts"—those leading wanderers, that mislead the rest. (Prov. iv. 23.) For wherever we see wandering eyes, wandering feet, and a wandering tongue, all flow from a heart, that has taken its own liberty in wandering from God. But with the law as our rule, and the Spirit as our guide, we shall be directed and kept in a safe and happy path.

Grant me thy law graciously. Grant me a clearer perception of its holy character—a more sensitive shrinking from transgressing it—a more cordial approval of its spirit—a more entire conformity to its directions.

30. *I have chosen the way of truth : thy judgments have I laid before me.*

Only two ways lie before us for our choice—" *the way of lying,*" and " *the way of truth.*" God by the light of his word guides us into one—Satan by his temptations allures us into the other. *The way of lying* is the natural choice of man. The *choice of the way of truth* is the Lord's work in the hearts of his people—the seal of his special eternal love. His teaching shows us *the way* (Ps. xxv. 4 ; xxxii. 8. Isa. xlviii. 17) ; and his grace enables us to " *choose*" it (Ps. cx. 3. Isa. xliv. 3–5). And who in his subsequent course has ever found reason to alter his first determination ? Does Mary regret her " choice of the good part?" (Luke, x. 42.) One whose solid and reflecting judgment was not likely to make a rash or hasty choice, tells us, of the outset of his course— " What things were gain to me, those I counted loss for Christ." The experience of twenty years—instead of bringing matter for repentance— only confirmed him in his choice : and he repeats his determination with increasing energy of expression ; " *Yea, doubtless, and I count all things but loss* for the excellency of the knowledge of Christ Jesus my Lord." (Philip. iii. 7, 8.) In the same spirit one of the ancient fathers expresses himself : ' If I have any possessions, health, credit, learning—this is all the contentment I have of them—that I may have *something to despise for Christ, who comprises in his own person all and every thing that is most desirable.*"*

The connexion of this verse with the preceding well illustrates the bias of the believer's heart. His experience

* " Totus desiderabilis, et totum desiderabile."—GREG. NAZ. *Orat.* i.

of the deceitfulness of sin, Satan, and his own heart, stirs up the prayer — " *Remove from me the way of lying.*" But *his choice* is expressed in this verse — " *I have chosen the way of truth.*" The sincere desire to have " *the way of lying re- moved from us,*" is a clear evidence, that we have already " *chosen the way of truth:*" that " the spirit of truth hath guided us to him" (John, xvi. 13, 14), who is indeed " *the way of truth*" — the true and only " way to God !" (John, xiv. 6.) And of all ways that could be set before the Christian, this is the way he would " *choose*" — as bringing most glory to his God, exalting the Saviour, honouring the Spirit of God, and securing the salvation of his own soul. Whatever becomes of me — the Christian would feel — ' I would have no other way than this. Yea, though I should perish, I would abide in it. So transcendant is the dis- covery of the glory of God — scarcely less clear than the glory of heaven itself !'

The practical pathway, however, is often rugged — always narrow. We may have to encounter not only the reviling of an ungodly world, but even the suspicions of our brethren, who may not always understand our motives. Yet if our heart is upright with God, " none of these things will move us. Our choice is made, and we are prepared to abide the cost." (Luke, xiv. 28. Acts, xx. 24.)

But that our choice may be daily established, let us not forget the treasury of our life, light, and grace. Let us *lay the " judgments of God before us.*" For we have always some new lesson to learn — some new duty to perform — some new snare to avoid. We must therefore walk by rule (see Gal. vi. 16 ; Philip. iii. 16,) — as under the eye of a jealous God, who enlightens and cheers our path — under the eye of the ungodly, who " watch for our halting" — under the eye of weak Christians, who might be stum- bled by our unsteady walk — under the eye of established

Christians, who will be yet further established by the testimony of our consistent profession. The Gospel affords
all the material for this strict and accurate walk. All is
given that is needed. The obedience that is enjoined is
secured. " God working in us " (Philip. ii. 12, 13. Isa.
xxvi. 12), enables us to work for him ; and while we are
humbly looking for further supplies, and diligently improving what has been already bestowed, he is pledged by promise to assist (Isa. xli. 10. Zech. x. 12), as we are bound
by duty to obey.

What then — let me inquire — is the choice which I
have made ? I would remember that it is for eternity.
And if, through the grace that has first chosen me, " *I
have chosen the way of truth*,"— is the effect of this choice
daily visible in a life and conversation well ordered according to the word of God ? If it is good to " hide that word
in my heart" (Verse 11), as a safeguard against sin ; it is
good also " *to lay it before*" my eyes, as the chart to guide
my course — the model to direct my work — the support to
uphold my weakness. (Josh. i. 8.)

31. *I have stuck unto thy testimonies; O Lord, put me not to
shame.*

We have just seen the *choice* of the man of God, and
the rule by which he acted upon it. Now we see his perseverance — *first choosing the way* — then *sticking to it*. While
he complained of " *his soul cleaving to the dust*" (Verse 25),
he would yet say — *I have stuck unto thy testimonies*. Thus
did he illustrate the apostle's delineation of the Christian's
two hearts (as a converted African expressed it), " I delight
in the law of God after the inward man ; but I see another
law in my members, warring against the law of my mind, and
bringing me into captivity to the law of sin, which is in my

members.   So then with the mind I myself serve the law
of God ; but with the flesh the law of sin."*   In the midst,
however, of the most painful conflicts, the child of God
holds fast his confidence.   He feels that he hates the sin
that he commits, and loves the Saviour, whom, in spite of
himself, he dishonours ; so that, with all his sins and unworthiness, he fears not to put in his claim among the
family of God.

But, reader, seriously ask yourself— How did you become a Christian ?   Was it by birth and education, or by
choice ?   If indeed by grace you have been enabled to
" *choose the way of truth*," then be sure you firmly *stick to it;*
or better, far better, that you had not made choice of it at
all.   " No man having put his hand to the plough, and
looking back, is fit for the kingdom of God.   If ye *continue*
in my word, then are ye my disciples indeed.   It had been
better for you not to have known the way of righteousness,
than, after you had known it, to turn from the holy commandment delivered unto you." (Luke, ix. 62. John, viii.
31. 2 Pet. ii. 21.)   Yet, praised be God for the security of
perseverance !   He that enabled you to " put your hand to
the plough" will keep it there in the habit of faith, firm
and stedfast.   " The Lord will perfect that which concerneth you." (Ps. cxxxviii. 8.)

* Rom. vii. 22, 23, 25. Thus does Augustine graphically describe
this conflict in his own mind—' The new will which began to be in
me, whereby I would love thee, O my God! the only certain sweetness, was not yet able to overcome my former will, confirmed by
long continuance.   So my two wills, the one old, the other new ;
the one carnal, the other spiritual, conflicted between themselves,
and rent my soul by their disagreement.   Then did I understand
by my own experience what I had read, how the " flesh lusteth
against the spirit, and the spirit lusteth against the flesh."   I was
myself on both sides, but more in that which I approved, than in
that which I condemned, in myself, because for the most part I
suffered reluctantly what I did willingly.'— *Confess.* Book viii. ch. 5.
Comp. Rom. vii. 15-20.

Yet this "cleaving to the Lord" (Acts, xi. 23), can only be maintained by unceasing conflict. The length and weariness of the way (Numb. xxi. 4), and the slowness of your progress, are sources of constant and harassing trial. Revert, then, to the ground of your original *choice*. Was it made under the Lord's light and direction? This reason may well bind you to "*stick to*" it. For are not the ways of God as pleasant—is not Christ as lovely—is not heaven as desirable—as at the beginning? Nay—have you not even more reason to adhere to your *choice*, than you had to make it? It was formed before at least you could fully know for yourself. Now "you have tasted" (1 Pet. ii. 3) —you have the seal of experience. Is not the crown more joyous in the nearer prospect?

Backslider! "has God been unto you a wilderness, and a land of darkness" (Jer. ii. 31), that you virtually give your testimony after trial,—'Satan is the better master, and I will return to him?' The world is the happiest path; and I will walk in it. This is, indeed, choosing a murderer in the stead of a Father—"forsaking the fountain" for the "broken cistern." (Jer. ii. 13.) Oh! must there not be repentance in this path? May that repentance come before it be too late! Ponder who it was, that befriended you in the moment of an awful extremity, and snatched you as "a brand from the burning." Ponder the endearing proofs of his love—condescending to become a man—"a man of sorrows" (Isa. liii. 3), and to die in the agony of the cross, bearing for you the eternal curse of God. (Gal. iii. 13.) And does not gratitude remind you, what returns of faithful service are due from a creature so infinitely indebted to him? Surely the stedfast perseverance with which his heart clave to his costly work (comp. Matt. xvi. 23; Luke, xii. 50; Heb. xii. 2, 3), may serve to put to shame your unsteadiness in "*sticking to his testimonies.*"

Believer! you are determined to abide by your choice
—but not in your own strength. Remember him, who one
hour declared, that he would sooner die with Christ than
deny him ; and the next hour denied him with oaths and
curses. (Matt. xxvi. 35, 74.) Learn, then, to follow up
your resolution with instant prayer—" *O Lord, put me not
to shame.*" Leave me not to myself, lest I become a *shame*
to myself, and an offence to thy Church. " I will keep thy
statutes. O forsake me not utterly." (Verse 8.) Dependence upon the Lord, in a deep sense of our weakness, is the
principle of perseverance. Never will he shut out the
prayer of his faithful servant. He hath promised—" My
people shall never be ashamed" (Joel, ii. 27) ; and therefore, taking firm hold of his promise, you may " go on
your way rejoicing."

32. *I will run the way of thy commandments, when thou shalt
enlarge my heart.*

A glowing picture of the Christian's delight in the
ways of God! If we " *have chosen the way of God's commandments,*" and have been able to " *stick unto*" this way,
surely we shall wish to " *run in it*" with constancy and
cheerfulness. We shall want to mend our pace. If we
walk, we shall long to " *run.*" There is always the same
reason for progress, that there was for setting out. Necessity, advantage, enjoyment, spur us on to the end. Whatever progress we have made, we shall desire to make more ;
we shall go on praying and walking, and praying that we
may walk with a swifter motion ; we shall be dissatisfied,
yet not discouraged—" faint, yet pursuing." (Judg. viii. 4.)
Now this is as it should be. This is after the pattern of
the holy Apostle :—" Brethren, I count not myself to have
apprehended : but this one thing I do ; forgetting those
things which are behind, and reaching forth unto those which

are before, I press toward the mark for the prize of the
high calling of God in Christ Jesus." (Philip. iii. 13, 14.)
But the secret as well as the pattern of Christian progress
is—looking beyond the Apostle, and the " so great cloud
of witnesses, with which we are encompassed"—and " looking unto Jesus." (Heb. xii. 1, 2.) Faith is the principle
of life, and supplies the daily motion of life ; directing
our eye to him as " the Author," until he " becomes the
Finisher," of our faith. This is at once our duty, our privilege, our happiness, and our strength. This is the
point, at which we begin to run ; and we " so run, that we
may obtain." (1 Cor. ix. 24.)

But let us more distinctly mark the medium through
which this spiritual energy flows — an enlarged heart. Without this influence how could we run this way of God's commandments? Such is the extent and latitude of the course
(see verse 96), that a straitened heart is utterly inadequate
to carry us through. There must be large treasures of
knowledge, in order that from a rich " treasure-house the
good things" may pour out abundantly. (See 1 Kings, iv.
29 ; with Matt. xii. 35.) For indeed spiritual "knowledge"
is the principle of " multiplied grace." (2 Pet. i. 2. Comp.
Col. i. 10.) Scriptural truths, divinely fixed in the understanding, powerfully influence the heart. Christian privilege also greatly advances this important end. In seasons
of depression we are " so troubled, that we cannot speak."
(Ps. lxxvii. 4.) We cannot pour out our hearts, as at
other times, with a large measure of spirit and life. But
when " we joy in God, having received the atonement"
(Rom. v. 11), the spirit is invigorated, as with oil on the
wheels, or as " with wings to mount" (Isa. xl. 31) on high
in the service of praise.

Very different, however, is this enlargement of heart from
enlargement of gifts. Fluency of utterance is too often
fearfully separated from the spiritual life, and utterly un-

connected with delight in *the way of God's commandments*. It is expression, not feeling—counterfeit grace—public, not secret or personal, religion. The yoke of sin is not broken, and the self-deceiver will be found at last among the deluded throng of gifted hypocrites, " punished with everlasting destruction from the presence of the Lord." (Matt. vii. 22, 23 ; with 2 Thess. i. 9.)

Indeed the spiritual principle is far too little realized. At the commencement of the course, conscious guilt straitens the approach to the throne of grace. Unbelief imprisons the soul. And even when the deliverer is known, who " sets at liberty them that are bruised" (Luke, iv. 18), still the body of death with all its clogging burden and confinement presses down the soul. Unbelief also continues to work, to narrow the conceptions of the gospel, and by the painful recollections of the past, to bring in distrust, distance, and bondage. And most painful is this restraint. For the soul, which is but beginning to see how desirable is the favour of God, feels also an earnest desire to honour him. And to him who—having fully " tasted that the Lord is gracious"—asks, " What shall I render unto the Lord ?" (Ps. cxvi. 12), this remaining influence of " the spirit of bondage" is more afflicting, than perhaps was a greater measure of it in a less enlightened stage of his way. Still, however, this legal spirit pursues him. His comforts, ebbing and flowing, according as he is dissatisfied or satisfied with his Christian progress, clearly evince a secret " confidence in the flesh," greatly hindering that " rejoicing in Christ Jesus," which so *enlarges the heart.* (Philip. iii. 3, 12–14.)

Thus by the shackles of sin, unbelief, and self-righteousness, we are indeed ' sore let and hindered in running the race set before us.' (Collect for Advent.) The light is obscured. Faith loses sight of its object. What otherwise would be a delight becomes a weariness. Obe-

dience is irksome ; self-denial intolerable ; the cross heavy.
The heart is, as it were, " shut up, and it cannot get forth."
(Ps. lxxxviii. 8.)   Faith is so low : desires are so faint ;
hopes so narrow, that it seems impossible to make progress.
Frequent defeats induce despondency. The world is resorted
to.   Sin ensnares and captivates.   Thus " we did run well;
but we have been hindered." (Gal. v. 7.)

This sad evil naturally leads us to inquire for the remedy.
The case is backsliding, not apostasy.   The remedy therefore is in that *engagement*, which embraces a wider expanse
of light, and a more full confidence of love.   We find that
we have not been " straitened" in God, but " in our own
bowels."   If then the rich fool thought of enlarging his
barns, when his stores had increased upon him (Luke, xii.
16–19), much more should we " enlarge the place of our
tent," that we may make more room for God, encourage
larger expectations, if we would have more full manifestations of him.   Let not the vessels fail, before the oil stays.
(See 2 Kings, iv. 6.)   Continually let the petition be sent
up —" Oh that thou wouldest bless me indeed, and enlarge
my coast !" (1 Chron. iv. 10.)   Whatever cause we have to
cry out —" My leanness, my leanness !" (Isa. xxiv. 16) —
still let us, in the exercise of faith and prayer, be waiting
for a more cheerful ability to love, serve, and praise.   Let
us be restless, till the prison-doors are again opened, and
the command is issued to the prisoners —" Go forth : and
to them that are in darkness — Show yourselves.   They
shall feed in the ways, and their pastures shall be in all
high places." (Isa. xlix. 9.)   Who knoweth but the Lord
will once more shine upon us ; once more unloose our fetters,
and renew our strength ?

But again and again must we be reminded that every
motion must begin with God. (Prov. xvi. 1.)   *I will run* —
but how ? not in my own strength, but by " the good hand
of my God upon me" (Ezra, vii. 9), delivering and *enlarging*

my heart. He does not say—I will make no efforts, unless thou work for me ; but if *thou wilt enlarge—I will run.* Weakness is not the plea for indolence, but for quickening grace. " Draw me"—saith the Church—" we will run after thee." (Cant. i. 4.) Effectual calling will issue in *running.* (Comp. Ps. cx. 3 ; Isa. lv. 5.) " Where the Spirit of the Lord is, there is liberty." The secret of Christian energy and success is a *heart enlarged* in the love of God.

Let me then begin betimes—make haste—keep straight on—fix my eye on the mark—" endure unto the end." I may yet expect in the joy of blessed surprise to exclaim— " Or ever I was aware, my soul made me like the chariots of Ammi-nadib." (Cant. vi. 12.) Godly sorrow had made me serious. Now let holy joy make me active. " The joy of the Lord is my strength" (Neh. viii. 10) ; and I am ready, under the power of constraining love (2 Cor. v. 14), to work and to toil — to run without weariness—to "march onward" without fainting ; * not measuring my pace by my own strength, but looking to him who " strengtheneth with all might by his Spirit in the inner man." (Eph. iii. 16.)

Happy fruit of wrestling prayer and diligent waiting on God ! Joy in God, and strength to walk with him, with increasing knowledge of him, increasing communion with him, and increasing confidence in him.

* Isa. xl. 31, " march onward."—BISHOP LOWTH'S Version.

PART V.

33. Teach me, O Lord, the way of thy statutes; and I shall keep it unto the end.

WE need no instruction in the way of sin. That has been our way, ever since Adam " sought out his own invention." (Eccles. vii. 29. Isa. liii. 6.) The ungodly " desire no knowledge of *the way of God's statutes*." (Job, xxi. 14.) The heart leads the judgment, and " their heart is enmity to the law of God." (Rom. viii. 7.) But for a child of God, this is a prayer for constant use. The outward revelation is of no avail without the inward teaching. The Divine Instructor must interpret and apply his own rule. However plain the word may be, the darkness must be removed from the understanding. Light will not show an object, except the faculty of sight be given. A blind man cannot see at noonday. We know nothing spiritually, except as we are taught of God. The more we are taught, the more we feel our need of teaching, and the more pressing will be our cries for this invaluable blessing. The blind man must be led in the plainest and most direct, as well as in the more difficult and rugged paths. And thus do we need the shining of light from above — not only in the " deep things of God " — but for the reception of the most elementary truths. And yet we want not this knowledge for its own sake — to feed pride or speculation — but for its practical influence. For of what avail is the dis-

covery even of important truth, if we be not moulded
into its likeness, and constrained " into the obedience of
faith?" The connexion of every thought with Christian
practice, here directed to its proper end, is a most striking
proof of the Divine origin of *the statutes*. The most clear
instructions for the regulation of our conduct flow from
single sentences or expressions in these " *statutes;*" and
this clearly proves an infinite wisdom in their distribution,
a reference in the eternal mind to every detail of practical
duty, and a Divine power and unction, applying the word
to the several circumstances of daily conduct. For, indeed,
what mind but the mind of God could have comprehended
in so small a compass such a vast system of instruction?
In this view, therefore, the Lord's teaching becomes the
spring of obedience. For how can we " *keep*" a way, which
we do not understand? And who was ever " *taught the
way of the Lord's statutes*," who had not his heart constrained and directed by their spiritual beauty and sweetness? In this path we realize union with the Saviour
(1 John, iii. 24); " the love of God is perfected in us"
(Ib. ii. 5); and our confidence is established before God
(Ib. iii. 21).

The object nearest to the believer's heart, and which
causes him many an anxious—and too often many an unbelieving thought—is the grace of perseverance. Now the
Lord's *teaching* is the principle of perseverance. It is " *the
light of life*" (John, i. 4; viii. 12), enlightening the mind,
and quickening the heart. Under this influence, therefore,
we live—we endure—we cannot fail of keeping *the way
unto the end*. (1 John, ii. 27.) Thus the end crowns the
work. For with this blessing of perseverance, is sealed to
us the hope of victory over our spiritual enemies, and the
participation of our Saviour's glory. (Rev. ii. 26–28.)
Confidence, indeed, without prayer and dependence upon

our glorious Head, is most daring presumption.   But that
" well-ordered and sure covenant," which " is all our salvation, and all our desire," engages for our continuance in
" *the way of the Lord's statutes.*"   " *I will put my fear in
their hearts, that they shall not depart from me.   I will put
my law in their inward parts, and write it in their hearts : and
I will be their God, and they shall be my people.*" (Jer. xxxii.
40 ; xxxi. 33 ; with 2 Sam. xxiii. 5.)

34. *Give me understanding, and I shall keep thy law ; yea, I
shall observe it with my whole heart.*

     ' He that is his own teacher'—says Bernard—and one
greater than Bernard (Prov. xxviii. 26), ' has a fool for his
master.'   Man cannot teach what he does not know ; and
of God, and of his law, he knows nothing.   Therefore the
beginning of wisdom is a consciousness of ignorance, a distrust of our own understanding, and the heartfelt prayer—
" *Give me understanding.*"   The spiritual *understanding* is the
gift of Jesus Christ. (1 John, ii. 20 ; v. 20.)   He directs
us to himself, as its fountain—" I am the light of the
world ; he that followeth me shall not walk in darkness,
but shall have the light of life." (John, viii. 12 ; also xii.
46.)   This *understanding* differs from mere intellectual discernment or speculative knowledge.   It is the spring of
spiritual activity in our walk with God (See Col. i. 9, 10) ;
so that our obedience is not outward and reluctant, but
filial delight and wholeness of heart :—we desire not only
to *keep the law of God to the end,* but every day *to the end*—
" *with our whole heart.*"— Such are our obligations towards
him, that we ought to study very accurately the character
of our walk with him ; always remembering that service
without *the heart—the whole heart*—is hateful in his sight
(Isa. i. 11–15. Hos. x. 2. Acts, v. 1–10) ; and that what is

now wilfully withheld, will gradually draw away the rest in apostasy from him. Now are we seeking more "engaged-ness of heart" for him? Then will this prayer be a suit-able expression of our need, and the utterance of a humble, resolute petitioner. It is not, however, enough, that we have once received, unless we are constantly receiving. We must ask, that we may receive; but after we have received, we must ask again. Yet is this prayer never offered up, until the soul has in part received what it is here seeking for. The natural man is "wise in his own conceit," and has therefore no idea of his need of Divine teaching.

But we must not be satisfied with even a clear appre-hension of the doctrines of the Bible, and of the "truth as it is in Jesus." "*Give me understanding*"—'not only that I may believe these doctrines, but that I may *keep and observe* them.' In every path of duty, this cry is repeated, with an importunity, that is never wearisome to the ears of our gracious Father. And in how many unnoticed in-stances has the answer been vouchsafed, when some clear and heavenly ray has darted unexpectedly into the mind, or some providential concurrence of unforeseen circumstances has disentangled a path before intricate and involved, and marked it before us with the light of a sunbeam! How many whispers of conscience! how many seasonable sug-gestions in moments of darkness and perplexity, may the observant child of God record, as the answer to this needful prayer! "Whoso is wise, and will observe these things, even they shall understand the loving-kindness of the Lord." (Ps. cvii. 43.) Nor will our growth in spiritual *understanding* fail to evidence itself in the steady consistency of a well-ordered conversation! "Who is a wise man, and endued with knowledge among you? Let him show out of a good conversation his works with meekness of wisdom." (Jam. iii. 13.) If then knowledge is valuable according to its usefulness, one ray of this practical knowledge—the result of prayer for heavenly teaching—is more to be prized than the highest attainments of speculative religion —flowing from mere human instruction.

35. *Make me to go in the path of thy commandments; for therein do I delight.*

We are equally ignorant of *the path of God's commandments*, and impotent to *go in it*. We need therefore double assistance. Our mind must be enlightened ; our hearts constrained ; else our knowledge of this humbling *path* would make us shrink from it. But under the complete influence of Divine grace, when *understanding has been given* to discern the beauty of it, the soul's warmest desire is fixed upon it. Conscious helplessness looks upward—*Make me to go:* and he who said to the paralytic—"Arise, take up thy bed, and go unto thy house," speaks the same word of quickening life and power to the soul "*giving heed*," "expecting to receive something of him." (Matt. ix. 6 ; with Acts, iii. 4, 5.) It is delightful to acknowledge of this work, that "all is of God"—that "it is he that worketh in us both to will and to do of his good pleasure." (2 Cor. v. 18. Philip. ii. 13.) To him only can it belong. For since the natural inclination "is not subject to the law of God, neither indeed can be" (Rom. viii. 7), Almighty power must introduce a new and active bias—" Turn thou me, and I shall be turned." (Jer. xxxi. 18.)—"*Make me to go in the path of thy commandments.*"

But even when brought into *this path*, still we want accelerated motion to run with increasing alacrity. We want to take " the Lord God for our strength ; and he shall make our feet like hinds' feet, and he shall *make us to walk* upon the high places." (Hab. iii. 19.) The *path*, indeed, is uninviting to the eye of sense. This distorted vision brings all its difficulties into full view ; hiding all its counter-

balancing enjoyments. Let us, howerer, exercise that
" faith," which is " the substance of things hoped for, the
evidence of things not seen." (Heb. xi. 1.)   Let us exhibit
our proper character, "walking by faith, and not by sight"
(2 Cor. v. 7), and our discernment of unseen things will be
more clear, and our enjoyment of them more permanent.
The prayer will then be with increasing earnestness—
" *Make me to go in the path of thy commandments.*"

But we must not be content with walking in this way ;
we must seek to " *delight in it.*"   Delight is the marrow of
religion. " God loveth a cheerful giver" (2 Cor. ix. 7), and
accepts obedience, only when it is given, not when it is
forced.   He loves the service of that man, who considers it
his highest privilege to render it, and whose heart rejoices
in the way, " as a giant to run his race." (Ps. xix. 5 ;
cxii. 1.)   Fervent prayer and cheerful obedience mark the
experience of the thriving Christian.   As a true " child of
Zion, he is joyful in his king" (Ps. cxlix. 2) ; he loves his
service, and counts it " perfect freedom"—the rule of love,
mercy, and grace.

But is the self-condemned penitent distressed by this
description of a child of God?   He cannot find the same
marks in himself ; and he too hastily concludes, that he
does not belong to the heavenly family ; not considering,
that his very grief is caused by his love to, and " *delight in*"
that way in which he is so hindered, and in which he daily
prays—" *Make me to go.*"   It was, probably, the same sense
of weakness and inability, " *to go in the path of God's commandments,*" which urged David's prayer ; and if it urges
yours, poor trembling penitent—if it sends you to a throne
of grace, you will, ere long, receive an answer of peace, and
" go on your way rejoicing."

This *delight in the path* is not only following the " man
after God's own heart ;" but it is the image of David's
Lord, and our forerunner in this path.   He could testify

to his Father—"I delight to do thy will, O my God"
(Ps. xl. 8; with Heb. x. 7); and to his disciples—"I have
meat to eat that ye know not of. My meat is to do the
will of him that sent me, and to finish his work." (John, iv.
32, 34.) And as a proof of the intenseness of his delight he
could, to their great amazement, "go before them" (Mark,
x. 32) to Jerusalem, unappalled by the "baptism" of blood
which awaited him; yea, even "straitened" with the un-
quenchable ardour of his love, "until it was accomplished."
(Luke, xii. 50.)

36. *Incline my heart unto thy testimonies, and not to*
covetousness.

But what "*makes us to go in the path of God's command-*
ments?" The force of his Almighty love effectually *inclines*
the will, as with a Divine touch. The day of his power, in
which he makes us willing, is a time of love. "I drew
them"—saith he—"with cords of a man, and with bands
of love." (Ps. cx. 3. Ezek. xvi. 8. Hos. xi. 4.) Every man,
who is conscious of the counteracting bias within, will
deeply feel the need of this prayer—"*Incline my heart.*"
The native principle of man draws him to his own self—
to his own indulgence—pleasure—*covetousness*—assuming
a thousand forms of gratifying self, at the expense of
love to God. Few but are ready to condemn this principle
in others, while perhaps it may be their own "easily-
besetting sin." When the mind is grasping after the world,
as if it were our portion, we have the greatest reason to
"take heed" to our Lord's admonition, and beware of
"covetousness" (Luke, xii. 15). When we invest earthly
gratifications with any inherent excellency—*virtually*
putting them in the place of God—then will be a season
for special supplication—*Incline my heart unto thy testi-*
monies, and not to covetousness.

There is probably no principle so opposed to the *Lord's testimonies*. It casts out the principle of obedience, since the love of God cannot co-exist with the love of the world (1 John, ii. 15); and the very desire to serve Mammon is a proof of unfaithfulness to God. (Matt. vi. 24.) We mark the deadly influence in direct breaches of the law of God. Balaam, in the indulgence of this propensity, set his will in mad contradiction to God (Num. xxii. 15–21. 2 Pet. ii. 14–16); Ahab was tempted to murder (1 Kings, xxi. 1–13); David, to murder and adultery (2 Sam. xi. 2–17); Achan, to steal (Josh. vii. 21); Judas, both to steal from his fellows, and to betray his Master (John, xii. 6. Matt. xxvi. 14–16); Gehazi and Ananias to lying. (2 Kings, v. 20–26. Acts, v. 1–8.) And besides—what is the matter of common but painful observation—how much of the good seed of the kingdom, that was springing up with the promise of a plentiful harvest, has this weed of rank luxuriance " choked, that it has become unfruitful!"* Our Lord's parables, therefore (Luke, xii. 16–21; xvi. 14, 19, &c.)— his providence (Matt. vi. 25–31)—his promises (Ib. verse 33. Ps. xxxiv. 9, 10. Isa. xxxiii. 15, 16. 1 Pet. v. 7)— his terms of discipleship (Matt. xvi. 24; xix. 27–29. Luke, xiv. 33)—his counsels (1 Cor. vii. 29–31. Philip. iv. 5)— his own example of poverty and renunciation of this world's comfort (Matt. viii. 20)— all are directed against this destructive principle. The power of the love of Christ delivered Matthew (Matt. ix. 9) and Zaccheus (Luke, xix. 1–10) from its influence, and " *inclined their hearts to the testimonies of God.*" And has not faith still the same power to turn the heart from the world, from sin, from self, to Christ? Learn, then, to rest upon the promise of his love (Heb. xiii. 5), and to delight in his *testimonies*. Earthly cares will be cast upon him, and earthly prospects will lose

* Mark, iv. 19.—The example of the rich young man, Matt. xix. 21, 22, Demas, 2 Tim. iv. 10.

their splendour.* This life of faith—living in union with a heavenly Saviour, involves the only effective principle of resistance. Those who are risen with Christ will be temperate in earthly things, "setting their affections on things above." Such—such alone—will "mortify the members that are upon the earth—evil concupiscence, and *covetousness, which is idolatry.*" (Col. iii. 1–5.)

We desire to sit loose to our earthly comforts. Are we enabled to check our natural discontent with the Lord's dealings with us, and to restrain our eagerness to "seek great things for ourselves" (Jer. vi. 13), by the recollection of his word—" Seek them not?" (Jer. xlv. 5.)

Let us not forget, that the inclination—even if it is not brought into active and perceptible motion, is fatally destructive of the life of religion. "They that *will be rich*† fall into temptation and a snare, and into many foolish and hurtful lusts, which drown men in destruction and perdition." Awful warning to professors!—" The love of money is the root of all evil; which while some have coveted after, they have erred from the faith, and pierced themselves through with many sorrows." (1 Tim. vi. 10.) A most important exhortation to the people of God!—" But thou, O man of God, flee these things, and follow after righteousness." (Ib. verse 11.) If the Lord loves you, he will not indeed lose you; but unless you "take heed, and beware of covetousness," he will not spare you. In the midst, therefore, of temptation without, and a world of sin within, go onwards, with the pilgrim's (1 Pet. ii. 11) prayer indelibly fixed on your heart—" *Incline my heart unto thy testimonies, and not to covetousness.*"

---

* Comp. Luke, xii. 15, with parallel verses, 16–21.

† Οἱ βουλομενοι πλουτειν. 1 Tim. vi. 9.—The very inclination to be rich is alienation from him, who by just right claims the supreme undisputed whole—"My son, give me thine heart." (Prov. xxiii. 26.)

37. *Turn away mine eyes from beholding vanity ; and quicken thou me in thy way.*

So strongly does the man of God deprecate temptation to self-indulgence, that he prays to be kept at the greatest possible distance from it. That his *heart* may not be *inclined to it :* he desires that *his eyes may be turned away from beholding it.* Keeping the eye is a grand means of " keeping the heart." (Num. xv. 39. Job, xxxi. 1.) Satan has so infused his poison into all the objects around us, that all furnish fuel for temptation : and the heart—naturally inclined to evil, and hankering after vanity—is stolen away in a moment. *Vanity* includes " all that is in the world— the lust of the flesh, the lust of the eye, and the pride of life." All is sin, " because it is not of the Father, but is of the world." (1 John, ii. 16.) Of all that belongs to earth—" the preacher, the son of David"—standing on the vantage-ground, and having taken within his view the widest horizon of this world's excellency, has pronounced his judgment—" Vanity of vanities, saith the preacher, vanity of vanities ! all is vanity." (Eccles. i. 1, 2 ; also ii. 11, xii. 8.) We have just mentioned "the lusts of other things choking" *many a promising profession.* Our Lord's solemn caution to his own disciples implies their injury to *a sincere profession*—" Take heed to yourselves, lest at any time your hearts be overcharged with surfeiting and drunkenness, and cares of this life ; and so that day come upon you unawares." (Luke, xxi. 34.) Some, indeed, seem to walk, as if they were proof against temptation. They venture to the very edge of the precipice, under a vain assurance that no danger is to be apprehended. But such a confidence is upon the brink of a grievous fall. (Prov. xvi. 18.) The tender-hearted child of God, trusting in the promise, that " Sin shall not have dominion over him" (Rom. vi. 14), knows that he can only enjoy the security of it, while he is shrinking from every occasion of sin. He " hates even the garment spotted by the flesh" (Jude, 23) ; and, remembering how often his outward senses have ministered to the workings of his weak and treacherous heart (see Prov. xxiii. 33 ; Josh. vii. 21), he continues in prayer—" *Turn away mine eyes from beholding vanity !*"

Probably the recollection of the circumstance of his own sin (2 Sam. xi. 2), would to the end of his life remind David of his special need of this prayer. Yet who that is conscious of his own weakness and corruption, will find the prayer unsuitable to his circumstances of daily temptation? But we must watch as well as pray. For as watchfulness without prayer is presumption, so prayer without watchfulness is self-delusion. To pray that " *our eyes*" may be " *turned from vanity*," without " making a covenant with our eyes" (Job, xxxi. 1), that they should not *behold* it, is like " taking fire in our bosoms," and expecting " not to be burnt" (Prov. vi. 27, 28), because we have prayed that we might not be burnt. If we pray not to be " led into temptation," we must " watch that we enter not into it." (Comp. Matt. vi. 13 ; with xxvi. 41.) The sincerity of our prayer will be proved by the watchfully avoiding the circumstances and occasions of temptation. The fear of sin will manifest itself by a fear of temptation to sin. " The knife will be put to the throat, if we be given to appetite." (Prov. xxiii. 2.) We shall be afraid of the wine sparkling in the glass. (Verses 31, 32.)

But where is the harm of *beholding vanity*, if we do not follow it ? When Eve *beheld* the forbidden fruit, perhaps she did not think of taking it : and when she took it, she did not think of eating it : but the beginning of sin " is as the letting out of water," whose progress once opened, beats down all before it. (Gen. iii. 6 ; with Prov. xvii. 14.) And who, after our " beguiled mother," has not found the eye

an inlet to sin?* When Bunyan's pilgrims were obliged
to pass through Vanity Fair, beset on every side with
temptations and allurements, they stopped their eyes and
ears, and quickening their pace, cried—" *Turn away mine
eyes from beholding vanity!*" A striking reproof to us, who
too often loiter and gaze, until we begin to covet those
vanities, to which, as Christians, we " are dead!" (See Col.
iii. 2, 3.)

Is it asked—What will most effectually " *turn my eyes
from vanity?*" Not the seclusion of contemplative retirement—not the relinquishment of our lawful connexion
with the world; but the transcendent beauty of Jesus unveiled to our eyes, and fixing our hearts. This will " *turn
our eyes from vanity*" in its most glittering forms. The
sight of the " pearl of great price" (Matt. xiii. 46) dims
the lustre of the " goodliest pearls" of earth; at once
deadens us to the enticements of the world, and urges us
forward in the pursuit of the prize. And is not this our
object? It is not enough, that through special mercy I
am preserved from temptations. I want to be *quickened* to
more life, energy, delight, and devotedness *in the way of my
God.* The secret of Christian progress is simplicity and
diligence. " *This one thing I do,*—forgetting the things
that are behind, and reaching forth to those things that are
before; I press towards the mark, for the prize of the high
calling of God in Christ Jesus." (Philip. iii. 13, 14.) The
Spirit leaves no wish in the heart for *beholding vanity.* The
world with all its flowery paths, is a dreary wilderness;
and Christ and heaven are the only objects of desire—" He
that shutteth his eyes from seeing evil, he shall dwell on
high; his place of defence shall be the munitions of rocks;

* Lot's wife, Gen. xix. 26; Shechem, xxxiv. 2; Potiphar's wife,
xxxix. 7; Achan, Josh. vii. 21; Samson, Judg. xvi. 1. Even the
man after God's own heart, 2 Sam. xi. 2. Comp. Prov. vi. 25; Matt.
v. 28; 2 Pet. ii. 14.

bread shall be given him, his water shall be sure. *" Thine eyes shall see the King in his beauty: they shall behold the land that is very far off."* (Isa. xxxiii. 15–17.)   Precious promises to those, that flee from temptation, and desire to walk in the ways of God!

38. *Stablish thy word unto thy servant, who is devoted to thy fear.*

Often—instead of being *quickened in the way*—I am fainting under the pressure of unbelief.   What then is my resource?   Only *the word* of promise.   Lord! seal—*stablish thy word unto thy servant*—*devoted* as I am—as I would be —*to thy fear.*   If " the fear of the Lord is the beginning of wisdom" (Ps. cxi. 10)—a " treasure" (Isa. xxxiii. 6)— a " strong confidence" (Prov. xiv. 26)—" a fountain of life" (Verse 27)—how wise—how rich—how safe—how happy—is he that " *is devoted to*" it!   " Blessed" indeed is he—with the favour of his God (Ps. xxxiii. 18), the secret of his love (Ps. xxv. 14), the teaching of his grace (Verse 12), and the mercy of his covenant. (Ps. ciii. 17.) The promises of the Old Testament are generally connected with the fear of God, as in the New Testament they are linked with faith.   But in truth, so identified are these two principles in their operation, that the faith, by which we apprehend the forgiveness of God, and the privileges of his kingdom, issues in a godly, reverential, filial fear. (Ps. cxxx. 4. Comp. Jer. xxxiii. 8, 9 ; Hos. iii. 5 ; also Heb. xii. 28.)   To be *devoted to this fear*, completes the character of *a servant of God*—the highest honour in the universe— the substantial joy of heaven itself. (Rev. vii. 15 ; xxii. 3.) It is an obedience of choice, of reverence, and of love. " Joining himself to the Lord, to serve him, and to love the name of the Lord—to be his servant." (Isa. lvi. 6.) ' Yes, gracious Lord, I had rather be bound than loosed.'

I only wish to be loosed from the bonds of sin, that I might
be bound to thee for ever.   My heart is treacherous ; lay
thine own bonds upon me.   " O Lord, truly I am thy servant : thou hast loosed my bonds" (Ps. cxvi. 16) ; *I am
" devoted to thy fear."*   Is this my desire, my mind, my determination, my character ?   Then let me plead my title to
an interest in the promises of the word—rich and free,
" exceeding great and precious" (2 Pet. i. 4),—all mine—
" yea and amen in Christ Jesus" (2 Cor. i. 20) ; let me
plead, that every *word* may be " *established*" in my victory
over sin, advancing knowledge of Christ, experience of his
love, conformity to his image, and, finally, in my preservation in him unto eternal life.

But how far *has* the fear of God operated with me as a
safeguard from sin (Gen. xxxix. 9. Neh. v. 15. Prov. xvi. 6),
and an habitual rule of conduct ? (Prov. xxiii. 17.)   David's
confidence in the promises of God, far from lessening his
jealousy over himself, only made him more " *devoted to the
fear*" of God.   And if my assurance be well grounded, it
will ever be accompanied with holy fear ; the influence will
be known by " standing more in awe of God's word" (Verse
161) ; having a more steady abhorrence of sin, and a dread
of " grieving the Holy Spirit of God."   Thus this filial
fear produces a holy confidence ; while confidence serves to
strengthen fear : and their mutual influence quickens devotedness to the work of the Lord.

It is interesting to remark, that the Christian privilege
of assurance is not confined to the New Testament dispensation.   David's pleading to have the " *word of his God
established unto him*," * was grounded upon the tried foundations of faith.   And this direct act of faith, as it regards
God in Christ, his engagements and his promises, cannot

* Mark this petition drawn out by David into a full pleading
with his God, 2 Sam. vii. 25, 28, 29. The expression also of the
same confidence will afterwards be noticed. Verse 49.

be too confident. The promises are made to the whole
Church, that we might each look for our part and interest
in them. God loves to have his own seal and hand-writing
brought before him. " Put me in remembrance"—saith
he : " let us plead together." " He cannot deny himself."
(Isa. xliii. 26. 2 Tim. ii. 13.)

Very cheering is it to mark, how the Lord *stablishes his
word* in our own experience. Every day he is fulfilling
some promise, and a word made good at one time encourages our confidence for another. (2 Cor. i. 10. 2 Tim. iv.
17, ·18. Comp. Matt. xvi. 9.) The word performed in
part is an earnest of the whole, assuring us of the time,
when we shall acknowledge his faithfulness, " who perform-
eth *all things* for us." (Ps. lvii. 2.) Thus, as *the word* is
eternally *stablished* on the foundation of the Divine engagements (Heb. vi. 17, 18), its certainty is sealed to our own
conviction. Our confidence is established, that if he has
spoken a word, he may be trusted for that word.

This, then, is the exercise and the power of faith. I
bring wants. I bring *thy word* of promise. *Stablish thy
word unto thy servant.* Thou hast bought me with a precious price ; thou hast made me thine : thou hast subdued
my heart to thyself, so that it is now " *devoted to thy fear.*"
Whatsoever, therefore, thy covenant has provided for my
sanctification, my humiliation, my chastisement, my present
and everlasting consolation—" *Stablish this word:*" let it
be fulfilled in me ; for I am " *thy servant, devoted to thy fear.*"

39. *Turn away my reproach which I fear: for thy judgments
are good.*

There is a *reproach*, which we have no cause to *fear*, but
rather to glory in. It is one of the chief privileges of the
Gospel (Matt. v. 10–12. Comp. Philip. i. 29)—the honourable badge of our profession. (Acts, v. 41 ; xxiv. 5 ;

xxviii. 22. Heb. xiii. 13. 1 Pet. iv. 12–16.) But it was
the "*reproach*" of bringing dishonour upon the name of
his God, that David *feared*,* and deprecated with most
anxious, importunate prayer. The fear of this *reproach* is
a practical principle of tender watchfulness and circumspection, and of habitual dependence upon an Almighty
upholding power. " Hold thou me up, and I shall be safe"
(Verse 117),—will be the constant supplication of one, that
fears the Lord, and fears himself. We do not, perhaps,
sufficiently consider the active malice of the enemies of the
gospel, "watching for our halting" (Jer. xx. 10); else
should we be more careful to remove all occasions of "*reproach*" on account of inconsistency of temper or conversation. None, therefore, that feel their own weakness, the
continual apprehension of danger, the tendency of their
heart to backslide from God, and to disgrace "that worthy
name by which they are called" (James, ii. 7), will think
this prayer unseasonable or unnecessary—" *Turn away my
reproach which I fear.*"

Perhaps also the conflicting Christian may find this a
suitable prayer. Sometimes Satan has succeeded in beguiling him into some worldly compliance, or weakened his
confidence, by tempting him to look to himself for some
warrant of acceptance (in all which suggestions he is aided
and abetted by his treacherous heart): and then will this
" accuser of the brethren" turn back upon him, and change
himself " into an angel of light," presenting before him a
black catalogue of those very falls, into which he had suc-

---

* 2 Sam. xii. 14. We find Saul strongly deprecating this *reproach*—"I have sinned; *yet honour me now*, I pray thee, before the
elders of my people, and before Israel." (1 Sam. xv. 30.) But how
different the principle in these two instances under a similar trial!
The one tremblingly alive, that the name of God might not be reproached through his shameful fall. The other earnest only to
secure his own reputation.

cessfully led him. Bunyan does not fail to enumerate
these " *reproaches*," as amongst the most harassing assaults
of Apollyon. In his desperate conflict with Christian, he
taunts him with his fall in the Slough of Despond, and
every successive deviation from his path, as blotting out
his warrant of present favour with the King, and blasting
all hopes of reaching the celestial city. Christian does not
attempt to conceal or palliate the charge. He knows it is
all true, and much more besides! but he knows that this
is true also—"Where sin abounded, grace hath much
more abounded." " The blood of Jesus Christ the Son of
God cleanseth from all sin." (Rom. v. 20. 1 John, i. 7.)
Believers! In the heat of your conflict remember the
only effective covering. " *Above all*, taking the shield of
faith, wherewith you shall be able to quench all the fiery
darts of the wicked." (Eph. vi. 16.) Do you not hate the
sins, with which you have been overtaken? Are you not
earnestly longing for deliverance from their power? Then,
even while the recollections of their guilt and defilement
humble you before the Lord, take fresh hold of the gospel,
and you shall " overcome by the blood of the Lamb." (Rev.
xii. 9–11.) Victory must come from the cross. And the
soul that is directing its eye thither for pardon, strength,
and consolation, may sigh out the prayer with acceptance
—" *Turn away my reproach which I fear.*"

But how deeply is the guilt of apostasy or backsliding
aggravated by the acknowledgment, which all are constrained to make—" *Thy judgments are good!*" How affecting is the Lord's expostulation with us!—" What iniquity
have your fathers found in me, that they are gone far from
me, and have walked after vanity, and are become vain?
O my people! what have I done unto thee, and wherein
have I wearied thee? testify against me. I have not caused
thee to serve with an offering, nor wearied thee with incense." (Jer. ii. 5. Mic. vi. 3. Isa. xliii. 23.) No, surely

we have nothing to complain of our Master, of his work, or of his wages : but much, very much, to complain of ourselves, of our unwatchfulness, neglect, backsliding ; and to humble ourselves on account of the consequent *reproach* upon our profession.

Never, however, let us cease to cry, that all *the reproach which we fear* on account of our allowed inconsistencies of profession, may, for the Church's sake, be " *turned away from us.*" Meanwhile, " let us accept it as the punishment of our iniquity" (Lev. xxvi. 41) ; and, in the recollection of the *goodness of the Lord's judgments*, still venture to hope and look for the best things to come out of it from our gracious Lord.

40. *Behold, I have longed after thy precepts; quicken me in thy righteousness.*

Behold ! An appeal to the heart-searching God— " Thou knowest that I love" (Comp. John, xxi. 17) *thy precepts!* The heartfelt acknowledgment of their *goodness* naturally leads us to *long after them.** The professor *longs after* the promises, and too often builds a delusive—because an unsanctifying—hope upon them. The believer feels it to be his privilege and safety to have an equal regard to both—to obey *the precepts of God* in dependence on his promises, and to expect the accomplishment of the promises, in the way of obedience to *the precepts.* The utmost extent of the professor's service is the heavy yoke of *outward conformity.* He knows nothing of an "*inward delight and longing after them.*" Of many of them his heart complains,—" This is a hard saying : who can hear it ?" (John, vi. 60.) The Christian can give a good reason for his delight even in the most difficult and painful *precepts.* The moments of

---

* Compare the same acknowledgment, Rom. vii. 12, connected with similar delight, v. 22.

deepest repentance are his times of sweetest " refreshing
from the presence of the Lord." *   Whatever be the pleasure of indulgence in sin, far greater is the ultimate
enjoyment arising out of the mortification of it.†   Most
fruitful is our Saviour's *precept*, which inculcates on his
followers self-denial and the daily cross. (Luke, ix. 23.)
For by this wholesome discipline we lose our own perverse
will ; the power of sin is restrained, the pride of the heart
humbled ; and our real happiness fixed upon a solid and
permanent basis. So that, whatever dispensation some might
desire for breaking the *precept* without forfeiting the promise, the Christian blesses God for the strictness, that
binds him to a steady obedience to it. To him it is grievous,
not to keep it, but to break it.   A *longing* therefore *after
the precepts*, marks the character of the child of God : and
may be considered as the pulse of the soul.   It forms our
meetness and ripeness for heaven.

There are indeed times, when the violence of temptation, or the paralysing effect of indolence, hides the movements of the " hidden man of the heart."   And yet even
in these gloomy hours, when the mouth is shut, and the
heart dumb, before God —" so troubled, that it cannot
speak" (Ps. lxxvii. 4)—even then, acceptable incense is
ascending before the throne of God.   We have a powerful
intercessor " helping our infirmities"— interpreting our desires, and crying from within, " with groanings that cannot
be uttered" (Rom. viii. 26) ; yet such as, being indited by
our Advocate within, and presented by our Advocate above

* Acts, iii. 19.   Luther says the practice of repentance was ever
sweeter to him, after hearing the expression of an old divine—' This
is kind repentance, which begins from the love of God.'

† See David's lively expression of gratitude—first to his God—
then to the instrument employed by him — (Abigail) in restraining
him from the gratification of most unjustifiable revenge.—1 Sam.
xxv. 32, 33.

(Heb. ix. 24. Rev. viii. 3, 4), are cheering earnests of their fulfilment. " He will fulfil the desire of them that fear him : he also will hear their cry, and will save them." (Ps. cxlv. 19.)

These *longings* might seem to betoken a vigorous exercise of grace. But shall I be satisfied, while the most fervent desires are so disproportioned to their grand object —so overborne by the corruption of the flesh (Rom. vii. 18–24)—and while a heartless state is so hateful to my Saviour? (Rev. iii. 16.) Idle confessions and complaints are unseemly and unfruitful. Let me rather besiege the mercy-seat with incessant importunity (Matt. xi. 12),— ' *Quicken me in thy righteousness.*' ' I plead *thy righteousness*—thy righteous promise for the reviving of my spiritual life. I long for more lively apprehensions of thy spotless *righteousness*. Oh! let it invigorate my delight, my obedience, my secret communion, my Christian walk and conversation.' Such *longings*, poured out before the Lord for a fresh supply of *quickening* grace, are far different from " the desire of the slothful, which killeth him" (Prov. xxi. 25), and will not be forgotten before God. " Delight thyself in the Lord ; and he shall give thee the desires of thine heart." (Ps. xxxvii. 4.) O for a more enlarged expectation, and a more abundant vouchsafement of blessing ; that we may burst forth and break out, as from a living fountain within (John, iv. 14 ; vii. 38), in more ardent *longings for the Lord's precepts!*

But it may be asked—What weariness in, and reluctance to duties, may consist with the principle and exercise of grace ? Where it is only in the members, not in the mind—where it is only partial, not prevalent—where it is only occasional, not habitual — where it is lamented and resisted, and not allowed—and where, in spite of its influence, the Christian still holds on in the way of duty— " grace reigns" in the midst of conflict, and will ultimately and gloriously triumph over all hindrance and opposition. But in the midst of the humbling views of sin that present themselves on every side, let me diligently inquire — Have I an habitual " hungering and thirsting after *righteousness* ?" And since, at the best, I do but get my longings increased, and not satisfied ; let the full satisfaction of heaven be much in my heart. " As for me, I will behold thy face in righteousness ; I shall be satisfied, when I awake, with thy likeness." (Ps. xvii. 15.)

And what an expectation is this to pretend to ! To think what the infinitely and eternally blessed God is — and what " man is at his best estate" (Ps. xxxix. 5) ; then to conceive of man — the worm of the dust — the child of sin and wrath — transformed into the likeness of God — how weighty is the sound of this hope ! What then must its substantiation be ? If the initial privilege be glorious (2 Cor. iii. 18), what will the fulness be ! (1 John, iii. 2.) Glory revealed to us ! transfused through us ! becoming our very being ! To have the soul filled — not with evanescent shadows — but with massive, weighty, eternal glory ! (2 Cor. iv. 17.) Worlds are mere empty bubbles, compared with this, our sure, satisfying, unfading inheritance.

PART VI.

41. *Let thy mercies come also unto me, O Lord; even thy salvation, according to thy word.*

A PRAYER of deep anxiety — large desire — simple faith! It is a sinner — feeling his need of mercy — yea, *mercies* — abundant mercy (Ps. li. 1) — mercies for every moment — looking for them only in the *Lord's salvation* — to be dispensed *according to his word.* Out of Christ we know only a God, of justice and holiness. In Christ we behold " a just God, and yet a Saviour" (Isa. xlv. 21); and in " his *salvation* mercy and truth are met together; righteousness and peace have kissed each other." (Ps. lxxxv. 9, 10. Comp. Rom. iii. 26.) Therefore general notions of *mercy* without a distinct apprehension of *salvation* have their origin in presumption, not in warranted faith. For can there be any communication of mercy from an unknown God? Can there be any intercourse with an angry God? " Acquaint now thyself with him, and be at peace; thereby good shall come unto thee" (Job, xxii. 21) — " *The Lord's mercies, even his salvation.*"

Can we conceive the moment, when this prayer is not suited to us? How can we be at any moment safe or happy without the spirit of it? To walk as a saved sinner, " accepted in the Beloved," conformed to his image, devoted to his service, sealed for his kingdom — this is, or should be, the sunshine of every day. Let this prayer live in the heart. Carry continually to the Lord the cry for all *his mercies*—specially for that, which is the seal and crown of them all—*his salvation.*

This prayer, however, is peculiarly suitable to the believer, longing to realize that which sometimes is clouded to his view—his personal interest in the *Lord's salvation!* It must *come to me;* or I shall never come to it. I want not a general apprehension—I am not satisfied with the description of it. *Let it come to me*—*Let thy mercies* be applied, so that I can claim them, and rejoice in them! I see *thy salvation* come to others. Who needs it more than I? *Let it come also unto me.* "*Look thou upon me, and be merciful unto me,* as thou usest to do to those that love thy name. *Remember me, O Lord, with the favour that thou bearest unto thy people;* O visit me with thy salvation; that I may see the felicity of thy chosen, that I may rejoice in the gladness of thy nation, that I may glory with thine inheritance." (Verse 132. Ps. cvi. 4, 5.)

Now, are we seeking the assurance of this *salvation?* Are we waiting to realize its present power, saving us from sin—Satan—the world—ourselves—and " blessing us with all spiritual blessings in Christ Jesus?" Should a trial of faith and patience be ordained for us, yet in the end we shall find an enriching store of experience from his wise dispensations. That he has kept us from turning our backs upon his ways, when we had no comfort in them; that he has upheld us with his secret supplies of strength—is not this the work of his own Spirit within, and the pledge of the completion of the work? That he has enabled us, against all discouragements, to " continue instant in prayer," is surely an answer to that prayer, which in our apprehensions of it, had been cast out. That in waiting upon him, we have found no rest in worldly consolation, is an assurance, that the Lord himself will be our soul-satisfying and eternal portion. And who is there now in the sensible enjoyment of his love, who does not bless that

Divine wisdom, which took the same course with them that has been taken with us, to bring them to these joys? When did a weeping seed-time fail of bringing a joyful harvest? (Ps. cxxvi. 5, 6.)

But let not the ground of faith be forgotten—*According to thy word,*—that it shall come fully—freely—eternally—to him that waiteth for it. (Ps. xxxiii. 22. Comp. ver. 81.) " Thou meetest him that rejoiceth and worketh righteousness; those that remember thee in thy ways." (Isa. lxiv. 5.) Many, indeed, are satisfied with far too low a standard of spiritual enjoyments. It is comfortless to live at a distance from our Father's house, when we might be dwelling in the secret of his presence, and rejoicing in the smiles of his love. But let us not charge this dishonourable state upon the sovereignty of the Divine dispensations. Let us rather trace it to its true source—want of desire—want of faith—want of prayer—want of diligence. What infinite need have we of heavenly influence! What gracious encouragement to seek it! The way was blocked up—mercy has cleared the path, opened our access—" The golden sceptre is always held out." (Esth. v. 2.) Earnest prayer will bring a sure answer. The blessing is unspeakable. *Let thy mercies—thy salvation, come unto me, O Lord.*

42. *So shall I have wherewith to answer him that reproacheth me; for I trust in thy word.*

What is the salvation which he had just been speaking of? The whole gift of the mercy of God,—redemption from sin, death, and hell—pardon, peace, and acceptance with a reconciled God—constant communication of spiritual blessings—all that God can give, or we can want; all that we are able to receive here, or heaven can perfect hereafter. Now if this *comes to us*—comes to our hearts—surely it will furnish us at all times with *an answer to him that reproacheth us.* The world casts upon us the *reproach* of the cross. " What profit is there that we have walked mournfully before the Lord of Hosts ? " (Mal. iii. 14.) What is there to counterbalance the relinquishment of pleasure, esteem, and worldly comfort ? The mere professor can give no answer. He has heard of it, but it has never *come to him.* The believer is ready with his *answer,* ' I have found in the *Lord's salvation* pardon and peace—" not as the world giveth"—and such as the world cannot take away. Here, therefore, do I abide, finding it *my happiness* not to live without the cross, and testifying in the midst of abounding tribulation, that there are no comforts like Christ's comforts.' This was David's *answer,* when family trials were probably an occasion of *reproach.* " *Although my house be not so with God, yet he hath made with me an everlasting covenant, ordered in all things and sure : for this is all my salvation and all my desire.*" (2 Sam. xxiii. 5.)

But there is a far heavier *reproach* than that of the world—when the grand accuser injects hard thoughts of God—when he throws our guilt and unworthiness—our helplessness and difficulties, in our face. And how severe is this exercise in a season of spiritual desertion ! Except the believer can stay his soul upon " a God that hideth himself, as still the God of Israel, the Saviour" (Isa. xlv. 15), he is unprepared with an *answer to him that reproacheth him.* Such appears to have been Job's condition (Job, vi. vii. ix.), and Heman's (Ps. lxxxviii.), not to speak of many of the Lord's most favoured people, at different stages of their Christian life. Most important, therefore, is it for us to pray for a realizing sense of *the Lord's mercies—even of his salvation*—not only as necessary for our peace and comfort— but to garrison us against every assault, and to enable us to throw down the challenge—" *Rejoice not against me, O mine enemy ; when I fall, I shall arise ; when I sit in darkness, the Lord shall be a light unto me.*" (Mic. vii. 8.)

Free grace has saved me — an unspotted righteousness
covers me — an Almighty arm sustains me — eternal glory
awaits me. Who shall condemn? "Who shall separate
us from the love of God which is in Christ Jesus our Lord?"
(Rom. viii. 33–39.)

Now, for this bold front to our enemies, nothing is
wanted beyond the reach of the weakest child of God. No
extraordinary holiness — no Christian establishment in experience — nothing but simple, humble faith — *For I trust
in thy word.* Faith makes this salvation ours, in all its
fulness and almighty power : and, therefore, our confidence
in the word will make us "ready always to give an
answer to every one that asketh us a reason of the hope
that is in us, with meekness and fear." (1 Pet. iii. 15.)
"No weapon that is formed against thee shall prosper;
and every tongue that riseth against thee in judgment,
thou shalt condemn. This is the heritage of the servants
of the Lord ; and their righteousness is of me, saith the
Lord." (Isa. liv. 17.)

But how often is our Christian boldness paralysed by
our feeble apprehensions of *the salvation of God!* Clear
and full evangelical views are indispensable for the effective
exercise of our weighty obligations. Any indistinctness
here, from its necessary mixture of self-righteousness and
unbelief, obscures the warrant of our personal interest, and
therefore hinders the firm grasp of Almighty strength.
Coldness and formality also deaden the power of Christian
boldness. Much need, therefore, have we to pray for a
realized perception of the freeness, fulness, holiness, and
privileges of the Gospel. Much need have we to use our
speedy diligence, without delay ; our painful diligence,
without indulgence : our continual diligence, without weariness ; that we be not satisfied with remaining on the
skirts of the kingdom ; that it be not a matter of doubt,
whether we belong to it or not ; but that, grace being

added to grace, " so an entrance may be ministered to us
abundantly, into" (2 Pet. i. 5–11) all its rich consolations
and everlasting joys.

43. *And take not the word of truth utterly out of my mouth ;*
for I have hoped in thy judgments.

For the sake of the church and of the world, no less
than for our own sakes, let us " give diligence" to clear
up our interest in the Gospel.   The want of personal assurance is not only a loss in our own souls, but a hindrance
to our Christian usefulness.   Hence our efforts are often
powerless in parrying off the attack of *him that reproacheth
us,* as well as to " strengthen the weak hands, and confirm
the feeble knees" (Isa. xxxv. 3) of our brethren.   The
charge of hypocrisy, or the want of the " constraining"
principle of " the love of Christ," stops the utterance of
the word of truth, and obscures our character as a " saint of
God " (Ps. cxlv. 10–12), and " a witness " for his name.
(Isa. xliii. 10.)   Justly, indeed, might he punish our unfaithfulness, by forbidding us any more to speak in his name.
And therefore the dread of this grievous judgment, and the
mourning over precious lost opportunities, stirs up the
prayer—' *Take not the word of truth utterly out of my mouth*
— Not only take it not *out of my heart ;* but let it be ready
in my *mouth* for the confession of my Master.'

This valuable prayer may preserve us from denying
Christ. Too apt are we to allow worldly intercourse, habits,
and conversation without a word of restraint.   Let the
whole weight of Christian responsibility be deeply felt—
faith in the heart, and confession with the mouth (Rom. x.
9, 10)—the active principle, and the practical exercise.
Should we be content with the dormant principle, where
would be the Church—the witness for God in the world?
Shall we shrink from the bold confession of Him, who

"despised the shame of the cross" for us? (Heb. xii. 2.)
Would not this imply distrust of our own testimony — *the
word of truth?*

It does indeed need wisdom to know when, as well as
what, to speak. There is "a time to keep silence," and
"the prudent shall keep silence in that time." (Eccles. iii.
7. Amos, v. 13.) But is it our cross to be "dumb with
silence?" And when we "hold our peace, even from good,"
is our "sorrow stirred — our hearts hot within us — the fire
burning"? (Ps. xxxix. 2, 3.) Nay — is not the plea of bashfulness or judicious caution often a self-deluding cover for
the *real* cause of restraint — the want of the personal apprehension of the Lord's mercy? "I believed, and therefore have
I spoken." (2 Cor. iv. 13.) Oh! let not the word of truth be
taken *utterly* out of our mouth. A stammering confession is
better than silence. If we cannot say all we want of, or for
our Saviour, let us say what we can. ' God's servants are
very sensible of the infinite value of the least atom of what
belongs to him.'* And a word spoken in weakness may
be a word of Almighty power, and a present help to some
fainting spirit. In our connexion with the world, many
occasions will unexpectedly occur, if the heart be but
wakeful and active to improve them. The common topics
of earthly conversation often furnish a channel for heavenly intercourse, so that our communications with the
world may be like Jacob's ladder, whose bottom rested
upon the earth, but the top reached unto the heavens.†

* Correspondence of the Rev. J. T. Nottidge (Seeleys) — a most
valuable treasure of experimental religion, p. 350.

† Gen. xxviii. 12. ' Why do I make any of my visits to any of
my neighbours, or countenance their visits unto me? Lord, I
desire to let fall something, that may be for the good of the company; even, that more may be known of thee, and done for thee,
for what passes in it. And when I propose to ingratiate myself
unto any people by the civilities of conversation, it shall be, that I
may gain thereby the better advantages to prosecute purposes upon

And oh! what a relief is it to the burdened conscience, to stammer out, if it be but a few words for God, even though there be no sensible refreshings of his presence! Yet if we would speak for him with power and acceptance, it must be out of the " good treasure and abundance of the heart." (Matt. xii. 34.) For it is only when " the heart is inditing a good matter, speaking of the things touching the King, that the tongue is as the pen of a ready writer." (Ps. xlv. 1, 2.)

But let us take up this petition as the expression of the Christian's exercises with his God. ' That word *utterly* ' —observes an eminently-tried believer—' though it seems to be beneath the notice of the mind, when one has got very low, is in reality one of the most blessed words in this most blessed book. How often, when I have formerly been upon the brink of giving up all for lost, and of saying— " Evil, be thou my good"—the thought has perhaps struck me, that, while I am struggling between despondency and rebellion, and too hard, too cold, too discouraged to look up to him, the blessed Redeemer is pitying the struggle of my soul; and it has kept me where I was, led me to put off despair at least till to-morrow; and then before to-morrow I have seen something of the grace and glory of the Gospel.'

What then is the advice, which this man of God gives from his own experience? ' When you are most deeply deploring your sins, never fail to thank the Lord, or at least to think how you would thank him, if you dared lift up a face overwhelmed with shame and defeat, that he has *not taken away his truth* UTTERLY; that he has left you clinging to some twig of hope, instead of leaving you to

them. In conversation, I would especially lay hold on all advantages to introduce as much as I can of a lovely Christ into the view of all that I come near unto.'— COTTON MATHER, *Student and Pastor*, pp. 74, 75.

find—what thousands who look outwardly very calm—have found—the depth of the precipice of despair.' *

The Psalmist's prayer here is the same confidence of faith, that was expressed in the preceding verse—*For I have hoped in thy judgments*, an acceptable spirit of approach to God, and an earnest of the revival of life and comfort in the Lord's best time and way.

44. *So shall I keep thy law continually for ever and ever.*

The heaping up of so many words in this short verse, appears to be the struggle of the soul to express the vehemency of its longings to glorify its Saviour. And, indeed, the Lord's return to us, unsealing the lips of the dumb, and putting his *word again into their mouth*, brings with it a fresh sense of constraining obligation. This fresh occupation in his praise and service is not only our present privilege, but an antepast of our heavenly employment, when the word will never more *be taken out of our mouth*, but we shall " talk of his wondrous works " (Verse 27) "*for ever and ever.*" The defects in the constancy and extent of our obedience (as far as our hearts are alive to the honour of God) must ever be our grief and burden ; and the prospect of its completeness in a better world, is that, which renders the anticipation of heaven so delightful. There we shall be blest with suitable feelings, and therefore be enabled to render suitable obedience—even one unbroken consecration of all our powers to his work. Then "*shall we keep his law continually for ever and ever.*" Once admitted to the " throne of God," we " shall serve him day and night in his temple " (Rev. vii. 15)—without sin—without inconstancy—without weariness—without end ! We speak of heaven ; but oh ! to be there ! To be engaged

* Nottidge, *ut supra*, pp. 350, 351.

throughout eternity in the service of love to a God of love ! In one day's continuance in the path of obedience even here, in the midst of the defilement which stains our holiest services, how sweetly do the moments roll away ! But to be ever employed for him, in that place, where " there shall in no wise enter anything that defileth" (Rev. xxi. 27)—this gives an emphasis and a dignity to the heavenly joy, which may well stamp it as " unspeakable and full of glory." (1 Pet. i. 8.) May we not then encourage the hope, that the Lord is making us meet for heaven, by the strength and constancy of our desires to *keep the laws of God*? And is it not evident, that heaven itself can afford no real delight to one, who feels the service of God on earth to be irksome ? He stands self-excluded by the constitution of his nature, by the necessity of the case. He has no heart for heaven, no taste for heaven, no capacity for enjoyment of heaven—" He that is unjust, let him be unjust still ; and he that is filthy, let him be filthy still ; and he that is righteous, let him be righteous still ; and he that is holy, let him be holy still." (Rev. xxii. 11.)

Heavenly, gracious Father ! who and what are we, that our hearts should be made the unworthy recipients of thy grace ? that our will should be subdued into " the obedience of faith ?" and that we should be permitted to anticipate that blessed period, when we shall " *keep thy law continually, for ever and ever?*" May this prospect realize the happiness of our present obedience ! May He, who has " bought us with a price" for his glory, reign in our hearts, and live upon our lips ; that each of us may have his mark upon our foreheads—the seal of his property in us, and of our obligation to him—" Whose I am, and whom I serve !" (Acts, xxvii. 23.)

45. *And I will walk at liberty: for I seek thy precepts.*

Not only perseverance but *liberty*, is the fruit of the Lord's mercy to our souls—not the liberty of sin—to do what we please—but of holiness—to do what we ought ; the one, the iron bondage of our own will ; * the other, the easy yoke of a God of love.   It was a fine expression of a heathen—" To serve God is to reign." †   Certainly in this service David found the liberty of a king.   *The precepts of God* were not forced upon him ; for he *sought them.*   " More to be desired than gold, yea, than much fine gold ; sweeter also than honey, and the honey-comb." (Ps. xix. 10.) The way of the Lord, which to the ungodly is beset with thorns and briers, is the king's highway of *liberty.*   The child of God walks here in the gladness of his heart and the rejoicing of his conscience.   Even in " *seeking these precepts,*" there is " *liberty*" and enlargement of heart ; a natural motion, like that of the sun in its course, " going forth as a bridegroom, and rejoicing as a strong man to run a race." (Verse 5.)   What must it be then, to walk in the full enjoyment of *the precepts!*   " Where the Spirit of the Lord is, there is liberty."   " They shall sing in the ways of the Lord,"—for " how great is his goodness ; how great is his beauty!" (2 Cor. iii. 17. Ps. cxxxviii. 5. Zech. ix. 17.)

---

* 'I am bound,' said Augustine—'not with another man's iron, but with my own iron will.   I gave my will to mine enemy, and he made a chain, and bound me with it.'—*Confess.* viii. 6.

† 'In regno vivimus.   Deo servire est regnare.'—SENECA. When the female martyr Agatha was upbraided, because, being descended of an illustrious parentage, she stooped to mean and humble offices—'Our nobility'—she replied—'lies in this; that we are the servants of Christ.'—BISHOP SUMNER's *Evidences*, pp. 359, 360.

Are we then obeying *the precepts* as our duty, or " *seeking*" them as our privilege ?   Do we complain of the strictness of the law, or of the corruption of the flesh ? Are the *precepts* of our own hearts our burden ?   Is sin or holiness our bondage ?   The only way to make religion easy, is to be always in it.   The glow of spiritual activity, and the healthfulness of Christian *liberty*, are only to be found in the persevering and self-denying pursuit of every track of the ways of God—" If ye continue in my word, then are ye my disciples indeed : and ye shall know the truth, and the truth shall make you free. If the Son, therefore, shall make you free, ye shall be free indeed." (John, viii. 31, 32, 36.) To have the whole stream of all our thoughts, actions, motives, desires, affections, carried in one undivided current towards God, is the complete and unrestrained influence of his love upon our hearts.

Let but our eyes be opened, our judgments clearly exercised, our consciences suffered to speak ; and this point is clear — Sin is slavery (John, viii. 34) — Holiness is liberty.   The sinner may live in bonds with as much delight as if he was in his element.   He may seem even to himself to be at large, while in fact he is " shut up, and cannot come forth."   For such is the tyranny under which he is bound, that he cannot help himself ; and (to use the confession of a heathen) while ' he sees and approves better things, he follows the worse.'*   Every sin is a fresh chain of bondage (Tit. iii. 3), under the check of a cruel master. On the other hand—the Lord's commands—as he himself declares, and all his servants testify—are " for our good alway." (Deut. vi. 24. Matt. xi. 29, 30. Comp. 1 John, v. 3.)   His ' service is perfect freedom.' (Liturgy.)   The life of liberty is to be under the bonds of holy love and duty.

---

* " Video meliora, proboque ;
Deteriora sequor."—*Medea in* OVID.

(Luke, i. 74, 75. Comp. Ps. cxvi. 16.) Let the trial be made of two Masters ; conviction must follow.

True it is, that the corrupt and rebellious inclinations will "lust" (Gal. v. 17) to the end. But as long as indulgence is denied, conflict excited, and the constant endeavour maintained to " bring every thought into captivity to the obedience of Christ" (2 Cor. x. 5), our liberty is established, even where it is not always enjoyed. Every fresh chain, by which we bind ourselves to the Lord, makes us more free.* While, then, they that " promise us liberty are themselves the servants of corruption" (2 Pet. ii. 19), let us live as the children of God — the heirs of the kingdom — grateful — free — blood-bought souls—remembering the infinite cost at which our liberty was purchased, and the moment of extreme peril when we were saved. When the flesh was weak, and the " law weak through the flesh" (Rom. viii. 3), and no resolution of ours could break us from the yoke of sin — then it was that " Christ both died, and rose, and revived, that he might be the Lord both of the dead and living" (Ib. xiv. 9), " delivering us from the hand of our enemies, that we might serve him without fear." (Luke, i. 74.) And then indeed do we " *walk at liberty*," when we " break the bands" of all other lords " asunder," and consecrate ourselves entirely to his *precepts*. " *O Lord our God, other lords beside thee have had dominion over us; but by thee only will we make mention of thy name.*" †

---

* " Jugum Christi non deterit, sed honestat colla."— BERNARD.

† Isa. xxvi. 13. An incident in the history of ancient Rome may furnish an illustration of that full liberty and entireness of heart, which forms the act of acceptable surrender to the Lord. When the people of Collatia were negotiating an unconditional capitulation to the Romans, Egerius, on the part of the Romans, inquired of the ambassadors—'Are the people of Collatia in their own power?' When an affirmative answer was given, it was next inquired—'Do you deliver up yourselves — the people of Collatia—

46. *I will speak of thy testimonies also before kings, and will not be ashamed.*

" *Liberty in walking*" in the Lord's ways will naturally produce boldness in *speaking* of them. Compare the conduct of the three unshaken witnesses for the truth before the Babylonish monarch. (Dan. iii. 16–18.) Mark the difference of the spirit displayed by the Apostles, and especially by Peter, before and after the day of Pentecost.* Look at Stephen before the council (Acts, vi. 15), and Paul before Felix (Acts, xxiv.), Festus (Acts, xxv.), and Agrippa (Acts, xxvi.). " God had not given to them the spirit of fear ; but of power, and of love, and of a sound mind." (2 Tim. i. 7.) Hear the great Apostle testifying of himself— " I am ready to preach the gospel to you that are at Rome also "— at the metropolis of the world, in the face of all opposition and contempt, and at the imminent hazard of my life—" *For* "—says he—" *I am not ashamed of the gospel of Christ.*" (Rom. i. 15, 16.) In the same determination of soul, he exhorts his dear son in the faith—" *Be not thou ashamed* of the testimony of our Lord, nor of me his prisoner." (2 Tim. i. 8.) To how many does " the fear of man

your city, your fields, your waters, your boundaries, your temples, your utensils, all your property, divine and human, into my power, and the power of the Roman people ?' ' *We surrender all.*' ' And so,' said he, ' I accept you.'— LIVY, Book i. Such may my surrender be to the Lord ! Disentangled from every other yoke, under no bonds that ought to bind me, Lord, I offer myself, and all that belongs to me, without exception or reserve, at thy feet. " But who am I, that I should be able to offer so willingly after this sort? For all things come of thee, and of thine own have I given thee." 1 Chron. xxix. 14,

* Contrast Matt. xxvi. 56, 69, 75 ; with Acts, ii. iii. iv. v. We can scarcely believe that the same persons are alluded to. But the explanation of the difficulty had been given by anticipation. (John, vii. 39.)

bring a snare?" (Prov. xxix. 25.) Many a good soldier
has faced the cannon's mouth with undaunted front, and
yet shrunk away with a coward's heart from the reproach
of the cross, and been put to blush even by the mention
of the Saviour's name. Far better — the Son of Man
"strengthening you" — to brave the fiery furnace, or the
den of lions in his service, than like Jonah, by flinching
from the cross, to incur the sting of conscience and the
frown of God. (Dan. iii. 16–18 ; vi. 16–22, with Jonah, i.
1–15.)

Professing Christians! Are we ready to bear our testimony for Jesus, against the sneer and ridicule of the ungodly? We are not likely to " be brought *before kings* and
rulers for the Son of Man's sake." (Luke, xxi. 12. Mark,
xiii. 9.) Yet no less do we need Divine help and strong
faith in withstanding the enmity of a prejudiced relative or
scornful neighbour. Young people! you are perhaps in
especial danger of being ashamed of your Bible, your religion, your Saviour. You may be brought under the snare
of the " fear of man," and be tempted to compromise your
religion, and to sacrifice your everlasting all from a dread
of " the reproach of Christ." But remember him, who for
your sake " before Pontius Pilate witnessed a good confession" (1 Tim. vi. 13); and shall the dread of a name
restrain you from sharing his reproach, and banish the
obligations of love and gratitude from your hearts? Have
you forgotten, that you once owned the service of Satan?
and will you not be as bold for Christ, as you were for him?
Were you once " glorying in your shame ;" and will you now
be ashamed of your glory? Oh! remember who hath said,
" Whosoever shall be ashamed of me and of my words, in
this adulterous and sinful generation, of him also shall the
Son of Man be ashamed, when he cometh in the glory of
his Father with the holy angels." (Mark, viii. 38.) Think

much and often of this word. Think on this day. Think
on the station of " the fearful and unbelieving" on the left
hand on that day. Think on their eternal doom (Rev.
xxi. 8). What is a prison, compared to hell? What need
to pray and tremble! If you are sincere in your determination, and simple in your dependence, then will the
" love of Christ constrain you" (2 Cor. v. 14), not to a cold,
calculating, reluctant service ; but to a confession of your
Saviour, bold, unfettered, and " faithful even unto death."
(Rev. ii. 10.) Every deviation from the straight path
bears the character of being *ashamed* of Christ. How much
have you to speak in behalf of *his testimonies*, his ways, his
love! When in danger of the influence of " the fear of
man," look to him for strength. He will give to you, as he
gave to Stephen—" a mouth and wisdom, which all your
adversaries shall not be able to gainsay or resist." (Luke,
xxi. 15, with Acts, vi. 10.) Thus will you, like them,
be strengthened " to profess a good profession before many
witnesses." (1 Tim. vi. 12.)

47. *And I will delight myself in thy commandments, which I*
have loved.

It is but poor comfort to the believer to be able to talk
well to others upon the ways of God, and even to " bear
the reproach" of his people, when his own heart is cold,
insensible, and dull. But why does he not rouse himself
to the active exercise of faith—" *I will delight* myself in
thy commandments?" That which is the burden of the
carnal heart is the delight of the renewed soul. The former
" is enmity against God : and therefore is not, and cannot
be, subject to his law." (Rom. viii. 7.) The latter can
delight in nothing else. If the gospel separates the heart
from *sinful* delights, it is only to make room for delights of

a more elevated, satisfying, and enduring nature.* Satan, indeed, generally baits his temptations with that seductive witchery, which the world calls pleasure. But has he engrossed all pleasure into his service? Are there no pleasures besides "the pleasures of sin?" Do the ways of the Lord promise nothing but difficulty and trial? What means then the experience of him, who could "rejoice in them, as much as in all riches," and who "loved them above gold, yea, above fine gold?" (Verses 14, 127.) The "fatted calf" of our Father's house is surely a most gainful exchange for "the husks" of the "far country." (Luke, xv. 13–24.) The delights of holiness go deeper than sensual pleasures. (Ps. iv. 7.) The joy of the saint is not that false, polluted, deadly joy, which is all that the worldling knows, and all that he has to look for: but it flows spontaneously from the fountain of living waters, through the pure channel of "the word of God, which liveth and abideth for ever." Nay, so independent is it of any earthly spring, that it never flourishes more than in the desolate wilderness, or the sick-bed solitude; so that, "although the fig-tree shall not blossom, neither shall fruit be in the vines, yet we will rejoice in the Lord, we will joy in the God of our salvation." (Hab. iii. 17, 18.) Men of the world see what religion takes away, but they see little of what it gives;† else would they reproach—not our folly—but their own blindness. "Thus saith the Lord God, Behold, my servants shall eat, but ye shall be hungry;

* 'Delectationes non amittimus, sed mutamus'—was the expression of one of the ancients. 'I live a voluptuous life'—said the excellent Joseph Alleine to his wife—'but it is upon spiritual dainties, such as the world know not, and taste not of.'

† Cyprian, in one of his epistles (ad Donat.), mentions the great difficulty he found in overcoming the false view of the gloom of religion—little suspecting that the cause of the gloom was in himself—not in the gospel. But this is explained, Matt. vi. 23.

behold, my servants shall drink, but ye shall be thirsty ;
behold, my servants shall rejoice, but ye shall be ashamed ;
behold, my servants shall sing for joy of heart, but ye shall
cry for sorrow of heart, and shall howl for vexation of
spirit." (Isa. lxv. 13, 14.)

The love and complacency of the soul first fixes on *the
commandments.*   Then how natural is the flow of *delight in
them !* even at the very time that we are " abhorring ourselves in dust and ashes" for our neglect of them ; and
God never has our hearts, until something of this *delight* is
felt and enjoyed.   But do we complain of the dulness of
our hearts, that restrains this pleasure ?   Let us seek for
a deeper impression of redeeming love.   This will be the
spring of grateful obedience and holy delight.   Let us turn
our complaints into prayers, and the Lord will quickly turn
them into praises.   Let us watch against everything, that
would intercept our communion with Jesus. Distance from
him must be accompanied with poverty of spiritual enjoyment.—" *They shall be abundantly satisfied with the fatness
of thy house : and thou shalt make them drink of the river of
thy pleasures.   For with thee is the fountain of life : and in
thy light shall we see light.*" (Ps. xxxvi. 8, 9.)

48. *My hands also will I lift up unto thy commandments,
which I have loved: and I will meditate in thy statutes.*

David seems at a loss for expressions adequately to set
forth the fervency of his love and delight in the ways and
word of God.   Here we find him *lifting up his hands*
with the gesture of one, who is longing to embrace the
object of his desire with both hands and his whole heart.
(See Ps. lxiii. 4 ; cxliii. 6.)   Perhaps also in *lifting up
his hands unto the commandments,* he might mean to express
his looking upward for assistance to keep them, and to live
in them. (See Ib. xxviii. 2.)   But how humbling this

comparison with ourselves! Alas! how often from the neglect of this influence of the Spirit of God, do our "hands hang down," instead of being *lifted up*, in these holy ways! We are too often content with a scanty measure of love : without any sensible " hungering and thirsting after righteousness ; " neither able to pray with life and power, nor to hear with comfort and profit, nor to " do good and communicate" with cheerfulness, nor to meditate with spiritual delight, nor to live for God with zeal and interest, nor to anticipate the endurance of the cross with unflinching resolution — the soul being equally disabled for heavenly communion and active devotedness. Shall we look for ease under the power of this deadening malady? Let us rather struggle and cry for deliverance from it. Let us subscribe ourselves before God as wretched, helpless, and guilty. He can look upon us, and revive us. Let us then "take hold upon his covenant," and plead that he will look upon us. Let us " put him in remembrance" of the glory of his name, which is much more concerned in delivering us out of this frame, by his quickening grace, than in leaving us, stupid, corrupt, and carnal in it. Professor! awake : or beg of the Lord to awaken you! For if your cold sleeping heart is contented with the prospect of a heaven hereafter, without seeking for a present foretaste of its joy, it may be a very questionable matter whether heaven will ever be yours.

Delight, however, will exercise itself in an habitual *meditation in the statutes.* (See Ps. i. 2.) The breathing of the heart will be — " *Oh, how love I thy law! it is my meditation all the day.*" (Verse 97.) It is in holy meditation on the word of God, that all the graces of the Spirit are manifested. What is the principle of faith, but the reliance of the soul upon the promises of the word? What is the sensation of godly fear, but the soul trembling before the threatenings of God? (Verse 120.) What is the object of

hope, but the apprehended glory of God? What is the
excitement of desire or love, but longing, endearing contemplations of the Saviour, and of his unspeakable blessings? Hence we can scarcely conceive of the influence of
grace separated from spiritual meditation on the word. It
is this which, under Divine teaching, draws out its hidden
contents, and exhibits them to the soul, as the objects
upon which the principles and affections of the Divine life
are habitually exercised. Not that any benefit can be expected from meditation, even upon the word of God, as an
abstract duty. If not deeply imbued with prayer, it will
degenerate into dry speculative study. Without some distinct practical application, it will be unedifying in itself,
and unsatisfactory for its important ends—the discerning
of the mind of God, and feeding upon the rich provision of
the Gospel.

Why then is the Bible read only—not *meditated on?*
Because it is not *loved.* We do not go to it, as the hungry
man to his food, as the miser to his treasure. The loss is
incalculable. Our superficial knowledge has no practical
influence. It is only as we " search," that we " know it for
our good." (Job, v. 27.)

Let it then be a matter of daily inquiry. Does my
reading of the word of God furnish food for my soul, matter
for prayer, direction for conduct? Scriptural study, when
entered upon in a prayerful spirit, will never, like many
other studies, be unproductive. The mind that is engaged
in it, is fitly set for bearing fruit; it will " bring forth
fruit in due season." (Ps. i. 2, 3.) Meditation kindles love,
as it is the effect of love, " While I was musing, the fire
burned." (Ps. xxxix. 3.) " Whoso looketh into the perfect
law of liberty, and continueth therein, this man is blessed
in his deed." (Jam. i. 25.) But let us take heed, that the
root of religion in the soul is not cankered by the indulgence of secret sin. The largest supply of Christian ordi-

nances will fail to refresh us, except the heart be kept right
with God in simplicity of faith, love, and diligence in the
service of Christ.

Come then, Christian, let us set our hearts to a vigorous, delighting devotedness to *the statutes of our God.* " It
is not a vain thing for us; because it is our life." (Deut.
xxxii. 46, 47.) But to regard *some* of the words only
would be to obey our own will, not God's. Let us *lift up
our hands to them all.* How shadowy is the joy of speculative contemplation, if it does not draw the heart to practical exercise ! Let faith return our obligations in the full
apprehension of the Lord's mercy. And then will love
constrain us to nothing less than " a living sacrifice" (Rom.
xi. 22, 30, xii. 1) to his service. If the professor sleeps in
notional godliness, let us employ our active *meditation* in
searching for the mine that lies not on the surface, but
which never fails to enrich diligent, patient, persevering
labour. (Prov. ii. 4, 5.)

PART VII.

49. Remember the word unto thy servant, upon which thou hast caused me to hope.

W<small>HAT</small> is faith ?   It is *hope upon God's word.*   The warrant of faith is therefore *the word.*   The object of faith is he that *causeth us to hope.*   He has not forgotten—he cannot forget, his *word.*   But he permits—nay, commands *his servants* to remind him of it (Isa. lxii. 6. M. R.) in order to exercise their faith, diligence, and patience.   Often, indeed, " *hope* deferred maketh the heart sick." (Prov. xiii. 12.)   But it is not needless delay (Hab. ii. 3)—not ignorance of the fittest time (Isa. xxx. 18)—not forgetfulness (Ps. cxi. 5)—not changeableness (Mal. iii. 6)—not weakness. (1 Sam. xv. 29.)   Meanwhile, however, constantly plead the promise—*Remember the word unto thy servant.* This is the proper use of the promises, as " arguments wherewith to fill our mouths, when we order our cause before God." (Job, xxiii. 4.)   When thus pleaded with the earnestness and humility of faith, they will be found to be the blessed realities of unchanging love.

Now—have not circumstances of Providence, or the distinct application of the Spirit, made some words of God especially precious to your soul ?   Such words are thus made your own, to be laid up against some future time of trial, when you may " put your God in remembrance" (Isa. xliii. 26) of them.   Apply this exercise of faith to such a word as this—" Him that cometh unto me, I will in no wise cast out." (John, vi. 37.) Then plead your interest in it as a coming sinner—" Lord, *I hope in this thy word.*" " *Thou hast caused me to hope*" in it. " *Remember this word unto thy servant.*" Thus is prayer grounded upon the promise, which it forms into a prevailing argument, and sends back to heaven ; nothing doubting, but that it will be verified in God's best time and way.*

Take another case; God has engaged himself to be the God of the seed of believers. His sacramental ordinance is the seal of this promise. (Gen. xvii. 7, 10, with Acts, ii. 38, 39.) The believer brings his child to this ordinance, as the exercise of his faith upon the faithfulness of God. Let him *daily* put his finger upon this promise, *Remember the word unto thy servant, upon which thou hast caused me to hope.* This is, as Augustine said of his mother, ' bringing before God his own hand-writing.' Will he not *remember his word?* Faith may be tried, perhaps long tried. " But he abideth faithful. He cannot deny himself." (2 Tim. ii. 13.) Faith trusts—not what the eye sees, but what the word promises.

Again—Have we ever found *God's word hoped on,* a covering and strength against besetting sin ? This will surely be an encouragement to cry under the same temptation—*Remember thy word.* " He who hath delivered, doth deliver, and will even to the end deliver." (2 Cor. i. 10.) He " hath done great things for us." And is not this an earnest of continued mercy ? " *Because thou hast been my help,* therefore under the shadow of thy wings will I rejoice." (Ps. lxiii. 7.) Thus may we confidently receive a

* We may observe Jacob making precisely this use of the word of promise to great advantage, at a time of personal extremity. Gen. xxxii. 9, 10, 12 ; with xxxi. 3, 13 ; xxviii. 13-15. Was not this in fact pleading—*Remember the word unto thy servant, upon which thou hast caused me to hope ?* Comp. also verse 38 of this Psalm.

promise as the distinct message to our soul, when we are conscious of a readiness to receive the whole word as the rule of our life. And does it not set an edge upon prayer, *to eye a promising God*, and to consider his promises — not as hanging in the air, without any definite direction or meaning, but as individually spoken and belonging to myself as a child and *servant of God?* This is the experience and comfort of the life of faith. This unfolds the true secret of living to God ; ending at last with the honourable death-bed testimony —" Behold, this day I am going the way of all the earth : and ye know in all your hearts and in all your souls, that not one thing hath failed of all the good things, which the Lord your God spake concerning you ; all are come to pass unto you ; and not one thing hath failed thereof." (Josh. xxiii. 14.)

50. *This is my comfort in my affliction; for thy word hath quickened me.*

. David was encouraged to plead *the word* of promise in prayer, from the recollection of its *comfort in his affliction.* For the man of God is not exempted from affliction, but he is comforted in it with God's comforts, flowing from the fountain-head. And truly no comforts are like God's comforts, and there are none beside his. (Ps. xciv. 19. 2 Cor. i. 3, 4.) They are indeed strong consolations, both in their foundation and their influence (Heb. vi. 18); supporting — not only in the prospect, but under the actual pressure of trouble, and fully proportioned to the need of the most sinking calamity. (2 Cor. i. 5.) Never therefore are we left unsupported in such a time, or called to drink a cup of unmingled tribulation. In the moments of our bitterest sorrow, how are we compelled to stand amazed at the tenderness, which is daily and hourly exercised towards us ! We have always some word exactly suited to our affliction,

and which we could not have understood without it ; and
" a word" *thus* " *spoken* in due season, how good is it !"*
One word of God, sealed to the heart, infuses more sensible
relief, than ten thousand words of man.   When therefore
the word assures of the presence of God in *affliction* (Isa.
xliii. 1, 2) ; of his continued pity and sympathy in his most
severe dispensations (Exod. iii. 7, 16) ; and of their certain issue to our everlasting good (Rom. viii. 28); must not
we say of it, *This is our comfort in our affliction?*   How does
the Saviour's love stream forth from this channel on every
side ; imparting life, refreshment, strength to those, who
but for this *comfort* would have " fainted" (Ps. xxvii. 13),
and " perished in their affliction !" (Verse 92.)   This indeed was the end, for which the Scriptures were written
(Rom. xv. 4) ; and such power of consolation have they
sometimes administered to the afflicted saint, that tribulation has almost ceased to be a trial, and the retrospect has
been the source of thankful recollection.

But first the word becomes life—then *comfort*.   And
those only, who have felt the *quickening power of the word*,
can realize its consolations.   Be thankful, then, Reader, if,
when dead in sins, it " *quickened you*" (Jam. i. 18. 1 Pet.

* Prov. xv. 23. ' I will show you a privilege that others want,
and you have in this case. Such as are in prosperity, and are filled with
earthly joys, and increased with children and friends ; though the
word of God, is indeed written for their instruction, yet to you who
are in trouble, and from whom the Lord hath taken many children,
and whom he hath otherwise exercised, there are some chapters,
some particular promises in the word of God, made in an especial manner, which would never have been yours, so as they now
are, if you had had your portion in this world like others. It is no
small comfort, that God hath written some scriptures to you, which
he hath not to others. Read these, and think God is like a friend,
who sendeth a letter to a whole house and family, but who speaketh
in his letter to some by name, that are dearest to him in the house.'
—RUTHERFORD's *Letters*.

i. 23); and, when sunk in trouble, once and again it has revived you. (Verses 81, 82.) Yet think not, that it is any innate power of its own, that works so graciously for you. No. The exhibition of the Saviour is the spring of life and consolation. It is because it " testifies of him" (John, v. 39), " the consolation of Israel" (Luke, ii. 25)—" afflicted in all our afflictions" (Isa. lxiii. 9)—and never failing to uphold with " grace sufficient for us." (2 Cor. xii. 9.) It is not, however, the word without the Spirit, nor the Spirit generally without the word ; but the Spirit by the word— first putting life into the word (John, vi. 63), and then by the word quickening the soul. The word then is only the instrument. The Spirit is the Almighty agent. Thus the work is the Lord's ; and nothing is left for us, but self-renunciation and praise.

51. *The proud have had me greatly in derision; yet have I not declined from thy law.*

The scorn of an ungodly world is one of the *afflictions*, which realize to us *the comfort of the word.* And this is a trial, from which no exemption is to be expected—" *All that will live godly in Christ Jesus* shall suffer persecution." (2 Tim. iii. 12. Comp. 1 Cor. iv. 13.) Not even David— though a king—a man of wisdom and prudence, and therefore not likely to give unnecessary offence ; and whose character and rank might be expected to command respect —not even was *he* shielded from *the derision of the proud* on account of the profession and service of his God. (Ps. xxxv. 15, 16 ; cxxiii. 3, 4.) Thus it ever was and ever will be. Faith in the doctrine of Christ, and conformity to the strict commandments of the gospel, must expose us to the taunts of the unbeliever and the worldling. Yet, where the heart is right with God, the *derision of the proud*, instead of forcing us to *decline from the law of*

God, will strengthen our adherence to it. David answered the bitter *derision* of Michal with a stronger resolution to abide by his God—" I will yet be more vile than thus." (2 Sam. vi. 20–22.) He counted it his glory, his duty, his joy. None, however, but a believer knows what it is to bear this cross : and none but a real believer can bear it. It is one of the touchstones of sincerity, the application of which has often been the means of " separating the precious from the vile," and has unmasked the self-confident professor to his own confusion. Oh ! how many make a fair profession, and appear " good soldiers of Jesus Christ," until the hour of danger proves them deserters, and they reap only the fruits of their self-confidence in their own confusion !

It is, therefore, of great importance to those who are just setting out in the warfare, to be well armed with the word of God. It kept David stedfast amidst the *derision of the proud;* and it will keep young Christians from being frightened or overcome by the sneer of an ungodly world. But that it may " dwell in us richly *in all wisdom*" (Col. iii. 16), and be suited to our own case, it will be well, under circumstances of reproach, to acquaint ourselves with the supporting promises and encouragements to suffer for righteousness' sake.* Above all, the contemplation of the great sufferer himself—meeting this poignant trial in meekness (Ps. xxii. 6–8. 1 Pet. ii. 23), compassion, and prayer (Luke, xxiii. 34), — will exhibit " a refuge from the storm, and a shadow from the heat, when the blast of the terrible ones is as the storm against the wall." (Isa. xxv. 4.) The mere professor knows not this refuge ; he possesses not this armour ; so that when " affliction or

---

* Such as the benediction of the Saviour, Luke, vi. 22, 23, confirmed by the recorded experience of the Lord's most favoured servants, the Apostles — Acts, v. 41 : Paul especially, 2 Cor. xii. 10 ; Col. i. 24,— the disciples of Thessalonica, 1 Thess. i. 6,— the Hebrew Christians, Heb. x. 34.

persecution ariseth for the word's sake, immediately he is
offended." (Mark, iv. 17.)

Christian! be satisfied with the approbation of your
God. Has he not adopted you into his family, stamped
you with his image, assured you by his Spirit, sealed you
for his kingdom? And is not this "honour that cometh
from God only" enough — far more than enough — to
counterbalance the *derision of the proud?* Think of the day,
when "the rebuke of the people shall be taken away from
off all the earth," when "he will confess their name before
his Father, and before his angels," when "the saints shall
judge the world," when "the upright shall have dominion
over them in the morning." Can we be Christians, if this
sure prospect does not infinitely more than compensate for
all "the hard speeches, which ungodly sinners have spoken
against us?" (Isa. xxv. 8. Rev. iii. 5. 1 Cor. vi. 2. Ps.
xlix. 14. Jude, 14, 15.)

Thus — blessed be God — the weapons of our warfare
are drawn from the Divine armoury; and therefore depending on the grace, and following the example, of Jesus, we
suffer, as the way to victory — the road to an everlasting
crown.

52. *I remembered thy judgments of old, O Lord; and have*
comforted myself.

The Lord's dealings with his people were a frequent
subject of meditation to the Psalmist (Ps. lxxvii. 5, 11,
12; cxliii. 5), and now were they his present support under
"the scourge of the tongue." (Job, v. 21.) Evidently they
are put upon record for the encouragement of future generations. (Ps. xliv. 1–3; lxxviii. 3–8; cv. 5, 6; cxlv. 4.
Joel, i. 3.) We are ready to imagine something peculiar
in our own case, and to "think it strange concerning the
fiery trial which is to try us, as though some strange thing

happened unto us. But when we *remember the Lord's judgments of old*, with his people, we *comfort ourselves* in the assurance, that "the same afflictions are accomplished in our brethren, that have been in the world" (1 Pet. iv. 12; v. 9); and that "as the sufferings of Christ have abounded in them, so their consolation also abounded by Christ." (2 Cor. i. 5.) They also encountered the same *derision of the proud*, and always experienced the same support from the faithfulness of their God. We do not sufficiently consider the mercy and gracious wisdom of God, in occupying so much of his written word with the records of his *judgments of old*. One class will pay a prominent attention to the preceptive, another to the doctrinal, parts of revelation — each forgetting that the historical records comprise a full and striking illustration of both, and have always proved most supporting grounds of consolation to the Lord's people. The important design in casting so large a portion of the small volume of Revelation into an historical form, is every way worthy of its author. "Whatsoever things were written aforetime, were written for our learning; that we through patience *and comfort of the Scriptures* might have hope" (Rom. xv. 4); and how admirably adapted the means are to the end, the diligent student in the Scripture field will bear ample witness. Wilfully, therefore, to neglect the historical portion of the sacred volume, from the idea of confining our attention to what we deem the more spiritual parts of scripture — would show a sad deficiency of spiritual apprehension, and deprive ourselves of the most valuable instruction, and most abundant comfort. This neglect would exclude us from one eminent means of increasing "patience," in the example of those "who through faith and patience inherit the promises;" of receiving "comfort," in the experience of the faithfulness of God manifested in every age to his people: and of enlivening our "hope," in marking the happy issue of the " patience of the saints," and the heavenly support administered unto them.* So far, therefore, are we from being little interested in the Scriptural records of past ages, that it is evident that the sacred historians, as well as the prophets, "ministered not unto themselves, but unto us the things which are now reported." (1 Pet. i. 12.)

Let us select one or two instances as illustrative of this subject. Why were the records of the deluge, and of the overthrow of the cities of the plain, preserved, but as exhibitions to the church, that " the Lord"— the Saviour of Noah, the eighth person, and the deliverer of just Lot— " knoweth how to deliver the godly out of temptations, and to reserve the unjust unto the day of judgment to be punished?" (2 Pet. ii. 5–9.) What a source of *comfort* then to the tempted people of God is the *remembrance of these judgments of old!* Take again the wonderful history of the overthrow of the Egyptians, and the consequent deliverance of God's ancient people. How often does the church recollect this interposition as a ground of assurance, that under similar circumstances of trial, the same illustrious displays of Divine faithfulness and love may be confidently expected! She looks back upon what the " arm of the Lord hath done in ancient days, and in the generation of old," as the pattern of what he ever would be, and ever would do, for his purchased people. (Isa. li. 9–11.) Thus also God himself recalls to our mind this overthrow and deliverance as a ground of present encouragement and support—"*According to the days of thy coming out of the land of Egypt* will I show unto him marvellous things" (Mic. vii. 15)—and the Church echoes back this remembrance in the expression of her faith, gratitude, and expectation for spiritual blessings:

* In this view, the recollection of the Lord's *judgments of old* " puts a new song into the mouth" of the Church, of "thanksgiving unto her God." Isa. xxv. 1–4.

"*He will subdue our iniquities*, and *thou wilt cast all their sins into the depths of* the sea." (Verse 19.) Such is the interesting use that may be made of the historical parts of Scripture! Such is the *comfort* to be derived from the *remembrance of the Lord's judgments of old!* And is not the recollection of his *judgments of old* with ourselves, productive of the same support? Does not the retrospect of his dealings with our own souls serve to convince us, that " all his paths are mercy and truth?" (Ps. xxv. 10.) The assurance is therefore warranted alike by experience and by Scripture—" We know that all things work together for good to them that love God, to them who are the called according to his purpose." (Rom. viii. 28.)

53. *Horror hath taken hold upon me,** *because of the wicked that forsake thy law.*

The *remembrance of the Lord's judgments of old*, while it brings *comfort* to his people as regards themselves, stirs up a poignancy of compassionate feeling for the ungodly. And indeed to a feeling and reflecting mind, the condition of the world must excite commiseration and concern! A " whole world lying in wickedness" (1 John, v. 19)! lying therefore in ruins! the image of God effaced! the presence of God departed! *Horror hath taken hold of me!* to see *the law* of Him, who gave being to the world, so utterly *forsaken!* so much light and love shining from heaven in vain! The earthly heart cannot endure that any restraint should be imposed; much less that any constraint, even of love, should be employed to change its bias, and turn it back to its God. Are you then a believer? then you will be most

* ' A burning horror hath seized me.'—AINSWORTH. ' Faintness and dejection of mind hath seized me.'—LXX.

tender of the honour of the law of God. Every stroke at
his law you will feel as a stroke at your own heart. Are
you a believer? then will you consider every man as your
brother; and weep to see so many of them around you,
crowding the broad road to destruction, and perishing as
the miserable victims of their own deceivings. The prospect on every side is, as if God were cast down from his
throne, and the creatures of his hand were murdering their
own souls.

But how invariably does a languor respecting our own
eternal interest affect the tenderness of our regard for the
honour of our God; so that we can look at *the wicked that
forsake God's law*, with comparative indifference! Awful
indeed is the thought, that it ever can be with us a small
matter, that multitudes are sinking! going down into perdition! with the name of Christ — under the seal of baptism
— partakers of the means of gospel grace — yet perishing!
Not, indeed, that we are to yield to such a feeling of *horror*,
as would paralyse all exertion on their behalf. For do we
owe them no duty — no prayer — no labour? (Acts, xvii.
16–18.)   Shall we look upon souls hurrying on with such
dreadful haste to unutterable, everlasting torments; and
permit them to rush on blinded, unawakened, unalarmed!
If there is a *horror* to see a brand apparently fitting for the
fire, will there not be a wrestling endeavour to pluck that
brand out of the fire?   Have we quite forgotten in our
own case the fearful terrors of an unconverted state — the
Almighty power of wrath and justice armed against us —
the thunder of that voice — " Vengeance belongeth unto
me, I will recompense, saith the Lord?" (Heb. x. 30;
with Deut. xxxii. 35.)   Oh! if the love of the Saviour and
the love of souls were reigning with more mighty influence
in our hearts, how much more devoted should we be in our
little spheres of labour! how much more enlarged in our

supplications, until all the kingdom of Satan were subject
to the obedience of the Son of God, and conquered by the
force of his omnipotent love!

But if the spirit of David, renewed but in part, was
thus filled with *horror* in the contemplation of the wicked,
what must have been the affliction — what the intensity of
his sufferings, " who was holy, harmless, undefiled, separate
from sinners" (Heb. vii. 26)—yea, " of purer eyes than to
behold iniquity" (Hab. i. 13. Comp. Ps. v. 5)—during
thirty-three years of continued contact with a world of sin!
What shall we say of the condescension of his love, in
wearing " the likeness of sinful flesh" (Rom. viii. 3)—
dwelling among sinners — yea, " receiving sinners, and
eating with them !" (Luke, xv. 2.)

Blessed Spirit! impart to us more of " the mind that
was in Christ Jesus," that the law of God may be increasingly precious in our eyes, and that we may be " exceedingly jealous for the Lord God of Hosts !" Help us
by thy gracious influence to plead with sinners for God,
and to plead for sinners with God!

54. *Thy statutes have been my songs in the house of my pilgrimage.*

Come, Christian pilgrim, and beguile your wearisome
journey heavenward by " singing the Lord's song in this
strange land." (Ps. cxxxvii. 4.) With *the statutes of God*
in your hand and in your heart, you are furnished with a
song for every step of your way—" The Lord is my shepherd ; I shall not want. He maketh me to lie down in
green pastures : he leadeth me beside the still waters. He
restoreth my soul: he leadeth me in the paths of righteousness for his name's sake. Yea, though I walk through the
valley of the shadow of death I will fear no evil ; for thou
art with me ; thy rod and thy staff, they comfort me.

Thou preparest a table before me in the presence of mine enemies : thou anointest my head with oil ; my cup runneth over. Surely goodness and mercy shall follow me all the days of my life ; and I will dwell in the house of the Lord for ever." (Ps. xxiii.) How delightfully does this song bring before you Him, who having laid down his life for you, engages himself as your Provider, your Keeper, your Guide, your faithful and unchangeable Friend ! Such a song, therefore, will smooth your path, and reconcile you to the many inconveniences of the way ; while the recollection that this is only *the house of your pilgrimage* and not your home ; and that " there remaineth a rest for the people of God" (Heb. iv. 9), will support the exercise of faith and patience to the end. How striking the contrast between *the wicked that forsake the law*, and the Christian *pilgrim*, who makes it the subject of his daily song, and the source of his daily comfort ! Yes, these same *statutes*, which are the yoke and burden of the ungodly, lead the true servant of the Lord from pleasure to pleasure ; and, cherished by their vigorous influence, his way is made easy and prosperous. Evidently, therefore, our knowledge and delight in the Lord's statutes will furnish a decisive test of our real state before him.

But it is important to remember that our cheerful song is connected with a pilgrim-spirit. Never forget that we are not at home (2 Cor. v. 6) ; only happy strangers on our passage homewards. Here we have no settled habitation (Heb. xiii. 14)—no rest. We are looking for a better country (Heb. xi. 10, 14–16): and as we look, we are seeking for it. Our " hearts are in the ways of it." (Ps. lxxxiv. 5.) Every day advances us nearer to it. (Rom. xiii. 11.) In this spirit *the statutes of the Lord will be our song*. Here are the deeds of conveyance — our title made sure to an estate — not small, of little account, or of uncertain interest — but " an inheritance" of incalculable value, made over

to us. (1 Pet. i. 3–5.)   Here we have sure direction —
such as cannot mislead us (Verse 105) — for the attainment
of it.   Here we are stimulated by the examples of our
fellow-pilgrims, who have reached their home (Heb. vi. 11,
12) ; and as we follow their track, many are the cordials
by the way, and home brightens in the nearer prospect.

What reason have we then every moment to guard
against the debasing, stupifying influence of the world,
which makes us forget the proper character of a pilgrim !
And what an habitual conflict must be maintained with
the sloth and aversion of a reluctant heart to maintain our
progress in the journey towards Zion !   Reader ! have you
entered upon a pilgrim's life ?   Then what is your solace
and refreshment on the road ?   It is dull, heavy, wearisome,
to be a pilgrim without a *song*.   And yet it is only the
blessed experience *of the Lord's statutes*, that will tune our
song.   " If therefore you have tasted that the Lord is
gracious" (1 Pet. ii. 3) ; if he has thus " put a new song
into your mouth" (Ps. xl. 3), oh ! do not suffer any carelessness or neglect to rob you of this heavenly anticipation.
And that your lips be not found mute, seek to maintain a
lively contemplation of the place whither you are going —
of Him who as your " forerunner is for you entered" (Heb.
vi. 20) thither — and of the prospect, that, having " prepared a place for you, he will come again, and take you to
himself ; that where he is, there you may be also." (John,
xiv. 2, 3.)   In this spirit, and with these hopes before you,
you may take up your song — " O God, my heart is fixed :
I will sing and give praise.   I will bless the Lord at all
times — his praise shall continually be in my mouth." (Ps.
cviii. 1 ; xxxiv. 1.)   Thus may you go on your *pilgrimage*
" singing in the ways of the Lord " (Ps. cxxxviii. 5), and
commencing a song below, which in the world of praise
above, shall never, never cease. (Rev. iv. 8.)

55. *I have remembered thy name, O Lord, in the night, and have kept thy law.*

How did this man of God live in the statutes of God! In the day they were his *pilgrim song—in the night* his happy meditation. (Ps. lxiii. 5, 6.) And, truly, if we can ever spend the waking moments of the night with God, " the darkness is no darkness with us, but the night shineth as the day." Many a tried believer has found this cordial for the restlessness of a wakeful night more restorative to the quiet and health of his earthly frame, than the most sovereign specifics of the medical world. " So he giveth his beloved sleep." (Ps. cxxvii. 2.) And if in any *night* of affliction we feel the hand of the Lord grievous to us, do we not find in *the remembrance of the Lord* a never-failing support? What does our darkness arise from, but from our forgetfulness of God, blotting out for a while the lively impressions of his tender care, his unchanging faithfulness, and his mysterious methods of working his gracious will? And to bring up as it were from the grave, the *remembrance of God's name,* as manifested in his promises, and in the dispensation of his love; this is indeed the " light that is sown for the righteous" (Ps. xcvii. 11), and which " springeth up out of darkness." (Ps. cxii. 4.) It is to eye the character of the Lord as All-wise to appoint, Almighty to secure, All-compassionate to sympathize and support. It is to recollect him as a " father pitying his children" (Ps. ciii. 13); as a " friend that loveth at all times" (Prov. xvii. 17), and that " sticketh closer than a brother." (Ib. xviii. 24.) And even in those seasons of depression, when unwatchfulness or indulgence of sin have brought the darkness of night upon the soul, though *the remembrance of the name of the Lord* may be grievous, yet it opens the way to consolation. It tells us, that there is a way made for our return ; that " the Lord waiteth, that he may be gracious" (Isa. xxx. 18) ; and that in the first step of our return to our Father, we shall find him full of mercy to his backsliding children. (See Luke, xv. 20–24.) Thus, though " weeping may endure for a night, joy cometh in the morning." (Ps. xxx. 5.)

Study the Lord's revelation of his own name; and what more full perception can we conceive of its support in the darkest midnight of tribulations ? " And the Lord descended in the cloud, and stood with him (Moses), and proclaimed the name of the Lord. And the Lord passed by before him, and proclaimed—The Lord, the Lord God, merciful and gracious, long-suffering, and abundant in goodness and truth, keeping mercy for thousands, forgiving iniquity, transgression, and sin, and that will by no means clear the guilty." (Ex. xxxiv. 5–7.) Can we wonder that such a name as this should be exhibited as a ground of trust ? " The name of the Lord is a strong tower : the righteous runneth into it and is safe." " They that know thy name will put their trust in thee." (Prov. xviii. 10. Ps. ix. 10.) Even our suffering Lord appears to have derived support from *the remembrance of the name of the Lord in the night* of desertion—" O my God, I cry in the day-time, and thou hearest not ; and in the night-season, and am not silent. *But thou art holy*, O thou that inhabitest the praises of Israel !" (Ps. xxii. 2, 3.) And from the experience of this source of consolation, we find the tempted Saviour directing his tempted people to the same support—" Who is among you that feareth the Lord, that obeyeth the voice of his servant, that walketh in darkness, and hath no light ? let him *trust in the name of the Lord*, and stay upon his God." (Isa. l. 10.)

The main principles of the Gospel are involved in this *remembrance of the Lord's name*. Memory is the storehouse, in which the substance of our knowledge is treasured up. Recollections without *faith* are shadowy notions. But we have confidence that our God in himself—and as engaged to us—is all that the Bible declares him to be. How vast then are our obligations to his dear Son—the only medium, by which his name could be known or *remembered*—"who hath" so "declared him!" (John, i. 18 ; also xiv. 6. Matt. xi. 27.) And here is the spring of practical religion. We shall *keep his law* when we *remember his name*. A sense of our obligations will impel us forward in diligence, heavenly-mindedness, and self-devotedness in our appointed sphere. Obedience will partake far more of the character of privilege than of duty, when an enlightened knowledge of God is the principle of action.

56. *This I had, because I kept thy precepts.*

How is it, believer, that you are enabled to *sing of the Lord's statutes*—and to *remember his name?* *This you have, because you keep his precepts.* Thus you are able to tell the world, that in keeping his "commandments there is great reward" (Ps. xix. 11),—that the "work of righteousness is peace ; and the effect of righteousness, quietness, and assurance for ever." (Isa. xxxii. 17.) Christian! let your testimony be clear and decided—that ten thousand worlds cannot bestow the happiness of one day's devotedness to the service of your Lord. For is it not in this path that you realize fulness of joy in "fellowship with the Father, and with his Son Jesus Christ?" "He that hath *my commandments*, and *keepeth* them, he it is that loveth me ; and he that loveth me shall be loved of my Father ; and I will love him, and will *manifest myself* to him — my Father will love him; and *we will come* unto him, and make our abode with him." (John, xiv. 21, 23, with 1 John, i. 3, 4 ; iii. 24.) If you were walking more closely with God in "the obedience of faith," the world would never dare to accuse religion as the source of melancholy and despondency. No man has any right to the hope of happiness in a world of tribulátion, but he that seeks it in the favour of his God. Nor can any enjoy this favour, except as connected, in the exercise of faith, with conformity to the will, and delight in the law, of his God. Thus not only are the "statutes of the Lord right," but they " rejoice the heart." (Ps. xix. 8.) There is a sweetness and satisfaction in the work, as well as a good flowing out of it—a current as well as a consequent privilege—cheering the soul in the act of exercise, just as the senses are regaled at the very instant with the object of their gratification.

But let us remark how continually David was enriching his treasury of spiritual experience with some fresh view of the dealings of God with his soul : some answer to prayer, or some increase of consolation, which he records for his own encouragement, and for the use of the Church of God. Let us seek to imitate him in this respect; and we shall often be enabled to say as he does—*This I had,*—this comfort I enjoyed—this support in trouble—this remarkable manifestation of his love—this confidence I was enabled to maintain—it was made my own, *because I kept thy precepts.*

This I had—not, this I hoped for. He speaks of " the promise of the life that now is"—that by which God clears away the charge,—" It is vain to serve him ; and what profit is it, that we have kept his ordinances?" (Mal. iii. 14.) Nor is it any boasting of merit, but only an acknowledgment of the gracious dispensation of his God. Such a reward for such poor service, can only be undeserved " mercy," (Ps. lxii. 12. Gal. vi. 16), having respect, not to the worthiness of the work, but to the faithfulness of the promise. Perfect keeping, according to the legal requirements, there cannot be. (Gal. iii. 10.) Evangelical perfection, in aiming at the mark, and constantly pressing onward towards it, there may be. (Phil. iii. 12–15.)

How important therefore is it—in the absence of this Christian confidence—to examine,—"Is there not a cause?" and what is the cause? Have not "strangers devoured my strength; and I knew it not?" (Hos. vii. 9.) Is the Lord "with me as in months past?" (Job, xxix. 2),—with me in my closet?—with me in my family?—with me at my table?—with me in my daily employments and intercourse with the world? When I hear the faithful people of God telling of his love, and saying—*This I had;* must I not, if unable to join their cheerful acknowledgment, trace it to my unfaithful walk, and say—*This I had* not, because I have failed in obedience to thy precepts; because I have been careless and self-indulgent; because I have slighted thy love; because I have "grieved thy Holy Spirit," and forgotten to ask for the "old paths, that I might walk therein, and find rest to my soul?" (Jer. vi. 16.) O let this scrutiny and recollection of our ways realize the constant need of the finished work of Jesus, as our ground of acceptance, and source of strength. This will bring healing, restoration, increasing devotedness, tenderness of conscience, circumspection of walk, and a determination not to rest, until we can make this grateful acknowledgment our own. At the same time, instead of boasting that our own arm, our own diligence, or holiness, "have gotten us" into this favour, we shall cast all our attainments at the feet of Jesus, and crown him Lord of all for ever.

PART VIII.

57. *Thou art my portion, O Lord; I have said that I would keep thy words.*

MAN, as a dependent being, must be possessed of some portion. He cannot live upon himself. It must, however, be not only good, but his own good—something that he may lay claim to as his own. It must also be a large portion, because the powers and capacities to be filled are large. If he has not a satisfying portion, he is a wretched empty creature. But where and how shall he find this portion? " There be many that say, Who will show us any good? Lord! lift thou up the light of thy countenance upon us." (Ps. iv. 6.) And then the goodness of the Lord, in having offered himself as the portion of an unworthy sinner! So that we can now lay claim to him, as having wholly and fully made himself over to us, and having engaged to employ his perfections for our happiness! " I will be thy God." (Jer. xxxi. 33.) Surely every good is centered in the chief good—the fountain of all blessings, temporal, spiritual, eternal. What, then, is the folly, madness, and guilt, of the sinner, in choosing his " portion in this life" (Ps. xvii. 14): as if there were no God on the earth, no way of access to him, or no happiness to be found in him? That such madness should be found in the heart of man, is a most affecting illustration of his departure from God. But that *God's own " people* should commit these two evils—forsaking the fountain of living waters, and hewing out for themselves broken cisterns"—this is the fearful astonishment of heaven itself. (Jer. ii. 12, 13.)

But we cannot know and enjoy God as our *portion*, except as he has manifested himself in his dear Son. And in the knowledge and enjoyment of him, can we envy those who "in their lifetime receive their good things" (Luke, xvi. 25 ; vi. 24), and therefore have nothing more to expect? Never, indeed, does the poverty of the worldling's portion appear more striking, than when contrasted with the enjoyment of the child of God (Comp. Ps. xvii. 14, 15),—" Soul"—said the rich fool—" thou hast much goods laid up for many years." But God said—" This night thy soul shall be required of thee." (Luke, xii. 19, 20.) Augustine's prayer was—" Lord, give me thyself!"* And thus the believer exults—" Whom have I in heaven but thee? and there is none upon earth that I desire but thee. Return unto thy rest, O my soul. The Lord himself is the portion of mine inheritance and of my cup. Thou maintainest my lot. The lines are fallen to me in pleasant places ; yea, I have a goodly heritage. I will bless the Lord, who hath given me counsel." (Ps. lxxiii. 25 ; cxvi. 7 ; xvi. 5–7.)

Elsewhere the believer makes this confession to himself —" The Lord is my portion—*saith my soul*." (Lam. iii. 24.) Here, as if to prove his sincerity, he " lifts up his face unto God." (John, xxi. 17. Job, xxii. 26.) " *Thou art my portion, O Lord*." And surely the whole world cannot weigh against the comfort of this Christian confidence. For it is as impossible, that his own people should ever be impoverished, as that his own perfections should moulder away. But a portion implies, not a source of ordinary pleasure, but of rest and satisfaction, such as leaves nothing else to be desired. Thus *the Lord* can never be enjoyed,

* " Da mihi te, Domine."

even by his own children—except *as a portion*—not only above all, but in the place of all. Other objects indeed may be subordinately loved : but of none but himself must we say—" He is *altogether lovely*." (Cant. v. 16.) " In all things he must have the pre-eminence" (Col. i. 18)—one with the Father in our affections, as in his own subsistence. (John, x. 30.) The moment that any rival is allowed to usurp the throne of the heart, we open the door to disappointment and unsatisfied desires.

But if we take the Lord as our *portion*, we must take him as our king. *I have said*—this is my deliberate resolution,—*that I would keep thy words.* Here is the Christian complete—taking *the Lord* as his *portion*, and his *word* as his rule. And what energy for holy devotedness flows from the enjoyment of this our heavenly *portion!* Thus delighting ourselves in the Lord, he gives us our heart's desire (Ps. xxxvii. 4) ; and every desire identifies itself with his service. All that we are and all that we have, are his ; cheerfully surrendered as his right, and willingly employed in his work. Thus do we evidence our interest in his salvation ; for " Christ became the *author of eternal salvation unto all them that obey him*." (Heb. v. 9.)

Reader ! inquire—was my choice of this Divine *portion* considerate, free, unreserved? Am I resolved that it shall be stedfast and abiding? that death itself shall not separate me from the enjoyment of it ? Am I ready to receive a Sovereign as well as a Saviour? (See Acts, v. 31.) Oh ! let me have a whole Christ for my *portion!* Oh ! let him have a whole heart for his possession. Oh ! let me call nothing mine but Him.

' The heart touched with the loadstone of Divine love : trembling with godly fear, yet still looking towards God by fixed believing—points at the love of election. He that loves may be sure he was loved first. (1 John, iv. 19.) He that chooses God in Christ for his delight and portion, may conclude confidently, that God has chosen him to enjoy him, and be happy in him for ever.'*

58. *I entreated thy favour with my whole heart; be merciful unto me according to thy word.*

Delight in the Lord as our *portion*, naturally leads us to *entreat his favour* as " life" (Ps. xxx. 5), and " better than life " (Ps. lxiii. 3), to our souls. And if we have *said that we would keep his words*, we shall still *entreat his favour* — to strengthen and encourage us in his way. We shall *entreat it with our whole hearts*, as though we felt our infinite need of it, and were determined to wrestle for it in Jacob's spirit—" I will not let thee go, except thou bless me." (Gen. xxxii. 26.) If we have known what unspeakable happiness it is to be brought into the *favour* of God " by the blood of Christ" (Eph. ii. 13) ; and if by " him also we have access unto that grace wherein we stand" (Rom. v. 1, 2), how shall we prize the sense of Divine *favour*, the light of our Father's countenance ! We shall never be weary of this source of daily enjoyment. It is to us as the light of the sun, which shineth every day with renewed and unabated pleasure. We " joy in God, through our Lord Jesus Christ, by whom we have now received the atonement." (Rom. v. 11.) Mercy, however, is the source of that *favour which we entreat;* and the word is the warrant of our expectation —*Be merciful unto us according to thy word.* As sinners, we need this *favour.* As believers, we *entreat* it in the assurance that praying breath, as the breath of faith, will not be spent in vain. Any indulged indolence, or neglect, or unfaithfulness— relaxing our diligence, and keeping back the *whole heart* from God—will, indeed, never fail to remove the sunshine

* Leighton on 1 Pet. i. 2.

from the soul. But the blood of Christ still opens the way
of return to the backslider, even though he may have
wandered, as it were, to the ends of the earth. For " if
from thence thou shalt seek the Lord thy God, thou shalt
find him, if thou seek him with *all thine heart and all thy
soul*." (Deut. iv. 29.) " *A whole heart*" in seeking the
Lord, is the seal of the Lord's heart in returning to us —
" I will rejoice over them" — saith he — " to do them good ;
and I will plant them in this land assuredly, *with my whole
heart, and with my whole soul*." (Jer. xxxii. 41.)

Reader ! if you are a child of God, *the favour of God*
will be to you the " one thing needful." In other things,
you will not venture to choose for yourself ; " for who
knoweth what is good for man in this life ?" (Eccles. vi.
12.) But in this choice you will be decided. This grand,
incomparable desire will fill your heart. This will be to
you as the portion of ten thousand worlds. Nothing will
satisfy besides.

You may, indeed, be a child of God without the enjoyment of the blessing ; but not so, if you be content to be
without it. If the wise sovereignty of our God is pleased
to withhold it, still the child in submission will *entreat* it.
Much more, when it is withdrawn in righteous chastening
of carelessness or folly, will the cry be reiterated upon the
ground of the covenant—*Be merciful unto me according to
thy word.* (Ps. lxxxix. 30–33.)

59. *I thought on my ways, and turned my feet unto thy
testimonies.*

The Psalmist's determination, lately mentioned, to *keep
God's word*, was not a hasty impulse, but a considerate resolve, the result of much *thinking on his* former *ways* of sin
and folly. How many, on the other hand, seem to pass
through the world into eternity without a serious *thought*

on their ways! Multitudes live for the world—forget
God and die! This is their history. What their state is,
is written as with a sunbeam in the word of truth—" The
wicked shall be turned into hell, and *all the nations that
forget God.*" (Ps. ix. 17.) When " no man repenteth him
of his wickedness, saying, *What have I done?*" (Jer. viii.
6)—this banishing of reflection is the character and ruin
of an unthinking world. Perhaps one serious thought
might be the new birth of the soul to God — the first step
of the way to heaven. For when a man is arrested by the
power of grace, he is as one awaking out of sleep, lost in
solemn and serious thoughts —' What am I?* where am
I? what have I been? what have I been doing? I have a
soul, which is my everlasting all—yet a soul without a
Saviour—lost—undone. What is my prospect for its
happiness? Behind me is a world of vanity, an empty void.
Before me a fearful unknown eternity. Within me an
awakened conscience, to remind me of an angry God, and a
devouring hell. If I stay here, I perish; if I go forward,
I perish; if I return home to my offended Father, I can
but perish.' (Comp. 2 Kings, vii. 4.) The resolution is
formed; ' " I will arise" (Luke, xv. 18), and fight my way
through all difficulties and discouragements to my Father's
house.' Thus does every prodigal child of God " come to
himself;" and this his first step of return to his God (Verse
17) involves the whole work of repentance. The wanderer
*thinks on his ways, and turns his feet unto the testimonies of his
God;* witnessing, to his joyful surprise, every hindrance
removed, the way marked with the blood of his Saviour,
and his Father's smiles in this way welcoming his return
homeward. This *turn is the practical exercise of a genuine
faith;* and " *because he considereth,* and *turneth away* from all

---

* How utterly unmeaning was the celebrated aphorism of
antiquity—' Know thyself'—until explained and illustrated by the
light of Revelation!

his transgressions that he hath committed, he shall surely live — he shall not die." (Ezek. xviii. 28.)

But this considerate exercise is needed, not only upon the first entrance *into the ways of God*, but in every successive step of our path. It will form the habit of daily " communion with our own heart" (Ps. iv. 4); without which, disorder and confusion will bewilder our steps. Probably David did not know how far his feet had backslidden from *the ways of his God*, until this serious consideration of his state brought conviction to his soul — so imperceptible is the declining of the heart from God! Nor is it a few transient thoughts or resolutions, that will effect this turn of the heart to God. *A man may maintain a fruitless struggle to return to God for many years in sincerity and earnestness ; while the simple act of faith in the power and love of Jesus will at once bring him back.* Thus, while " *thinking on his ways*," let him walk in Christ as the way of return — and he will walk in the way of *God's testimonies* with acceptance and delight. In this spirit of simplicity, he will listen to the first whisper of the convincing voice of the Spirit, which marks the early steps of return from secret declension from God. (See Isa. xxx. 21.) He will also thankfully accept the chastening rod, as the Lord's appointed instrument of restoring his wandering children to himself. For so prone are they to *turn their feet* away from the Lord — so continually are they " turning aside like a deceitful bow " (Ps. lxxviii. 57), — and so deaf are they, from the constitution of their sinful nature, to the ordinary calls of God; that, in love and tender faithfulness to their souls, he is often constrained, by the stroke of his heavy hand, to arrest them in their career of thoughtlessness, and turn them back to himself. Most suitable then for such a state is the prayer of Basil — ' Give me any cross, that may bring me into subjection to thy cross ; and save me in spite of myself !'

60. *I made haste, and delayed not, to keep thy commandments.*

A superficial conviction brings with it a sense of duty, without constraining to it. Men stand reasoning and doubting, instead of *making haste.* But a sound conviction sweeps away all excuses and delays. No time will be lost between making and performing resolutions. Indeed, in a matter of life and death—of eternal life and eternal death (see Deut. xxx. 15–19)—the call is too clear for debate, and there is no room for delay. Many a precious soul has been lost by waiting for " a more convenient season " (Acts, xxiv. 25)—a period, which probably never arrives, and which the wilful neglect of present opportunity provokes God to put far away. To-day is God's time. To-morrow ruins thousands. To-morrow is another world. " *To-day—while it is called to-day* ; if ye will hear his voice " (Heb. iv. 7)—" *make haste, and delay not.*" Resolutions, however sincere, and convictions, however serious, " will pass away, as the morning cloud and as the early dew" (Hos. vi. 4. Comp. xiii. 3), unless they are carefully cherished, and instantly improved. The bonds of iniquity will soon prove too strong for the bonds of your own resolutions ; and in the first hour of temptation, conviction left to chance to grow, will prove as powerless as the " seven green withs" to bind the giant Samson. (Judg. xvi. 7–9.) If ever delays are dangerous, much more are they in this concern of eternity. If therefore convictions begin to work, instantly yield to their influence. If any worldly or sinful desire is touched, let this be the moment for its crucifixion. If any affection is kindled towards the Saviour, give immediate exprèssion to its voice. If any grace is reviving, let it be called forth into instant duty. This is the best—the only—expedient to fix and detain the motion of the Spirit now striving in the heart : and who knoweth but the improvement of the

present advantage may be the moment of victory over difficulties hitherto found insuperable, and may open the path
to heaven with less interruption, and more steady progress?

It is from the neglect of this *haste* that convictions
often alternately ebb and flow so long, before they settle
in a sound conversion. Indeed the instant movement—
making haste, and delaying not—marks the principle of
the spiritual life. This was the prodigal's resolution, no
sooner formed than in action. He said—" I will arise, and
go to my father—and *he arose*, and came to his father."
(Luke, xv. 18–20.) When Matthew heard the voice—
" Follow me—*he left all, rose up* and followed him." (Luke,
v. 27, 28. Comp. Matt. iv. 18–22.) When Zaccheus was
called from the top of the sycamore-tree—" *Make haste,* and
come down, for to-day I must abide at thy house—*he made
haste*, and *came* down, and received him joyfully."*

Ah! as you prize a hope for eternity ; as you wish to
" flee from the wrath to come," and to " flee for refuge to
the hope set before you "—beware of smothering early convictions. They may prove the first dawn of eternal day
upon the soul—the first visit of the quickening Spirit to
the heart. Guard them with unceasing watchfulness.
Nourish them with believing prayer. " Exercise " them
unto practical " godliness." (1 Tim. iv. 7.) " Quench not
the Spirit." (1 Thess. v. 19.) Let not the spark be ex-
tinguished by opposition of the world. Let it not expire
for want of the fuel of grace. Let it not lie dormant or
inactive. " Stir up the gift of God which is in thee." (2
Tim. i. 6.) Every exercise, every motion, adds grace to
grace, and increases its vigour, health, and fruitfulness. The
more we do, the more we find we can do. The withered
hand, whenever stretched forth in obedience to the Saviour's
word, and in dependence on his grace, will never fail of a

---

* Luke, xix. 5, 6. Comp. also the example of Paul, Gal. i. 15, 16.

supply of spiritual strength. (Mark, iii. 5.) Every successive act strengthens the disposition, until a continual suc-
cession has formed the ready and active habit of godliness.
Thus the Lord works in setting us to work. Therefore
think — determine — turn — *make haste, and delay not;* and
we wish you God speed ; " we bless you in the name of
the Lord." (Ps. cxxix. 8.)

Professor ! did you realize eternity, would you hover as
you do between heaven and hell ? If you were truly alive
and awake, no motion would be swift enough for your desire to " flee from the wrath to come"— to " flee for refuge
to lay hold on the hope set before you." (Matt. iii. 7. Heb.
vi. 18.) If ever God should touch your heart to feel the
heavenly sweetness of communion with him, will there be
no regret, that the privilege was not sooner sought and enjoyed ? Had I betaken myself earlier to a *hearty* interest
in the ways of God, how much more knowledge, experience,
and comfort should I have attained ! how much more honour
should I have brought to God ! how much more profit to
my fellow-sinners ! Remember, every day of carnal pleasure or lukewarm formality is a day lost to God — to your
own happiness — to eternity.

A word to the believer— Have you any doubts to clear
up, any peace to regain in the ways of the Lord ? *Make
haste* to set your heart to the work. *Make haste* to the
blood of atonement. Be on the watch to " hear the Shepherd's voice"(John, x. 27), even if it be the voice of reproof.
Promptness is a most important exercise of the habit of
faith. Delay brings guilt to the conscience. The blessing
of conviction—the comfortable sense of acceptance—the
freedom of the Lord's service—is sacrificed to sloth and
procrastination. The work that is hard to-day will be
harder still to-morrow, by the resistance of this day's convictions. A greater cost of self-denial, a heavier burden
of sorrow, and increasing unfitness for the service of God,

will be the issue of *delay*. Be continually therefore looking for some beam of light to descend, and some influence
of grace to flow in upon you from your exalted Head. A
simple and vigorous faith will quickly enliven you with
that love, delight, rejoicing in the Lord, readiness to work,
and cheerfulness to suffer, which will once again make the
ways of God " pleasantness and peace" to your soul.

61. *The bands of the wicked have robbed me; but I have not*
forgotten thy law.

Are we not too apt to cull out the easy work of the
Gospel, and to call this love to God? Whereas true love
is supreme, and ready to be at some loss, and to part with
near and dear objects, knowing that he " is able to give
us much more than" we lose for him. (2 Chron. xxv. 9.
Comp. Job, xlii. 10–12.) Our resolution to *keep his commandments* will soon be put to the test. Some trial to the
flesh will prove whether we flinch from the cross, or study
to prepare ourselves for it. Few of us, perhaps, have literally known this trial of David. (See 1 Sam. xxx. 1–3.)
But the lesson to be learnt from his frame of mind under
it, is of great importance to all who profess to have their
" treasure in heaven." It teaches us, that only exercised
faith will sustain us in the time of trouble. This faith
will enable us instantly to recollect our heavenly portion,
and to assure our interest in it, in a remembrance of
the law of our God. Had David *forgotten God's law*, no
other resource of comfort opened before him. But it was
ready—substantiating to his mind " the things that were
not seen and eternal." (2 Cor. iv. 18. Heb. xi. 1.) Look
again at the Apostle's deliberate estimate of this very trial
—not only bearing his loss, but absolutely forgetting it in
the enjoyment of his better portion —" Yea, doubtless, and
I count all things but loss for the excellency of the know-

ledge of Christ Jesus my Lord, *for whom I have suffered the loss of all things ; and do count them but dung, that I may win Christ.*" (Phil. iii. 8.)

The temper of mind under such trials as this, serves indeed most clearly to discover the real bent of the heart. If we are in possession of a spiritual and heavenly portion, we shall bear to be *robbed by the bands of the wicked*, and yet, "hold fast our profession." David, under this calamity, "encouraged himself in the Lord his God." (1 Sam. xxx. 6.) Job, under the same visitation, " fell upon the ground, and worshipped." (Job, i. 13–17, 20.) The blessings, indeed, we lose, are but as a feather compared with the blessings which we retain. The Providence of God is an abundant support for his children. Their prospects (not to speak of their present privileges) effectually secure them from ulti- mate loss, even in the spoiling of their worldly all. (See Mark, x. 29, 30.) Thus the early Christians suffered *the bands of the wicked to rob them* — nay — " they took joyfully the spoiling of their goods ; *knowing in themselves, that they had in heaven a better and an enduring substance.*" (Heb. x. 34.) We have, indeed, little reason to be frightened from religion by the anticipation of its trials. The exchange of the world for God, and of the service of sin for the ways of heaven, leaves no room for regret in life, in death, or in eternity. The Christian's darkest houɪ is ten thousand times brighter than the brightest day of the ungodly. The hope of the crown will enable us to bear the cross, and to realize its sanctifying support as a matter for unbounded praise.

But how desolate are the poor votaries of the world in the hour of trouble ! Ignorant of the all-sufficiency of the refuge of the gospel ; instead of being driven to it by the gracious visitations of God, they would rather retreat into any hiding-place of their own, than direct their steps back- ward to him. Their circumstances of distress are most intensely aggravated by the sullen rebellion of the heart, which refuses to listen to those breathings of the Saviour's love, that would guide them to himself, as their sure, peaceful, and eternal rest! (See Matt. xi. 28.) Would that we could persuade them to cast their souls in penitence and faith before his blessed cross! (1 Pet. v. 7.) The burden of sin, as Bunyan's pilgrim found, would then drop from their backs. And this burden once removed — other burdens, before intolerable, would be found comparatively light; nay — all burdens would be removed in the enjoyment of the Christian privilege of casting all, — sin — care — and trouble, upon Jesus. Contrast the state of destitution without him, with the abundant resources of the people of God. We have a double heaven — a heaven on earth, and a heaven above — one in present sunshine — the other in " the city, which hath no need of the sun " (Rev. xxi. 23) — where our joys will be immediate — unclouded — eternal. Thus our portion embraces both worlds. Our present " joy no man taketh from us" (John, xvi. 22); and we have " laid up treasures in heaven," where *the bands of the wicked* can "never break through, nor steal." (Matt. vi. 20.)

Christian! does not your faith realize a subsistence of things not seen? The only realities in the apprehension of the world are " the things that are seen, and are temporal." Your realities are " the things that are not seen, and are eternal." (2 Cor. iv. 18.) Then, remember — if you be *robbed* of your earthly all, your treasure is beyond the reach of harm. You can still say — " I have all, and abound." (Phil. iv. 18; also 2 Cor. vi. 10.) You can live splendidly upon your God, though all is beggary around you. You confess the remembrance of the law of your God to be your unfailing stay — " *Unless thy law had been my delights, I should then have perished in my affliction.*" (Verse 92.)

62. *At midnight I will rise to give thanks unto thee : because of thy righteous judgments.*

Another exercise of sacred pleasure is the ways of the Lord! His portion was always satisfying to this holy man, and he was daily feeding upon it with fresh delight. There was no occasion for the painful restrictions and mortifications of a monastery to oblige him to self-denying observances. Much less was there any desire, by these extraordinary services, to work out a righteousness of his own, to recommend him to the favour of God. His diligence in this heavenly work was the spontaneous effusion of a heart " filled with the Spirit." (Eph. v. 18.) Presenting the morning and the evening service " seven times a day" (See verses 147, 148, 164), was not enough for him ; but he must *rise at midnight* to continue his song of praise. These hours sometimes had been spent in overwhelming sorrow. (See Ps. lxxvii. 3, 4.) Now they were given to the privileged employment of praise. (Ps. xlii. 8. Comp. Job, xxxv. 10.) Indeed it seems to have been his frequent custom to stir up his gratitude by a *midnight* review of the Lord's daily manifestations of mercy. (Ps. cxxxix. 17, 18.) A most exciting example — especially for the child of sorrow, when " wearisome nights are appointed to him," and he " is full of tossings to and fro unto the dawning of the day !" (Job, vii. 3, 4.) Thus " let the saints be joyful in glory ; *let them sing aloud upon their beds.*" (Ps. cxlix. 5.) We observe this Christian enjoyment under circumstances of outward trial. When " *at midnight* — their feet made fast in the stocks — Paul and Silas prayed, and *sang praises to God*" (Acts, xvi. 24, 25) : *they gave thanks, because of his righteous judgments.*

We often complain of our want of spirituality in the Divine life — how much our body hinders the ascent of the

soul heavenwards—how often drowsiness overcomes our
evening communion with our God ; the " weakness of the
flesh" overpowering the " willingness of the Spirit."
(Matt. xxvi. 41.)   But, after making all due allowances
for constitutional infirmity, how far are we " instant in
season and out of season" in the mortification of the
flesh ? (1 Cor. ix. 27.)   Do we earnestly seek for a heart
delighting in heavenly things ?   The more the flesh is
denied for the service of God, the more we shall be elevated
for the enjoyment, and realize the privilege of the work ;
and instead of having so often to mourn that our " souls
cleave unto the dust" (Verse 25), we shall " mount up-
wards with eagles' wings" (Isa. xl. 31), and even now by
anticipation, take our place before " the throne of God and
the Lamb."   Such is the active influence of self-denial in
exercising our graces, and promoting our comfort !   Oh !
how much more fervent would be our prayers — how much
more fruitful in blessings—were they enlivened with more
abundant delight in the ' angelic work of praise!' (Baxter.)
The theme is always before us.   The subject of the heavenly
song should constantly engage our songs on earth—Jesus
and his love—the "worthiness of the Lamb that was slain"
—his " power, and riches, and wisdom, and strength, and
honour, and glory, and blessing." (Rev. v. 12.)   *Midnight*
wakefulness would be far sweeter than slumber ; yea, night
itself would be turned into day, did *the judgments of God*,
as manifested in the glory of the Saviour, thus occupy our
hearts. (See Rev. xv. 3, 4.)   Lord ! tune my heart to thy
praise, and then no time will be unseasonable for this
blessed employment.   Time thus redeemed from sleep will
be an antepast of the unwearied service of heaven. (Rev.
iv. 8.)

63. *I am a companion of all them that fear thee, and of them that keep thy precepts.*

Those that love the Lord's service naturally associate with kindred spirits—with those that *fear him, and keep his precepts.* These two features identify the same character (Comp. Ps. ciii. 17, 18): as cheerful obedience is always the fruit of filial *fear.* These then are the Lord's people; and union with him is in fact union with them. Sometimes the society of the refined and intelligent of this world may be more congenial to our natural taste. But ought there not to be a restraint here? Ought not the Christian to say—" Surely the fear of God is not in this place" (Gen. xx. 11)? and " should I love them that hate the Lord?" (2 Chron. xix. 2.) Let those of us, who live in close, and to a certain degree necessary, contact with the world, subject their hearts to an evening scrutiny on this subject. ' Has the society of this day refreshed my soul, or raised my heart to spiritual things? Has it promoted a watchful temper? Or has it not rather " quenched the spirit" of prayer, and restrained my intercourse with God? To meet the Christian in ordinary courtesy, *not in unity of heart*, is a sign of an unspiritual walk with God. Fellowship with God is " walking in the light." " Fellowship one with another" is the natural flow. " The communion of saints" is the fruit and effect of communion with God. (See 1 John, i. 3–7.)

The calls of duty, or the leadings of Providence, may indeed unavoidably connect us with those, who " have no fear of God before their eyes." Nor should we repel them, by religiously affecting a sullen or uncourteous habit. (See 1 Pet. iii. 8.) But such men, whatever be their attractions, will not be the companions of our choice. Fellowship with them is to " remove the ancient landmark" (Prov. xxii.

28) ; to forget the broad line of separation between us and them ; and to venture into the most hazardous atmosphere. If indeed our hearts were ascending, like a flame of fire, with a natural motion heavenwards, and carrying with them all in their way, the choice of the *companions* of our pilgrimage would be a matter of little importance. But so deadening to our spirit is the conversation of the men of this world (however commanding their talents, or interesting their topics), that even if we have been just before enlivened by the high privilege of communion with God, the free and self-indulgent interchange of their society will benumb our spiritual powers, and quickly freeze them again. To underrate therefore the privileged association with *them that fear God*, is to incur — not only a most awful responsibility in the sight of God ; but also a most serious hazard to our own souls.

If then we are not ashamed to confess ourselves Christians, let us not shrink from walking in fellowship with Christians. Even if they should exhibit some repulsive features of character, they bear the image of him, whom we profess to love inexpressibly and incomparably above all. They will be our *companions* in our eternal home ; they ought therefore to be our brothers now. How sweet, and holy, and heavenly, is this near relation with them in our common Lord! Shall we not readily consent to his judgment, who pronounced " the righteous to be more excellent than his neighbour?" (Prov. xii. 26.) " Iron sharpeneth iron." (Ib. xxvii. 17.) If then "the iron be blunt," this will be one of the best means of " whetting the edge." (See Eccles. x. 10.) The most established servants of God gladly acknowledge the sensible refreshment of this union of heart. (Comp. 1 Sam. xxiii. 16. Ps. xvi. 3. Acts, xxviii. 15, Rom. i. 11, 12. 2 Cor. vii. 6, 7.) It is marked in the word of God, as the channel of the communication of heavenly wisdom (Prov. xiii. 20)—as a feature in the

character of the citizens of Zion (Ps. xv. 1, 4. Comp. xvi.
3, and especially 1 John, iii. 14)—and as that disposition,
which is distinguished with manifest tokens of the Saviour's
presence (Luke, xxiv. 15, 32); and which the great day
will crown with the special seal of his remembrance. " They
that feared the Lord spake often one to another ; and the
Lord *hearkened, and heard*" it ; " and a book of remembrance was written before him for them that feared the
Lord, and that thought upon his name.   And they *shall be
mine*, saith the Lord of Hosts, in that day when I make up
my jewels." (Mal. iii. 16, 17.)

64. *The earth, O Lord, is full of thy mercy: teach me thy
statutes.*

What full provision is made for man's happiness ! The
first creation was *full of mercy*. God knew that he had
created a being full of want. Every faculty wanted some
suitable object, as the source of enjoyment in the gratification—of suffering in the denial ; and now has he charged
himself with making provision for them all—so perfect,
that no want is left unprovided for.

But what a picture does the earth now present on every
side—a world of rebels ! yet a world *full of the mercy of
the Lord !* " O Lord, how manifold are thy works ! in
wisdom hast thou made them all. The earth is full of thy
riches. The eyes of all wait upon thee, and thou givest
them their meat in due season. Thou openest thine hand,
and satisfiest the desire of every living thing." (Ps. civ.
24 ; cxlv. 15, 16.) And how does the contemplation of
the Lord's *mercy* in providence encourage our faith, in
the expectancy of spiritual privileges ! " O Lord ! thou
preservest man and beast. How excellent is thy loving-
kindness, O God ! *therefore* the children of men put their
trust under the shadow of thy wings. They shall be

abundantly satisfied with the fatness of thy house ; and thou
shalt make them drink of the river of thy pleasures." (Ps.
xxxvi. 6–8.) ' As thou dost largely bestow thy blessings
upon all creatures according to their nature and condition,
so I desire the spiritual blessings of the lively light of thy
law and word, which are fitting and convenient for the
being and happiness of my soul.'* As an ignorant sinner,
" what I see not, teach thou me." (Job, xxxiv. 32.) *Teach
me thy statutes;* that which thou hast appointed, as the
way of duty, and the path to glory—that path which I am
utterly unable to discover, or when discovered, to walk in,
without the help of thy grace. And indeed the hearts of
his people are the vessels, into which the Lord is continually
pouring more and more of himself, until they shall " be
filled with all the fulness of God." (Eph. iii. 19.) Every
good, according to its character and degree, is diffusive.
And thus the goodness or *mercy of God* pervades his
whole universe—natural—plentiful—free—communica-
tive. (Verse 68.)

Yet none but a believer will understand how to use the
plea which is here employed The *mercy* that he sees on
every side, is to him a pledge and earnest of that *mercy*,
which his soul needs within. The world indeed in its present fallen state, when seen through the medium of pride
and discontent, exhibits a picture of misery, not of *mercy;*
and only ministers occasion for complaint against the
Creator. But the believer—feeling the infinite and eternal

---

* Diodati. 'It is worthy of special notice, how often and in
what varied connexions, David in this Psalm prays to be taught
the statutes of God, though he seems to have been more intimately
acquainted with the sacred oracles, as then extant, than almost any
other man ; but he knew that Divine teaching alone could enable
him rightly to understand the Scriptures, and to apply general rules
to all the variety of particular cases, which occurred in the course
of his life.'—Scott.

desert of sin — cannot but know, that the lowest exercise of goodness in God is an act of free undeserved *mercy*. No wonder then that he sees *mercy* in everything — in every part of the universe of God — a world *full of mercy*. The very food we eat, our raiment, our habitations, the contrivances for our comfort, are not mere displays of goodness, but manifestations of *mercy*. Having forfeited all claim upon the smallest consideration of God, there could have been no just ground of complaint, had all these blessings been made occasions of suffering, instead of comfort and indulgence.

Indeed is it not a marvel, that when man — *full of mercy* — is lifting up his hand against his God — employing against him all the faculties, which his *mercy* gave and has preserved — that God should be so seldom provoked to strike by their aggravated provocations? What multitude — what weight — what variety of mercy doth he still shower upon us! Even our hair, though seemingly so unimportant, the seat of loathsome, defiling, and even mortal disease — is the object of his special care. (Matt. x. 30.) All the limbs of the body, all the faculties of the mind, all the affections of the heart, all the powers of the will : keeping us in health, and capable of acting for our own happiness — how does he restrain them from those exercises or movements which might be fatal to our happiness!

And then the question naturally recurs — and to a spiritual mind will never weary by its recurrence — Whence flows all this *mercy?* Oh! it is delightful indeed to answer such an inquiry — delightful to contemplate him, " in whom" we are not only " blessed with all spiritual blessings" (Eph. i. 3); but who is also the medium, through which our temporal comforts are conveyed to us. How sweet to eye these mercies, as bought with the most precious blood that ever was known in the world, and to mark the print of the nails of our crucified Friend stamped upon the

least of them ! We allow it to add a relish to our enjoyments, that we can consider them as provided by some
beloved friend ; and should not our mercies be doubly sweet
in remembrance of that munificent Friend, who purchased
them for us so dearly ; who bestows them upon us so richly;
yea, who gives himself with them all ?

Have we heard of this mercy of God ? And do we feel
the need of it for ourselves — for every moment ? Then let
us apply to the throne of grace in the free and open way of
acceptance and access. Let us go to the King (as Ben-
hadad's servants to the king of Israel, 1 Kings, xx. 31)
in the spirit of self-condemnation and faith. Our acceptance does not depend (as in the case referred to) upon
a " peradventure ;" but it rests upon the sure word of promise —" Him that cometh to me, *I will in no wise cast out.*"
(John, vi. 37.)

PART IX.

65. *Thou hast dealt well with thy servant, O Lord, according unto thy word.*

THERE is a time for all things in the believer's experience — for confession, prayer, and praise. This Psalm mostly expresses the confessions and prayers of the man of God — yet mingled with thankful acknowledgments of mercy. He had prayed — "*Deal bountifully with thy servant.*" (Verse 17.) Perhaps here is the acknowledgment of the answer to his prayer — *Thou hast dealt well with thy servant, O Lord, according unto thy word.* And who among us has not daily reason to make the same acknowledgment? Even in those trials, when we have indulged hard thoughts of God, a clearer view of his judgments, and a more simple dependence upon his faithfulness and love, will rebuke our impatience and unbelief, and encourage our trust.* Subsequent experience altered Jacob's hasty view of the Lord's dealings with him. In a moment of peevishness, the recollection of the supposed death of a beloved son, and the threatened bereavement of another, tempted him to say —

* 'If all the sad losses, trials, sicknesses, infirmities, griefs, heaviness, and inconstancy of the creature, be expounded to be, as I am sure they are, the rods of the jealousy of a Father in heaven, contending with all your lovers on earth, though there were millions of them, for your love, to fetch it home to heaven, single. unmixed; you will forgive (if we may use that word) every rod of God, and "let not the sun go down upon your wrath" against any messenger of your afflicting and correcting Father.'—RUTHERFORD'S *Letters.*

"*All these things are against me.*" (Gen. xlii. 36.) At a brighter period of his day, when clouds were beginning to disperse, we hear that " the spirit of Jacob *revived:* And Jacob said, *It is enough;* Joseph my son is yet alive, I will go and see him before I die." (Gen. xlv. 27, 28.) And when his evening sun was going down almost without a cloud, in the believing act of " blessing the sons of" his beloved " Joseph" (Heb. xi. 21), how clearly does he retract the language of his former sinful impatience!— " God, before whom my fathers, Abraham and Isaac, did walk — the God which fed me all my life long unto this day— *the Angel which redeemed me from all evil*, bless the lads !" (Gen. xlviii. 15, 16.) This surely was in the true spirit of the acknowledgment — *Thou hast dealt well with thy servant, O Lord, according unto thy word.*

And how is it that any of us have ever harboured a suspicion of unbelief? Has God in any one instance falsified his promise? Has " the vision" failed to come at the end? Has it ever " lied?" (Hab. ii. 3.) Has he not " confirmed his promise by an oath," " that we might have two immutable things" as the ground of " *strong* consolation?" (Heb. vi. 17, 18.) Any degree less than *the full credit* that he deserves, is admitting the false principle, that God is a man, that he should lie, and the son of man, that he should repent. It weakens the whole spiritual frame, shakes our grasp of the promise, destroys our present comfort, and brings foreboding apprehensions of the future. Whereas, if we have faith and patience to wait,—" in the mount the Lord shall be seen." (Gen. xxii. 14. See Scott *in loco.*) " All things" may seem to be " against us," while at the very moment, under the wonder-working hand of God, they are " working together for our good." (Rom. viii. 28.) When therefore we " are in heaviness through manifold temptations," and we discover a " needs-be" for it all; and

" the trial of faith is found unto praise and honour and glory" (1 Pet. i. 6, 7)—when we are thus reaping the fruitful discipline of our Father's school (Heb. xii. 11), must we not put a fresh seal to our testimony — *Thou hast dealt well with thy servant, O Lord?* But why should we delay our acknowledgment till we come out of our trial? Ought we not to give it even in the midst of our " heaviness?"* Faith has enabled many, and would enable us, to " glorify God in the fires" (Isa. xxiv. 15); to " trust" him, even when " walking in darkness, and having no light" (Ib. l. 10); and, even while smarting under his chastening rod, to acknowledge, that he *has dealt well with us.*

But if I doubt the reasonableness of this acknowledgment, then let me, while suffering under trials, endeavour to take up different language. ' Lord, thou hast dealt ill with thy servant; thou hast not kept thy word.' If in a moment of unbelief my impatient heart, like Jacob's, could harbour such a dishonourable suspicion, my conscience would soon smite me with conviction—' What! shall I, who am " called out of darkness into marvellous light"— shall I, who am rescued from slavery and death, and brought to a glorious state of liberty and life, complain? Shall I, who have been redeemed at so great a price, and who have a right to " all the promises of God in Christ Jesus" (2 Cor. i. 20), and who am now an " heir of God, and joint heir with Christ" (Rom. viii. 17), murmur at my Father's will? Alas, that my heart should prove so foolish, so weak, so ungrateful! Lord! I would acknowledge with thankfulness, and yet with humiliation, *Thou hast dealt well with thy servant, according unto thy word.'* But how sinfully do we neglect these honourable and cheering acknow-

---

* Verses 71, 75. " In everything (*therefore including affliction*) by prayer and supplication, *with thanksgiving,*" &c. Philip. iv. 6. Comp. also 1 Thess. v. 18.

ledgments! Were we habitually to mark them for future remembrance, we should be surprised to see how their numbers would multiply. " If we should count them, they are more in number than the sand." (Ps. cxxxix. 18.) And truly such recollections—enhancing every common, as well as every special mercy—would come up as a sweet savour to God " by Christ Jesus." (Heb. xiii. 15.) " Bless the Lord, O my soul, and *all that is within me*, bless his holy name ; and forget not all his benefits." (Ps. ciii. 1, 2.)

66. *Teach me good judgment and knowledge; for I have believed thy commandments.*

If the perception of the Lord's merciful dealings with my soul is obscure— *Teach me good judgment and knowledge.* Give me a clear and enlarged apprehension, that I may be ready with my acknowledgment—" *All the paths of the Lord are mercy and truth.*" (Ps. xxv. 10.) Or even with an enlightened assurance of his wise and faithful dispensations, still would I urge this petition before him, as needful for every step of my path. Indeed this prayer illustrates the simplicity and intelligence of Christian faith—always desiring, asking, and expecting the most suitable blessings. For what blessings can be more suitable to an ignorant sinner, than *good judgment and knowledge: knowledge* of ourselves, of our Saviour, of the way of obedience—and *good judgment*, to apply this knowledge to some valuable end ? These two parts of our intellectual furniture have a most important connexion and dependence upon each other. *Knowledge* is the speculative perception of general truth. *Judgment* is the practical application of it to the heart and conduct. No school, but the school of Christ—no teaching, but the teaching of the Spirit—can ever give this *good judgment and knowledge.* Solomon asks it for himself (1 Kings, iii. 9)—Paul for his people. (Phil. i.

9, 10. Col. i. 9.) Both direct us to God as the sole fountain and author.*

We cannot fail to observe a very common defect in
Christians;—warm affections connected with a blind or
loose judgment. Hence, too often, a lightness in religion,
equally unsteady in profession and in practice — easily
satisfied with a narrow compass in the vast field of Scripture, instead of grasping a full survey of those truths,
which are so intimately connected with our Christian
establishment and privilege. Much perplexing doubt, dis-
couragement, and fear ; much mistaken apprehension of
important truth, much coldness and backsliding of heart
and conduct, arises from the want of an accurate and full
apprehension of the scriptural system.

This prayer has a special application to the tender and
sensitive child of God. The disease of his constitution is
too often a scrupulous conscience—one of the most active
and successful enemies to his settled peace and quietness.†

---

* Prov. ii. 6. 1 Cor. i. 5. 2 Tim. i. 7. It is recorded of one of
the Reformers, that, when he had well acquitted himself in a public
disputation, a friend begged to see the notes, which he had been
observed to write, supposing that he had taken down the arguments
of his opponents, and sketched the substance of his own reply.
Greatly was he surprised to find that they consisted simply of these
ejaculatory petitions—'More light, Lord,—more light,—more
light!' How fully was the true spirit of prayer compressed in
these short aspirations! Could they fail of success? "If any of
you lack wisdom, let him ask of God, who giveth to all men liberally,
and upbraideth not ; *and it shall be given him.*" Jam. i. 5. Greenham, being asked his judgment of some important matters, answered—'Sir, neither am I able to speak, nor you to hear; *for we
have not prayed.* I may, indeed, talk, and you may answer, as natural
men : but we are not now prepared to confer as children of God.'—
Works, p. 19.

+ 'Scruple,' as Bishop Taylor justly observes—'is a little stone
in the foot. If you set it on the ground, it hurts you. If you hold
it up, you cannot go forward. It is a trouble, when trouble is over,

The faculty of conscience partakes, with every other power of man, of the injury of the fall ; and therefore, with all its intelligence, honesty, and power, it is liable to misconception. Like a defect of vision, it often displaces objects : and, in apparently conflicting duties, that which touches the feeling, or accords with the temper, is preferred to one, which, though more remotely viewed, really possessed a higher claim. Thus it pronounces its verdict from the predominance of feeling, rather than from the exercise of judgment—more from an indistinct perception of the subject presented to the mind, than from a simple immediate reference " to the law and testimony." Again — matters of trivial moment are often insisted upon, to the neglect of important principles. (Col. ii. 18.) External points of offence are more considered, than the habitual mortification of the inward principle. Conformity to the world in dress and appearance is more strongly censured than the general spirit of worldliness in the temper and conduct of *outward non-conformists ; while the spirit of separation from the world (which may exist in a somewhat wider range of Christian liberty, than the narrow perception of some professors has conceived.* See 1 Cor. viii. 4, 7), is totally disregarded. Thus are non-essentials confounded with fundamentals — things indifferent with things unlawful, from a narrow misconception of what is directly forbidden and allowed.* Conscience, therefore, must not be trusted without the light of the word of God ; and most

a doubt, when doubts are resolved ; a little party behind the hedge, when the main army is broken and cleared : and when conscience is instructed in its way, and girt for action, a little trifling reason, or an absurd fear, hinders it from beginning the journey, or proceeding in the way, or resting at the journey's end.'—*Duct. Dub.* Book i. chap. vi. See Calvin's lively description of scrupulosity, Institutes, Book iii. c. xix. § 7–11. See also Scott's Continuation of Milner, iii. 503.

* ' Measuring actions by atoms is the way, not to govern, but to disorder conscience.' — BISHOP TAYLOR, *ut supra.*

important is the prayer — *Teach me good judgment and knowledge.*

The exercises of this state of feeling are both endless and causeless. In the well-intended endeavour to guard against a devious track, the mind is constantly harassed with an over-anxious inquiry, whether the right path is accurately discovered ; and thus at once the pleasure and the progress of the journey are materially hindered. The influence therefore of this morbid sensibility is strenuously to be resisted. It renders the strait way more strait. It retards the work of grace in the soul. It is usually connected with self-righteousness. It savours of, and tends to produce, hard thoughts of God. It damps our cheerfulness in his service, and unfits us for the duty of the present moment. What however is more than all to be deprecated, is, that it multiplies sin ; or, to speak more clearly, it superinduces another species of sin, besides the actual transgression of the law of God. For opposition to the dictates of conscience in any particular is sin, even though the act itself may be allowed by the law of God. We may therefore sin in the act of doing good, or in obedience to the liberty and enjoyment of the gospel, as well as in the allowed transgression of the law. Indeed, under the bondage of a scrupulous conscience, we seem to be entangled in the sad necessity of sinning. The *dictates of conscience, even when grounded upon misconception, are authoritative.**
Listening to its suggestions may be sinning against " the liberty, wherewith Christ has made us free," and in which

* See Rom. xiv. 14. " To him *that esteemeth anything to be unclean* (though " clean" by the express appointment of God. Acts, x. 9–13. 1 Tim. iv. 3–5, and only *"unclean" therefore by the misconception of conscience*) " *to him it is unclean*"—i. e.—*he must not touch it, upon the ground of conscience*—though the gospel allowed the use of it, and it was an infringement of Christian liberty to abstain from it. Thus did his ignorance make to himself an occasion of sin.

we are commanded to " stand fast." (Gal. v. 1, with iv. 9, 10.) No human authority can free from its bonds. Resistance to its voice is disobedience to God's vicegerent, and therefore, *in a qualified sense at least*, disobedience to God himself. And thus it is sin, even when that which conscience condemns may be innocent. (Comp. Rom. xiv. 20–23.)

The evil of a scrupulous conscience may often be traced to a diseased temperament of body, to a naturally weak or perverted understanding, to the unfavourable influence of early prejudice — to a want of simple exercise of faith, or perception of the matters of faith. In these cases faith may be sincere, though weak ; and the sin, such as it is, is a sin of infirmity, calling for our pity, forbearance, prayer, and help. In many instances however, wilful ignorance, false shame that will not inquire, or a pertinacious adherence to deep-rooted opinion, is the source of the disease. Now such persons must be roused, even at the hazard of wounding the conscience of the more tenderly scrupulous. But as the one class decidedly sin, and the other too frequently indulge their infirmity, the excitement will probably be ultimately useful to both. Both need to have the conscience enlightened ; and to obtain " a right judgment in all things" — by a more diligent " search in the Scriptures " — by " seeking the law at the mouth of the priest"* — and, above all, by earnest prayer with the Psalmist — *Teach me good judgment and knowledge.* Thus they will discern between what is imperative, and what is indifferent ; between what is lawful, and what is expedient. If " whatsoever is not of faith is sin," then the only prospect of the removal of the doubt will be increase of faith — that is, a more full persuasion of the Divine warrant and in-

---

* Mal. ii. 7. See the example of the primitive church. Acts, xv. 1, 2.

struction. (Rom. xiv. 5; with 23.) " Howbeit there is not in
every one this knowledge" (1 Cor. viii. 7) : yet the exhortation speaks alike to all—" Grow in grace, and in the knowledge of our Lord and Saviour Jesus Christ." (2 Pet. iii.
18.) Indeed the most favourable symptoms of scrupulosity
(except where the disease originates in external causes)
partake of the guilt of wilful ignorance ; because none can
be said sincerely to ask for *good judgment and knowledge,*
who do not diligently improve all means of obtaining it.
If therefore, the scrupulous shrink from honestly seeking
the resolution of their difficulties in private conferences
(where they are to be had) with Ministers or experienced
Christians, so far they must be considered as wilfully
ignorant. We would indeed " receive them," " bear with
their infirmities" (Rom. xiv. 1 ; xv. 1), and encourage
them to expect relief from their hard bondage in the way
of increasing diligence, humility, and prayer. While their
minds are in doubt concerning the path of duty, their
actions must be imperfect and unsatisfactory. Let them
therefore wait, inquire, and pray, until their way be made
plain. This done, let them act according to their conscience, allowing nothing that it condemns, neglecting
nothing which it requires. The responsibility of error
(should error be eventually detected) will not be—the too
implicit following of the guidance of conscience—but the
want of due care and diligence for its more clear illumination. Generally, however, the rule will apply—" If thine
eye be single, thy whole body shall be full of light."*
    But, *besides the scrupulous conscience, the imperfectly*

___

* Matt. vi. 22. Comp. Prov. xxiv. 5. For a similar view of this
case, see Baxter's Christian Directory, Book i. chap. ii´. The
sacrifices appointed for sins of ignorance under the law (Lev. iv.),
mark God's sense of this case : while the frequent breaches of
Christian unity and forbearance arising from it may well justify this
extended consideration of it.

enlightened conscience presents a case equally to be deprecated. Often does it charge to a sinful source those incessant variations of feelings, which originate in bodily
indisposition, or accidental influence of temptation. Sins
of infirmity are confounded with sins of indulgence : occasional with habitual transgressions of duty. Only a part
of the character is brought under cognisance : and while
short-comings or surprisals are justly condemned : yet the
exercise of contrition, faith, love, and watchfulness, is passed
by unnoticed. Thus the gospel becomes the very reverse
of the appointment of its gracious Author. (Comp. Isa. lxi.
3.) It brings ashes for beauty, mourning for the oil of
joy, and the spirit of heaviness for the garment of praise.
If this evil is " not a sin unto death," it is " a sore evil
under the sun," which may often give occasion for the
prayer— *Teach me good judgment and knowledge;* that, in
the simplicity of faith, I may be blessed with a tender conscience, and be delivered from the bondage of a scrupulous,
and from the perplexity of an unenlightened, conscience.
Let my heart never condemn me where it ought not. Let
it never fail to condemn me where it ought.

But, alas! the perception of our need of this *good
judgment and knowledge,* is far too indistinct and uninflu-
ential. We need to cry for these valuable blessings with
deeper earnestness, and more diligent and patient waiting
upon God. Divine wisdom is a treasury, that does not
spend by giving ; and we may ask to be enriched to the
utmost extent of our wants, " in full assurance of faith."
But this faith embraces the whole revelation of God—*the
commandments as well as the promises.* And thus it becomes
the principle of Christian obedience. For can we *believe
these commandments* to be as they are represented—" holy,
just, and good," and not delight in them ? (Rom. vii. 12,
with 22.) " In those is continuance"— said the prophet —
" and we shall be saved." (Isa. lxiv. 5.) Convinced of their

perfection, acknowledging their obligations, loving them, and living in them, we shall "come to full age" in the knowledge of the Gospel, and, " by reason of use have our senses exercised to discern both good and evil." (Heb. v. 14.)

67. *Before I was afflicted I went astray; but now have I kept thy word.*

The *teaching of good judgment and knowledge* will lead us to deprecate, instead of desiring, a prosperous state. But should the Christian, by the appointment of God, be thrown into the seductive atmosphere, he will feel the prayer that is so often put into his lips, most peculiarly expressive of his need — " *In all time of our wealth — Good Lord, deliver us!*" (Litany.) A time of wealth is indeed a time of special need. It is hard to restrain the flesh, when so many are the baits for its indulgence. Such mighty power is here given to the enemy, while our perception of his power is fearfully weakened! Many and affecting instances are recorded of the hardening of the heart even of the Lord's people, in the deadening influence of a proud and worldly spirit.* But the fate of the ungodly is written as with a sunbeam for our warning — " When Jeshurun waxed fat, he kicked — I spake unto thee in thy prosperity ; but thou saidst, I will not hear." (Deut. xxxii. 15. Jer. xxii. 21.) But how awful will be the period, when the question shall speak to the conscience with all the poignancy of self-conviction — " What fruit had ye then in those things whereof ye are now ashamed?" What is the end of this flowery path ? " Death !" (Rom. vi. 21.) " Surely thou didst set them in slippery places : thou castest them down into destruction. How are they brought into desolation as in a moment !

* The histories of David, 1 Chron. xxi. 1–4 ; Solomon, 1 Kings, xi. 1–8 ; Uzziah, 2 Chron. xxvi. 16 ; and Hezekiah, 2 Chron. xxxii. 25–32, will readily occur to the mind.

They are utterly consumed with terrors" (Ps. lxxiii. 18,
19) ; " the prosperity of fools shall destroy them." (Prov.
i. 32.)

Our Saviour's allotment for his people—" In the world
ye shall have tribulation" (John, xvi. 33. Acts, xiv. 22.
1 Thess. iii. 3)—marks not less his wisdom than his love.
This is the gracious rod, by which he scourges back his
prodigal children to himself.   This is the wise discipline,
by which he preserves them from the poisoned sweetness of
carnal allurements, and keeps their hearts in a simple
direction towards himself, as the well-spring of their everlasting joy.   With all of them this one method has been
pursued.   All have been taught in one school.   All have
known the power of affliction in some of its varied forms of
inward conflict or outward trouble.   All have found a time
of affliction a time of love.   All have given proof, that the
pains bestowed upon them have not been in vain.   Thus
did Manasseh in affliction beseech " the Lord, and humble
himself greatly before the Lord God of his fathers."
(2 Chron. xxxiii. 12. Comp. Dan. iv. 36, 37.)   Thus also
in afflictions the Lord " heard Ephraim bemoaning himself" (Jer. xxxi. 18, 19) ; and beheld Israel " seeking him
early" (Hos. v. 15 ; vi. 1, 2), and the forlorn wandering
child casting a wishful, penitent look towards his Father's
house, as if the pleasures that had enticed his heart from
home, were now embittered to the soul. (Luke, xv. 16, 17.)

And thus the Christian can give some account of the
means, by which his Father is leading and preparing him
for heaven.   Perhaps he did not at first see the reason.
(See Heb. xii. 11.)   It was matter of faith, not of consciousness.   But in looking back, how clear the path, how
valuable the benefit, *Before I was afflicted, I went astray:
but now have I kept thy word.*   ' I never prized it before.   I
could indeed scarcely be said to know it.   I never understood its comfort, until affliction expounded it to me.   I

never till now saw its suitableness to my case.' But what
an heightened aggravation of guilt, when these especial
mercies fail of their gracio s end — when vanity, worldliness, and sin still reign with uncontrolled sway! Ah!
when sinners are unhumbled " under the mighty hand of
God" — when they are afflicted, and not purged by affliction — when it is said of them — " They received not correction" (Zeph. iii. 2)—it seems the forerunner of that
tremendous judgment—" Why should ye be stricken any
more ?" (Isa. i. 5.)

Heavenly Father ! keep thy poor, weak, erring child from
this fearful doom.   Let not that measure of prosperity,
which thou mayest be pleased to vouchsafe, prove my curse.
But especially let every cross, every affliction which thou
art pleased to mingle in my cup, conform me more to my
Saviour's image, restrain my heart from its daily wanderings, endear thy holy ways and word to my soul, and give
me sweeter anticipations of that blessed home, where I
shall never wander more, but find my eternal happiness in
keeping thy word.

68. *Thou art good, and doest good: teach me thy statutes.*

The blessed effects of chastisement, as a special instance
of the Lord's *goodness*, might naturally lead to a general
acknowledgment of the *goodness* of his character and dispensation.   Judging in unbelieving haste, of his providential and gracious dealings, feeble sense imagines a frown,
when the eye of faith discerns a smile, upon his face ; and
therefore in proportion as faith is exercised in the review
of the past, and the experience of the present, we shall be
prepared with the ascription of praise — *Thou art good.*
This is indeed the expression (Heb. xi. 6) — the confidence
(Nah. i. 7)—the pleading (Ps. xxv. 7 ; lxxxvi. 5)—of
faith.   It is the sweet taste of experience — restraining the

legality of the conscience, the many hard and dishonourable thoughts of God, and invigorating a lively enjoyment of him. Indeed ' this is the true and genuine character of God. He is good (Ps. xxxiv. 8, with Mic. vii. 18)—He is goodness. Good in himself—good in his essence—good in the highest degree. All the names of God are comprehended in this one of *Good.** All the acts of God are nothing else but the effluxes of his goodness distinguished by several names according to the object it is exercised about. When he confers happiness without merit, it is grace. When he bestows happiness against merit, it is mercy. When he bears with provoking rebels, it is long-suffering. When he performs his promise, it is truth. When he commiserates a distressed person, it is pity. When he supplies an indigent person, it is bounty. When he succours an innocent person, it is righteousness. And when he pardons a penitent person, it is mercy. All summed up in this one name—Goodness. None so communicatively good as God. As the notion of God includes goodness, so the notion of goodness includes diffusiveness. Without goodness he would cease to be a Deity ; and without diffusiveness he would cease to be good. The being good is necessary to the being God. For goodness is nothing else in the notion of it but a strong inclination to do good, either to find or to make an object, wherein to exercise itself, according to the propension of its own nature ; and it is an inclination of communicating itself, not for its own interest, but for the good of the object it pitcheth upon. Thus God is good by nature ; and his nature is not without activity.

* The revealed "goodness" of God made to Moses in answer to his prayer—" I beseech thee, show me thy glory"—shows it to be not a single attribute, or a display of any particular feature of the Divine character, but rather the combined exercise of all his perfections. Exod. xxxiii. 18, 19; with xxxiv. 5-7.

He acts consistently with his own nature — *Thou art good, and doest good.*'*

How easily is such an acknowledgment excited towards an earthly friend! Yet who has not daily cause to complain of the coldness of his affections towards his God? It would be a sweet morning's reflection to recollect some of the innumerable instances, in which the goodness of God has been most distinctly marked, to trace them in their peculiar application to our own need ; and above all to mark, not only the source from which they come, but the channel through which they flow. A view of covenant love does indeed make the goodness of God to shine with inexpressible brightness " in the face of Jesus Christ" (2 Cor. iv. 6) ; and often when the heart is conscious of backsliding, does the contemplation of this *goodness* under the influence of the Spirit, prove the Divinely appointed means of " leading us to repentance." (Rom. ii. 4.) Let us therefore wait on, even when we see nothing. Soon we shall see, where we did not look for it. Soon we shall find *goodness* unmingled — joy unclouded, unspeakable, eternal.

Meanwhile, though the diversified manifestations — the materials of our happiness, in all around us, be countless as the particles of sand, and the drops of dew ; yet without heavenly *teaching* they only become occasions of our deeper misery and condemnation. It is not enough that the Lord gives — he must *teach us his statutes.* Divine truths can only be apprehended by Divine *teaching.* The scholar, who has been longest taught, realizes most his need of this teaching, and is most earnest in seeking it. Indeed, " the earth is full of the goodness of the Lord," yet we may be

---

* CHARNOCK'S Works, vol. i. 581, 585, 588. For another exquisite view (parallel, in some degree identical, with Charnock) of this ' perfecting perfection, which crowns and consummates all the rest,' — see HOWE'S Works, 8vo. edit. 1822, viii. pp. 107–114.

utterly ignorant of it.   The instances of goodness in the
shape of a cross, we consider to be the reflection on it.
Nothing is goodness in our eyes, that crosses our own
inclination.   We can hardly bear to hear of the cross,
much less to take it up.   We talk of goodness, but yield
to discontent.   We do not profess to dislike trial—only
the trial now pressing upon us—any other cross than this ;
that is, my will and wisdom rather than God's.   Is there
not, therefore, great need of this prayer for Divine *teaching*,
that we may discern the Lord's mercies so closely crowded
together, and make the due improvement of each ?   Twice
before had the Psalmist sent up this prayer and plea.
(Verses 12, 64. Comp. Ps. xxv. 8.)   Yet he seems to make
the supplication ever new by the freshness and vehemency
of his desires.   And let me ever make it new by the remembrance of that one display of goodness, which casts every
other manifestation into the shade—" God so loved the
world, that he gave his only-begotten Son." (John, iii. 16.)

This constitutes of itself a complete mirror of infinite
and everlasting goodness — the only intelligent display of
his goodness — the only manifestation, that prevents from
abusing it.   What can I say to this—but *Thou art good,
and doest good?*   What may I not then expect from thee !
' " *Teach me thy statutes.*"   Teach me the Revelation of
thyself—Teach me the knowledge of thy Son.   For " this
is life eternal, that I might know thee, the only true God,
and Jesus Christ whom thou hast sent." ' (John, xvii. 3.)

69. *The proud have forged a lie against me ; but I will keep
thy precepts with my whole heart.*

If the Lord *does us good*, we must expect Satan to do
us evil.   Acting in his own character, as a " liar and the
father of it" (John, viii. 44), he readily puts it into the
hearts of his children to *forge lies against* the children of

God! But all is overruled by the ever-watchful care and providence of God, for the eventual good of His church. The cross frightens the insincere, and removes them out of the way; while the stedfastness of his own people marvellously displays to the world the power and triumph of faith. A most delightful source of encouragement in this fiery trial is, to take off the eye from the objects of sense, and to fix it upon Jesus as our pattern, no less than our life. For every trial, in which we are conformed to his suffering image, supplies to us equal direction and support. Do " *the proud forge lies against us ?* " So did they against him. (Comp. Matt. xxvi. 59–61.) " The disciple is not above his master, nor the servant above his lord. It is enough for the disciple, that he be as his master, and the servant as his lord. If they have called the Master of the house Beelzebub, how much more shall they call them of his household?" (Matt. x. 24, 25.) " *Consider him, therefore, that endured such contradiction of sinners against himself, lest ye be wearied and faint in your minds.*" (Heb. xii. 3.)

But is it always *lies that are forged against us?* Is there no worldliness, or pride, or inconsistency in temper and walk, that opens the mouths of the enemies of the gospel, and causes " the way of truth to be evil spoken of?" (2 Pet. ii. 2.) Do they not sometimes " say all manner of evil" against some of us, for Christ's sake; yet alas! not altogether " falsely"? (See Matt. v. 11); " Woe unto the world, because of offences! for it must needs be that offences come; but woe to that man, by whom the offence cometh!" (Matt. xviii. 7.) If, however, the reproach of the world be " the reproach of Christ," " let us hold fast the profession of our faith without wavering; for he is faithful that promised." (Heb. x. 23.) Insincerity of heart can never support us to a consistent and persevering endurance of the cross. A heart divided between God and the world will ever be found faulty and backsliding.

(Comp. Hos. x. 2 ; Jer. iii. 10.) *Wholeness of heart in the precepts of God* adorns the Christian profession, awes the ungodly world, realizes the full extent of the Divine promises, and pours into the soul such a spring-tide of enjoyment, as more than counterbalances all the reproach, contempt, and falsehood, which the forge of the great enemy is employing against us with unceasing activity, and relentless hatred. Yet forget not, believer, that these proofs of the malicious enmity of the proud must often be received as the gentle stroke of your Father's chastisement. Let the fruits of it, then, be daily visible in the work of mortification — in the exercise of the suffering graces of the gospel — in your growing conformity to his image — and in a progressive meetness for the world of eternal uninterrupted love.

70. *Their heart is as fat as grease; but I delight in thy law.*

An awful description of the hardened state of *the proud forgers of lies!* Yet not of their state only, but of every sinner, who stands out in wilful rebellion against God. The tremendous blow of almighty justice has benumbed his heart, so that the pressure of mountains of sin and guilt is unfelt ! The heart is left of God, " seared with a hot iron" (1 Tim. iv. 2), and therefore without tenderness ; " past feeling " (Eph. iv. 19) ; unsoftened by the power of the word : unhumbled by the rod of providential dispensations, given up to the heaviest of all spiritual judgments ! But it is of little avail to stifle the voice of conscience, unless the same power or device could annihilate hell. It will only " awake out of sleep, like a giant refreshed with wine" (Ps. lxxviii. 66. P. T.), and rage with ten-fold interminable fury in the eternal world, from the temporary restraint, which for a short moment had benumbed its energy. Wilful resistance to the light of the gospel, and the strivings of the Spirit, constrained even from a God of love the message of judicial abandonment—"Make the heart of this people fat, and make their ears heavy, and shut their eyes ; lest they see with their eyes, and hear with their ears, and understand with their heart, and convert, and be healed." (Isa. vi. 9, 10.) Who then among us will not cry—*From hardness of heart, and contempt of thy word and commandment, Good Lord! deliver us!* (Litany.) Tenderness is the first mark of the touch of grace, when the heart becomes sensible of its own insensibility, and contrite on account of its own hardness. ' Nothing'—said Jerome, in a letter to a friend—'makes my heart sadder, than that nothing makes it sad.' But when " the plague of our own heart" begins to be " known" (1 Kings, viii. 38), and becomes a matter of confession, humiliation, prayer ; the promise of " a new heart" is as life from the dead. (Ezek. xxxvi. 26.) The subject of this promise *delights in God's law;* and this amidst the sometimes overwhelming power of natural corruption, gives a satisfactory witness of a change " from death unto life."

Christian ! can you daily witness the wretched condition of the ungodly, without the constraining recollection of humiliation and love ? What sovereign grace, that the Lord of glory should have set his love upon one so vile ! (Eph. ii. 4, 5.) What mighty power, to have raised my insensible heart to that *delight in his law,* which conforms me to the image of his dear Son ! (See Ps. xl. 8.) Deeply would I " abhor myself :" and gladly would I acknowledge, that the service of ten thousand hearts would be a poor return for such unmerited love. What, oh, " what shall I render to the Lord !" (Ps. cxvi. 12.)—Prayer for them who are still lying in death—praise for myself quickened from

death.   But what can give the vital breath, pulse, feeling,
and motion?   " Come, from the four winds, O breath;
and breathe upon the slain, that they may live." (Ezek.
xxxvii. 9.)

Let us apply, for the purpose of daily self-examination,
this description of the heart, either as given up to its natural insensibility, or as cast into the new mould of *delight in the law of God*.   Such an examination will prove
to us, how much even renewed souls need the transforming,
softening influences of grace.   " The deceitfulness of sin
hardens the heart" (Heb. iii. 13) to its original character,
as fat as grease, unfeeling, incapable of impression,
without a Divine touch.   O Lord, let not my heart be
unvisited for one day, one hour, by that melting energy
of love, which first made me feel, and constrained me
to love.

71. *It is good for me that I have been afflicted; that I might
learn thy statutes.*

If I mark in myself any difference from the ungodly—
if I can feel that my natural insensibility is yielding to the
influence of grace—if I am enabled to " *delight in God's
law*," which before I had neglected as a " strange thing"
(Hos. viii. 12), if this softening transformation (Job, xxiii.
16) has been wrought in the school of affliction ; let me
thankfully acknowledge—*It is good for me that I have been
afflicted*.   None indeed but the Lord's scholars can know
the benefit of this school and this teaching.   The first
lessons are usually learned under the power of the word
pricking and piercing the heart; yet issuing in joyous
good. (Acts, ii. 37–47 ; xvi. 27–34.)   All special lessons
afterward will probably be learned here. (See Job, xxxvi.
8–10.)   ' I never '—said Luther—' knew the meaning of
God's word, until I came into affliction.   I have always

found it one of my best schoolmasters.'* This teaching
distinguishes the sanctified from the unsanctified cross,
explaining many a hard text, and sealing many a precious
promise—the rod expounding the word, and the Divine
Teacher effectually applying both.

Indeed, but for this discipline we should miss much of
the meaning and spiritual blessing of the word. For how
can we have any experimental acquaintance with the promises of God, except under those circumstances for which
the promises are made? When, for example, but in the
day of trouble, could we understand the full mercy of such
a gracious word, as—" *Call upon me in the day of trouble:
I will deliver thee, and thou shalt glorify me?* " (Ps. l. 15.)
And how much more profitable is this experimental learning than mere human instruction! When, therefore, we
pray for a clearer apprehension and interest in the blessed
book, and for a deeper experience of its power upon our
hearts; we are, in fact, often unconsciously supplicating
for the chastening rod of our Father's love. For it is the
man " whom the Lord chasteneth," that he " teacheth out
of his law."† Peter, indeed, when on the mount of trans-

---

* On another occasion, referring to some spiritual temptation
on the morning of the preceding day, he added to a friend (Justin
Jonas), 'Doctor, I must mark the day; I was yesterday at school.'
MILNER, v. 484. In one of his works, he most accurately calls
affliction 'the theology of Christians—theologium Christianorum.'
To the same purport is the testimony of a learned French divine
and tried saint of God—' I have learned more divinity'—said Dr.
Rivet, confessing to God of his last days of affliction—' in these ten
days that thou art come to visit me, than I did in fifty years before.
Thou hast brought me to myself. "Before I was afflicted I went
astray," and was in the world; but now I am conversant in the
school of God; and he teacheth me after another manner than all
those doctors, in reading whom I spent so much time.'—MIDDLE-
TON'S *Biog. Evan.* iii. 248.

† Ps. xciv. 12. The use of the word παιδια in the acceptation

figuration, said, "*It is good* for us to be here. Let us build here three tabernacles." Here let us abide, in a state of comfort, indulgence, and sunshine. But well was it added by the sacred historian—" Not knowing what he said." (Luke, ix. 33.) The judgment of David was far more correct, when he pronounced, that *it was good for him that he had been afflicted.* For so often are we convicted of inattention to the voice of the Lord — so often do we find ourselves looking back upon forsaken Sodom, or lingering in the plain, instead of pressing onward to Zoar (Comp. Gen. xix. 17–23), that the indulgence of our own liberty would shortly hurry us along the pathway of destruction. Alas! often do we feel the spirit of prayer to be quenched for a season by " a heart overcharged with the cares of this life" (Luke, xxi. 34) — or by the over-prizing of some lawful comfort — or by a temper inconsistent with our Christian profession — or by an undue confidence in the flesh. And at such seasons of backsliding, we must count among our choicest mercies the gracious discipline, by which the Lord schools us with the cross, *that we may learn his statutes.*

After all, however, this must be a paradox to the unenlightened man. He can only " count it" all grief—not " *all joy*—when he falls into divers temptations." (James, i. 2.) His testimony is — It is evil—not *it is good—for me that I have been afflicted.* And even God's children, as we have before remarked, do not always take up this word while smarting under the rod. The common picture of happiness is freedom from trouble, not, as Scripture describes it (Job,

of chastening (LXX. in this verse, and Heb. xii. 5) is remarkable, as describing literally the instruction, by which a child is trained to the acquisition of useful knowledge, which, however, not being generally effected without chastening, accounts for the use of the word, to mark the discipline which usually attends instruction.

v. 17), the portion of trouble. Yet how true is God's judgment, when it is the very end of affliction to remove the source of all trouble (Isa. xxvii. 9), and consequently to secure — not to destroy — solid happiness! We must however determine the standard of real good by its opposition — not its accordance — to our own fancy or indulgence. The promise of "every good thing" may be fulfilled by a plentiful cup of affliction. (Ps. xxxiv. 10, 19.) Present evil may be "working together for" ultimate "good." (Rom. viii. 28. Comp. Jer. xxiv. 5.) Let God take his own way with us. (Jer. xxix. 11. John, xvi. 6, 7.) Let us interpret his providences by his covenant (Gen. xxxii. 10–12) — his means by his end (Jam. v. 11) — and instead of fainting under the sharpness of his rod, we shall earnestly desire the improvement of it.

Are you, then, tried believer, disposed to regret the lessons you have already learned in this school? Or have you purchased them at too dear a cost? Do you grieve over the bleedings of a contrite heart, that have brought you under the care of the healing physician? Or could you by any other way have obtained so rich a knowledge of his love, or have been trained to such implicit obedience to his will? As Jesus, "though he were a Son, yet learned he obedience by the things which he suffered" (Heb. v. 8); so may we "rejoice, inasmuch as we are partakers of his sufferings" (1 Pet. iv. 13), and be thankful to learn the same obedience, as the evidence and fruit of our conformity to him.

The Lord save us from the greatest of all afflictions, an affliction lost! (Comp. 1 Kings, xiii. 33; 2 Chron. xxviii. 22.) "Be thou instructed, O Jerusalem, lest my soul depart from thee; lest I make thee desolate, a land not inhabited." (Jer. vi. 8.) "He that being often reproved, hardeneth his neck, shall suddenly be destroyed, and that without remedy." (Prov. xxix. 1.) A call to tremble and repent, to watch and pray, and " turn to him that smiteth us !" (Isa. ix. 13.)

Oh ! is there one of that countless throng surrounding the everlasting throne, who has not sung—" *It is good for me that I have been afflicted?*" " And one of the elders answered, saying unto me, What are these which are arrayed in white robes? and *whence came they?* And I said unto him, Sir, thou knowest. And he said unto me, These are they which *came out of great tribulation*, and have washed their robes, and made them white in the blood of the Lamb." (Rev. vii. 13, 14.)

72. *The law of thy mouth is better unto me than thousands of gold and silver.*

Well might David acknowledge the benefit of *affliction*, since he had thus *learned in God's statutes* something that was *better to him than thousands of gold and silver.* This was indeed an enlightened judgment for one to form, who had so small a part of *the law of God's mouth*, and so large a portion of this world's treasure. And yet, if we study only his book of Psalms to know the important uses and privileges of *this law*, and his son's book of Ecclesiastes, to discover the real value of paltry *gold and silver* (Eccles. v. 9–20 ; vi. 1, 2), we shall, under Divine teaching, be led to make the same estimate for ourselves. Yes, believer, with the same, or rather with far higher delight than the miser calculates his *thousands of gold and silver*, do you tell out the precious contents of *the law of your God.* After having endeavoured in vain to count the *thousands* in your treasure, one single name sums up their value— " the unsearchable riches of Christ." (Eph. iii. 8.) Would not the smallest spot of ground be estimated at *thousands of gold and silver*, were it known to conceal under its surface a mine of inexhaustible treasure? This it is that makes the word so inestimable. It is the field of the "hidden treasure." "The pearl of great price" (Matt. xiii. 44–46) is known to be concealed here. You would not, therefore, part with one leaf of your Bible for all the *thousands of gold and silver*. You know yourself to be in possession of the substance—you have found all besides to be a shadow. "I lead"—saith the Saviour—"in the way of righteousness, in the midst of the paths of judgment; *that I may cause them that love me to inherit substance; and I will fill their treasures*." (Prov. viii. 20, 21.) The grand motive, therefore, in "searching the Scriptures," is because "they testify of Christ." (John, v. 39.) A sinner has but one want—a Saviour. A believer has but one desire—to "know and win Christ." (Phil. iii. 8–10.) With a "single eye," therefore, intent upon one point, he studies this blessed book. "With unveiled face he beholds in this glass the glory of the Lord" (2 Cor. iii. 18): and no arithmetic can compute the price of that, which is now unspeakably *better to him than* the treasures of the earth.

Christian! bear your testimony to your supreme delight in the book of God. You have here opened the surface of much intellectual interest and solid instruction. But it is the joy that you have found in the revelation of the Saviour, in his commands, in his promises, in his ways, that leads you to exclaim, "More to be desired are they than gold, yea, than much fine gold!" (Ps. xix. 10.) Yes, indeed—every promise—every declaration—centering in him, is a pearl; and the word of God is full of these precious pearls. If then they be the richest who have the best and the largest treasure, those who have most of the word in their hearts, not those who have most of the world in their possession—are justly entitled to this pre-eminence. "Let then the word of Christ dwell in us *richly* in all wisdom." (Col. iii. 16.) For those who are rich in this heavenly treasure are men of substance indeed.

True—this is a correct estimate of the worth of God's law—*better* than this world's treasure. But is it *better to me?* Is this my decided choice? How many will inconsiderately acknowledge its supreme value, while they yet hesitate to relinquish even a scanty morsel of earth for an interest in it! Do I then habitually prefer *this law of God's mouth* to every worldly advantage? Am I ready to forego every selfish consideration,* if it may only be the means of uniting my heart more closely to the Book of God? If this be not my practical conviction, I fear I have not yet opened the mine. But if I can assent to this declaration of the man of God, I have made a far more glorious discovery than Archimedes; and therefore may take up his expression of joyful surprise—'I have found it! I have found it!' What? That which the world could never have given me—that of which the world can never deprive me.

Yet how affecting is it to see men poor in the midst of great riches! Often in the world we see the possessor of a large treasure—without a heart to enjoy it—virtually therefore a pauper. Oftener still in the Church do we see professors (may it not be so with some of us?) with their Bibles in their hands—yet poor even with the external interest in its "unsearchable riches." Often also do we observe a want of value for *the whole law* or revelation of God's mouth. Some parts are highly honoured to the depreciation of the rest. But let it be remembered that the

---

* A Jewish Rabbi, when induced by the prospect of a lucrative situation to fix his settlement in a place *where there was no synagogue*, is said to have resisted the temptation by the recollection of this verse. Poli Synopsis—in loco. A reproof to Christians, who, in choosing "the bounds of their habitation," have not always eyed their Master's rule, Matt. vi. 33.

whole of Scripture " is given by inspiration of God and is *therefore* profitable" for its appointed end. (2 Tim. iii. 16, 17.) Oh ! beware of resting satisfied with a scanty treasure. Prayer and diligence will bring out not only " things new," but the " old" also with a new and brighter glow. Scraping the surface is a barren exercise. Digging into the bowels is a most enriching employ. No vein in this mine is yet exhausted. And rich indeed shall we be, if we gather only one atom of the gold each day in prayerful meditation. But as you value your progress and peace in the ways of God —as you have an eye to your Christian perfection—put away that ruinous thought—true as an encouragement to the weak (Zech. iv. 10), but false as an excuse to the slothful (Prov. xiii. 4)—that a little knowledge is sufficient to carry us to heaven.

And—Lord—help me to prize *the law* as coming from *thy mouth.* (1 Thess. ii. 13.) Let it be for ever written upon my heart. Let me be daily exploring my hidden treasures. Let me be enriching myself and all around me with the present possession and interest in these heavenly blessings.

PART X.

73. *Thy hands have made me and fashioned me: give me understanding, that I may learn thy commandments.*

IN the vast universe of wonder, man is the greatest wonder—the noblest work of God. A council of the Sacred Trinity was held respecting his creation—" God said, Let us make man in our image, after our likeness." (Gen. i. 26.) Every part of creation bears the impress of God. Man—man alone—bears his image, his likeness. Everywhere we see his track—his footsteps. Here we behold his face. What an amazing thought, that the three Eternal subsistents in the glorious Godhead, should have united in gracious design and operation towards the dust of the earth! But thus man was formed—thus was he raised out of his parent dust, from this low original, to be the living temple, and habitation of Divine glory—a Being full of God. The first moment that he opened his eyes to behold the light and beauty of the new-made world, the Lord separated him for his own service, to receive the continual supply of his own life. His body was fitted as a tabernacle for his soul, " curiously wrought" by the hand of God ; and all its parts and " members written in this book, which in continuance were fashioned, when as yet there was none of them." Most naturally therefore does the contemplation of this " perfection of beauty" raise the adoring mind upward—" I will praise thee ; for I am fearfully and wonderfully made ; marvellous are thy works ; and that my soul knoweth right well." (Ps. cxxxix. 14–16.)   *Thy hands have made me and fashioned me.*

Could we suppose that man was formed to eat, to sleep, and to die — that, after taking a few turns upon the grand walk of life, he was to descend into the world of eternal silence, we might well ask the question of God — " Wherefore hast thou made all men in vain ?" (Ps. lxxxix. 47.) But the first awakening of man from his death-like sleep enlightens him in the right knowledge of the end of his creation.   If I am conscious of being the workmanship of God, I shall feel my relationship to him, and the responsibility of acting according to it.   I would plead then this relation before him in asking for light, life, and love.   I cannot serve thee as a creature, except I be made a new creature.   Give me a spiritual being, without which my natural being cannot glorify thee.   Thou hast indeed " curiously wrought" my frame ; but sin has marred all. Make me thy spiritual " workmanship, created in Christ Jesus." (Eph. ii. 10.)   *Give me understanding* — spiritual knowledge, *that I may learn thy commandments* — " Renew a right spirit within me." (Ps. li. 10.)

But the natural man feels no need of this prayer.   No, he is puffed up in his own wisdom.   He cannot receive the Divine testimony, which levels him, while he "understandeth not," with " the beasts that perish" (Ps. xlix. 20), and tells him, that he must " become a fool, that he may be wise." (1 Cor. iii. 18.)   But should he ever know his new state of existence, he will offer up this prayer eagerly and frequently ; and every step of his way heavenward he will feel increasing need of Divine " wisdom and spiritual understanding."

How does the song of heaven remind us of this end of our creation !—" Thou art worthy, O Lord, to receive glory, and honour, and power ! for thou hast created all things ; *and for thy pleasure they are,* and were created." (Rev. iv.

11.)   In harmony with this song we must acknowledge, that the " Lord hath made all things for himself" (Prov. xvi. 4)—that he " created all things for his glory." (Isa. xliii. 7.)   And the recollection that he " created us by Jesus Christ" (Eph. iii. 9. Col. i. 16. John, i. 1–3), brings before us the grand work of redemption, and the work of the new creation consequent upon it.   He who created us in his own image, when that image was lost, that he might not lose his property in us, put a fresh seal upon his natural right, and " purchased us with his own blood."   Oh ! let us not be insensible to this constraining motive to *learn his commandments.*   " Ye are not your own, for ye are bought with a price ; therefore glorify God in your body and in your spirit, which are God's." (1 Cor. vi. 19, 20.)

74. *They that fear thee, will be glad when they see me: because I have hoped in thy word.*

How cheering is the sight of a man of God !   How refreshing his converse !   How satisfactory and enlivening is the exhibition of his faith !   The goodness of God to one becomes thus the joy and comfort of all.   What an excitement is this to close communion with our God, that the light which we thus receive will shine on those around us !   What a comfort will it be even in our own hour of temptation, that the hope, which we may then be enabled to maintain in the word of God, shall prove the stay, not only of our own souls, but of the Lord's people !   Many a desponding Christian, oppressed with such fears as this — " I shall one day perish by the hand of Saul" (1 Sam. xxvii. 1)—when he hears of one and another exercised in the same trials, and who have *hoped in God's word,* and have not been disappointed, *will be glad when he sees them.* Thus David recorded his conflicts, that we may not despair of our own ; and his triumphs, that " in the name of our

God we might set up our banners." (Ps. xx. 5.) " I had
fainted, unless I had believed to see the goodness of the
Lord in the land of the living.   Wait on the Lord, be of
good courage, and he shall strengthen thine heart : wait, I
say, on the Lord." (Ps. xxvii. 13, 14.)   Thus also, under
affliction, he was comforted with the thought of comforting
others with the history of his own experience—" *My soul
shall make her boast in the Lord: the humble shall hear thereof,
and be glad.   O praise the Lord with me, and let us magnify
his name together.*   He hath put a new song in my mouth,
even praise unto our God.   Many shall see it, and fear, and
shall trust in the Lord.   Bring my soul out of prison, that
I may praise thy name ; the righteous shall compass me
about, for thou shalt deal bountifully with me." (Ps. xxxiv.
2, 3, P. T. ; xl. 3 ; cxlii. 7. Comp. also lxix. 30–32.)

In this view, the believer, who has been " sifted in the
sieve " of temptation, without the least " grain " of faith
or hope " falling upon the earth" (Amos, ix. 9), stands
forth as a monument of the Lord's faithfulness, to
" strengthen the weak hands, and confirm the feeble knees,
and to say to them that are of fearful heart, Be strong, fear
not." (Isa. xxxv. 3, 4.)   Those that are " fearful, and of
little faith," *are glad when they see him.*   They " thank
God" for him, and " take courage" (Acts, xxviii. 15) for
themselves.   What a motive is this to keep us from despondency ; that, instead of destroying by our unbelief, those
who are already " cast down," we may enjoy the privilege
of upholding their confidence, and ministering to their comfort !   And how should the weak and distressed seek for
and prize the society of those, who have been instructed by
the discipline of the Lord's school !

Believer ! what have you to tell to your discouraged
brethren of the faithfulness of your God ?   Cannot you put
courage into their hearts, by declaring that you have never
been " ashamed of your hope ? "   Cannot you tell them

from your own experience, that Jesus " is for a foundation-stone, a tried stone, a sure foundation ?" (Isa. xxviii. 16.) Cannot you show them, that, because he has borne the burden of their sins, he is able to " bear their griefs, and to carry their sorrows" (Isa. liii. 4)? that you have tried him, and that you have found him so ? Oh! be animated to know more of Christ yourself; let your hope in him be strengthened, that you may cause gladness in the hearts of those *that, see you;* so that, " whether you be afflicted, or whether you be comforted, it may be for their consolation and salvation." (2 Cor. i. 6.)

But, O my God! how much cause have I for shame, that I impart so little of thy glorious light to those around me! Perhaps some poor trembling sinner *has been glad when he saw me*, hoping to hear something of the Saviour from my lips, and has found me straitened, and cold, and dumb. Oh! that I may be so " filled with the Spirit," so experienced in thy heavenly ways, that I may invite " all that fear thee to come to me," that I may " declare what thou hast done for my soul" (Ps. lxvi. 16); so that, " when men are cast down, they may say, There is lifting up." (Job, xxii. 29.)

75. *I know, O Lord, that thy judgments are right, and that thou in faithfulness hast afflicted me.*

This is the Christian's acknowledgment—fully satisfied with the dispensation of God. This is his confidence— so invigorating to his own soul—so cheering to the church. The Lord's dealings are called *his judgments*—not as having judicial curses, but as the acts of his justice in the chastening of sin. (1 Pet. iv. 17.) Perhaps also—as the administration of his wise judgments in their measure and application. (Jer. x. 24. Comp. Isa. xxvii. 8.) But here is not only the confession of the Lord's general judgment,

but of his especial *faithfulness* to himself. And this he
knew — not from the dictates of the flesh (which would have
given a contrary verdict), but from the testimony of the
word (Deut. xxxii. 4), and the witness of his own experience. (Verse 137 ; cxlv. 17.) It could not be doubted —
much less denied —' *I know, O Lord*, that thy rules of proceeding are agreeable to thy perfect justice and wisdom ;
and I am equally satisfied, that the afflictions that thou
hast laid upon me from time to time, are only to fulfil thy
gracious and faithful promise of making me eternally happy
in thyself.' Blessed fruit of affliction! when we can thus
" see the end of the Lord, that the Lord is very pitiful, and
of tender mercy" — that his " thoughts towards us are
thoughts of peace, and not of evil!" (Jam. v. 11. Jer. xxix.
11.) " The patience and faith of the saints" teach this
difficult but most consoling lesson, in deciphering the mysterious lines in God's providence.

The child of God under the severest chastisement must
acknowledge justice. Our gracious reward is always more
— our " punishment always less, than our iniquities deserve." (Ezra, ix. 13. Comp. Job, xi. 6.) " Wherefore
should a living man complain?" (Lam. iii. 39.) In trouble
he is indeed — but not in hell. If he complain, let it be of
none but himself, and his own wayward choice. *I know, O
Lord, that thy judgments are right* — and who can doubt the
wisdom? Who would charge the operator with cruelty, in
cutting out the proud flesh, that was bringing death upon
the man? Who would not acknowledge the *right judgment*
of his piercing work? Thus, when the Lord's painful work
separates us from our sin, weans us from the world, and
brings us nearer to himself, what remains for us, but thankfully to acknowledge his righteousness and truth? Unbelief is put to rebuke ; and we, if we have indulged
suspicion " that God hath forgotten to be gracious," must
confess, " This is our infirmity." (Ps. lxxvii. 7–10.)

This assurance of the Lord's perfect justice, wisdom, and intimate knowledge of our respective cases, leads us to yield to his appointments in dutiful silence. Thus Aaron, under his most afflictive domestic calamity, "held his peace." (Lev. x. 1–3.) Job under a similar dispensation was enabled to say—"The Lord gave, and the Lord hath taken away : blessed be the name of the Lord !" (Job, i. 21. Comp. ii. 10.) Eli's language in the same trial was, " It is the Lord ; let him do what seemeth him good." (1 Sam. iii. 18.) David hushed his impatient spirit—" I was dumb ; I opened not my mouth, because thou didst it." And when Shimei cursed him, he said, " Let him alone ; let him curse ; for the Lord hath bidden him." (Ps. xxxix. 9. 2 Sam. xvi. 11, 12.) The Shunamite, in the meek resignation of faith, acknowledged—" It is well." (2 Kings, iv. 26.) Hezekiah kissed the rod, while it was smiting him to the dust—" Good is the word of the Lord which thou hast spoken." (Isa. xxxix. 8.) Thus uniform is the language of the Lord's people under chastisement—*I know, O Lord, that thy judgments are right.*

But the confession of justice may be mere natural conviction. (Exod. ix. 27. Judges, i. 7. 2 Chron. xii. 6.) Faith goes further, and speaks of *faithfulness.* David not only acknowledges God's right to deal with him as he saw fit, and even his wisdom in dealing with him as he actually had done, but his *faithfulness in afflicting*—not his faithfulness *though he afflicted*—but *in afflicting him;* not as if it were consistent with his love, but as the very fruit of his love. It is not enough to justify God. What abundant cause is there to praise him ! It is not enough to forbear to murmur. How exciting is the display of *his faithfulness* and love ! Yes—the trials appointed for us are none else than the faithful performance of his everlasting engagements. And to this cause we may always trace (and it is our privilege to believe it, where we cannot *visibly* trace it) the reason of much that is painful to the flesh. (Ps. lxxxix. 30–32. Deut. viii. 16. Comp. Ps. cvii. 43.) Let us only mark its gracious effects in our restoration*—instruction (Verse 71, and texts),—healing of our backslidings (Hos. ii. 6, 7, 14), and the continual purging of sins (Isa. xxvii. 9 ; xlviii. 10. Zech. xiii. 9. John, xv. 2)—and then say—' Is not the *faithfulness* of God gloriously displayed?' The Philistines could not understand Samson's riddle—how " Meat could come out of the eater, and sweetness out of the strong." (Judg. xiv. 14.) As little can the world comprehend the fruitfulness of the Christian's trials ; how his gracious Lord sweetens to him the bitter waters of Marah (see Exod. xv. 23–25), and makes the cross not so much the punishment as the remedy of sin. He finds therefore no inclination, and he feels that he has no interest in having any change made in the Lord's appointments, revolting as they may be to the flesh. He readily acknowledges that his merciful designs could not have been accomplished in any other way ; while under trials many sweet tokens of love are vouchsafed, which, under circumstances of outward prosperity, could not have been received with the same gratitude and delight.

You that are living at ease in the indulgence of what this poor world can afford, how little does the Christian envy your portion ! How surely in some future day will you be taught by experience to envy his ! The world's riches are daily becoming poorer, and its pleasures more tasteless ; and what will they be, and how will they appear, when eternity is at hand ! Whereas affliction is the special token of our Father's love (Heb. xii. 6. Rev. iii. 19), conformity to the image of Jesus, and preparation for his ser-

---

* Verse 67, and texts referred to on that verse.

vice and kingdom. It is the only blessing that the Lord
gives, without requiring us to ask for it.*   We receive it,
therefore, as promised, not as threatened ; and when the
" peaceable fruits of righteousness,"† which it worketh in
God's time and way, spring up in our hearts, humbly and
gratefully will we acknowledge the *righteousness* of his
judgments, and the *faithfulness* of his corrections.

76. *Let, I pray thee, thy merciful kindness be for my comfort :*
    according to thy word unto thy servant.

What ! does the Psalmist then seek his comfort from
the very hand that strikes him ?   This is genuine faith,
" Though he slay me, yet will I trust in him." (Job,
xiii. 15.)   The very arm that seems to be uplifted for my
destruction, shall be to me the arm of salvation.

Several of the preceding verses have spoken of affliction.
(Verses 67, 71, 75.)   The Psalmist now prays for alleviation under it.   But of what kind ?   He does not
" beseech the Lord, that it might depart from him."
(2 Cor. xii. 8.)   No.   His repeated acknowledgments of
the supports vouchsafed under it, and the benefits he had
derived from it, had reconciled him to commit its measure
(Jer. x. 24) and continuance to the Lord.   All that he
needs, and all that he asks for, is, a sense of his *merciful
kindness* upon his soul.   Thus he submits to his justice in
accumulated trials, and expects consolation under them,
solely upon the ground of his free favour.   Indeed, it is
hard to hold on under protracted affliction without this

* Philip. i. 29.   Lord Bacon remarks, that 'prosperity is the
blessing of the Old Testament, adversity is the blessing of the
New, which carries the greater benediction, and the clearer revelation of God's favour.'— *Essay on Adversity.*

† Such as patience, experience, hope — the work of tribulation.
Heb. xii. 11 ; with Rom. v. 3–5.

precious support. Patience may restrain murmuring—
but a sense of love alone keeps from fainting. Holiness
is our service—affliction is our exercise—*comfort* is our
gracious reward. All the candles in the world, in the
absence of the sun, can never make the day. The whole
earth, in its brightest visions of fancy, destitute of the
Lord's love, can never cheer nor revive the soul. Indeed,
it matters little where we are, or what we have. In the
fulness of refreshing ordinances, unless the Lord meets us,
and blesses us with his *merciful kindness for our comfort*,
it is " a thirsty land, where no water is." Absalom might
as well have been at Geshur as at Jerusalem, so long as
he " saw not the king's face." (Comp. 2 Sam. xiv. 23, 24.)
Nothing that the Lord " gives us richly to enjoy" will
satisfy, if this source of refreshment be withheld. The
worldling's inquiry is—" Who will show us any good?"
The Christian forms his answer into a prayer—" Lord!
lift thou up the light of thy countenance upon me." (Ps.
iv. 6.) *Let thy merciful kindness be for my comfort.* This
gives the enjoyment of every real good, and supplies the
place of every fancied good. It is a blessing that never
cloys, and will never end : and every fresh taste quenches
the thirst for earthly pleasures. " Whosoever drinketh of
this water"—saith our Divine Saviour—" shall thirst
again. But whosoever drinketh of the water that I shall
give him shall never thirst !" (John, iv. 13, 14.) " Delight
thyself in the Lord ; and he shall give thee the desires of
thine heart." (Ps. xxxvii. 4.)

But, Reader, do you wish to realize this comfort?
Then seek to approach your God by the only way of access.
Learn to contemplate him in the only glass in which a
God of love is seen — " in the face of Jesus Christ."
(2 Cor. iv. 6. Comp. John, xiv. 6.) Guard against looking for comfort from any other source. Beware especially
of that satisfaction in creature-cisterns which draws you

away from " the fountain of living waters." (Jer. ii. 13.)
Learn also to prize this comfort supremely, and not to be
content without some enjoyment, or even with a scanty
measure of enjoyment ; but rather let every day's refreshment be made a step for desiring and attaining renewed
and sweeter refreshment for to-morrow.   Some, however,
appear to look at David's experience, as if *at present* they
could hardly expect to reach its happiness : and so they go
on in a low, depressed, and almost sullen state, refusing
the privileges, which are as freely offered to them as to
others.   But such a state of mind is highly dishonourable
to God.   Let them earnestly plead their interest in the
word of promise — *According to thy word unto thy servant.*
Let them lay their fingers upon one or all of the promises
of their God.   Let them spread before the Lord his own
handwriting and seals ; and their Saviour hath said —
" According to your faith be it unto you."*   " The king

---

* Matt. ix. 29. The writer cannot forbear indulging himself
with a transcript of the prayer of Monica, Augustine's mother, as a
beautiful example of this earnestness and simplicity of faith in
pleading the promises of the word —' Lord, these promises were
made to be made good to some, and why not to me? I hunger ;
I need ; I thirst ; I wait. Here is thy hand-writing in thy word ;
and in the last sacrament, I had thy seal affixed to it. I am resolved
to be as importunate till I have obtained, and as thankful afterwards,
as by thy grace I shall be enabled ; being convinced that I am
utterly lost and undone, if thou hearest not the desires of the
humble : and if thou dost hear and grant, I am so well acquainted
with myself and with my own heart, that I have nothing to glory in ;
but I shall wholly glory in the Lord ; and I do resolve and believe,
that I shall to all eternity celebrate and magnify the riches of thy
grace.   Thy promises are the discoveries of thy purposes, and
vouchsafed as materials for our prayers ; and in my supplications
I am resolved every day to present and tender them back to thee ;
and if thou wilt have regard to them, and appear to be a " God of
truth " to my soul ; a poor creature, that hath long feared to burn
in hell for hypocrisy, will be secured and made happy for ever.   I
am resolved to wait upon thee, and to cast down my soul upon thee

is held in the galleries" (Cant. vii. 5 ; also, vi. 5) ; and, if
he should " make as though he would go farther," he is
willing that we should " constrain him, saying, Abide with
us."*   No veil now but the veil of unbelief need hinder us
from seeing an unclouded everlasting smile of *merciful
kindness* upon our heavenly Father's reconciled face. Only
let us see to it, that he is the first, the habitual object of
our contemplation, the satisfying well-spring of our delight—that he is the one desire, to which every other is
subordinate, and in which every other is absorbed.

Lord Jesus ! I would seek for a renewed enjoyment in
thy merciful kindness.   I would not forget, that it was
this that brought thee down from heaven—that led thee
to endure the death of the cross—that has washed me in
thy precious blood—that visits me with many endearing
tokens of thy love.   Oh, let all my days be spent in the sense
of this *merciful kindness for my comfort,* and in rendering
to thee the unworthy returns of grateful, filial service.

77. *Let thy tender mercies come unto me, that I may live ; for
thy law is my delight.*

Sin is no light trouble to the man of God.   Mercy,
therefore, is to him no common blessing.   Never can he
have—never can he ask, enough.   Hence his repeated
cries.   Mercy brought him out of sin and misery.   Mercy
keeps — holds him on — assures him to the end. (Ps.
cxxxviii. 8.)   Every blessing comes in the way of mercy.

in this way ; and thou hast assured me, thou art a " God of Judgment."   Thou didst promise in judgment.   Thou knewest what
thou didst in making such promises ; and thou wilt be a " God of
Judgment ;" thou knowest when and where to make them good ;
and thou hast pronounced—" Blessed are they that wait for thee."
On thee I will wait, and for this blessing I will hope and look.'

* Comp. Luke, xxiv. 28, 29; with Gen. xxxii. 26-29. Comp. the
invitation given, Cant. iv. 16, instantly accepted, v. 1.

(Ps. cxxxvi. 23–25.) The most careful walker according
to the gospel rule (Gal. vi. 16), needs mercy. The elect
are "vessels of mercy" (Rom. ix. 23)—filled up to the
brim with mercy. The crown of glory at last is received at
the hands of mercy. (Matt. xxv. 34.)

The distinguishing character of God is, that his mercies
are *tender mercies* (Ps. li. 1 ; lxxix. 8)—a father's pitying
(Ps. ciii. 13)—yearning mercies. (Hos. xi. 8. Jer. xxxi.
20.) When his returning prodigal expected probably up-
braiding looks, if not a frown of banishment, how did these
tender mercies bury, not only his sins, but also his very confessions in the depths of the sea, and welcome him without
a cloud to his forsaken home! (Comp. Luke, xv. 20–24.)
The same *tender* considerations put away from his children
all anxiety respecting "what they shall eat, or what they
shall drink, or wherewithal they shall be clothed. (Matt. vi.
25–34.) As a Father he also "chasteneth" (Deut. viii. 5)
them—" he suffereth their manners" (Acts, xiii. 18)—he
"spareth them, as a man spareth his own son that serveth
him" (Mal. iii. 17) ; and, finally, he determineth respecting
each of them by an act of sovereign power—"Thou *shalt call*
me, My Father, and shalt not depart from me." (Jer. iii.
19.) In a yet more endearing character he speaks—"As
one whom *his mother comforteth*, so will I comfort you.
They may forget; yet will I not forget thee." (Isa. lxvi.
13 ; xlix. 15.)

Yet have we no just apprehension of these *tender mercies*, unless they *come unto us*. In the midst of the wide
distribution, let me claim my interest. *Let them come unto
me.* (Verse 41.) Praised be God! the way is open to me.
The mere report is unfruitful. I cannot speak of them
with glow and unction. The application of them is *life*—
not the mere breathing of spiritual existence, but the life
of my life—the living principle of devotedness and enjoyment—living to and for God in every form and sphere, in

every hour and action of the day ; my feebleness becoming strength in the Lord ; " walking up and down in his name." (Zech. x. 12.) This truly is " reigning in life" (Rom. v. 17) ; rising to more of its honour and dignity, and reaching forth to more of its excellence and happiness.

But let us not lose sight of the abundant overflowing spring, from which our life is maintained. " In Christ was life" (John, i. 4) ; and he " came that we might have life, and that we might have it more abundantly." (John, x. 10.) There can be, therefore, no exercises of life without a vital union to Christ—the source of life. Shall we then give up the hope of believing in Christ, till we feel the influence of this spiritual principle ? This would be indeed like refusing to abide in the vine, till we could bring forth fruit ; whereas the branch, while separated from the vine, must ever be fruitless and withered. (John, xv. 4–6.) *We must receive life from Christ, not bring it to him.* Faith implants us in him ; and " Christ dwelling in the heart by faith" becomes the life of the soul, animating it in the ways of God. (Comp. Gal. ii. 20, with Ezek. xxxvi. 27.)

This life, therefore, will manifest itself in *delight in God's* law. We shall not be satisfied to live upon the mere surface of the gospel (which is barren and unproductive, as any other surface, in spiritual usefulness), but we shall search into its hidden treasures, and draw forth its real life and consolation. This " *delight*" will furnish a plea for our use at the throne of grace. ' If this is the fruit and acting of the life of thine own implanting, Lord ! cherish it. Let me live by the influence of *thy tender mercies.* I venture to plead my *delight in thy law,* as an evidence of my adoption into thy family. And, therefore, I would renew my plea and my petition—*Let thy tender mercies come unto me,* that my life may be not only existence, but enjoyment—the beginning, the earnest, of the everlasting life and bliss of heaven.'

78. *Let the proud be ashamed: for they dwelt perversely with me without a cause: but I will meditate in thy precepts.*

The prophecy with which God himself condescended to open the history of the church, has ever since been in the course of accomplishment. (Gen. iii. 15. Comp. Rev. xii. 17.) " Enmity between the seed of the serpent and the seed of the woman," has been the prevailing character and course of the world. " An unjust man is an abomination to the just ; and he that is upright in the way is abomination to the wicked." (Prov. xxix. 27.) David, however, prayed for the confusion of his enemies—not in a vindictive spirit, as if thirsting for their destruction ; but as opening the way for his own more free service of God (Verse 134), and as a chastening, that might eventually turn to their salvation—" Fill their faces with shame, *that they may seek thy name, O Lord!*" (Ps. lxxxiii. 16.) That his prayer was the expression of his tender compassion, rather than of resentful feeling, is sufficiently evident from his affectionate weeping concern for their immortal interests. (Verses 53, 136, 158.) Prayers of the same deprecating character dropped from the lips of the gentle and compassionate Saviour (Ps. lxix. 21–23) : while the objects of his awful deprecations were interested in the most yearning sympathies of his heart. (Comp. Matt. xxiii. 37.) A regard also for the honour of God dictated this prayer. David knew that the malice of his enemies against him was only the working of their enmity against God ; that it was not so much him that they hated and persecuted, as God in him. And therefore as a servant of God he could appeal — " Do not I hate them, O Lord, that hate thee ? and am not I grieved at those that rise up against thee ? *I hate them with perfect hatred; I count them mine enemies.*" (Ps. cxxxix. 21, 22.) The followers of a despised Saviour must indeed expect to be sorely distressed with the *perverse-ness of the proud.* But when, like their Master, they can testify that it is *without a cause* (Ps. xxxv. 19 ; lxix. 4, with John, xv. 25), how cheering are their Master's words! " Blessed are ye, when men shall revile you, and persecute you, and shall say all manner of evil against you falsely for my sake. Rejoice, and be exceeding glad ; for great is your reward in heaven." (Matt. v. 11, 12.)

And have you, reader, been exercised with trials from an ungodly world ? Has the derision of the proud, or the slight or ill-treatment of the ungodly, never excited re-vengeful feelings within? Have you always been enabled to set your Saviour's example before you, and " in patience possessing your soul," to refer your cause to your Almighty Friend? " O Lord, I am oppressed, undertake for me." (Isa. xxxviii. 14. Comp. Ps. cxl. 12, 13.) Remember, he has engaged to take up your cause—" Shall not God avenge his own elect, which cry day and night unto him, though he bear long with them ? *I tell you that he will avenge them speedily.*" (Luke, xviii. 7, 8.)

But learn in the hour of trial where to go, and what to do. Go to the word of God for direction and support. *Meditate in his precepts.* There is often a hurry of mind in times of difficulty, which unhinges the soul from the simple exercise of faith. But habit brings practice, and steadiness, and simplicity, enabling us most sweetly to fix our hearts upon the word of God, and to apply its directions and encouragements to the present exigency. Our enemies fight against us with an arm of flesh. We resist them with the armour of the word of God. And how inestimably precious is the armour, refuge, strength, and consolation, here provided for us against every effort to disturb our peace, " or separate our hearts from the love of God, which is in Christ Jesus our Lord ! "

79. *Let those that fear thee turn unto me, and those that have known thy testimonies.*

As the believer finds trouble from the world, he prays that he may find help from the Lord's people. The very sight of our Father's family is cheering. It brings not only fellowship but help. For the wise distribution of gifts in the body—each having his own gift—was ordained for the mutual help and sympathy of the several members. (1 Cor. xii. 7. Eph. iv. 15, 16.) It is painful therefore to see Christians often walking aloof from each other, and suffering coldness, distance, differences and distrust to divide them from their brethren. Who then will not pray, that he, who has the hearts of all his people in his hand, would *turn the hearts of those that fear him and know his testimonies,* unto their brethren? It was the honour of Mordecai, that he was " accepted of the multitude of his brethren." (Esth. x. 3.) In the primitive church, " Demetrius had good report of all men, and of the truth itself " (3 John, 12); and the members of the church generally " did eat their meat with gladness and singleness of heart ; praising God, and *having favour with all the people.*" (Acts, ii. 46, 47.) ' Then,' as Chrysostom exultingly exclaims, ' the Church was a little heaven.' Then they could say to each other—" Behold, how good and pleasant it is for brethren to dwell together in unity !"* and even their Heathen neighbours were awed and con-

---

* Ps. cxxxiii. 1.   Most truly catholic was the rule of the excellent Philip Henry, and most consistently exemplified in his Christian conduct, determining ' in those things, in which all the people of God are agreed, to spend my zeal; and as for other things about which they differ, to walk according to the light God hath given me, and charitably to believe others to do so too.'—Life, WILLIAMS' *Edition,* p. 127.

strained into the confession—" See how these Christians love one another."

Alas! that our Jerusalem should no longer exhibit the picture of a " city compact together" (Ps. cxxii. 3)—that so many " walls of partition" should separate brother from brother, so that our Zion has very rarely been exhibited in her " perfection of beauty," when " the multitude of them that believed were of one heart and of one soul." (Ps. l. 2, with Acts, iv. 32.) Prejudice and misconception divided Job from his friends. (Job, vi. 29.) Want of forbearance cankered the union of the members of the church of Rome (Rom. xiv., xv. 1–7), and even prevailed to separate chief friends—Paul and Barnabas. (Acts, xv. 37.) Diversity of sentiment injured the influence of brotherly love at Corinth. (1 Cor. i. 10–12.) And thus it has been in every successive age of the church; so that the full answer to the Redeemer's prayer, and the grand display to the world of the Divine original of the gospel, is yet to be manifested. (John, xvii. 21.) But as " the communion of saints" was the peculiar feature of primitive Christianity, and ever since has formed an article of her faith; in proportion as we return to the primitive standard, we shall hold closer fellowship with each other—as " members of one body" (1 Cor. xii. 12–27)—" considering one another, to provoke unto love and to good works" (Heb. x. 24)—"bearing one another's burdens" (Gal. vi. 2; v. 13);—and " receiving one another, as Christ also received us, to the glory of God." (Rom. xv. 7.)

Want of Christian self-denial presents the main hindrance to this " keeping the unity of the spirit in the bond of peace." But—admitting that some of the brethren are " weak in the faith" in comparison with ourselves—are we then to be ' rolling endlessly the returning stone,'* obtruding always the same stumbling-offence upon them?

* Morning Exercises, Oct. 1682.

(Rom. xiv. 1.)   We are " not to please ourselves" in com-
pelling them to adopt our views ; but rather to " receive
them, and bear their infirmities." (Rom. xv. 1.)   Accursed
be that charity, that is preserved by " the shipwreck of
faith !" But though scriptural truth must never be denied,
there are times when it may be forborne.   The Apostle
" knew and was persuaded of the Lord Jesus, that there
was nothing unclean of itself" (Rom. xiv. 14) ; yet he
would rather allow even the misconception of conscience,
until clearer light should be given, than endanger the unity
of the church.   Liberty must give place to love ; and for
himself, he would rather restrain himself from lawful indulgence, than hazard the safety of a weaker brother, or
turn from one that loved his Saviour. (Rom. xiv. 15, 16.
1 Cor. viii. 13. Comp. Phil. iii. 15, 16.)   Wherever, therefore, in the judgment of Christian charity, we discover
those " that love our Lord Jesus Christ in sincerity" (Eph.
vi. 24. Comp. 1 John, iii. 14), we must be ready to give
them our very hearts, to view them as brethren, as one with
ourselves, and to welcome them with brotherly love, as those
whom, with all their infirmities, Jesus " is not ashamed to
call his brethren." (Heb. ii. 11, 12.) We must be ready to
turn to them, as those *that fear God, and have known his
testimonies.*

And does not the believer's anxiety for the company and
assistance of the Lord's people rebuke Christian professors,
who are far too closely linked to the society of the world?
Surely, if the lovely attraction of many of its most avowed
votaries can compensate for the absence of their Saviour's
image, they can have but little relish for that heavenly
enjoyment, which unites the children of God together in
close and hallowed communion with God.   And do we not
see a proof of the deteriorating influence of this worldly
spirit, in their readiness to feel disgust at the infirmities of
the real brethren of the Lord, and to neglect the image of

Christ in them, from the unsightliness of the garb, which may sometimes cover it?

But let us mark the completeness of the Christian — combining the fear with the knowledge of God. Knowledge without fear would be self-confidence. Fear without knowledge would be bondage. But *the knowledge of his testimonies*, connected with *an acquaintance with his ways*, moulds the character of men of God into the spirit of love; and qualifies them, " as fathers" (1 John, ii. 13, 14) in the gospel, to counsel the weak and inexperienced. Should we, however, be excluded from the privilege of their intercourse; or should they be prevented from *turning unto us;* may it not be the appointed means of leading us to a more simple dependence on Divine teaching and grace, and to a more blessed anticipation of our Father's house in heaven, where all will be harmony, peace, and love? ' We shall carry truth and the knowledge of God to heaven with us; we shall carry purity thither, devotedness of soul to God and our Redeemer, Divine love and joy, if we have these beginnings here, with whatsoever else of permanent excellence, that hath a settled, fixed seat and place in our souls now: and shall there have them in perfection. But do you think we shall carry strife to heaven? shall we carry anger to heaven? Envyings, heart-burnings, animosities; shall we carry these to heaven with us? Let us labour to divest ourselves, and strike off from our spirits everything that shall not go with us to heaven, or is equally unsuitable to our end and way, that there may be nothing to obstruct and hinder our " abundant entrance" at length into the everlasting kingdom.'*

* Howe's *Works*, vol. iv. 126, 127 —' It will be one of the felicities of heaven,' (as Milner sweetly remarks upon the prejudices subsisting between Bernard and the supposed heretics of his day), ' that saints shall no longer misunderstand each other.'—Milner's *History of the Church*, iii. 384.

80. *Let my heart be sound in thy statutes, that I be not ashamed.*

The *perverseness of the proud* will be sure to put them to *shame.* (Verse 78.) As the preservative from this *shame,* David prays therefore for *a sound heart*—filled with solid principle—delivered into the mould of the word (Rom. vi. 17, Gr.)—like the sacrifices of the law—entire for God. (Lev. xxii. 22, 23. Comp. Mal. i. 8.) Often had he prayed for Divine teaching (Verses 12, 33, 64, 68)—now he begs for *soundness in the Lord's statutes.* How many "have made shipwreck of faith and of a good conscience" (1 Tim. i. 19), from an unsound heart! Ignorant of the spirituality of God's requirements, and resting in an outward obedience, they falsely conceive themselves to be "alive without the law" (Rom. vii. 9), and "touching the righteousness that is of the law, blameless." (Phil. iii. 6.) Others go a little beyond the surface; while the want of "simplicity and godly sincerity," of brokenness of heart, love to the Saviour, and dependence upon his grace, sooner or later discovers to their eternal confusion, that "the root of the matter is" not "in them." "Their root shall be as rottenness, and their blossom shall go up as dust. Their goodness is as a morning cloud, and as the early dew it goeth away." (Isa. v. 24. Hos. vi. 4. Comp. Matt. xiii. 20, 21.) An unsound professor, like beautiful fruit, may attract the careless eye; but a more narrow inspection will show a worm at the core, which has spoiled nearly to the surface.* Such religion is only a shrivelled mass of inactive formality —a dead image of a living thing.

Alas! how common is it to profess to take Christ for a

* 'Quæ splendent in conspectu hominis, sordent in conspectu judicis.' Comp. Luke, xvi. 15. 1 Sam. xvi. 7.

Saviour, while the heart is evidently worshipping Mammon
as its God!—constrained—not inclined—to the Lord's
statutes! How possible is it to be "carnally-minded" in
the daily routine of spiritual exercises! How important
is the recollection, that no change of place, of company, or
of circumstances, can of itself effect a change of heart!
"Saul among the prophets" was Saul still; with "another
heart" (1 Sam. x. 9–12) indeed, but not a new heart. Sin
was restrained, but not crucified. He "went out," therefore, as one of his progenitors, "from the presence of the
Lord" (Gen. iv. 16), and perished, a miserable apostate from
the statutes of his God. Will profession—knowledge—
gifts—feelings—privileges—avail for a *sound heart?*
Need we speak of Judas—a follower—nay, even, an
apostle of Jesus Christ—living in a familiar intercourse with
his Lord—yet with all his privileges—all his profession,
"gone to his own place" (Acts, i. 25)—the melancholy
victim of his own self-deceitfulness? Need we allude to
Balaam—"the man whose eyes were open—which heard
the words of God—which saw the vision of the Almighty"
—who could in the ken of his eye mark the goodliness of
the Lord's inheritance, and even in the distant horizon
catch a glimpse of "Jacob's star and sceptre," *and yet*
"*loved the wages of unrighteousness?*" (Numb. xxiv. 2–5,
17. 2 Pet. ii. 15.) Need we bring to the mind's eye
Ananias and Sapphira? (Acts, v. 1–10.) Alexander (Acts,
xix. 33, 34, with 1 Tim. i. 20; 2 Tim. iv. 14) and Demas
(Col. iv. 14. Philem. 24, with 2 Tim. iv. 10)—and others
of like stamp—all of whom once shone as stars (Rev. xii.
4) in the firmament of the church—need we speak of the
end of these men, to give energy to the prayer—*Let my
heart be sound in thy statutes?*

How fearful the thought of being "a branch in the
true vine" only by profession! to be "taken away" at
length—"cast forth as a branch—withered—gathered—

cast into the fire—burned!" (John, xv. 2, 6.) It is in the inner man that hypocrisy sets up its throne; whence it commands the outward acts into whatever shape or form may be best suited to effect its purpose. The upright Christian will therefore begin with calling in the help and light of God to ascertain the *soundness of his heart.* " Search me, O God, and know my heart; try me, and know my thoughts; and see if there be any wicked way in me." (Ps. cxxxix. 23, 24.) Can there be a true and solid work, where there is a professed change of heart, and no manifested change of temper and conduct? Can that *heart*, which is found upon inquiry to be earthly—unprofitable under the power of the word (Heb. vi. 8)—"regarding" secret "iniquity" (Ps. lxvi. 18)—seeking bye-ends of praise (2 Kings, x. 16), reputation (John, xii. 43), or gain (John, vi. 26. 1 Tim. vi. 5)—and for the attainment of these ends shrinking from the appointed cross — can that *heart be sound in the Lord's statutes?* Impossible.

But, on the other hand, do you find that your trust in God is sincere, your desire towards him supreme, your obedience to him entire? Prize those evidences of *soundness of heart.* Thank God for them. They are the workings of his mighty Spirit in your heart—perhaps the answer to the prayer which that same Spirit had indited, *Let my heart be sound in thy statutes.* Diligently improve all the means of grace for keeping your heart in a vigorous state. Be daily—yea, continually—abiding in the vine, and receiving life and health from its fulness. (John, xv. 4, 5.) Be much conversant with the word of God — loving it for itself—its holiness—its practical influences. Be chiefly afraid of inward decays—of a barren, sapless notion of experimental truth; remembering, that except your profession be constantly watered at the root, " the things that remain in you will be ready to die." (Rev. iii. 2.) Specially " commune with your own heart." Watch it jealously,

because of its pioneness to live upon itself—its own graces
or fancied goodness (a sure symptom of unsoundness)—
instead of " living by the faith of the Son of God." Examine your settled judgment, your deliberate choice, your
outgoing affections, your habitual, allowed practice ; applying to every detection of unsoundness the blood of
Christ, as the sovereign remedy for the diseases of a " deceitful and desperately wicked heart."

But it may be said—will not these exercises of godly
jealousy hinder our Christian assurance ? Far from it.
They will form an efficient preservative from carnal security.
They will induce increasing tenderness, activity, and circumspection, in our daily walk ; and thus, instead of retarding the enjoyment of our heavenly privilege, they will
settle the foundation of a peaceful temperament. (Verse 6.
1 John, iii. 20, 21.) *It is a light and careless frame*, that is
the real hindrance to confidence. An unsound professor
knows nothing of the true spirit of adoption—nothing of
that holy familiarity, with which a child of God unbosoms
himself to his heavenly Father ; and if he preserves an
empty name in the church, he will be *put to shame* before
the universe of God. (Comp. Dan. xii. 2. Luke, xii. 1, 2.)
But the *sound heart* is connected with " a hope that maketh
not ashamed"—the full blessing of scriptural confidence.
For the heart is made *sound* by the " sprinkling of the
blood of Christ ;" and when thus " sprinkled from an evil
conscience," we " have boldness" to " draw near"—yea,
even to " enter into the holiest,"—" in full assurance of
faith." (See Heb. x. 19–22.) Blessed privilege of access
and communion with our reconciled God ! Every moment
endears the Saviour to our souls, and enlivens the hope of
his glorious coming, as the joyful consummation of all the
prospects of faith—" Herein is our love made perfect, *that
we may have boldness in the day of judgment.*" (1 John,
iv. 17.)

PART XI.

81. My soul fainteth for thy salvation; but I hope in thy word.

THE salvation of the Gospel was the constant object of faith and desire to the Lord's people under the old dispensation. Long had the church triumphed in the glowing anticipation, as if in the full possession of the promised blessing — " It shall be said in that day, Lo, this is our God ; we have waited for him, we will be glad and rejoice in his salvation. I will greatly rejoice in the Lord ; my soul shall be joyful in my God ; for *he hath clothed* me with the garments of salvation ; he hath covered me with the robe of righteousness ; as a bridegroom decketh himself with ornaments, and as a bride adorneth herself with her jewels." (Isa. xxv. 9 ; lxi. 10.) And as it was the joy of their living moments, so was it the support and consolation of their dying hours. " I have waited for thy salvation, O Lord !" (Gen. xlix. 18), was the expression of the dying patriarch's faith. And how cheering were the last words of this " sweet Psalmist of Israel," whose *soul was now fainting for God's salvation*, even in his dark and foreboding family prospect ! " Although my house be not so with God, yet hath he made with me an everlasting covenant, ordered in all things and sure : for this is *all my salvation*, and all my desire, although he make it not to grow." (2 Sam. xxiii. 5.) Good old Simeon, in the break of the gospel-day, was ready to " depart in peace, for his eyes had

seen God's salvation." (Luke, ii. 28–30, also 25.)   And
shall not we, under this heavenly influence, naturally appropriate these feelings of ancient believers to ourselves ?
What interpreter but experience will be needed to explain
them ?   The uneasiness felt by any interruption of our enjoyment, will show the soul to be *fainting for this salvation.*
Nothing will satisfy but the Saviour.   The tempting offer
of " all the kingdoms of the world, and the glory of them,"
will fail in attraction.   Still the cry will be—" Say unto my
soul, I am thy salvation. (Ps. xxxv. 3.)   *Let thy mercies
come also unto me, O Lord; even thy salvation, according to
thy word."* (Verse 41.)

As the lowest expectant of this salvation, am not I
richer than the sole possessor of this world's portion ?   And
therefore if the Lord hides his face, I would look to no other
quarter ; I would stay by him, and " wait on him," though
days and months and years may pass away, " until he have
mercy upon me." (Ps. cxxiii. 1, 2. Comp. Isa. viii. 17. Mic.
vii. 9.)   *My soul fainteth for his salvation:* and—pressing to
my lips the fullest cup of earth's best joy—my heart would
burst with despair of satisfaction, " but" that " *I hope in
his word."* (Ps. cxxx. 5.)   " By this hope I am saved."
(Rom. viii. 24.)   In " the patience of hope" (1 Thess. i. 3)
I am resolved to wait until the last moment, lying at the
footstool of my Saviour.   I am looking for the " assurance
of this hope" (Heb. vi. 11)—when, in the joyous anticipation of eternity, and with " the earnest of" the heavenly
" inheritance" in my soul, I shall echo the voice of my
coming Saviour—" Even so come, Lord Jesus." (Rev.
xxii. 20.)

Oh, how precious and important a part of our armour is
Hope !   As a " helmet" (Eph. vi. 17. 1 Thess. v. 8), it has
" covered our head in the day of battle" from many a " fiery
dart of the wicked."   In times of darkness—when the restless foe hides the prospect from the eye of faith, and the

child of God can scarcely, if at all, mount up and sing —
even then hope remains, and lights a taper in moments dark
as the chamber of the grave — " *Yet* the Lord will command
his loving-kindness in the day-time ; and in the night-
season his song shall be with me, and my prayer unto the
God of my life." (Ps. xlii. 8.) And when the afflicted,
tempest-tossed soul is trembling at the prospect of impending danger — at this moment of infinite peril, Hope holds
out the " anchor sure and stedfast" (Heb. vi. 19) ; so that
in the awful crisis, when " deep calleth unto deep, and all
the waves and billows are going over us" (Ps. xlii. 7), most
unexpectedly " an entrance is ministered unto us *abundantly*," in the Lord's best time, into our desired haven. (2 Pet.
i. 11. Ps. cvii. 30.) And it is this hope alone that sustains
us. Were we to conceive of God according to the notions
of our own hearts, we should give way to most unbelieving patience. But the Divine character — as it shines forth
in the word with such love and wisdom, such tenderness and
grace — invigorates our hope. The strength of the strongest of God's people proves but small, when afflictions press
heavily, and expected help is delayed. But though the *soul
fainteth*, it cannot fail. We depend not on what we see or
feel, but on what *the word* promises. If God has engaged,
it must be fulfilled, be the difficulties — nay, impossibilities
— what they may. Fixed, therefore, upon this sure foundation, with our father Abraham, "against hope" from what
we see, "we believe in hope" from what God has promised.
(Rom. iv. 18.) Thus *the word* is faith's sure venture for
eternity — stamped with such a marvellous, mysterious impression of Divine glory and faithfulness, and communicating such Divine power and refreshment, that the believer
cannot but produce his experience of its efficacy for the
support of his tempted brethren — " I had fainted, unless I
had believed to see the goodness of the Lord in the land of
the living. Wait on the Lord : be of good courage, and he

shall strengthen thine heart : wait, I say, on the Lord."
(Ps. xxvii. 13, 14.)

82. *Mine eyes fail for thy word, saying, When wilt thou comfort me?*

Though the believer may be enabled, in the habitual
working of faith, to sustain his *hope in the word*, yet " hope
deferred maketh the heart sick." (Prov. xiii. 12.)   Still,
Christian, as you value the promise, trust the assurance.
Do not be discouraged by present appearances.   The sunshine is behind the cloud.   " The vision is for an appointed
time ; though it tarry, wait for it." (Hab. ii. 3.)   " The
Lord is not slack concerning his promise," but we are hasty
in looking for it. (Comp. 2 Pet. iii. 9, with Isa. v. 19 ;
xxviii. 16.)   *The failing of our eyes* is the impatience of the
will, " limiting God" (Ps. lxxviii. 41) to our own time,
ways, and means.   Faith may be exercised in not seeing his
reasons—not being able to harmonize his promises with his
providences, or his outward dispensations with his Divine
perfections. (Jer. xii. 1.)   But let us leave this to him, and
be " still, and know that he is God." (Ps. xlvi. 10.)   We
shall find in the end, that perseverance in waiting has
turned to double advantage ; and that even when the present answer to prayer, and also sensible comfort and acceptance have been withheld ; yet that important blessings
have been accomplished, and the merciful purposes vouchsafed in bringing the wayward will into more entire subjection to himself.   Yes—the blessing will be so much the
sweeter, from being vouchsafed in the Lord's best time.
Waiting time—whatever weariness may attend it—is precious time, and not a moment of it will be lost.   The Lord
secretly upholds faith and patience, so that every step of
feeble perseverance in the way brings with it unspeakable
delight.   Even while *our eyes fail* for the fulfilment of *the*

word, peace is found in submission and joyful expectation ; and instead of a time of hardness, indolence, or carelessness, the Lord's return is anticipated the more intensely, as his absence had been felt to be the most painful trial.   For as well might the stars supply the place of the sun, as outward comforts, or even the external duties of religion, supply to the waiting soul the place of an absent God.

Never, however, let us forget, that the real cause of separation between God and a sinner is removed.   The way of access is opened by the blood of Jesus (Heb. x. 19, 20) ; and in this way we must be found waiting, until he look upon us.   Here will our cry—" *When wilt thou comfort me?*" be abundantly answered ; and though the sovereignty of God be exhibited in the time and measure of his consolations, yet the general rule will be—" According to your faith, be it unto you." (Matt. ix. 29.)

But if unbelief clouds our comfort, turn the eye more simply to the " *word*" as testifying of Jesus.   Here alone is the ground of comfort ; and the more confidently we expect, the more patiently we will look.   Nor shall we ever look in vain.   Sin will be rebuked (Ps. lxxxix. 30–32). But restoration and acceptance are assured.   We shall obtain—not the spurious comfort of delusion—but those wholesome comforts, founded upon the word of promise, and connected with contrition, peace, love, joy, and triumph. The gospel shows hell deserved, and heaven purchased— thus combining conviction and faith.   Indeed, conviction without faith, would be legal sorrow ; as assurance without conviction would be gospel presumption.   Paul's experience happily united both.   Never was man at the same moment more exercised with conflict, and yet more established in assurance. (Comp. Rom. vii. 14–25 ; viii. 33–39.)   Thus may we maintain our assurance *as really* in wrestling trouble as in exulting joy ; honouring the Lord by an humble, patient spirit—in Bernard's resolution—' I will never come away from thee without thee'—in the true spirit of the wrestling patriarch—" I will not let thee go, except thou bless me." (Gen. xxxii. 26.)

But we sometimes seem to go " mourning without the sun" (Job, xxx. 28),—" shut up, and we cannot come forth " (Ps. lxxxviii. 8),—straitened in our desires and ex-pectations—doing little for the Lord—with little enjoy-ment in our own souls, and little apparent usefulness to the Church.   At such seasons it is our clear duty and privilege to " wait upon the Lord, that hideth his face from the house of Jacob, and to *look for him*." (Isa. viii. 17.)   " He waiteth that he may be gracious.   He is a God of Judg-ment ; and blessed are all they that wait for him."*   He waits—not because he is reluctant to give, but that we may be fitted to receive.

83. *For I am become like a bottle in the smoke, yet do I not*
forget thy statutes.

What an affecting picture of misery !   Not only were his patience and hope—but his very body—" dried up" by long-continued affliction. (Prov. xvii. 22.)   This is he, who in the prime of youth was " ruddy and of a beautiful coun-tenance, and goodly to look to" (1 Sam. xvi. 12),—now shrivelled up like a *bottle* of skin (Josh. ix. 4. Matt. ix. 17), hung up *in the smoke !*   Such is the mark that the rod of

---

* Isa. xxx. 18. ' Thou mayest seek after honours, and not obtain them ; thou mayest labour for riches, and yet remain poor; thou mayest dote on pleasures, and have many sorrows.   But our God, of his supreme goodness, says—Who ever sought me, and found me not ? Who ever desired me, and obtained me not ? Who ever loved me, and missed of me ?   I am with him, that seeks for me.   He hath me already, that wisheth for me ; and he that loveth me, is sure of my love. The way to come to me, is neither long nor difficult.'—Augustine.

" chastening" leaves on the body of humiliation.* The soul is strengthened—the body withers—under the stroke.

What might naturally have been expected to have been the result of this lengthened exercise? Saul, under protracted trial, resorted to the devil for relief. (1 Sam. xxviii. 6, 7.) An infidel nation took occasion from thence to throw off the yoke. (Mal. iii. 13, 14, with ii. 17.) Even a good man, under a few hours' trial, murmurs against God—nay, even defends his murmuring. (Jonah, iv. 7–9.) How did this man of God behave? When his *soul was fainting, his hope in the word* kept him from sinking. (Verse 81.) Under the further continuance of the trial, the same recollection gives him support—*yet do I not forget thy statutes.* (Comp. Verses 51, 61, 109, 141 ; xliv. 17–19.)

Now—Christian—do not expect a new way to heaven to be made for you. Prepare for the cross. It may be— as with David—a heavy, long-continued burden, and, should it come—look on it as your appointed trial of faith, and your training discipline for more enduring conflicts. And remember that your determined resolution rather to pine away in affliction, than " make a way of escape" by sin—is the proof of the reality of his own grace in you, and of his faithful love towards you. Think how honourably he manifests your relation to Christ, by causing " his sufferings to abound in you," and making you " bear in your body the marks of the Lord Jesus." (2 Cor. i. 5. Gal. vi. 17. Comp. 1 Pet. iv. 13.) And do you not thus realize, as you could not otherwise do, the sympathy of our High Priest, who was himself " a root out of a dry ground, having no form nor comeliness, and no beauty that he should be desired—despised and rejected of men" (Isa. liii. 2, 3) to the end? Oh, what a

* Ps. xxxix. 11. Comp. xxxi. 12; cii. 3. The history of Job: xxx. 30. The woeful misery of the church: Lam. iv. 8; v. 10. The sufferings of the Saviour: Ps. xxii. 15. Isa. lii. 14.

supporting cordial to his afflicted people is the sympathy of
this suffering, tempted Saviour! (Heb. iv. 15 ; ii. 18.)

But to look at David, under his long-continued trials,
preserving his recollection of *the Lord's statutes*—what a
striking evidence of the presence of his God, and the sustaining power of his word! If we then—blessed with much
larger Scriptures than he—fail in deriving from them the
same support, it can only be, that we do not search them in
a dependent, prayerful, and humble spirit—that we do not
simply look for the revelation of Christ ; to mark his glory,
and to increase in the knowledge of Him. (John, v. 39.)
In this spirit we should have more to say of the comfort of
remembering *the Lord's statutes;* and of their upholding
influence, when all other stays were found as " the trust in
the shadow of Egypt—shame and confusion." (Isa. xxx·
1–3.)

Job's history strikingly illustrates both the trial and its
sanctified results. When " scraping himself with a potsherd,
and sitting down among the ashes,"—the temporary victim
of Satanic power—he might well have taken up the complaint, *I am become like a bottle in the smoke.* But when
in this hour of temptation he was enabled to resist the
tempter in the person of his own wife, and commit himself
with implicit resignation into the hands of his faithful God,
" What! shall we receive good at the hand of God, and
shall we not receive evil?" (Job, ii. 7–10)—was not this
the confidence,—*Yet do I not forget thy statutes?*

This confidence is indeed an encouraging seal of the
Lord's love to our souls. For we never should have remembered *his statutes*, had he not written his covenant
promises upon our hearts. (Jer. xxxi. 31–34.) And how
much more honourable to our God is it than the desponding
complaint—" The Lord hath forsaken me, and my God hath
forgotten me!" (Isa. xlix. 14.) Let us watch then against

a proud sullenness under every little trial—such as the coldness of friends, the unkindness of enemies, or our Father's providential dispensations. How sinful to allow hard thoughts of him, whose name and character, "without variableness or shadow of turning," is "Love!" A steady trust in the long and wearisome seasons of tribulation, is indeed "to glorify God in the fires." (Isa. xxiv. 15.) Nothing honours him so much as this enduring, overcoming faith, persevering in despite of opposition, in destitution of all outward prospects of relief. It is when "against hope we believe in hope, not staggering at the promise of God through unbelief," that we are "strong in faith, giving glory to God." (Rom. iv. 18–20.)

84. *How many are the days of thy servant? When wilt thou execute judgment on them that persecute me?—*
85. *The proud have digged pits for me, which are not after thy law.*

Though a steady confidence in severe and protracted exercise may enable us, *not to forget the statutes;* yet we shall hasten to carry our complaint before him. *How many are the days of thy servant?*—my days of affliction under the "fury of the oppressor." To complain *of* God is dishonourable unbelief. (Jonah, iv. 1–3.) To complain to God is the mark of his "elect, which cry day and night unto him, though he bears long with them." (Luke, xviii. 7, with Ps. vi. 3; xiii. 1, 2.) Christians! study this instructive pattern; and, when exposed to the lawless devices of *the proud,* forget not your hiding-place. God in Christ is your stronghold, "whereunto you may continually resort. He *hath given commandment to save you.*" (Ps. lxxi. 3.) Your trial has done its appointed work, when it has brought you to him; and inclined you, after your blessed Master's example, instead of taking the vengeance into your own hands, to commit yourself and your cause " to him that judgeth righteously."* 'And this,' as Archbishop Leighton excellently observes, ' is the true method of Christian patience — that which quiets the mind, and keeps it from the boiling tumultuous thoughts of revenge ; to turn the whole matter into God's hands ; to resign it over to him, to prosecute when and as he thinks good. Not as the most, who had rather, if they had power, do for themselves, and be their own avengers : and, because they have not power, do offer up such bitter curses and prayers for revenge unto God, as are most hateful to him, and differ wholly from this calm and holy way of committing matters to his judgments. The common way of referring things to God is indeed impious and dishonourable to him, being really no other than calling him to be a servant and executioner of our passion. We ordinarily mistake his justice, and judge of it according to our own precipitate and distempered minds. If wicked men be not crossed in their designs, and their wickedness evidently crushed, just when we would have it, we are ready to give up the matter as desperate ; or at least to abate of those confident and reverent thoughts of Divine justice which we owe him. However things go, this ought to be fixed in our hearts, that he that sits in heaven judgeth righteously, and executes that his righteous judgment in the fittest season.'

Usually the Psalmist is expressing his love for the law. Here he is complaining against his enemies ; yet still implying the same spirit, that *the pits, which the proud dug for him* (Ps. xxxv. 7), *were not after God's law.* The martyr's cry under the altar shows the acceptance of this complaint (see Rev. vi. 9–11) ; " seeing it is a righteous thing with God to recompense tribulation to them that trouble" his people, " and to them that are troubled rest." (2 Thess. i.

---

* 1 Pet. ii. 23, and Archbishop Leighton on the passage.

6, 7.) Some of us indeed have known but little of " cruel mockings" (Heb. xi. 36) and bitter *persecutions.* Let such be thankful for the merciful exemption from this " hardness" (2 Tim. ii. 3) : but let them gird on their armour for the conflict. Let none of us, in the determination to " live godly in Christ Jesus," expect to escape " persecution." (2 Tim. iii. 12.) Let us " count the cost" (Luke, xiv. 28) of suffering for Christ, whether we shall be able to abide it. For the mere spiritless notions, or for the unenlivened forms of religion, of which we have never felt the power, nor tasted the sweetness, it would be little worth our while to expose ourselves to inconvenience. But if we understand the grand substantials of the gospel — if we are clearly assured of their reality, practically acknowledge their influence, and experimentally realize their enjoyment, we shall dare the persecuting malice of *the proud* in defence of a treasure dearer to us than life itself. Should we, however, be too rich to part with all for Christ, or too high in the estimation of the world to confess his despised followers, it will be no marvel, or rather a marvel of mercy, if he should sweep away our riches, and suffer *the proud to dig pits for us.* To make this world " a wilderness or a land of darkness" to us, may be his wisely-ordained means to turn us back to himself as our portion, to his word as our support, to his people as our choice companions, and to heaven as our eternal rest.

86. *All thy commandments are faithful: they persecute me wrongfully; help thou me.*

In the lengthened duration of trials, the *eyes fail with looking upward,* the voice of prayer grows faint, and in a moment of weakness, the faithfulness of God is almost questioned, as if we should go mourning to the very end of our days. It is at such a season that he who delights to

"comfort them that are cast down" (2 Cor. vii. 6), realizes
to the view of faith the unchangeable *faithfulness of his
commandments* with respect to his people.   In this recollection we can "look up and lift up our heads," and "go on
our way," if not "rejoicing," yet at least with humble acquiescence ; assured, that in the perseverance of faith and
hope, we shall ultimately be "more than conquerors through
him that loved us." (Rom. viii. 37.)

Many Old Testament histories beautifully illustrate the
reward of this simplicity of faith in temporal emergencies.*
When Asa's "hands were *made strong* by the *hands of the
mighty God of Jacob*," "*his bow abode in strength*." (Gen. xlix.
24.)   When at a subsequent period he "*trusted in man, and
made flesh his arm, and his heart departed from the Lord*"
(Comp. Jer. xvii. 5–8), he *became, like Samson*, "*weak, and as
another man*." (Judg. xvi. 7, with 2 Chron. xvi. 7.)   So true
is it, that no past communications of Divine strength can
stand in the stead of the daily habit of dependence upon
the Lord, without which we are utterly helpless, and are
overthrown in every conflict.   Our best prosperity, therefore, is to leave our cause in his hands, looking upward in
the simplicity of wretchedness for his help : '*All thy commandments are faithful; they persecute me wrongfully; help
thou me.*   Wretched and forlorn I am ; but thy truth is my
shield.'

Believer !   This is your only posture of resistance.
Should you enter the field of conflict without this "shield
of faith," some crevice will be found in your panoply,
through which a "fiery dart" will inflict a poisonous
wound." (Eph. vi. 16.)   But how can faith be exercised
without a distinct acquaintance with the object of faith ?
We cannot repose trust in, or expect help from, an unknown

---

* The examples of Asa, 2 Chron. xiv. 10–12, and Jehoshaphat,
2 Chron. xx. 1–30, may be referred to.

God—an offended God, whom every day's transgression has made our enemy. There must, then, be reconciliation, before there can be help. Those, therefore, who are unreconciled by the death of Christ, cry for help to a God, who does not hear, accept, or answer, them. But when Christ is known as " the peace," and the way of access to God, what instance can there be of trial or difficulty, when our reliance upon the Lord will fail? Not indeed that we shall always return from the throne of grace with the wished-for relief. For too often we bring our burden before the Lord, and yet through distrust neglect to *leave* it with him. Oh! let us remember, when we go to Jesus, that we go to a tried, long-proved, and faithful friend. Dependence upon him is victory. " The good fight" is the fight " of faith." (1 Tim. vi. 12.) We are best able to resist our enemy upon our knees; and even such a short prayer as this—*Help thou me*—will bring down the strength of Omnipotence on our side. But we might as well expect to crush a giant with a straw, as to enter the spiritual conflict with weapons of carnal warfare. Every trial realizes experimentally the help of a faithful Saviour. He does indeed deliver gloriously; and leaves us nothing to do, but to " stand still," wonder, and praise. " Fear ye not, stand still, and see the salvation of the Lord, which he will show to you to-day; for the Egyptians, whom ye have seen to-day, ye shall see them again no more for ever." (Exod. xiv. 13.)

87. *They had almost consumed me upon earth; but I forsook not thy precepts.*

And why did they not *quite consume him?* Because " the eyes of the Lord run to and fro throughout the whole earth, to show himself strong in behalf of them, whose heart is perfect toward him." (2 Chron. xvi. 9.) " Surely the wrath of man shall praise thee; the remainder of wrath

shalt thou restrain." (Ps. lxxvi. 10.)   And why have not
our spiritual enemies *consumed us upon earth?*   " Satan
hath desired to have us, that he may sift us as wheat."
But—saith the Saviour—" *I have prayed for you, that your
faith fail not.*" (Luke, xxii. 31, 32.)   " My sheep shall never
perish ; neither shall any pluck them out of my hand."
(John, x. 28.)   Stedfastness of profession is the evidence of
the life of faith : grounded upon this security, the more we
are shaken, the more we shall hold fast.   Neither long-
continued distress (Verse 83), nor determined opposition,
will turn us from the ways of God.   We would rather
forsake all that our heart held dear upon earth, than *the
precepts* of our God.   With whatever intensity of affection
we love father and mother (and the influence of the Gospel
has increased the sensibilities of relative affection), we remember who hath said—" He that loveth father and mother
more than me, is not worthy of me." (Matt. x. 37.)   Unlike the deluded professor (Matt. xiii. 21), we have counted
the cost of the " tribulation and persecution " of the Gospel;
and the result has only served to confirm our love and adherence to our heavenly Master.   Shall not we find in
heaven — nay, do not we find in the gospel — a far better
portion than we lose ? (Matt. xix. 29.)

When, therefore, we are tempted to neglect *the precepts*,
or when we fail to live in them, and to delight in them, let
us each bring our hearts to this test : ' What would I take
in exchange for them ?   Will the good-will and approbation of the world compensate for the loss of the favour of
God ?   Could I be content to forego my greatest comforts,
to " suffer the loss of all things" (Phil. iii. 8), yea, of life
itself (Acts, xx. 24), rather than forsake one of the ways of
God ?   When I meet with such precepts as link me to the
daily cross, can I throw myself with simple dependence upon
that Saviour, who has engaged to supply strength for what
he has commanded ?'   How often in times of spiritual

temptation, if not of temporal danger, *they had almost consumed us upon earth!* but "in the mount" of difficulty "the Lord has been seen."* Oh! let each of us mark our road to Zion with multiplied Ebenezers, inscribed *Jehovah-jireh, Jehovah-nissi.* (Exod. xvii. 15.) " By this I know thou favourest me, because mine enemy doth not triumph over me. And as for me, thou upholdest me in mine integrity, and settest me before thy face for ever." (Ps. xli. 11, 12.)

What a fine testimony of the upholding grace of God! How could a helpless believer stand against such an appalling array? Yet it is a great, but a true word, suitable for a babe in Christ, as well as for an Apostle—" I can do all things through Christ that strengtheneth me." (Phil. iv. 13.) Yes, I can " wrestle even against principalities and powers" of darkness, if I be " strong in the Lord, and in the power of his might." (Eph. vi. 10–12.)

88. *Quicken me after thy loving-kindness : so shall I keep the testimony of thy mouth.*

We need continual *quickening* to maintain our stedfastness *in the precepts.* " God, who is rich in mercy, for his great love wherewith he loved us, even when we were dead in sins, *hath quickened us,* together with Christ." (Eph. ii. 4, 5.) But without daily *quickening after the same lovingkindness,* " the things which remain will be ready to die." For every breath of prayer, Divine influence must flow— " *Quicken us, and we shall call upon thy name.*" (Ps. lxxx. 18.) For the work of praise, without the same influence we are dumb.—" *Let my soul live, and it shall praise thee.*" (Verse 175.) For the exercise of every spiritual grace, there must be the commanding voice of our Divine Head

---

* ' In the mount the Lord shall be seen, or shall appear,' *Jehovah-jireh.* (Gen. xxii. 14.)—SCOTT, *in loco.*

—" *Awake, O north wind; and come, thou south: blow upon my garden, that the spices thereof may flow out.*" (Cant. iv. 16.) Thus is the creature laid in the dust, and all the glory is given to God. " Not that we are sufficient of ourselves to think anything as of ourselves ; but our sufficiency is of God." (2 Cor. iii. 5.)

Why is it, then, that at one time we spring to duty as the joy of our life ; while at other times the soul is so chained down under the power of corruption, that it scarcely can put forth the feeblest exercise of life ? The source of our life is the same ; — " Hid with Christ in God." (Col. iii. 3.) But the power of the flesh hinders its every motion. (See Gal. v. 17.) Such a spiritual sloth has benumbed us — such backwardness to prayer, and disrelish for heavenly things ! These are sins deeply humbling in themselves, and aggravated by the neglect of the plentiful provision laid up in Christ, not only for the life, but for the peace, joy, and strength of the soul. Nothing but indolence or unbelief straitens our supplies. Oh ! stir up the prayer for *quickening* influence, and we shall be rich and fruitful. Sometimes also self-confidence paralyzes our spiritual energy. We expect our recovery from a lifeless state by more determined resolutions, or increased improvement of the various means of grace. Let these means indeed be used with all diligence, but with the fullest conviction that all means, all instruments, all helps of every kind, without the influence of the Spirit of grace, are dead. " It is the Spirit that quickeneth ; the flesh profiteth nothing." (John, vi. 63.)

These records of David's prayers strikingly mark the intensity of his desire to live to God. Every decay of strength and activity was, as it were, death to him, and awakened his reiterated cries. Do we desire to *keep the testimony of his mouth?* Do we mourn over our shortcomings in service ? Oh ! then, for our own sake, for the Lord's sake, and for the church's and the world's sake, let our petitions be incessant each one for himself—' *Quicken me*— Quicken this slothful heart of mine.   Enkindle afresh the sacred spark within, and let me be all alive for thee.' Let faith be kept alive and active at the throne of grace, and all will be alive ; our obligation will be deeply felt, and practically acknowledged.

The title here given to the directory of our duty—*the testimony of God's mouth*—adds strength to our obligations. Thus let every word we read or hear be regarded as coming directly from the *mouth of God.* (Comp. Judg. iii. 20.) What reverence, what implicit submission does it demand! May it ever find us in the posture of attention, humility, and faith, each one of us ready to say—" Speak, Lord, for thy servant heareth !" (1 Sam. iii. 9, 10.)

PART XII.

89. For ever, O Lord, thy word is settled in heaven. 90. Thy faithfulness is unto all generations; thou hast established the earth, and it abideth. 91. They continue this day according to thine ordinances, for all are thy servants.

THE Christian extends his survey far beyond the limits of his individual sphere. His view of the operations of God in creation enlarges his apprehensions of the Divine attributes, and especially that of unchanging *faithfulness.* Indeed, the very fact of a creation in ruins—a world in rebellion against its Maker, failing of the grand end of existence, and yet still continued in existence—manifests *his faithfulness unto all generations.* (Gen. viii. 22.) How different is the contemplation of the Christian from that of the philosopher! His is not a mere cold, speculative admiration, but the establishment of his faith upon a clear discovery of *the faithfulness of God.* Thus he stays his soul upon the assured unchangeableness of the Divine word— *"Concerning thy testimonies, I have known of old, that thou hast founded them for ever. Thy word is true from the beginning: and every one of thy righteous judgments endureth for ever."* (Verses 152, 160.) How striking is the contrast between the transient glory of man's goodliness, and the solid foundation of all the promises, hopes, and prospects of the children of God!—" The grass withereth, and the flower fadeth ; but the word of our God shall stand for ever." (Isa. xl. 6–8. Comp. 1 Pet. i. 24, 25.) " Unbelief" is the

character of our " evil hearts." (Heb. iii. 12.) Man chooses
his own measure and objects of faith ; he believes no more
than he pleases. But it is a fearful prospect, that the
threatenings of God rest upon the same solid foundation
with his promises. " Heaven and earth shall pass away :
but my word shall not pass away." (Comp. Luke, xxi.
28–33.)

Need we any further proof of his *faithfulness?* Look
at *the earth established* by his word of power. (Ps. xxxiii. 9.
Heb. i. 3.) See how " he hangeth it upon nothing " (Job,
xxvi. 7), as if it might fall at any moment ;—and yet it is
immoveably fixed (Ps. xxiv. 2 ; xciii. 1; civ. 5 ; cxlviii. 6)—
it abideth (Eccles. i. 4) — and with all its furniture, *continueth
according to his ordinances.* This—though the scoff of the
infidel (2 Pet. iii. 4) — is the encouragement to Christian
faith. It is at once a token of his covenant with nature,
that " while the earth remaineth, seed-time and harvest,
and cold and heat, and summer and winter, and day and
night, shall not cease" (Gen. viii. 22) ; and an emblem of
his covenant with the seed of David, that he " will not cast
them off for all that they have done." (Jer. xxxi. 35, 36 ;
xxxiii. 20, 21, 25, 26.) Thus every view of the heavens —
yea— every time we set our foot on the earth (Isa. liv. 9,
10)—shows the unchangeableness of his everlasting covenant, and the security of the salvation of his own people.

In this vast universe, *all are his servants.* " The stars
in their courses"— " fire and hail, snow and vapours, stormy
wind—fulfil his word. He sendeth forth his commandment upon earth : his word runneth very swiftly." (Judg.
v. 20. Ps. cxlviii. 8 ; cxlvii. 15. Comp. Job, xxxvii. 12.
Isa. xlviii. 13.) Man—the child of his Maker (Deut.
xxxii. 6)—" created in his image" (Gen. i. 27 ; v. 1)—
destined for his glory (Isa. xliii. 7)—is the only rebel and
revolter. Most affecting is the appeal, that his own Father
and God is constrained to make concerning him—" Hear,

O heavens, and give ear, O earth ; for the Lord has spoken. I have nourished and brought up children, and they have rebelled against me!" (Isa. i. 2.)

Is not then the universe of nature a parable of grace —setting out on every side—in every view—a cheering display of *the faithfulness of God?* (Ps. lxxxix. 2.) If his providence fails not, will the promise of his covenant disappoint us? Why should he change? Does he see or know anything now, that he has not foreseen and foreknown from eternity? What more sure ground of salvation than the unchangeableness of God? (Mal. iii. 6. Heb. vi. 17, 18 ; vii. 21–25.) If I can prove *a word* to have been spoken by God, I must no more question it than his own Being. It may seem to fail on earth ; but *it is for ever settled in heaven.* The decrees of the kings of the earth, " settled" on earth, are exposed to all the variations and weakness of a changing world. They may be revoked by themselves or their successors, or they may die away. The empty sound of the " law of the Medes and Persians that altereth not" (Dan. vi. 8), has long since been swept away into ̤oblivion. But while " the word settled" on earth has " waxed old like a garment," and perished ; *the word settled in heaven*—is raised above all the revolutions of the universe, and remaineth as the throne of God—unshaken and eternal ; exhibiting the foundation of the believer's hope and of the unbeliever's terror to be alike unalterably fixed.

But we also remark the foreknowledge as well as the *faithfulness* of God. From the eternity that is past, as well for the eternity that is to come, *thy word is settled in heaven.* Before this fair creation was marred, yea, before it was called into existence, its ruin was foreseen, and a remedy provided. " The Lamb was slain from the foundation of the world" (Rev. xiii. 8), and fore-ordained before (1 Pet. i. 20) that æra. Coeval with this period, a people " were chosen in him" (Eph. i. 4), and *for ever the word was settled in heaven.*—" All that the Father giveth me *shall come to me.*" (John, vi. 37.) For the establishment of the Redeemer's kingdom upon earth " the decree is declared ;" however earth and hell may combine against it—" Yet have I set my king upon my holy hill of Sion." (Ps. ii. 6–8.) And what a blessed encouragement in the grand work of bringing back " the lost sheep of the house of Israel" (Matt. xv. 24), and those " other sheep" with them, " which are not of this fold" (John, x. 16) is it, that we do not depend upon the earnestness of our prayers, the wisdom of our plans, or the diligence of our endeavours ; but upon " the *word*" *for ever settled in heaven!*—" The Redeemer shall come to Zion, and unto them that turn from transgression in Jacob, *saith the Lord.* As for me, this is my covenant with them, saith the Lord— My Spirit that is upon thee, and my words which I have put in thy mouth, shall not depart out of thy mouth, nor out of the mouth of thy seed, nor out of the mouth of thy seed's seed, *saith the Lord, from henceforth, and for ever.*" " I have sworn by myself, *the word is gone out of my mouth* in righteousness, and *shall not return,*— That unto me every knee shall bow, every tongue shall swear." (Isa. lix. 20, 21 ; xlv. 23.)

92. *Unless thy law had been my delights, I should then have perished in mine affliction.*

The support of the word is as sure as its basis—and that in the time when other supports sink—in *affliction.* David—like his great prototype—was a man of affliction (Ps. cxxxii. 1),—sometimes ready to *perish*—always kept up by *the law* of his God. How many a false professor has been tried and cast by this hour of *affliction!* But he who has been sifted by temptation—who has " endured the hardness" of persecution, as a " good soldier of Jesus

Christ" (2 Tim. ii. 3),—and who is ready rather to be " *consumed upon earth*" (Verse 87), than to shrink from his profession—this is he whom his Master " will lift up, and not make his foes to rejoice over him." (Ps. xxx. 1.) It is the established rule of the kingdom—" Them that honour me I will honour." (1 Sam. ii. 30.) " Because thou hast kept the word of my patience, I also will keep thee from the hour of temptation, which shall come upon all the world, to try them that dwell upon the earth." (Rev. iii. 10.)

The law of God opens to us a clear interest in every perfection of his Godhead—every engagement of his covenant. What wonder then, that it brings *delights*, which the world can never conceive, when bowed down with accumulated *affliction?* However the believer's real character may be hidden from the world, the hour of trial abundantly proves, both what the *law* can do for him, and what a lost creature he would have been without it. In affliction, friends mean well ; but of themselves they can do nothing. They can only look on, feel, and pray. They cannot "speak to the heart." This is God's prerogative (Isa. xl. 2. Hos. ii. 14, Margin) : and his *law* is his voice.

But for this support, Jonah probably would have *perished in his affliction.* In the belly of the fish, as " in the belly of hell," he appears to have recollected the experience of David under deep and awful desertion ; and in taking his language out of his mouth, as descriptive of his own dark and terrific condition, a ray of light and hope darted upon his dungeon-walls.* Indeed it is a mystery, how a sinner, destitute of the support and comfort of the word of God, can ever uphold himself in his trials. We marvel not, that often "his soul should choose strangling, and death, rather than his life." (Job, vii. 15. Comp. 2 Cor. vii. 10.)

* Jonah, ii. 3; with Ps. xlii. 7. The phraseology in the LXX. is identical, as if it were a clear and distinct recollection of the Psalmist's expressions, when describing his own state of desertion.

But in order to derive support from the *law*, it must be *our delights**—yea—that it may be *our delights* it must be the matter of our faith. For what solid *delight*, can we have in what we do not believe? (Ps. xxvii. 13.) Must it not also be our joy in prosperity, if we would realize its support in *affliction?* For this, how ineffectual is the mere formal service! Who ever tasted its tried consolations in the bare performance of the outward duty? It must be read in reality; it will then be taken as a cordial. Let it be simply received, diligently searched, and earnestly prayed over; and it will guide the heavy-laden to Him, who is their present and eternal rest.† The tempest-tossed soul will cast anchor upon it.—"*Remember the word unto thy servant, upon which thou hast caused me to hope.*" (Verse 49.) One promise applied by the Spirit of God is worth ten thousand worlds. And each promise is a staff—if we have but faith to lean upon it—able to bear our whole weight of sin, care, and trial.

Is then *affliction* our appointed lot? If " man is born " —and the child of God twice born—" to trouble, as the

* ' Delights '—instar omnium—instead of all manner of delights.

+ Matt. xi. 28. It was the speech of a holy man—after God had made this precious text the messenger to open his dungeon of spiritual distress, and bring him into the light of inward joy—that he had better be without meat, drink, light, air, earth, life, and all, than without this one comfortable Scripture. ' If one single promise '—as Gurnal sweetly remarks in giving this story—' like an ear of corn rubbed in the hand of faith, and applied by the Spirit of Christ—can afford such a full satisfying meal of joy to the hunger-bitten, pining soul; oh, what a price can we set upon the whole field of Scripture, which stands so thick with promises every way as cordial as this!'—GURNAL on Eph. vi. 17. Well might Luther say—' I have covenanted with my Lord, that he should not send me visions, or dreams, or even angels. I am content with this one gift of the Scriptures, which abundantly teaches and supplies all that is necessary both for this life and that which is to come.'

sparks fly upward" (Job, v. 7),—how important is it to lay
in a store of supply from this inexhaustible treasury,
against the time when all human support will fail! Supplied hence with heavenly strength, we shall be borne up
above the weakness and weariness of the flesh. And as
the riches of this storehouse are "the riches of Christ"
(Eph. iii. 8. John, v. 39), let those parts be most familiar
to us,* which mark his person (Isa. liii. 1, 2), his character (Ib. verse 9), offices (verses 4, 5, 12), life (verse 3),
sufferings (verses 7, 8), and death (verse 9), resurrection
and glory (verses 10, 12), together with the promises, encouragements, and prospects directly flowing from this
blessed subject—and oh! what a treasure-house shall we
find, richly furnished with every source of delight, and
every ground of support!

93. *I will never forget thy precepts; for with them thou hast
quickened me.*

An admirable resolution! the blessed fruit of the quickening power of the word in his deep *affliction.* He had before acknowledged this supernatural efficacy—" *Thy word
hath quickened me.*" (Verse 50.) Now he more distinctly
mentions it, as the *instrumental* only — *not the efficient
— cause—With them thou hast quickened me.* Had the
power been in the word, the same effect would have immediately and invariably followed. Nor should we have been
constrained to lament the limited extent of its influence.
How many, Christian, shared with you in the outward
privileges; but perhaps unto none was the life-giving
blessing vouchsafed, save unto yourself—the most unlikely
—the most unworthy of all! (Comp. Luke, iv. 25, 26.)

---

* Such as Isa. liii. which, in the compass of a single chapter
sketches out his whole history. See the text.

Thus does " God work in us both to will and to do"—not
according to any prescribed law, but "*of his good pleasure.*" (Philip. ii. 13.) *The grace therefore is not from, but
through, the means.* Almighty God is the source of the
life. The word is the instrument—yet so " quick" (Heb.
iv. 12), so melting (Jer. xxiii. 29), so attractive (Matt. xi.
28), that we might ask, out of what rock was that heart
hewn, that is proof against its power? Yet while *the precepts* work nothing without the agents (1 Cor. iii. 7) they
are the ordinary course, *by which the Lord quickeneth* whom
he will. (John, v. 21. Rom. x. 17.)

And do not we find them still lively channels of refreshment? Surely, then, we will hold to our purpose of
not forgetting the precepts. The leaves of the word of God
are the leaves of the tree of life, as well as of the tree of
knowledge. They not only enlighten the path, but they
supply life for daily work and progress. " The words that
I speak unto you"—said Jesus—" *they are spirit, and they
are life*" (John, vi. 63) : so that the times when we have
been most diligent in our meditation and obedience to *the
precepts*, have been uniformly the seasons of our most holy
consolation.

Men of the world, however, with accurate recollections
of all matters, connected with their temporal advantage,
are remarkably slow in retaining the truths of God. They
plead their short memories, although conscious that this
infirmity does not extend to their important secular engagements. But what wonder that they *forget the precepts*,
when they have never been quickened *with them*—never
received any benefit from them? The word of God is not
precious to them : they acknowledge no obligation to it :
they have no acquaintance with it. It has no place in
their affections, and therefore but little abode in their
remembrance.

But this resolution is the language of sincerity, not of

perfection.   The child of God is humbled in the conscious
forgetfulness of the Lord's precepts.   And this consciousness keeps his eye fixed upon Jesus for pardon and acceptance : while every fresh sense of acceptance strengthens
his more habitual remembrance.   Then, as for his natural
inability to preserve an accurate recollection of Divine
things — let him not estimate the benefit of the word by
the results in the memory, so much as by the impression
upon the heart.   The word may have darted through the
mind, as a flash of lightning, that strikes and is gone ; and
yet the heart may have been melted, and the passing flash
may have shed a heavenly ray upon a dubious path.   If
the heart retains the quickening power, the *precepts are
not forgotten,* even though the memory should have failed
to preserve them.

But whatever word of conviction, direction, or encouragement, may have come to us, affix this seal to it —
I will never forget thy precepts.   It may be of signal use in
some hour of temptation.   The same Spirit that breathed
before upon it may breathe again ; if not with the same
present sensible power, yet with a seasonable and refreshing
recollection of past support.

94. *I am thine; save me ; for I have sought thy precepts.*

What a high and honourable character is stamped upon
the meanest believer !   He is the Saviour's unalienable
property (1 Cor. iii. 23), his portion (Deut. xxxii. 9), the
" workmanship " (Eph. ii. 10) of his hand, the purchase
of his blood (Ps. lxxiv. 2. Acts, xx. 28. 1 Cor. vi. 19, 20),
the triumph of his conquering love. (Isa. liii. 10–12.
Luke, xi. 21, 22.)   He is given to him by his Father
(John, vi. 37 ; x. 29 ; xvii. 6–11)—" preserved in him,
and called." (Jude, 1.)   The evidence of his character is
found in *seeking the Lord's precepts.*   " Whom we serve "

will prove "whose we are." (Acts, xxvii. 23.) " His servants ye are, to whom ye obey." (Rom. vi. 16.) " Know that the Lord hath set apart him that is godly for himself." (Ps. iv. 3.) " The carnal mind is not subject to the law of God, neither indeed can be. So then they that are in the flesh" cannot *seek the Lord's precepts.* (Rom. viii. 7, 8.) A new and spiritual bias, therefore, is the visible stamp and seal of the Lord's interest in us.

True it is, that our Divine Saviour can never be robbed of his property—that his people are saved in him, beyond the reach of earth and hell to touch them. Yet are they dependent still—always sinners—every day's provocation making them more sinners than before ; needing, therefore, from day to day, fresh power, fresh keeping, and, above all, fresh cleansing and acceptance. But what a powerful plea for mercy may we draw from the Lord's interest in us ! Will not a man be careful of his children, his treasure, his jewels ? ' Such am I. (Heb. ii. 13. Exod. xix. 5. Mal. iii. 17.) Thy sovereign love hath bought me—made me *thine* (Isa. xliii. 3, 4)—*I am thine ; save me.* Thou hast saved me ; " thou hast delivered my soul from death ; wilt thou not deliver my feet from falling ?" (Ps. lvi. 13.) Save me from the love of sin, from the daily guilt and power of sin ; from the treachery of my own foolish heart : from all this, and all besides, which thou seest ensnaring to my soul. If I am not thine, whence this desire, this endeavour to *seek thy precepts ?* What mean my privileged moments of communion with thee ? What mean the yet unsatisfied desires after a conformity to thine image ? Lord, I would humbly plead thine own act, thy free and sovereign act, that made me thine. *Save me,* because thou hast brought thy salvation near to me, and sealed me thine. I need mercy to begin with me ; mercy to accompany me ; mercy to abide with me for ever. *I am thine ; save me.'*

And what irresistible energy does it give to our plead-ing, that this was the sole purpose, that brought down the Son of God from Heaven! " I came down"—said he— " from heaven, not to do mine own will, but the will of him that sent me. *And this is the Father's will which hath sent me, that of all which he hath given me I should lose nothing.*" (John, vi. 38, 39.)   Of this purpose he was enabled to tes-tify at the conclusion of his work—" *Those that thou gavest me I have kept, and none of them is lost, but the son of per-dition.*" (John, xvii. 12 ; xviii. 9.)

But some cry for *salvation*, who neglect duty, and thus make void their plea.   Can we make our interest good, by *seeking his precepts?*   Is it the way in which we love to walk?   Then let us not desist from our plea before God, until our heart listens to the voice of love, centering every blessing of creation, redemption, and heavenly calling, in the privilege of adoption—" Thus saith the Lord, that created thee, O Jacob, and he that formed thee, O Israel : Fear not, for I have redeemed thee : I have called thee by thy name ; *thou art mine.   Thou art my servant ;* O Israel, thou shalt not be forgotten of me.   I have blotted out, as a thick cloud, thy transgressions ; and as a cloud thy sins." (Isa. xliii. 1 ; xliv. 21, 22.)   I have regarded this thy plea. I have heard this thy prayer—*I am thine, save me.**

95. *The wicked have waited for me to destroy me ; but I will consider thy testimonies.*

Am I, as a believer, safe as the Lord's property, and in the Lord's keeping ?   Yet must I expect that *the wicked*, the ungodly, as the instruments of Satan, will not cease to distress me.   The Psalmist had before alluded to this

---

* The same plea is urged in prayer, Ps. cxliii. 12 ; lxxxvi. 2. Margin. Comp. also verse 125.

trial, as driving him to his refuge. (Verses 78, 87. Comp.
verses 114, 115.) And, indeed, this is the constant character of the believer's walk—enduring the enmity of the
ungodly, and seeking his refuge in the word of God—in
that hiding-place of safety to which the word directs him.
How striking is the proof of the irreconcileable variance
between God and the world—the world encouraging all
that is contrary to God, and persecuting his image in his
people! Yet the word opens to us a sure defence. If our
" soul is among lions" (Ps. lvii. 4), cannot we testify to
the astonishment of the world—" My God hath sent his
angel, and hath shut the lions' mouths, that they have not
hurt me?" (Dan. vi. 22.) We hear indeed the roaring of
the winds and waves; but we hear also the voice hushing
the storm to rest—" Peace, be still." (Mark, iv. 39.)

The experience of this trial and support beautifully
illustrates the promise—" He that believeth shall not
make haste." (Isa. xxviii. 16.) He whose hope is firmly
fixed on that " tried corner-stone," which God himself
hath " laid in Zion as a sure foundation"—" shall not be
greatly moved;" nay—he " shall not be moved"* at all,
by *the wicked waiting for him to destroy him.* In the hour
of difficulty, instead of perplexing himself with successive expedients for his safety (sought more from human
contrivance, than from asking counsel at the mouth of
God) he " possesses his soul in patience," and calmly
commits all events to the Lord. Such a man " shall not
be afraid of evil tidings! his heart is fixed, trusting in the
Lord." (Ps. cxii. 7.) ' This trust is grounded on the word
of God, revealing his power and all-sufficiency, and withal
his goodness, his offer of himself to be the stay of the soul,
commanding us to rest upon him. People wait on I know

* Ps. lxii. 2, 6. His confidence increased in the recollection
of his support—"I shall not be *greatly* moved—I *shall not be
moved.*"

not what persuasions and assurances ; but I know no other
to build faith on but the word of promise.   The truth and
faithfulness of God opened up his wisdom, and power, and
goodness, as the stay of all those that, renouncing all other
props, will venture on it, and lay all upon him.   " He that
believes, sets to his seal that God is true :" and so he is
sealed for God ; his portion and interest secured.   " If you
will not believe, surely ye shall not be established."'*

But it is the *considering* of the Lord's testimonies
that draws out their staying support.   The soul must be
fixed upon them, as " tried words, purified seven times in
the fire." (Ps. xii. 7. P. B. Trans.)   And in this frame,
I will, under all distresses, all circumstances of trial,
or even of dismay, *consider thy testimonies.   I will consider* the faithfulness of those blessed declarations —
" There shall not an hair of your head perish.   Touch not
mine anointed." (Luke, xxi. 18. Ps. cv. 15.)   " He that
toucheth you, toucheth the apple of mine eye." (Zech.
ii. 8.)   With this armour of defence, I shall not be afraid,
even should I hear the " evil tidings," that *the wicked
have waited for me, to destroy me.*   Or even should I be
destroyed, I know that *thy testimonies* cannot fail—that
my rock is perfect—" that there is no unrighteousness in
him" (Ps. xcii. 15) ; and therefore, " though a host should
encamp against me, my heart shall not fear ; though war
should rise against me, in this will I be confident." (Ps.
xxvii. 3.)   Whether, then, I am delivered from *the wicked,*
and live, " I live unto the Lord ;" or whether I fall into
their snare, and " die—I die unto the Lord" (Rom.
xiv. 8) ; for *I will consider thy testimonies,* assured that
all thy purposes shall be accomplished concerning me, as
thou hast said—" I will never leave thee, nor forsake
thee." (Heb. xiii. 5.)   " Thou wilt keep him in perfect

* LEIGHTON's Sermon on Ps. cxii. 7.

peace, whose mind is stayed on thee, because he trusteth
in thee." (Isa. xxvi. 3.)

96. *I have seen an end of all perfection; but thy commandment is exceeding broad.*

A deeper insight into the Lord's *testimonies* is the
sure result of *considering* them. Weigh them in the
balances against this world's excellency; the world and
the word — each with all its fulness. Of the one *perfection
we see an end* — of the other — none. This world is a
matter of experience and observation. *We have seen an
end* — not of some — but *of all its perfection.* It wants
sufficiency. It stands us in no stead in the great emergencies of affliction — death — judgment — eternity. *It
wants solidity in its best substance.* " In its wisdom is
grief!" (Eccles. i. 18.) All its delicacies and indulgencies
— after having, like the King of Jerusalem, " not withheld the heart from any joy" — all end in the verdict of
disappointment — " Behold! all was vanity and vexation
of spirit!" (Eccles. ii. 10, 11.) *Its continuance* is but *for
a moment.* The soul is born for eternity. Therefore it
must have a portion to last as long as itself. But the
world, with its lusts and fashions, passeth away. (1 John,
ii. 17.) All that it can offer is a bubble — a shadow. In
its best riches, honours, and pleasures — in the utmost that
its *perfection* can yield — in its height and prime of enjoyment — what is it in itself — what is it able to do for us?
" All is vanity." (Eccles. i. 2. 1 Cor. vii. 31.) And yet
such is the alienation of the heart from God, that it is
first tried to the very uttermost, before any desire to
return homeward is felt or expressed. And even then,
nothing but the Almighty power of God can bring the
sinner back. He would rather perish in his misery, than
" return to his rest."

Now contrast with the emptiness of the world the fulness of *the commandment of God*. Our whole duty to our God, our neighbour, and ourselves, is here laid open before us — commanding without abatement, and forbidding without allowance — making no excuse for ignorance — frailty or forgetfulness — reaching not only to every species of crime, but to everything tending to it. This is *perfection*, of which we never *see an end*. Every fresh view opens — not the extent — but the immensity of the field ; and compels us at length to shut up our inquiries with the adoring acknowledgment — *Thy commandment is exceeding broad.* Its various parts form one seamless piece ; so that no particle can be separated without injury to the whole. As all the curtains of the tabernacle connected by taches and loops, made but one covering for the ark, and the loosening or disjunction of the smallest point disannulled the fitness of the whole ; so it belongs to the perfection of *the commandment*, that " whosoever shall keep the whole law, and yet offend in one point, he is guilty of all." (Jam. ii. 10, 11.) The spirituality of its requirements equally illustrates its Divine *perfection*. An angry look is murder (Matt. v. 21, 22. Comp. 1 John, iii. 15); an unchaste desire is adultery (Matt. v. 27) ; the " stumbling-block of iniquity" (Ezek. xiv. 7)—" covetousness" (Eph. v. 5)—in the heart is idolatry ; the thought (Prov. xxiv. 9. Comp. xxiii. 7) as well as the act—the first conception of sin, as well as the after-commission—brings in the verdict— Guilty — Death.

Can we, then, endure the sight of its *exceeding breadth ?* Yes — for *the commandment* of the gospel (John, vi. 28, 29. 1 John, iii. 23) is equally *broad*, and covers all. (Rom. iii. 22.) We know who hath stood in our place — who hath satisfied Sinai's unalterable requirements, and borne its awful curse. (Gal. iv. 4, 5 ; iii. 13.) *Broad* as it may be, the love which hath fulfilled it is

immeasurable.   As a covenant, therefore, it has now lost
its terrors.   As a rule, we love it for its extent, and for its
purity ; for the comprehensiveness of its obligations, and
for the narrowness of its liberty for indulgence ; nor would
we wish to be subject to a less severe scrutiny, or a more
lenient administration.

Reader! if you have learnt *the exceeding breadth* and
spirituality of the law (the first lesson that is taught and
learnt in the school of Christ), your views of yourself and
your state before God will be totally changed.   Before,
you were " thanking God" in your heart, " that you were
not as other men are."   Now you will be " smiting upon
your breast, saying—God be merciful to me a sinner!"
(Luke, xviii. 9–13.)   Before, perhaps, you might have
thought yourself, " touching the righteousness which is
of the law, blameless."   Now you will glory in your new
and more enlightened choice — " What things were gain
to me, those I counted loss for Christ." (Philip. iii. 6, 7.)
Once you considered yourself " alive," when you were really
dead.   Now that " the commandment is come" in its
heart-searching spirituality and conviction to your soul,
you " die " (Rom. vii. 9) that you may live.   Blessed
change from the law to the gospel — " from death to life !"
" I through the law am dead to the law, that I might live
unto God." (Gal. ii. 19.)

Such is the effect of the transition from a legal to an
evangelical ground.   Before, we were reckless of sin, and
therefore reckless of the gospel.   As the one fell lightly
upon our conscience, the other held a light estimation in
our judgment.   While we had no disturbance from the
law, we had no delight in the gospel.   But now that
we see in the true mirror, we are at once alarmed and
enlightened.   Praised be God! we now take the true
estimate—we degrade to the uttermost righteousness by
works—we exalt to the uttermost righteousness by faith.
In the one we see pollution—in the other perfection.

PART XIII.*

97. *O how love I thy law! it is my meditation all the day.*

MARK the man of God giving utterance to his feelings of
heavenly delight—expressing most, by intimating that
he cannot adequately express what he desires.   He seems
unable to restrain his acknowledgments of Divine influence
springing up in his heart — *O how love I thy law!* This
experience is most distinctive of a spiritual character.
The professor may read, and understand, and even *externally*
obey the law ; but the believer only *loves* it ; and he lives
in it, as if he could not live without it ; To the professor it
is a task imposed to satisfy conscience ; " the veil upon the
heart" (2 Cor. iii. 15) darkens all his spiritual apprehension, and consequently excludes spiritual delight.   To the
child of God, it is food and medicine, light and comfort—
yea, " life from the dead."   The law of precept in the
word is a " law of liberty" (Jam. i. 25)—a law of love—
in his heart.   His former obedience was the bondage of
fear.   But how different is the effect of constraining love !
He now delights to view it in every lineament.   He dwells
upon every feature with intense enjoyment.   Before, it was
his confinement—his chain.   Now, it is his liberty—his
ornament. He is not what he was—" Old things are passed
away : behold, all things are become new." (2 Cor. v. 17.)

* ' I enjoyed a solemn seriousness in learning MEM in the 119th
Psalm.'—MARTYN's *Journals,* vol. i. p. 191.

Think what good reason there is to *love the law*. It is the epistle of our most beloved friend — not to be slighted, but to be placed in our bosom, nearest our hearts. It sets out that relief, without which the conscience would have been tortured by the never-dying worm. (2 Cor. v. 19.) There is more of glory — more of God — in this, than in any other manifestation of his name. (Ps. cxxxviii. 2. Eph. iii. 10. 2 Tim. i. 10.) It has ever been the mirror, that has reflected Christ to his church. The spiritual eye discerns him in every part.* Now — Reader — do you search for him in *his law?* Do you *love his law*, because it " testifies of him?" Do you pray for his Spirit, that his law may guide you to him? This is the evidence that you have " turned unto the Lord, when the veil is taken away," and you " with *unveiled* face behold in this glass the glory of the Lord." (2 Cor. iii. 15–18.) Then if you do *love his law*, you will love the whole of it — its obligations as well as its privileges. You will love it *at all times* (Verse 20), even when it is thwarting your own will and way. The whole law is light and love — wisdom and faithfulness.

* John, v. 39. 'Were I to enjoy Hezekiah's grant, and to have fifteen years added to my life, I would be much more frequent in my applications to the throne of grace. Were I to renew my studies, I would take my leave of those accomplished triflers — the historians, the orators, the poets of antiquity — and devote my attention to the Scriptures of truth. I would sit with much greater assiduity at my Divine Master's feet, and desire to " know nothing save Jesus Christ and him crucified." This wisdom, whose fruits are peace in life, consolation in death, and everlasting salvation after death — this I would trace — this I would seek — this I would explore through the spacious and delightful fields of the Old and New Testament.' Such was the testimony of one, who had cultivated the classic fields with no inconsiderable success, and who above most men had enriched his soul with the glorious treasures of the word of God — whose praise is in all the churches as the author of ' Theron and Aspasia.'

But *love of the law* fastens the soul to the beloved object, *It is my meditation all the day.* (Ps. i. 2.) When you cannot have it in your hand, it will be found, if indeed your soul is in a prosperous state, " hid in your heart." There it is kept as your most precious treasure ; while you live upon it with unwearied appetite as your daily bread, and exercise yourself in it as your daily rule. Oh, how worthy is it of all the love of the warmest heart ! The deepest students are most humbled for their want of suitable enlargement.

But this heavenly spirit can only be grounded upon a sense of reconciliation. Can an unreconciled sinner be interested in *the law*, in every page of which he reads his own condemnation ? This explains the enmity of the ungodly. (Comp. 1 Kings, xxii. 8.) But the cultivation of this spirit *upon the ground of the gospel* is a most important principle of the Christian stedfastness, the want of which has been the source of fearful delusion (See 2 Thess. ii. 10, 11) ; and in the exercise of which we shall realize a deeper insight and more spiritual discernment of Scriptural truth. Warm affections will be far more influential than talent, or mere external knowledge.

This habit of love and holy meditation will spread its influence over our whole character. It will fill our hearts with heavenly matter for prayer, diffuse a sweet savour over our earthly employments, sanctify the common bounties of Providence (1 Tim. iv. 4, 5), realize the presence of God throughout the day, command prosperity upon our lawful undertakings (Ps. i. 3. Comp. Josh. i. 7, 8), and enlarge our usefulness in the church. (1 Tim. iv. 15.) Thus the man of God is formed in his completeness, symmetry, and attraction — such as the world is often constrained secretly to admire, even where the heart is unready to follow.

Lord ! implant in my heart a supreme *love to thy law*. Write it upon my heart — even that new law, " the law of the Spirit of life in Christ Jesus." (Rom. viii. 2.) May I love it so, that I may be always meditating upon it, and by continual meditation yet more enlarging my love and delight in it! So let it prove an ever-springing source of heavenly enjoyment and holy conversation!

98. *Thou through thy commandments hast made me wiser than mine enemies; for they are ever with me.* 99. *I have more understanding than all my teachers: for thy testimonies are my meditation.* 100. *I understand more than the ancients, because I keep thy precepts.*

What a fruitful harvest did David reap from his glowing love, and "*daily meditation on the law of God!*" He became *wiser than his enemies* in "subtlety" (Prov. i. 1, 4)—*than all his teachers* in doctrine—*than the ancients* in experience. Yet he is not speaking of his extraordinary gifts as a prophet, but of his knowledge gained by ordinary means. Nor is he here boasting of his own attainments: but commending the grace of God in and towards him —*Thou through thy commandments hast made me wiser.* (Prov. ii. 6. Jam. i. 17.) How much more wisdom does the persecuted believer draw from the word of God, than his persecutors have ever acquired from the learning of this world! Those, however, who have been *effectually* taught of God, need to be *daily* taught of him. While they rest upon their God, and seek counsel in his word, they are wise indeed; yet when they trust to their own wisdom, and turn to their own counsel, they become a bye-word and occasion of offence by their own folly. Was David *wiser than his enemies or his teachers*, when he dissembled himself before Achish (1 Sam. xxvii.)—or when he yielded to the indulgence of lust (2 Sam. xi.)—or when in the pride of his heart he numbered the people? (2 Sam.

xxiv.) Alas! how often do even God's children befool themselves in the ways of sin!

But how did David attain this Divine wisdom? Not by habits of extensive reading—not by natural intelligence—but by a diligent *meditation in the testimonies.** In order to avail ourselves, however, of this means—*a simple reception of the Divine testimony is of absolute importance.* We can never obtain that assurance of the certainty of our faith, which is indispensable to our peace, or resist the influence of unenlightened *teachers,* or the long-established worldly maxims of *the ancients, except by entire submission to the supreme authority of Scripture.* Many sincere Christians—especially at the outset of their course—are much hindered—either by the scepticism of others, or of their own minds; or from their previous habit of studying the Bible in the light of carnal wisdom, or in dependence upon human teaching. Such need special prayer for humility of mind and simplicity of faith. Under this gracious influence they will discern that path to glory, which in infinite condescension is made so plain, that " the wayfaring men, though fools, shall not err therein," and the unlearned believer, who has the word before his eyes, in his heart, and in his life, shall become " perfect, thoroughly furnished unto all good works." (Isa. xxxv. 8. 2 Tim. iii. 17.)

In our Christian progress, David's habit of scriptural *meditation* will prove of essential service. For while those who " confer with flesh and blood" cannot have their counsellors always at hand; we, seeking our wisdom from the word of God, have the best Counsellor *ever with us,* teaching us what to do, and what to expect. Obedience also, as well as meditation, directs our way. David found

---

* This was bound upon him as a king. Deut. xvii. 18, 19.

understanding, because he kept the precepts. And David's Lord has pointed out the same path of light: "*If any man will do God's will, he shall know of the doctrine.*" (John, vii. 17.) "*Thou meetest him that rejoiceth, and worketh righteousness—those that remember thee in thy ways.*" (Isa. lxiv. 5. Comp. John, xiv. 21–23.) Thy ways truly are ways of light, joy, and love!

Now let us turn in, and inquire—What is our daily use of the word of God? Are we satisfied with a slight looking, or do we seek an intimate acquaintance with it! Is its influence ever present—ever practical? Do we prize it as a welcome guest? Is it our delightful companion and guide? Oh! *meditate* in this blessed book. " Eat the word," when you " have found it ; and it will be unto you the joy and rejoicing of your heart." (Jer. xv. 16.) The name of Jesus—its great subject—will be more precious—your love will be inflamed (Ps. xxxix. 3)—your perseverance established (Verses 23, 95)—and your heart enlivened in the spirit of praise. (Ps. lxiii. 5, 6.) Thus bringing your mind into close and continual contact with *the testimonies of God*, and pressing out the sweetness from the precious volume, it will drop as from the honeycomb, daily comfort and refreshment upon your heart.*

---

* Thus Luther recommends us to 'pause at any verse of Scripture we choose, and to shake, as it were, every bough of it; that, if possible, some fruit at least may drop down to us. Should this mode'—he remarks—' appear somewhat difficult at first, and no thought suggest itself immediately to the mind capable of affording matter for a short ejaculation; yet persevere, and try another and another bough. If your soul really hungers, the Spirit of God will not send you away empty. You shall at length find in one, and that perhaps a short verse in Scripture, such an abundance of delicious fruit, that you will gladly seat yourself under its shade, and abide there, as under a tree laden with fruit.'

101. *I have refrained my feet from every evil way, that I might keep thy word.*

David's wisdom was of a practical—not of a merely intellectual or speculative—character. It taught him to "*keep the Lord's precepts;*" and in order to this, to *refrain his feet from every evil way.* And will not advancing wisdom show itself by increasing tenderness of conscience and carefulness of conduct? The professor is afraid of hell; the child of God—of sin. The one *refrains* from the outward act—the other seeks to be crucified to the love of sin. Observe not only the practice, but the motive —that *he might keep the word.* Shall we not "abhor that which is evil," that we might "cleave to that which is good" (Rom. xii. 9)—"abstaining from all appearance of evil" (1 Thess. v. 22), lest unconsciously we should be drawn into the atmosphere of sin—"hating even the garment spotted by the flesh" (Jude, 23)—fearing the infection of sin worse than death? But how fearful the danger of self-deception! What need to entreat the Lord to "see if there be any wicked way in us?" (Ps. cxxxix. 24.) Oh! for the large supply of grace and unction, to maintain an upright walk before a heart-searching God; to "keep ourselves from our iniquity" (Ps. xviii. 23); and in dependence upon the promises, and in the strength of the gospel, to "perfect holiness in the fear of God!" (2 Cor. vii. 1.)

But how awful to hear men talk of *keeping the word* in a loose and careless profession! For how can it be kept, if the heart has not felt its holiness? For this is its beautiful peculiarity; that, in order to *keep* it, there must be a separation from sin. The two things are incompatible with each other. The two services are at variance at every point; so that the love of sin must be cast out, where the love of God is engrafted in the heart. Yet so strongly are we disposed to *every evil way*, that only the Almighty power of grace can enable us to *refrain from* one or another crooked path. Often is the pilgrim (yea, has it not too often happened to ourselves?) held back by a temporary ascendancy of the flesh—by a little license given to sin—or by a relaxed circumspection of walk. At such seasons, the blessed privilege of *keeping the word* is lost. We are sensible of a declining delight in those spiritual duties, which before were our " chiefest joy." And " is there not a cause?" Have we not provoked our gracious God by harbouring his enemy in our bosom—nay more— by pleading for its indulgence? Has not " the Holy Spirit been grieved" by neglect, or by some worldly compliance : so that his light has been obscured, and his comforting influence quenched? No consolations, consistent with the love and power of sin, can ever come from the Lord. For the holiness of the word of God cannot be either spiritually understood, or experimentally enjoyed, but in a consistent Christian walk. And yet, such is the true blessedness of the word, that the very expectation of *keeping it* may operate as a principle of restraint *from every evil way.*

Is there any bondage in this restraint from sin? Oh, no ! Sin is slavery ; and therefore deliverance from it is " perfect freedom." There is indeed a *legal restraint* much to be deprecated, when the conscience is goaded by sins of omission or of wilfulness ; and the man, ignorant of, or imperfectly acquainted with, the only way of deliverance, hopes to get rid of his burden by a more circumspect walk. But not till he casts it at the foot of the cross, and learns to look wholly to Jesus his deliverer, can he form his resolution upon safe and effectual grounds. Oh, may I therefore seek to abide within a constant view of Calvary ! Sin will live everywhere but under the cross of Jesus. Here it withers and dies. Here rises the spring of that holiness, contrition, and love, which refreshes and quickens the soul.　Here let me live : here let me die.*

Blessed Lord! thou knowest that I desire to *keep thy word.*　Prepare my heart to receive and to retain it. May I so "abide in Christ," that I may receive the sanctifying help of his Spirit for every moment's need!　And while I rejoice in him as my Saviour, may I become daily more sensible of every deviation from the straight path! May my eye guide my feet!　"Looking to Jesus," may I have light and grace!　And may daily grace be given to *refrain my feet from every evil way, that I may keep thy word!*

102. *I have not departed from thy judgments; for thou hast taught me.*

If *I have refrained my feet from* sin—if *I have not departed from God's judgments*—to him be all the glory. Oh, my soul! art thou not a wonder to thyself?　So prone to depart—to be carried away by uncertain notions—by the oppositions of Satan—by the example or influence of the world—how is it, that thou art able to hold on thy way?　Because the covenant of the Lord engages thy perseverance,—" I will put my fear in their hearts, that *they shall not depart* from me." (Jer. xxxii. 40.　Comp. xxxi. 33. 1 John, ii. 27.)　While conscious of my own corrupt bias to depart, let me humbly and thankfully own the work of Divine teaching.　Man's teaching is powerless in advancing the soul one step in Christian progress.　The teaching from

* ' When I am assaulted by some wicked thought, I then betake me to the wounds of Christ.　When my flesh casteth me down, by the remembrance of my Saviour's wounds, I rise up again.　Am I inflamed with lust?　I quench that fire with the meditation of Christ's passion.　Christ died for us.　There is nothing so deadly, that is not cured by the death of Christ.'—AUGUSTINE.

above is " the light of life." (John, viii. 12. Comp. Eph.
v. 14.) It gives not only the light, but the principle to
make use of it. It not only points the lesson, and makes
it plain : but imparts the disposition to learn, and the
grace to obey. So that now I see the beauty, the pleasantness, the peace, and the holiness of *the Lord's judgments*,
and am naturally constrained to walk in them. Oh, how
much more frequent would be our acknowledgment of the
work of God, did we keep nearer to the Fountain-head of
life and light! (Ps. xxxvi. 9.) How may we trace every
declension in doctrine⁀ and practice—all our continual
estrangement *from the Lord's judgments*—to following our
own wisdom, or depending upon human teaching! " Trusting in man," is the departing of the heart from the Lord.
(Jer. xvii. 5.) I never shall depart from sin by the influence of human persuasion. I never shall depart from
the Lord, so long as I have the witness in my heart—
Thou teachest me.

Reader! what has been your habit and progress *in
the judgments of God?* Have you been careful to avoid
bye-paths? Has your walk been consistent, steady, advancing " in the fear of the Lord, and in the comfort of
the Holy Ghost?" (Acts, ix. 31.) If there has been no
allowed departure from the ways of God, it has been the
blessed fruit of " ceasing from your own wisdom" (Prov.
xxiii. 4), and the simple dependence upon the promise
" written in the prophets—And they shall be all taught of
God." And how delightfully does this heavenly teaching
draw your heart with a deeper sense of need and comfort
to the Saviour! For, as he himself speaks, " *Every man
therefore that hath heard, and hath learned of the Father,
cometh unto me.*" (Isa. liv. 13, with John, vi. 45.) Remember—it was no superior virtue or discernment that has
restrained your departure from God, but — *Thou hast*

taught me the way to come to God ; the way to abide in
him — Christ the way — Christ the end. And his teaching will abide with you. (1 John, ii. 24, 27.) It will win
you by light and by love, and by a conquering power
allure your heart with that delight in his judgments, and
fear of offending against them, that shall prove an effectual
safeguard in the hour of temptation. Watch the first step
of departure,— the neglect of secret prayer,— the want of
appetite for the sincere word — the relaxing of diligence —
the loss of the savour of godliness. Be careful therefore
that the teaching of the Lord be not lost upon you.
Inquire into your proficiency in his instructive lessons.
And do not forget to prize his teaching rod — that loving
correction, of which David had felt the blessing (Verse 67),
and which he so often uses, to keep his children from
departing from his judgments.

Lord! do thou lead me by the hand, that I may make
daily progress in *thy judgments.* Restrain my feet from
" perpetual backsliding." All human instruction will be
ineffectual to keep me from *departing from thy judgments,*
except *thou teachest me.* Neither grace received, nor experience attained, nor engagements regarded, will secure
me for one moment without continual teaching from thyself.

103. *How sweet are thy words unto my taste! yea, sweeter
than honey to my mouth.*

None but a child of God could take up this expression.
Because none besides has a spiritual taste. The exercises
of David in this sacred word were delightfully varied. Its
majesty commanded his reverence. (Verses 129, 161.) Its
richness called forth his love. (Verses 72, 127. Ps. xix. 10.)
Its sweetness excited his joy. Its holy light, keeping his
heart close with God (Verse 102), naturally endeared it to

his soul.* How barren is a mere external knowledge of the Gospel! The natural man may talk or even dispute about its precious truths. But he has never tasted them —at least not so as to relish and feed on them. The highest commendation cannot explain the *sweetness of honey* (Prov. xxiv. 13, 14) to one who has never tasted it. Thus nothing but experience can give a spiritual intelligence. But what we have really tasted, we can warmly commend —" Oh! taste and see that the Lord is good." (Ps. xxxiv. 8.) Having once tasted of his Divine goodness, the sweetest joys of earth will be insipid, distasteful, and even bitter.

Do we ask—what is it that gives this unutterable sweetness to the word? (Ps. xix. 10. Job, xxiii. 12.) Is it not that name, which " is as ointment poured forth?" (Cant. i. 3.) Is it not " the savour of the knowledge of Christ" (2 Cor. ii. 14), that revives the soul in every page with the breath of heaven? For can the awakened sinner hear, that " God so loved the world, that he gave his only-begotten Son, that whosoever believeth in him should not perish, but have everlasting life" (John, iii. 16)—and not be ready to say—*How sweet are thy words unto my taste! yea, sweeter than honey unto my mouth?* Can the weary soul listen to the invitation to " all that labour and are heavy-laden" (Matt. xi. 28. Comp. Prov. xvi. 24); and not feel the *sweetness* of those breathings of love? Who can tell the *sweetness* of those precious *words* to the conflicting, tempted soul — displaying the Divine sovereignty in choosing him, the unchanging faithfulness in keeping him, and the Almighty power of the Divine will in the gift of eternal life? (John, x. 28.) And how can the believer hear his Saviour " knock at the door" of

* Verse 102. Thrice in one short Psalm does he stir up his habit of praise of the word, and of the God who gave it. See Ps. lvi. 4, 10.

his heart, calling him to fresh communion with himself
(Rev. iii. 20): and not turn to him with the ardent excitement of his love—"All thy garments smell of myrrh,
and aloes, and cassia, out of the ivory palaces, whereby
they have made thee glad!" (Ps. xlv. 8.)

But are there not times, when we gather no *sweetness*
from the word? It is with the spiritual, as with the
natural food—a want of appetite gives disgust, instead of
sweetness and refreshment. An indolent reading of the
word without faith—without desire—without application
—or with a taste vitiated by contact with the things of
sense—deadens the palate—"The full soul loatheth an
honeycomb : but to the hungry soul every bitter thing is
sweet." (Prov. xxvii. 7.)

But how melancholy is the thought of the multitudes,
that hear, read, understand the word, and yet have never
tasted its sweetness! Like Barzillai, they have no sense
to "discern between good and evil." (2 Sam. xix. 35.)
Full of the world, or of their own conceits—feeding on
the delusive enjoyments of creature-comforts—nourishing
some baneful corruption in their bosoms (See 1 Pet. ii.
1, 2)—or cankered with a spirit of formality—they have no
palate for the things of God ; they are "dead in trespasses
and sins." But *how sweet is the word* to the hungering and
thirsting *taste!* We eat, and are not satisfied. We drink,
and long to drink again. "If so be we have tasted that
the Lord is gracious, as new-born babes" we shall "desire
the sincere milk of the word, that we may grow thereby."
(1 Pet. ii. 2, 3.) We shall take heed of any indulgence of
the flesh, which may hinder the spiritual enjoyment, and
cause us to "loathe" even "angels' food" as "light bread."
(Ps. lxxviii. 25. Num. xxi. 5.) Instead of resting in our
present experience of its sweetness, we shall be daily
aspiring after higher relish for the heavenly blessing.*

* "*Castæ deliciæ meæ* sunt Scripturæ tuæ."—AUGUSTINE.

And will not this experience be a "witness in ourselves" of the heavenly origin of the word? For what arguments could ever persuade us that honey is bitter, at the moment when we are tasting its sweetness? Or who could convince us that this is the word of man, or the imposture of deceit, when its blessed influence has imparted peace, holiness, joy, support, and rest, infinitely beyond the power of man to bestow? But let this enjoyment — as the spiritual barometer — the pulse of the soul — accurately mark our progress or decline in the Divine life. With our advancement in spiritual health, the word will be increasingly *sweet to our taste:* while our declension will be marked by a corresponding abatement in our desires, love, and perception of its delights.

104. *Through thy precepts I get understanding : therefore I hate every false way.*

The Psalmist having spoken of the pleasure, now speaks of the profit — of the word — the teaching connected with its sweetness. (Prov. ii. 10, 11 ; xvi. 21.) Before, he had mentioned the avoiding of sin in order to profit (Verse 101) — now, as the fruit of profit. So closely are they linked together. Man's teaching conveys no *understanding* — God's teaching not only opens the Scriptures, but "opens the understanding to understand them," and the heart to feel their heavenly warmth of life. (Comp. Luke, xxiv. 45, 32.) Thus having learned "the principles of the doctrine of Christ," we shall "go on to perfection" — "growing in grace, in the knowledge of Christ." (Heb. vi. 1. 2 Pet. iii. 18.) Many inconsistencies belong to the young and half-instructed Christian. But when *through the precepts he gets understanding,* he learns to walk more uniformly and steadily, *abiding in the light.* In this spirit and atmosphere springs up a constant and irreconcileable *hatred of every false way;* as contrary to the God he loves. These ways will include a thousand devious paths —all meeting in one fearful end—often discovered too late. (Prov. v. 11. Matt. xxv. 11, 12.) In doctrine can we too much turn away from the thought of putting any-thing—the Church, ordinances, repentance, prayers—in the place of Jesus—another "foundation" in the stead of that which God himself "laid in Zion?" Oh, for spiritual *under-standing to hate this false way* with a deadly hatred! What think we of the ways of the sinful world—so long trusted to for happiness—yet so delusive? The sinner thinks that he has found a treasure, but it proves to be glittering trash—burdensome instead of enriching—only leaving him to the pain of disappointed hope. Rightly are such ways called *false ways;* and of those that tread in them, it is well said—" This their way is their folly." (Ps. xlix. 13.) Strewed they may be with the flowery "pleasures of sin." But they are "hard" (Prov. xiii. 15) in their walk, and ruinous in their end. (Matt. viii. 12. Philip. iii. 19.) In-quire of those, whose past wanderings justly give weight and authority to their verdict—' What is your retrospective view of these ways?' Unprofitableness. ' What is your present view of them?' Shame. ' What prospect for eternity would the continuance in them assure to you?' " Death." (Rom. vi. 21.) Let them then be not only avoided and forsaken, but abhorred; and let every devi-ation into them from the straight path, however pleasing, be " resisted" even " unto blood." (Heb. xii. 4.)

But let me ask myself, Have I detected the *false ways* of my own heart? Little is done in spiritual religion, until my besetting sins are searched out. And let me not be satisfied with forbearance from the outward act. Sin may be restrained, yet not mortified; nor is it enough that I leave it for the present, but I must renounce it for ever. Let me not part with it as with a beloved friend, with the hope and purpose of renewing my familiarity with it at a " more convenient season " (Acts, xxiv. 25) : but let me shake it from me, as Paul shook off the viper into the fire (Acts, xxviii. 5), with determination and abhorrence. What! can I wish to hold it ? If *through the precepts of God I have got understanding,* must not I listen to that solemn, pleading voice, " Oh ! do not this abominable thing that I hate ?" (Jer. xliv. 4.) No, Lord : let me " pluck it out" of my heart, " and cast it from me." (Matt. v. 29.) Oh, for the high blessing of a tender conscience ! such as shrinks from the approach, and " abstains from all appearance of evil" (1 Thess. v. 22) ; not venturing to tamper with any self-pleasing way ; but *hating* it as *false,* defiling, destructive ! I have marked the apple of my eye — that tenderest particle of my frame — that it is not only offended by a blow or a wound ; but that, if so much as an atom of dust find an entrance, it would smart, until it had wept it out. Now such may my conscience be — sensitive of the slightest touch of sin — not only fearful of resisting, rebelling, or " quenching the Spirit," but grieving for every thought of sin that grieves that blessed Comforter — that tender Friend ! To *hate every false way,* so as to flee from it, is the highest proof of Christian courage. For never am I better prepared to " endure hardness as a good soldier of Jesus Christ" (2 Tim. ii. 3), than when my conscience is thus set against sin. Would not I then submit to the greatest suffering, rather than be convicted of unfaithfulness to my God ?

Lord ! turn my eyes, my heart, my feet, my ways, more and more to thy blessed self. Shed abroad thy love in my heart, that sin may be the daily matter of my watchfulness, grief, resistance, and crucifixion.

PART XIV.

105. *Thy word is a lamp unto my feet, and a light unto my*
path.

THE nightly journeys of Israel were guided by a pillar of
fire (Exod. xiii. 21, 22)—directing not only their course,
but every step and movement. (Numb. ix. 15–23.) Thus
is our passage in a dark and perilous way irradiated by the
lamp and light of the word. But except *the lamp* be lighted
—except the teaching of the Spirit accompany *the word,* all
is darkness—thick darkness. Let us not then be content
to read *the word* without obtaining some *light* from it in
our understanding—in our experience—in our providential path. Did we more habitually wait to receive, and
watch to improve the light, we should not so often complain of the perplexity of our path. It would generally
determine our steps under infallible guidance : while in the
presumptuous neglect of it—like Israel of old (Numb. xiv.
44, 45)—we are sure to come into trouble.

Yet it may sometimes be difficult to trace our light to
this heavenly source. *A promise may seem to be applied to*
my mind, as I conceive, suitable to my present need. But how
may I determine, whether it is *the lamp of the word;* or
some delusive light from him, who can at any time, for the
accomplishment of his own purpose, transform himself
"into an angel of light?" Or if a threatening be impressed upon my conscience, how can I accurately distinguish between the voice of " the accuser of the brethren,"

and the warning of my heavenly guide? Let me mark the
state of my own mind. If I am living in the indulgence
of any known sin, or in the neglect of any known duty —
if my spirit is careless, or my walk unsteady ; a consoling
promise, being unsuitable to my case, even though it
awakened some excitement of joy, would be of doubtful
application. *The lamp* of God *under the circumstances
supposed*, would rather reflect the light of conviction than
of consolation. For, though God as a Sovereign may speak
comfort when and where he pleases ; yet we can only expect him to deal with us according to the prescribed rules
of his own covenant ; chastening, not comforting, his backsliding people. (Comp. Ps. lxxxix. 30–32.) In a spirit of
contrition, however, I should not hesitate to receive a word
of encouragement, as *the lamp of God* to direct and cheer
my progress ; being conscious of that state of feeling, in
which the Lord has expressly promised to restore and guide
his people. (Comp. Isa. lvii. 18.) Let me also inquire
into the terms and character of the promise. When he
" that dwelleth in the high and holy place," engages to
dwell " with him also that is of a contrite and humble
spirit" (Isa. lvii. 15) ; any symptoms of tenderness and
humility would naturally lead me to consider this word of
promise, as sent by my kind and watchful Father, to be
a lamp unto my feet, and a light unto my path.

Again — a distinct and experimental view of the Saviour in his promises, endearing him to me, and encouraging my trust in his faithfulness and love — this is manifestly
light from above. (Comp. 2 Cor. i. 20.) Or if the purpose of the promise answers any proper end — to excite or
to encourage to any present duty connected with the promise ; I cannot doubt, but *the lamp of the Lord* is directing
my path.

For example — when the promise was given to Joshua,
" I will not fail thee, nor forsake thee" (Josh. i. 5) ; he

could not misconstrue " a word" so " fitly spoken" " in a time of need." And when the same promise was subsequently given to the Church, the application was equally clear, as a dissuasive from inordinate attachment to the things of time and sense, and an encouragement to entire dependence upon the Lord. (Heb. xiii. 5.)

Further—The practical influence of the word will also enable me clearly to distinguish the light of heaven from any illusion of fancy or presumption. The effect of an *unconditional promise* of deliverance given to the Apostle in a moment of extremity, was exhibited in a diligent use of all the appointed means of safety. (Acts, xxvii. 24, 31.) An *absolute* promise of prolonged life given to Hezekiah when lying at the point of death, produced the same practical result, in a scrupulous attention to the means for his recovery. (Isa. xxxviii. 5, 21.) Upon the warrant of a general promise of Divine protection, Ezra and the Jews " fasted, and besought their God for this." (Ezra, viii. 21–23.) Now in these and other instances, the power of the word, working diligence, simplicity, and prayer, evidently proved its sacred origin. An assurance of safety proceeding from another source, would have produced sloth, carelessness, and presumption; and therefore may I not presume the quickening word in darkness and perplexity, to be the Lord's *lamp unto my feet*, and light *unto my path*, " to guide my feet into the way of peace?"

Let me apply the same test to the threatenings of the word. Their influence, meeting me in a watchful and humble walk with God, I should at once consider as the suggestion of the great enemy of the soul, ever ready to whisper distrust and despondency to the child of God. But in a self-confident, self-indulgent state, I should have as little hesitation in marking an alarming word to be *the light of the word of God*. It would be well for me at such a time to be exercised with fear (Comp. 1 Cor. ix. 27); not as arguing any insecurity in my state; but as leading me to " great searchings of heart," to increasing watchfulness, humiliation, and prayer. " The commandment is a lamp, and the law is a light : and reproofs of instruction are the ways of life." (Prov. vi. 23.) Oh, that I may be enabled to make use of this *lamp* to direct every step of my heavenly way !

Whence then — it may be asked — the various tracks even of the sincere servants of God ? Though there is clear light in the word, yet there is remaining darkness in the most enlightened heart. There is no eye without a speck, no eye with perfect singleness of vision — consequently without some liability to error. There is light for the teachable — not for the curious ; — light to satisfy faith — not cavilling. Add to this the office of the ministry — the Lord's gracious ordinance for Christian instruction (Mal. ii. 7) and establishment (Eph. iv. 11–14) ; not to enslave (2 Cor. i. 24. 1 Pet. v. 3), but to direct (2 Cor. xiii. 10. Eph. iv. 13. 1 Thess. iii. 10) the judgment in the light of the word. To honour this ordinance is therefore the path of light. To neglect it, is the the exposure to all the evils of a wayward will and undisciplined judgment. (2 Tim. iv. 3, 4.)

Lord ! as every action of the day is a step to heaven, or hell — Oh ! save me from ever turning my face away from the path, into which thy word would guide me. Enable me to avail myself of its light, in the constant exercise of faith, prudence, and simplicity.

106. *I have sworn, and I will perform it, that I will keep thy righteous judgments.*

The blessing of the guidance of the Lord's word naturally strengthens our resolution to walk in its path. And as if a simple resolution would prove too weak, the Psalmist strengthens it with an oath. Nay more, as if an oath was hardly sufficient security, he seconds it again with a firm resolution—*I have sworn, and I will perform it.* 'There shall be but one will between me and my God; and that will shall be his, not mine.' Some timid Christians, under a morbid sense of their own weakness, would shrink from this solemn engagement. And some, perhaps, may have burdened their consciences with unadvised or self-dependent obligations.* Still, however, when it is a free-will offering, it is a delightful service, well-pleasing to God. Such it was in the days of Asa, when "all Judah *rejoiced at the oath: for they had sworn with all their heart, and sought him with their whole desire; and he was found of them."* (2 Chron. xv. 12–15.) Vows under the law were both binding and acceptable. (Numb. xxx. 1. Deut. xxiii. 21–23.) Nor are they less so—*in their spirit at least*—under "the perfect law of liberty." A holy promise originating in serious consideration, and established by a more solemn obligation, so far

---

* It is related of Mr. Pearce, by his excellent biographer, that at the period of the first awakening of his mind—'having read Doddridge's 'Rise and Progress of Religion,' he determined formally to dedicate himself to the Lord in the manner recommended in the seventeenth chapter of that work. The form of a covenant there drawn up he also adopted as his own; and that he might bind himself in the solemn and affecting manner, signed it *with his blood.* But, afterwards, failing in his engagements, he was plunged into the greatest distress, and almost into despair. On a review of his covenant, he seems to have accused himself of pharisaical reliance upon the strength of his resolutions, and, therefore, taking the paper to the top of his father's house, he tore it into small pieces, and threw it from him to be scattered by the wind. He did not, however, consider his obligation to be the Lord's as thereby nullified; but feeling more suspicious of himself, he depended solely *upon the blood of the cross.'*—FULLER's *Life of Pearce,* pp. 3, 4. This instance must be considered, not as an example of the entangling nature of covenant engagements, but as an illustration, by way of contrast, of the enlightened deliberation and simplicity with which they should ever be undertaken. See some admirable remarks on this subject from Newton's pen. *Life of* GRIMSHAWE, pp. 16–18.

from being repugnant to the liberty of the gospel, appears
to have been enjoined by God himself;* nay, his people are
described as animating each other to it, as to a most joyous
privilege (Jer. l. 4, 5); as a renewed act of faith and daily
dedication.

Yet we would warn the inconsiderate Christian not to
entangle his conscience by *multiplied vows* (as if they were
—like prayer—a component part of our daily religion);
nor *by perpetual obligation*—whether of restraint or of
extraordinary exercises; nor *by connecting them with trifles*
—thus weakening the deep solemnity of the purpose.
Christian simplicity must be their principle. Our engagements to God must be grounded on his engagements to us.
His faithfulness—not ours (Contrast Matt. xxvi. 35)—
must be our confidence. There is no innate power in these
obligations; and except they be made in self-renouncing
dedication, they will only issue in despondency and deeper
captivity in sin.

But the inconsiderateness of the unwary is no legitimate argument against their importance. If Jephthah was
entangled in a rash and heedless vow (Judg. xi. 35), David
manifestly enjoyed the "perfect freedom" of the "service"
of his God, when "binding his soul with a bond" equally
fixed, but more advised, in its obligation. (Ps. cxvi. 12–
14.) And have we, with "the vows of God upon us"
(Ps. lvi. 12), baptismal vows—perhaps also confirmation
or sacramental vows—found our souls brought into
bondage by these solemn engagements? Does not a
humbling sense of forgetfulness suggest sometimes the
need of a more solemn engagement? And may we not
thus secure our duty without being ensnared by it? Have
not covenanting seasons often restrained our feet from
devious paths, and quickened our souls in his service?
Daily, indeed, do we need "the blood of sprinkling" to par-

* Isa. xix. 21. Comp. also Isa. xliv. 5, and SCOTT on this verse.

don our innumerable failures, and the Spirit of grace to strengthen us for a more devoted obligation. (Gen. xxxv. 1, with xxviii. 20–22. Comp. 2 Pet. i. 9.) But yet in dependence upon the work and Spirit of Christ, often have these holy transactions realized to us a peace and joy, that leads us to look back upon such times and seasons of favoured enjoyment. " If," therefore, " we sin" in a " perpetual backsliding" (Jer. viii. 5) from these engagements, it is still our privilege without presumption to believe, that " we have an advocate with the Father, Jesus Christ the righteous ; and he is the propitiation for our sins." (1 John, ii. 1, 2.) And as for necessary grace, there is One who hath said —" My grace is sufficient for thee " (2 Cor. xii. 9) ; and that One has given no less a proof of his interest in us, than by dying for us. May we not therefore trust, that he will " perfect that which concerneth us" (Ps. cxxxviii. 8) ; that he will " work all our works in us" (Isa. xxvi. 12)—" to will and to do of his good pleasure ?" (Phil. ii. 13.)

Perhaps however " a messenger of Satan" may " buffet us." " Thou hast broken thy bond ; now will it be worse with thee than before." But did not Jesus die for sins of infirmity, and even of presumption ? Does every failing annul the marriage covenant ? So neither does every infirmity or backsliding dissolve our covenant with God. Was our faithfulness the basis of this covenant ? Rather, does not " the blood of this covenant " (Heb. xiii. 20) make constant provision for our foreseen unfaithfulness ? And does not our gracious God overrule even our backsliding to establish a more simple reliance upon himself, and a more circumspect and tender walk before him ?

But let us take a case of conscience. A Christian has been drawn away from a set season of extraordinary devotion by some unforeseen present duty, or some unlooked-for opportunity of actively glorifying God. Has he then broken his obligation ?   Certainly not.   It was, *or ought to have been, formed* with an implied subserviency to paramount duty.   It cannot, therefore, be impaired by any such providential interference.   Yet let it not be a light matter to remove a free-will offering from the altar.   Let godly care be exercised to discover the subtle indulgence of the flesh in the service of God.   Let double diligence redeem the lost privilege of more immediate and solemn self-dedication. In guarding against legal bondage, let us not mistake the liberty of the flesh for the liberty of the Gospel.   Let us be simple and ready for self-denying service ; and the Lord our God will not fail to vouchsafe " some token for good."

" Come " then, my fellow-Christian, " and let us join ourselves to the Lord in a perpetual covenant, never to be forgotten " (Jer. l. 5) by God : never to be forsaken by us. Let each of us renew our surrender—" O Lord, truly I am thy servant ;" I offer myself to thee : " Thou hast loosed my bonds " (Ps. cxvi. 16) ; oh ! bind me to thyself with fresh bonds of love, that may never be loosed.   Glad am I that I am anything — though the meanest of all ; that I have anything — poor and vile as it is — capable of being employed in thy service. I yield myself to Thee with my full bent of heart and will, entirely and for ever ; asking only, that I may be " a vessel for the Master's use." (2 Tim. ii. 21.)

107. *I am afflicted very much : quicken me, O Lord, according to thy word.*

It would seem, that this holy saint's covenanting season was a time of deep *affliction :* while his determined resolution to *keep* God's word of obedience, gave boldness to his pleading, that God would perform his word of promise — *Quicken me, O Lord, according to thy word.* And this is our high privilege, that we are permitted to pour our troubles into the ear of One, who is able perfectly to enter into, and to sympathize with us in them ; " who knoweth our frame" (Ps. ciii. 14), who hath himself laid the affliction upon us (Ps. xxxix. 9) : yea, more than all, who in " all our affliction is" himself " afflicted" (Isa. lxiii. 9) ; and who " suffered being tempted, that he might be able to succour them that are tempted." (Heb. ii. 18.)   There are none—not even those most dear to us—to whom we can unbosom ourselves, as we do to our heavenly Friend. Our wants, griefs, burdens of every kind — we roll them all upon him, with special relief in the hour of affliction.   An affecting contrast to those who are indeed *afflicted very much;* whose souls, " drawing near unto death," and knowing no refuge, are ready to burst with their own sorrows, " the sorrow of the world"—unmitigated—unrelieved— " working death !" (2 Cor. vii. 10.)

There is a " needs-be" (1 Pet. i. 6, 7) for the *afflictions* of the Lord's people.   The stones of the spiritual temple cannot be polished or fitted to their place without the strokes of the hammer.   The gold cannot be purified without the furnace.   The vine must be pruned for greater fruitfulness. (John, xv. 2.)   The measure of discipline varies indefinitely.   But such is the inveteracy of fleshly lusts, that *very much affliction* may often be the needful regimen. (2 Cor. xii. 7.)   Yet will it be tempered by one, who knows the precise measure (Job, xxxiv. 23), who can make no mistakes in our constitutions, and whose fatherly pity will chasten " not for his pleasure, but for our profit." (Ps. ciii. 13, 14. Heb. xii. 10.)   And need we speak of the alleviations of our trials, that they are infinitely disproportioned to our deserts (Ezra, ix. 13)—that they are " light, and but for a moment," compared with eternity (2 Cor. iv. 17)—that greater comfort is vouchsafed in the endurance of them, than we even ventured to anticipate from their removal (2 Cor. xii. 8–10)—that the fruit at the end more than balances the trials themselves? (Deut. viii. 15, 16. Jer. xxix. 11.) Need we say—how richly they ought to be prized, as conforming us to the image of our suffering Lord (1 Pet. iv. 13); how clearly we shall one day read in them our Father's commission, as messengers of love; and how certainly " the end of the Lord" will be " that the Lord is very pitiful aud of tender mercy?" (Jam. v. 11, with Job, xlii. 10–12.)

Perhaps affliction—at least *very much affliction*—may not be our present lot. Yet it is our duty, and wisdom, as the good soldier in the time of truce, to burnish our armour for the fight. " Let not him that girdeth on his harness boast himself as he that putteth it off. Because the wicked have no changes, therefore they fear not God." (1 Kings, xx. 11. Ps. lv. 19.) The continual changes in Christian experience may well remind us of the necessity of " walking humbly with God," that we may not, by an unprepared spirit, lose the blessing of the sanctified cross. How many of the Lord's dear children may bear Ephraim's name—"*For God hath caused me to be fruitful in the land of my affliction!*" (Gen. xli. 52.) Sometimes they are so conscious of the present good, that they dread affliction *leaving* them, more, probably, than the inexperienced professor dreads its *coming*.

But great affliction is as hard to bear as great prosperity. Some whose Christian profession had drawn out the esteem of others—perhaps also their own complacency—have shown by " faintness in the day of adversity their strength to be small" (Prov. xxiv. 10. Comp. Jonah, iv. 5–9), and themselves to be almost untaught in this school of discipline—shaken, confused, broken. Special need indeed have we under the smart of the rod, of *quickening* grace to preserve us from stout-heartedness or dejection. We think we could bear the stroke, did we know it to be paternal, not judicial. Have we, then, " forgotten the exhortation, which speaketh unto us *as unto* children?" Do " we despise the chastening of the Lord? ' *Quicken me, Lord*, that I may be preserved in a humble, wakeful, listening posture, to hear and improve the message of thy blessing of the sanctified cross.' Do we " faint, when we are rebuked of him?" (Heb. xii. 5.) " *Quicken me, O Lord*," that I sink not under the "blow of thy hand." (Ps. xxxix. 10; xxxviii. 1–3.) Thus will this Divine influence save us from the horrible sin of being offended with God in our fretting spirit. We shall receive his chastisement with humility without despondency, and with reverence without distrust; hearkening to the voice that speaks, while we tremble under the rod that strikes: yet so mingling fear with confidence, that we may at the same moment adore the hand which we feel, and rest in mercy that is promised. (Mic. vii. 8, 9.) Our best support in the depths of affliction is, prayer for *quickening according to thy word!* and which of the exercised children of God has ever found one jot or one tittle of it to fail? " Patience working experience, and experience hope, and hope making not ashamed," in the sense of " the love of God shed abroad upon the heart by the Holy Ghost which is given unto us " — all this is the abundant answer to our prayer, " Thou which hast showed me great and sore troubles, *shalt quicken me again*, and shalt bring me up again from the depths of the earth. Thou shalt increase my greatness, and comfort me on every side." (Rom. v. 3–5, with Ps. lxxi. 20, 21.) Nothing will bear looking back to with comfort, like those trials, which though painful to the flesh, have tended to break our spirit, mould our will, and strengthen the simplicity of our walk with God.

108. *Accept, I beseech thee, the free-will offerings of my mouth, O Lord: and teach me thy judgments.*

As the first-fruits of his entire self-devotion to the

Lord (Verse 106); as the only sacrifice he could render in his affliction ; and as an acknowledgment of his answered prayer for *quickening* grace (Verse 107), behold this faithful servant of God presenting *the free-will offerings of his mouth for acceptance.* Such he knew to be an acceptable service. For the sacrifices of the Old Testament were not only typical of the One sacrifice for sin, but of the spiritual worship of the people of God. (Comp. Ps. li. 16, 17. Mal. iii. 3, with Philip. iv. 18. Heb. xiii. 15, 16. 1 Pet. ii. 5.) To those who are interested in the atonement of Jesus, there needeth " no more sacrifice for sin." That which is now required of us, and in which we would delight, is to " take with us words, and turn to him, and say unto him — Take away all iniquity, and receive us graciously ; so will we render *the calves of our lips.*" (Hos. xiv. 2.)

No offering but a *free-will offering* is accepted. Such was the service under the law (Num. xxix. 39. Deut. xvi. 10. 2 Chron. xxxi. 14. Amos, iv. 5) : such must it be under the gospel. (Rom. xii. 1. 2 Cor. v. 14, 15 ; viii. 5.) Yet neither can this offering be accepted, until the offerer himself has found acceptance with his God. " The Lord had respect," first to the person of " Abel," then " to his offering." (Gen. iv. 4, 5.) But if our persons are covered with the robe of acceptance—if the " offering up of the body of Jesus Christ once for all" has " perfected" us before God (Heb. x. 10, 14) : however defiled our services may be, however mixed with infirmity, and in every way most unworthy ; even a God of ineffable holiness " beholds no iniquity" (Num. xxiii. 21) in them. No offering is so pure as to obtain acceptance in any other way ; no offering so sinful as to fail of acceptance in this way. Most abundant, indeed, and satisfactory is the provision made in heaven for the continual and everlasting acceptance of our polluted and distracted services—" Another angel came, and stood at the altar, having a golden censer ; and there was given unto him much incense, that he should offer it, with the prayers of all saints, upon the golden altar which was before the throne. And the smoke of the incense, which came with the prayers of the saints, ascended up before God out of the angel's hand." (Rev. viii. 3, 4.) With such a High Priest and Intercessor, not only is unworthiness dismissed, but boldness and assurance of faith is encouraged. (Heb. iv. 14–16 ; x. 21, 22.)

But, as we remarked, it was a *free-will offering* that we here presented—the overflowings of a heart filled with love. No constraint was necessary. Prayer was delightful. He was not forced upon his knees. Let me seek fellowship with him in presenting my *free offering* before my God. Does not he love it? (2 Cor. ix. 7.) Does not his free love to me deserve it? (Eph. ii. 4, 5.) Did not my beloved Saviour give *a free-will offering* of delight and of joy? (Ps. xl. 8. Heb. xii. 2.) And shall not his free-flowing love be my pattern and my principle? (2 Cor. v. 14, 15.) Shall his offering be free for me, and mine, be reluctant for him? Shall he be ready with his blood for me, and I be backward with my mouth for him? O my God, work thine own Almighty work—make me not only living, but "*willing* in the day of thy power." (Ps. cx. 3.) Let the stream flow in the full tide of affectionate devotedness. Blessed Jesus! I would be thine, and none other's. I would tell the world, that I am captivated by thy love, and consecrated to thy service. Oh, let me "*rejoice for that I offered willingly.*" Great grace is it, that he is willing to accept my service. For what have I to offer, that is not already "his own?" (1 Chron. xxix. 9, 14, 17.) But let me not forget to supplicate for further instruction—'*Teach me thy judgments,* that I may be directed to present a purer offering ; that by more distinct

and accurate knowledge of thy ways, my love may be enlarged, and my obedience more entire, until I "stand perfect and complete in all the will of God."' (Col. iv. 12.)

109. *My soul is continually in my hand, yet do I not forget
thy law.* 110. *The wicked have laid a snare for me : yet
I erred not from thy precepts.*

Precarious health, or familiarity with dangers, may
give peculiar emphasis to the phrase — *My soul is continually
in my hand.* (Comp. Judg. xii. 3. Job, xiii. 14.) David,
in his early public life, was in constant apprehension from
the open violence (Comp. 1 Sam. xix. 5 ; xxviii. 21) and
the secret machinations (1 Sam. xviii. 10, 11 ; xix. 9, 10)
of his bitter enemy.* Hunted down " as a partridge in the
mountains" (1 Sam. xxvi. 20), and often scarcely escaping
the snare *which the wicked laid for him.* (1 Sam. xviii. 10 ;
xix. 11–17) ; at one time he could not but acknowledge —
" there is but a step between me and death" (1 Sam. xx. 3);
at another time he was tempted to say, " I shall now perish
one day by the hand of Saul." (1 Sam. xxvii. 1.) Subsequently the hand of his own son was aimed at his throne
and his life. (2 Sam. xv. 13, 14 ; xvii. 1–3.) Yet could
no peril shake his undaunted adherence to *the law and precepts of God.* (Verse 87.)

What was the life of Jesus upon earth? Through the
enmity of foes — various, opposite, yet combined (Luke,
xxiii. 12) — his *soul was continually in his hand.* Yet how
wonderful was his calmness and serenity of mind, when
surrounded by them all, like " lions" in power, " dogs" in
cruelty, wolves in malice ! (Ps. xxii. 16, 20, 21, with
Isa. liii. 7.) A measure of this spirit belongs to every

* The men of Keilah, 1 Sam. xxiii. 11, 12. The Ziphites, Ib.
xxiii. 19 ; xxvi. 1.

faithful disciple—not natural courage, but "the spirit of power," as the gift of God (2 Tim. i. 7), enabling him in the path of *the precepts* "to withstand in the evil day, and having done all, to stand." (Eph. vi. 13.)

Let us again mark this confidence, illustrated in the open trials of the servants of God. Mark the Apostle, when "the Holy Ghost witnessed to him in every city, that bonds and imprisonment awaited him. None of these things"—said he—"move me. I am ready not to be bound only, but also to die at Jerusalem for the name of the Lord Jesus." (Acts, xx. 23, 24 ; xxi. 13.) He could look "tribulation, or persecution, or peril, or sword," in the face ; and, while he *carried his soul continually in his hand*, in true Christian heroism, in the most exalted triumph of faith, he could say in the name of himself and his companions in tribulation—"Nay, in all these things we are more than conquerors." Nothing could make him flinch. Nothing could turn him back. Nothing could wring the love of the service of his God out of his heart. His principle was found invincible in the hour of trial— not, however, as a native energy of his heart, but "*through him that loved him*." (Rom. viii. 37.) Did he not speak and live in the spirit of this fearless confidence—*Yet do I not forget thy law?* Daniel's history again shows the utter impotency of secret devices to produce apostasy in the children of God. When *the wicked*, after many an ineffectual attempt to "find occasion or fault," were driven to *lay a snare for him* in "the law of his God" (Dan. vi. 5), this noble confessor of the faith continued to "kneel upon his knees three times a-day, and prayed and gave thanks before his God, as *he did afore-time*." (Verses 6–10.) The den of lions was far less fearful in his eyes than one devious step from the straight and narrow path. (Comp. Luke, xii. 4, 5.) Sin was dreaded as worse than a thousand deaths. He surely then could have said—*Yet I erred not from thy precepts.*

But how striking must it have been to David, in his imminent peril, to have seen the " counsel of Ahithophel "—regarded as oracular, when employed in the cause of God—now, when directed against the church, " turned to foolishness !" (Comp. 2 Sam. xvi. 23, with xv. 31 ; xvii. 14) — an instance, only " one of a thousand," of the ever-watchful keeping of the Great Head and Guardian of his Church. (Isa. xxvii. 3.) Thus does he over-rule the devices of the enemy for the establishment of his people's dependence upon himself. " The wrath of man praiseth him" (Ps. lxxvi. 10), and he " taketh the wise in his own craftiness." (Job, v. 3, with 1 Cor. iii. 19.)

But the day of difficulty is a " perilous time" in the church. " Many shall be purified, and made white, and tried." (Dan. xii. 10.) Have we been able to sustain the shock in a steady adherence to *the law and precepts of God?* (Verses 51, 69. Rev. ii. 10.) This is indeed the time, when genuine faith will be found of inestimable value. In such a time, David experienced the present blessing of having chosen the Lord for his God. When clouds began to gather blackness, and surrounding circumstances to the eye of sense engendered despondency — faith realized All-sufficient support ; and " David encouraged himself in the Lord his God." (1 Sam. xxx. 6.) And is not David's God " our God, the health of our countenance" (Ps. xlii. 11), the guide of our path (Ps. xlviii. 14), the God of our salvation ? (Ps. lxviii. 20.) Oh, let us not rest, till his confidence becomes ours—" What time I am afraid, I will trust in thee." (Ps. lvi. 3.)

But the cross, which proves and establishes the Christian, sifts the unsound professor as chaff. Nothing but this *solid principle* of faith can resist either the persecution (Matt. xiii. 20, 21) or *the snare.* (1 Kings, xiii.

11–19.) Many desire conformity to Christ and his people in everything but in their ʻcross. They would attain their honour without the steps that led them to it. Dread this flinching spirit. Reject it—as did our Lord—with indignation. It "savoureth not of God." It is the voice of Satan (Matt. xvi. 22, 23), who would promise a pillow of carnal ease under our heads—a path of roses under our feet—but a path of slumber, of delusion, and of ruin.

The time of special need is at hand with us all, when we shall need substance and reality for our support—the true confidence of a living faith. Those who have never felt the nearness of eternity, can have but a faint idea of what we shall need in the hour when "flesh and heart fail" (Ps. lxxiii. 26), to fix a sure unshaken foot upon "the Rock of ages." "Watch, therefore," for ye know not (Mark, xiii. 35, 36) how soon ye may be ready to say, *My soul is in my hand,* quivering on the eve of departure to the Judge. " Let your loins be girded about, and your lights burning! and ye yourselves like unto men that wait for the Lord, when he will return from the wedding ; that when he cometh and knocketh, they may open unto him *immediately.* Blessed are those servants, whom the Lord, when he cometh, shall find watching ; verily I say unto you, that he shall gird himself, and make them to sit down to meat, and will come forth and serve them." (Luke, xii. 35–37.)

111. *Thy testimonies have I taken as an heritage for ever, for they are the rejoicing of my heart.*

' Precious Bible : what a treasure !' *The testimonies of God*—the declaration of his will in doctrine—obligation —and privilege ! David had felt their value, as the stay of his soul in shaking and sifting trial. (Verses 109, 110.) But how did he claim his interest in them ? Not by purchase, or by merit, it was his *heritage*. As a child of Abraham, he was an " heir according to promise." (Gal. iii. 29.) *They*—all that is contained in them, " the Lord himself," the sum and substance of all, " was the portion of his *inheritance*." (Ps. xvi. 5.) Man looks at his *heritage*. ' This land—this estate—or this kingdom is mine.' The child of God looks round on the universe—on both worlds —on God himself with his infinite perfections—and says, " All things are mine." (1 Cor. iii. 21, 22.) My title is more sure than to any earthly *heritage*. Every promise is sprinkled with " the blood of the everlasting covenant," as the seal of its blessings, and the pledge of their performance.

But not only are they *my heritage;*—by my own intelligent choice *I have taken* them to be so. A blessing is it to have them. But the blessing of blessings is to have them made good—applied—sealed—*made my own;* so that, like the minor come to age, I take possession of my *heritage*, I live on it, I live in it, it is my treasure, my portion. If a man is known by his *heritage*, let me be known by mine. Let it " be known and read of all men," that I count not the world my happiness, but that I take my Bible, ' Here is my *heritage*. Here I can live royally— richer upon bare promises than all the treasures of earth could make me. My resources never fail when all besides fail. (Hab. iii. 17, 18. Ps. lxxiii. 26.) When all earthly heritage shall have passed away, mine endureth *for ever*.' (1 Pet. i. 24, 25.)

Let me not then entertain a low estimate of this precious *heritage*. " Heirs of promise" are entitled to " strong consolation." (Heb. vi. 17, 18.) What belongs to a " joint-heir with Christ," interested in the unchanging love of Jehovah from eternity, but the language of triumphant exultation ? (Rom. viii. 17–34.) The first view, as it passed before my eyes, was the *rejoicing of my heart;* and never could I be satisfied, till I had *taken it* as my soul-satisfying and eternal portion.

Need we then entreat you, believer, to show to the world, that the promises of your *heritage* are not an empty sound—that they impart a Divine reality of support and enjoyment—and that an interest in them habitually realized is a blessed, a heavenly portion? Should your heart, however, at any time be captivated by the transient prospect before your eyes : should you be led to imagine some substantial value in this world's treasures—you will have forgotten the peculiar pre-eminence of your heritage—its enduring character. But what are the gaudy follies—the glittering emptiness of this passing scene, in comparison with your heavenly prospects, or even of your present sources of enjoyment!

We can readily account for the affecting indifference with which "the men of the world" barter away these treasures, as Esau did his birthright, for very trifles. (Heb. xii. 16. Gen. xxv. 29–34.) They have no present interest in them. "They have their portion in this life. They have received their consolation." (Ps. xvii. 14. Luke, vi. 24.) But, oh! how soon, having spent their all, will they "begin to be in" infinite, eternal "want!" (Luke, xv. 14.) Yet, having no interest in this heavenly *heritage*, they can have no pleasure in surveying it. If, therefore, conscience imposes upon them the drudgery of casting their careless eye over it, what wonder if they should find nothing to enliven their hopes, or to attract their hearts? What communion can worldly hearts hold with this heavenly treasure? What spiritual light, as the source of heavenly comfort, can penetrate this dark recess? As well might the inhabitant of the subterraneous cavern expect the cheerful light of the sun, as the man, whose eyes and heart are in the centre of the earth, enjoy the spiritual perception of an interest in *the heritage* of the people of

God. If, however, the darkness and difficulties of the
word are pleaded in excuse for ignorance ; let those indolent triflers confess, how small a portion of that persevering devotedness, which has been employed in gathering together the perishing stores of this world, has been
given to search into this hidden mine of unsearchable
riches !

O my soul, if I can lay claim to this blessed *heritage*, I envy not the miser his gold ! Rather would I
adore that grace, which has " made me to differ" from
him ; and given me a far happier and far richer *heritage*.
But let me be daily enriching myself from this imperishable store ; so that, poor as I am in myself, and seeming
to " have nothing," I may in reality be " possessing all
things." (2 Cor. vi. 10.) Let the recollection of the rich
heritage of light, comfort, peace, and strength, furnished
in the word, be my abundant joy : and bind my heart to
a closer adherence to its obligations, and to a more habitual
apprehension of its privileges.

112. *I have inclined mine heart to perform thy statutes alway,
even unto the end.*

The Psalmist had just been rejoicing in his privileges.
He now binds himself to his obligations — and *that* not for
a day — but *even to the end.* Observe where he begins his
work — not with the eye — the ear — the tongue — but
with *the heart*, " for out of the heart are the issues of life."
(Prov. iv. 23.) And yet this *inclining of the heart to the
Lord's statutes* is as much the work of God as to create a
world ; and as soon could " the Ethiopian change his skin,
or the leopard his spots," as we could " do good, who are
accustomed to do evil." (Jer. xiii. 23.) David was very
far from meaning, that any act of his own power could
turn the channel of his affections out of their natural

course. But prayer, such as he had often poured out (Verses 36, 37), sets every principle of the soul in action, and, in dependence upon the Holy Spirit, he *inclines his heart.* Thus we do what we do ; but God enables us, 'preventing us, that we may have a good will, and working with us, when we have that good will' (Art. X.)—not working without or against us, but in us—through us—with us—by us. His preventing grace makes the first impressions, and his assisting grace enables us to follow. (Jer. xxxi. 18.) Weak indeed are our purposes, and fading our resolutions, unsupported by Divine grace. Yet renewing strength is given to the "waiting" Christian, even to " mount up on eagles' wings, to run without weariness, and to walk without fainting." (Isa. xl. 31.) Conscious as we are, that " without Christ we can do nothing," it is no less true, that we " can do all things through Christ which strengtheneth us." (John, xv. 5, with Phil. iv. 13.) Let us exercise, then, the grace already given, in dependence upon a continued supply ; and turning to him with freedom and delight, we shall *incline our hearts* with full purpose *to perform his statutes alway, even unto the end.* This is God's way of quickening the dead soul to life and motion ; alluring it by an inexpressible sweetness, and at the same moment, by an invincible power, drawing it to himself.

Every step indeed to the end will be a conflict with indwelling sin, in the form of remaining enmity, sloth, or unbelief. But how encouraging is it to trace every tender prayer, every contrite groan, every spiritual desire, to the assisting, upholding influence of the " free spirit of God !" (See Rom. viii. 26. Ps. li. 12.) The continual drawing of the Spirit will be the principle to perseverance. The same hand that gave the new bias for a heavenward motion will be put forth to quicken that motion even unto the end. ' I can hardly hold on,'—the believer might say,—' from one step to another.' How can I then dare to hope, that I shall hold on a constant course — a daily conflict *unto the end?* But was it not Almighty power that supported the first step in your course? And is not the same Divine help pledged to every successive step of difficulty? Doubt not, then, that " He is faithful that hath promised" (Heb. x. 23): dare to be " confident of this very thing, that He which hath begun a good work in you, will perform it until the day of Jesus Christ." (Philip. i. 6.) And in this confidence go on to " work out your salvation with fear and trembling ; for it is God which worketh in you both to will and to do of his good pleasure." (Philip. ii. 12, 13.)

PART XV.

113. I hate vain thoughts, but thy law do I love.

THE fall of man has misplaced his affections. Love was originally made for God and *his law ;*—hatred, for sin. Now man loves what he ought to hate (John, iii. 19. Rom. i. 32 ; vi. 12), and hates what he ought to love. (Job, xxi. 14. Ps. xiv. 1. Rom. viii. 7.) The work of Divine grace is to restore the disordered affections to their proper centre, and to bestow them on their right object ;—*hating vain thoughts, and loving the law of God.* Few think of the responsibility of their thoughts ; as if they were too trifling to be connected with any solemn account. The enlightened soul, however, learns to make a conscience of his thoughts. Here is the seminal principle of sin. (Gen. vi. 5. Prov. xxiii. 7 ; xxiv. 9.) How must a radical remedy be applied ?

Vain thoughts are the natural produce of the unrenewed heart, and of the yet unrenewed part of the believer's heart. Who that " knows the plague of his own heart," and the spirituality of the Christian walk with God, does not constantly complain of their baneful influence ? The child of God longs that his " every thought may be brought into captivity to the obedience of Christ." (2 Cor. x. 5.) But he " sees another law in his members, warring against the law of his mind ;" so that " when he would do good, evil is present with him." (Rom. vii. 21, 23.) When he would " attend upon the Lord without distraction" (1 Cor. vii. 35) ; many times, even in a single exercise, does he forget his sacred employment. Sin seems to enter into every pore of his soul ; and a cloud of *vain thoughts* darkens every avenue to communion with God. He would gladly say, " My heart is fixed, my heart is fixed" (Ps. lvii. 7) ; but he finds his affections wandering, as " the eyes of the fool, in the ends of the earth" (Prov. xvii. 24), as if there were no object of Divine attraction to his soul. We do not hear the worldling, or indeed the servant of God in his worldly employments, complaining of this burden. He can bring to deep, important, and anxious concerns of this world, all that intensity and fixedness of attention which the emergency may demand. Indeed, the wily adversary would rather assist than hinder this concentration of mind, as diverting the soul from the far more momentous and interesting subjects of eternity. But never do the " sons of God come to present themselves before the Lord," except " Satan comes also among them." (Job, i. 6.)

Vain thoughts are his ceaseless hindrances to our spiritual communion with God. Are we aware of the subtlety, and therefore the peculiar danger, of this temptation ? We should instinctively start from an enticement to open transgression. The incursion of defiling or blasphemous thoughts would be such a burden, that we should " have no rest in our spirit," while they remain undisturbed within us. But perhaps neither of these temptations are so formidable as the crowd of thoughts of every kind, incessantly running to and fro in the mind ; the indulgence of which, though not actually sinful in itself, yet as effectually restrains the soul from intercourse with God, as the most hateful injections. These are " the little foxes, that spoil the tender grapes." (Cant. ii. 15.) Nay—the *thoughts* may be even spiritual in their nature, and yet *vain* in their tendency ; because unsuitable to the present frame, and calculated, and indeed intended by the great enemy, to divert the mind from some positive duty. Who has not felt a serious thought upon an unseasonable subject, and an unseasonable time, to be in its consequences a *vain thought*—the secret impulse of the false " angel of light" (2 Cor. xi. 14), dividing the attention between two things, so that neither of them may be wholly done, done to any purpose, done at all?* If at any time " iniquity has been regarded in the heart ;" if the world in any of its thousand forms has regained a temporary ascendancy ; or if lusting imaginations are not constantly " held in" as " with bit and bridle ;" these *vain thoughts*, ever ready to force their entrance, will at such seasons " get an advantage of us." Restless in their workings, they keep no sabbaths : and can only be successfully met by a watchful and unceasing warfare.

It may indeed be sometimes difficult, in the midst of this continual trial, to maintain a clear sense of adoption. But this is the distinctive mark of Christian sincerity :— Do we cordially *hate* them, as exceedingly sinful in the

---

* Greenham (one of the most valuable of the Puritan writers upon experimental subjects) used to bring distractions of mind to this test—" If they brought any past sin to mind for his humiliation, or any comfort to excite his thankfulness, or any instruction suitable to the present moment—he took them to be of God. But if they *drew off his mind from present duty* to rove after other subjects, he suspected their source, and girded himself to prayer for increasing steadiness of application to the matter in hand." See his Works, folio, p. 23. Being asked to account for distractions in holy meditations, he said—" It was either want of preparation and sanctifying the heart by prayer before we set upon so holy an exercise, and therefore a rebuke from the Lord for our ' presumption in being bold to work upon holy matters in our own strength '—or else a dependence upon a general purpose of thinking good, or restraining evil, without fastening our minds upon some particular object, but rather ' ranging up and down,' leaving some part of our mind and meditation void for other matters, without wholly and seriously setting on a thing propounded. When any complained to him of blasphemous thoughts, he would say—' Do not fear them, but abhor them.' "

sight of God (Prov. xxiv. 9), hurtful to our own souls (Cant. ii. 15, and Scott, *in loco*) and contrary to our new nature? (Rom. vii. 22.) If we cannot altogether prevent their entrance, or eject them from their settlement, are we careful not to invite them, not to entertain them, not to suffer them to " *lodge within us?* " (Comp. Jer. iv. 14.) This active *hatred* is a satisfactory proof that they are not so much the natural suggestion of the heart, as the injections of the enemy of our peace. They are at least so directly opposed to our better will and dominant bias, that we may say, " If I do that I would not, it is no more I that do it, but sin that dwelleth in me." (Rom. vii. 20.) Our affliction and conflict with them prove that they dwell with us—not as welcome guests, or as the family of the house—but as " thieves and robbers." Their indulgence *constitutes our sin.* Their indwelling may be considered *only as our temptation.* They supply, indeed, continual matter for watchfulness, humiliation, and resistance; yet so far as they are abhorred and resisted, they are rather our infirmities than our iniquities, and leave no stain of actual guilt upon the conscience. An increasing sense of the sinfulness of sin, and of the extent of duty, will indeed show their deeper aggravations and more persevering opposition. Still, however, even while we groan under their defiling, distracting influence, in our best services, we may assure our confidence in him, who " spareth us, as a man spareth his own son that serveth him" (Mal. iii. 17), and who will gather up the broken parts of our prayers with merciful acceptance.

But the subjugation of this evil—even though we be secured from its condemnation—is a matter of the deepest concern. Forget not—oh, may the impression be indelible! —that it was for these *vain thoughts* that the Saviour was nailed to the cross. Here lies the ground of self-loathing —the quickening principle of conflict and exertion. Let the heart—the seat of this evil disease—be continually washed in the cleansing blood of Calvary; for until the corrupt fountain be cleansed, it must ever "send forth bitter waters." (Comp. 2 Kings, ii. 19–22. Jer. iv. 14.) Let it be diligently "kept" (Prov. iv. 23), and carefully filled, so that it may be a "good treasure bringing forth good things." (Matt. xii. 35.) Let there be the continued exercise of that "watchfulness" "which is unto prayer" (Matt. xxvi. 41), combined with an unflinching adherence to plain and obvious duty. Let the temptation to desist awhile from services so polluted, that they appear rather to mock God than to worship him, be met on the onset with the most determined opposition. Once admit this suggestion, and our active enemy will pour in successive incursions of *vain thoughts* into our perplexed and yielding minds, to turn us back step by step in our attempts to approach God. If, therefore, we cannot advance as we could wish, let us advance as we can. If a connected train of thought or expression fails us, let us only change—not surrender—our posture of resistance; substituting sighs, desires, tears, and "groanings"—for words, and casting ourselves upon our God in the simple confidence of faith, "Lord, all my desire is before thee, and my groaning is not hid from thee. Thou tellest my wanderings: put thou my tears into thy bottle: are they not in thy book?" (Ps. xxxviii. 9; lvi. 8.) It is far better to wander *in* duty than *from* it. For if *any duty* be neglected on account of the defilement that is mingled with it, for the same reason we must neglect *every other duty*, and, as the final consequence, the worship of God would be abolished from the earth.

Much of our successful warfare, however, depends upon an accurate and well-digested acquaintance with our own hearts—upon a discovery of the bias of the mind in our unoccupied moments, and of the peculiar seasons and circumstances that give most power to temptation. This once known, set a double watch against those doors, by which the enemy has been accustomed to find his most convenient and unobstructed entrance.

But we must not forget the effective means suggested by David's experience—the *love of God's law*. Here rises the native enmity against God—not as the Creator, but the Law-giver—and therefore against his law as the dictate of his will. (Rom. viii. 7.) Here, then, is the power of grace subduing this enmity. Not only I fear, and therefore through fear I keep, but *I love thy law*. And ' He that loves a holy law '—remarks an excellent old writer— ' cannot but hate a vain thought.'* For if the law be the transcript of the image of God, the thoughts affectionately drawn out towards him must naturally fix the image of the beloved friend upon the mind, and by a sweet constraint fasten down the thoughts to Divine contemplation. Are we then ever winged with an elevating love to the Saviour? And do we not find our hearts start out from their worldly employments with frequent glances and flights towards the object of our desire? And will not this communion of love gradually mould the soul into a fixed delight, exciting our *hatred*, and strengthening our resistance of every sinful affection? Thus, as *love to the law* stirs up the powers of the renewed man, " spiritual wickedness" will be abhorred, conflicted with, and overcome.

Yet these defilements will remain to die with the last breathings of the old man ; which, though crucified indeed and expiring, will struggle with fearful strength and unabated enmity to the end. And let them remain, as humbling mementos of our unclean nature, " shapen in iniquity, and conceived in sin" (Ps. li. 5) ; and as enlivening our anticipations of that blessed place, where " shall in no wise

---

* STEELE's Antidote against Distractions.

enter anything that defileth" (Rev. xxi. 27); where *vain thoughts*, and whatever beside might " separate between us and our God," will be unknown for ever.   Meanwhile let them endear to us the free justification of the Gospel; let them lead us daily and hourly to " the fountain opened for sin and for uncleanness" (Zech. xiii. 1); and enhance in our view that heavenly intercession, which provides for the perfect cleansing and accepting of services even such as ours.

Blessed contemplation! Jesus prays not for us, as we do for ourselves. His intercession is without distraction —without interruption. If we are then so dead, that we cannot, and so guilty, that we dare not, pray, and so wandering in our *vain thoughts*, that our prayers appear to be scattered to the winds, rather than to ascend to heaven— if on these accounts combined, we " are so troubled, that we cannot speak" (Ps. lxxvii. 4): yet always is there One to speak for us, of whom " a voice from heaven" testified for our encouragement, " saying—This is my beloved Son, in whom I am well pleased." (Matt. iii. 17.) With such hopes, motives, and encouragements, let us " continue instant in prayer" (Rom. xii. 12), *until we pray, and that we may pray.* Let us supplicate our Lord with restless importunity, that his omnipotent love would take hold of these hearts, which every moment sin and Satan seem ready to seize. At the same time, conscious of our hatred of every interruption to his service, and of the simplicity of our affection to his holy law, let us hold fast that confidence before him, which will issue in perfect peace and established consolation.

114. *Thou art my hiding-place, and my shield; I hope in thy word.*

We have seen the unremitting vigilance of the enemy

pursuing the man of God in his secret retirement with painful distraction. See how he runs to *his hiding-place.* Here is our main principle of safety—not our strivings or our watchfulness, but our faith. Flee instantly to Jesus. (Ps. cxliii. 9. Prov. xviii. 10.) He is the sinner's *hiding-place,* " the man,"—that wondrous man, " in whom dwelt all the fulness of the Godhead bodily." (Isa. xxxii. 2. Col. ii. 9.) Yes, Jesus exposed himself to the fury of " the tempest," that he might become *a hiding-place,* for us. The broken law pursued with its relentless curse—' The sinner ought to die'—But *thou art my hiding-place,* who hast " redeemed me from the curse of the law, being made a curse for me." (Gal. iii. 10, 13.) " The fiery darts " pour in on every side : but the recollection of past security awakens my song of acknowledgment—" Thou hast been a strength to the poor, a strength to the needy in his distress, a refuge from the storm, a shadow from the heat, when the blast of the terrible ones is as a storm against the wall." (Isa. xxv. 4.) Our *hiding-place* covers us from the power of the world. " In me "—saith our Saviour—" ye shall have peace. Be of good cheer ! I have overcome the world." (John, xvi. 33.) Helpless to resist the great enemy, our Lord brings us to his wounded side, and hides us there. We " overcome him by the blood of the Lamb." (Rev. xii. 11.) To all accusations from every quarter, our challenge is ready—" Who shall lay anything to the charge of God's elect ?" (Rom. viii. 33, 34.) From the fear of death, our *hiding-place* still covers us. " Jesus through death hath destroyed him that had the power of death." (Heb. ii. 14, 15.) Against the sting of this last enemy, a song of thanksgiving is put into our mouth—" O death ! where is thy sting ? O grave ! where is thy victory ? Thanks be to God, which giveth us the victory through our Lord Jesus Christ. ' (1 Cor. xv. 55, 57.) Thus is " the smoking flax," which the malice of Satan strives to extinguish, not " quenched ; " nor is " the bruised reed," which seems beyond the hope of restoration, " broken."

But the completeness of our security is graphically portrayed—*Thou art my hiding-place*, to cover from danger, —*my shield* (Gen. xv. 1. Ps. iii. 3 ; v. 12. Comp. Eph. vi. 16), also to protect me in it. Either I shall be kept *from* trouble, that it shall not come ; or *in* trouble, that it shall not hurt me. The *hiding-place* alone would be imperfect security, as being limited to one place. But *my shield* is moveable, wherever be the point of danger or assault. I can " quench the dart" that is aimed at my soul.

But *a hiding-place* implies also secrecy. (Ps. xxxi. 20.) And truly the believer's is "a hidden life" (Col. iii. 3), beyond the comprehension of the world. He mixes with them in the common intercourse of life. But while seen of man, he is dwelling " in the secret of the Lord's tabernacle" (Ps. xxvii. 5), safe in the midst of surrounding danger, guarded by invincible strength. (Isa. xxvi. 1.) Often, indeed, must the world be surprised at his constancy, amidst all their varied efforts to shake his stedfastness. They know not " the secret of the Lord, which is with them that fear him." (Ps. xxv. 14.) And never could he have had a just conception of the all-sufficiency of his God, until he finds it above him, around him, underneath him, in all the fulness of everlasting love — *his hiding-place, and his shield.* Thus in the heart of the enemy's country " he dwelleth on high, and his place of defence is the munitions of rocks." (Isa. xxxiii. 16.)

But are we acquainted with this *hiding-place?* How have we discovered it ? Are we found in it, and careful to abide in it ? Within its walls " that wicked one toucheth us not." (1 John, v. 18.) Yet never shall we venture outside the walls unprotected, but his assault will give us some painful remembrance of our unwatchfulness. And then

do we *prize our shield*, and run behind it for constant security. Remember, every other *hiding-place* " the waters will
overflow." (Isa. xxviii. 16, 17.) Every other shield is a
powerless defence. Surely then the *word* which has discovered this security to us, is a firm warrant for our *hope*.
And, therefore, every sinner, enclosed in the covert of love,
will be ready to declare—*I hope in thy word.*

115. *Depart from me, ye evil-doers ; for I will keep the commandments of my God.*

Safe and quiet in *his hiding-place*, and behind *his shield.*
David deprecates all attempts to disturb his peace—*Depart
from me, ye evil-doers.* He had found them to be opposed
to his best interests ; and he dreaded their influence in
shaking his resolution for his God. Indeed such society
must always hinder alike the enjoyment and the service of
God. " Can two walk together, except they be agreed ? "
(Amos, iii. 3.) And can we be " agreed," and walk in fellowship with God, except we be at variance with the principles, the standard, and conduct of a world that is " enmity
against him ? " (Comp. Matt. vi. 24. Jam. iv. 4.) Not
more needful was the exhortation to the first Christians
than to ourselves—" Save yourselves from this untoward
generation." (Acts, ii. 40.) True fellowship with God
implies therefore a resolute separation from the ungodly.
Secure in the *hiding-place*, and covered with the *shield* of
our covenant God, let us meet their malice, and resist their
enticements, with the undaunted front of " a good soldier
of Jesus Christ." (2 Tim. ii. 3.)

Not that we would indulge morose or ascetic seclusion.
We are expressly enjoined to courtesy and kindness (1 Pet.
iii. 8) ; to that wise and considerate " walk towards them
that are without" (Col. iv. 5), which " adorns the doctrine
of God our Saviour" (Tit. ii. 10), and indeed in some in-

stances has been more powerful even than the word itself (Comp. 1 Pet. iii. 1, 2), to " win souls to Christ." But when they would tempt us to a devious or backsliding step — when our connexion with them entices us to a single act of conformity to their standard, dishonourable to God, and inconsistent with our profession — then must we take a bold and unflinching stand—*Depart from me, ye evil-doers : for I will keep the commandments of my God.*

This resolution gives no countenance to the self-delusive notion of maintaining an intimate connexion with professed *evil-doers*, for the kind purpose of recommending our religion to their acceptance — a scheme, which requires a rare degree of caution and simplicity to attempt without entangling the conscience ; and which, for the most part at least, it is to be feared, is only a specious covering for the indulgence of a worldly spirit. If the men of the world are to be met, and their society invited, for the accomplishment of this benevolent intention, it must be upon the principle of the Lord's command to his prophet—"*Let them return unto thee : but return not thou to them.*" (Jer. xv. 19.) The amiable desire to " please our neighbour" is limited to the single end, that it should be "*for his good to edification.*" (Comp. Rom. xv. 2.) And whenever this end and restriction has been overlooked, it is sufficiently evident that self-gratification has been the moving principle : *and that the distinctive mark of the Christian character — bearing the cross, and confessing the name of our Divine Master—has been obscured.*

Sometimes, however, in the struggle of conscience, an apprehension of danger, is not altogether forgotten, and the question is asked, with some trembling of spirit—" *How far may I conform to the world, without endangering the loss of my religion ?*" But, not to speak of the insincerity and self-deception of such a question, it would be better answered by substituting another in its place—" *How far may I be separate from the world, and yet be destitute of the vital principle?*" Scrutinize, in every advancing step toward the world, the workings of your own heart. Suspect its reasonings. Listen to the first awakened conviction of conscience. Though it be only a whisper, or a hint, it is probably the indication of the Divine will. And never forget, that this experiment of worldly conformity, often as it has been tried, has never answered the desired end. However this compromise may have *recommended ourselves*, no progress has been made in *recommending our Master;* since his name — whether from unwatchfulness or cowardice on our part, or from the overpowering flow of the world on the other side — has probably in such society scarcely passed over our lips with any refreshment or attentiveness. Indeed, so far from commending our religion by this accommodation, we have succeeded in ingratiating ourselves in their favour, only so far as we have been content to keep it out of sight; while at the same time, our yielding conformity to their taste, and habits, and conversation, has virtually sanctioned their erroneous standard of conduct; and tended to deceive them with the self-complacent conviction, that it approaches as near to the Scriptural elevation, as is absolutely required. The final result, therefore, of this attempt to recommend the Gospel to those who have no " heart for it," is — that our own consciences have been ensnared, while they retain all their principles un- altered.

It must surely be obvious, that such a course is plainly opposed to the revealed declarations of Scripture, and bears the decisive character of unfaithfulness to our Great Master. We might also ask, whether our love to the Lord can be in fervent exercise, while we " love them that hate him ?" (2 Chron. xix. 2) — whether our hatred of sin can be active and powerful, while we can find pleasure in the society of those, whose life " without God in the world" (Eph. ii. 12),

is an habitual, wilful course of rebellion against him?*—
whether we can have any deep or experimental sense of our
own weakness, when thus venturing into temptation?—
whether by unnecessary contact with the world, we can
expect to " go upon hot coals," and our " feet not be
burned?" (Prov. vi. 28) — or, in fact, whether we are not
forgetting the dictates of common prudence in forsaking
the path of safety for a slippery, but more congenial path?
Is no harm to be anticipated from a wilful, self-pleasing
association? Is it likely to be less dangerous to us than
it was to an Apostle (Matt. xxvi. 51, 69–75)? or, because
we conceive ourselves to have more strength, shall we use
less watchfulness, and show more presumption?

But, supposing Scripture not to determine the path of
duty with infallible certainty; let this line of conduct be
subjected to the impartial scrutiny of our own hearts, and
of the effects, whether neutral or positively detrimental,
which have resulted from it to ourselves, or to the church.
Have we not felt this fellowship with *evil-doers* to be an
hindrance in *keeping the commandments of our God?* If it
has not always ended in open conformity to their maxims;
or if, contrary to our apprehensions, it does not appear to
sanction their principles, yet have we realized no deadening
unfavourable influence? Has the spirit of prayer sustained
no injury in this atmosphere? Have we never felt the
danger of imbibing their taste,— the spirit of their conversation and general conduct; which, without fixing any
blot upon our external profession, must insensibly estrange
our best affections from God! And have we never considered the injury of this worldly association to the Gospel
in weakening by an apparent want of decision " on the
Lord's side" (Comp. Exod. xxxii. 26. Judg. v. 23. Matt.

* Who are the wicked, but those that forget God? Ps. ix. 17;
x. 4.

xii. 30), the sacred cause which we are pledged to support ; and obscuring the spiritual character of the people of God as a distinct and separate people? (Comp. Numb. xxiii. 9. John, xvii. 16.) In a providential connexion with *evil-doers*, we go safely in the spirit of humility, watchfulness, and prayer ; and this connexion, felt to be a cross, is not likely to prove a snare. (Ps. cxx. 5, 6.)   But does not union of spirit with them, to whom David says, with holy determination—*Depart from me,*—and to whom David's Lord will one day say—" Depart!" (Matt. xxv. 41)—prove a want of fellowship with his spirit, and an essential unfitness for communion with the society of heaven?   The children of this world can have no more real communion with the children of light, than darkness has with light. (2 Cor. vi. 14.)   As great is the difference between the Christian and the world, as between heaven and hell—as between the sounds, " Come, ye blessed," and, " Depart, ye cursed." (Matt. xxv. 34, 41.)   The difference, which at that solemn day will be made for eternity, must, therefore, be visibly made now.   They must depart from us, or we from God.   We cannot walk with them both.   ' Defilement '—as Mr. Cecil remarks—' is inseparable from the world.'*   We cannot hold communion with God, in the spirit of the world ; and, therefore, separation from the world, or separation from God, is the alternative.   Which way—which company—is most congenial to our taste ? Fellowship will be a component part of our heavenly happiness. (Heb. xii. 22–24.)   Shall we not then walk on earth with those, with whom we hope to spend our eternity, that our removal hence may be a change of place only, not of company?   May we have grace to listen to our Father's voice of love—" Wherefore, come out from among them, and be ye separate, saith the Lord ; and touch not the unclean

---

* CECIL's " Remains."

thing: and I will receive you, and will be a Father to you, and ye shall be my sons and daughters, saith the Lord Almighty." (2 Cor. vi. 17, 18.)

116. *Uphold me according unto thy word, that I may live: and let me not be ashamed of my hope.*

Lest the Psalmist should seem to have been self-confident in his rejection of the society of the ungodly, and his determination to adhere to his God ; here, as on former occasions,* mindful of his own weakness, he commits himself to the *upholding* grace of God. He does not content himself with commanding the *evil-doer to depart.* He pleads for his God to come to him. He wants not only the hindrances to be removed, but the vouchsafement of present supporting grace. Such is our urgent continual need! Every circumstance has its temptation. Every change of condition is specially trying—and what is he in himself? unstable as water! Indeed the highest Archangel before the throne stands only as he is upheld by the Lord, and may unite with the weakest child in the Lord's family in the acknowledgment,—" By the grace of God I am what I am."† Much more, therefore, must I, pressed on every side with daily conflict and temptation, and conscious of my own weakness and liability to fall, " come to the throne of grace," for " grace to help in time of need." (Heb. iv. 16.) My plea is the word of promise—*according to thy word*—" as thy days, so shall thy strength be." (Deut. xxxiii. 25.) " Fear thou not"—is the language of

* Verses 8, 31. The same frame is marked—Ps. xvii. 4, 5.
  † 1 Cor. xv. 10. Comp. 2 Pet. ii. 4.
  ' Man's wisdom is to seek
        His strength in God alone;
     And e'en an angel would be weak,
        Who trusted in his own.'—COWPER: *Olney Hymns,* iii. 74.

my upholding God—" for I am with thee ; be not dismayed, for I am thy God : I will strengthen thee : yea, I will help thee : *yea, I will uphold thee* with the right hand of my righteousness." (Isa. xli. 10.) Blessed be the goodness that made the promise, and that guides the hand of my faith, as it were, to fasten upon it !

But why do I need the promise ? why do I plead it ? but *that I may live*—that I may know that life, which is found and enjoyed " in the favour" of God ? (Ps. xxx. 5.) Nothing seems worth a serious thought besides ; nothing else deserves the name. And therefore new life—" life more abundantly" (John, x. 10)—let it be the burden of every prayer—the cry of every moment. Thus upheld by the Lord's grace, and living in his presence, I hope to feel the increasing support of my Christian hope. . Though I have just before expressed it in *God's word*—though I have " made my boast in the Lord," as *my hiding-place and my shield* (Verse 114), yet conscious helplessness leads me earnestly to pray—*Let me not be ashamed of my hope.*

Yes—Jesus is the sinner's hope—" the hope set before" his people, to which they " flee for the refuge" of their souls. And well may our " hope" in him be called " an anchor of the soul, sure and stedfast." (Heb. vi. 18, 19.) How does the distressed church plead with *the hope of Israel*, and put her God in remembrance of this his own name (Jer. xiv. 8), that she might *not be ashamed of her hope!* And how does she—with every member of her body—eventually learn by this pleading, to say in the confidence of faith—"*I know whom I have believed!*" (2 Tim. i. 12.) And is there not a solid ground for this confidence ? Is not the " stone that is laid in Zion for a foundation," a " tried stone ?" Has it not been tried by thousands and millions of sinners—nay, more, tried by God himself, and found to be " a sure foundation ?" (Isa. xxviii. 16.) Yet still, that I may " hold fast the beginning of my confidence," and " the rejoicing of my hope, firm unto the end " (Heb. iii. 6, 14), I must persevere in prayer—*Uphold me according unto thy word.*

David, when left to his own weakness, was *ashamed of his hope :*—" I said in my haste, I am cut off from before thine eyes." (Ps. xxxi. 22.) At another time, when upheld in a season of accumulated trial, " he encouraged himself in the Lord his God." (1 Sam. xxx. 6.) Thus I see " wherein my great strength lieth," and how impotent I am, when left to myself. What a mercy, that my salvation will never for a single moment be in my own keeping ! what need have I to pray to be saved from myself ! How delightful is the exercise of faith in going to the Strong for strength ! The issue of my spiritual conflicts is certain. He who is the author, will ever be the upholder, of the " hidden life " in his people. It is a part of his own life, and therefore can never perish. The Tempter himself will flee, when he marks the poor, feeble, fainting soul, *upheld according to the word of his God,* and placed in safety beyond the reach of his malice. (See 1 Pet. i. 5.) Not, however, that, as I once supposed, my weakness will ever be made strong ; but that I shall daily grow more sensible of it, shall stay myself more simply upon infinite everlasting strength ; and " most gladly shall I glory in my infirmities, that the power of Christ may rest upon me." (2 Cor. xii. 9.)

117. *Hold thou me up, and I shall be safe ; and I will have respect unto thy statutes continually.*

Such is my sense of need and peril, that my only refuge lies in " continuing instant in prayer." (Rom. xii. 12.) I must send up one cry after another into my Father's ear for the support of his *upholding* grace. For not only the consciousness of my weakness, but the danger of the slippery path before me, reminds me, that the safety of every moment depends upon my *upholding* faithful God. The ways of temptation are so many and imperceptible—the influence of it so appalling—the entrance into it so deceitful, so specious, so insensible—my own weakness and unwatchfulness so unspeakable—that I can do nothing but go on my way, praying at every step—*Hold thou me up, and I shall be safe.* Often, indeed, can I remember, when " my feet were almost gone, my steps had well-nigh slipped" (Ps. lxxiii. 2): that I have been enabled to record—" Thy mercy, O Lord, held me up." (Ps. xciv. 18.)

How beautiful is the picture given of the church of old ! " Who is this that cometh up from the wilderness, *leaning upon her Beloved?*" (Cant. viii. 5.) This state of dependence was familiar to the Psalmist, and aptly delineates his affectionate, though conflicting, confidence. " My soul followeth hard after thee : thy right hand upholdeth me." (Ps. lxiii. 8.) The recollection of the care of his God, from his earliest life, supplied encouragement for his present faith, and matter for unceasing praise—*"By thee have I been holden up from the womb;* thou art he that took me out of my mother's bowels: my praise shall be continually of thee." (Ps. lxxi. 6.) We cannot wonder, then, that this confidence should sustain his soul in the contemplation of the remaining steps of his pilgrimage, and his prospects for eternity. " Nevertheless "— saith he—" I am continually with thee : *thou hast holden me* by thy right hand. *Thou shalt guide me* with my counsel, and afterwards receive me to glory." (Ps. lxxiii. 23, 24.) And, indeed, the more lively my spiritual apprehensions are, the more I shall realize the Lord by the operations of his grace as well as of his providence, " compassing my path and my lying down" (Ps. cxxxix. 3) ; lest any hurt me, keeping me night and day." (Isa. xxvii. 3.)

Is it inquired—how the Lord *holds up* his people in

this slippery path? "Of the fulness of Jesus they all receive, and grace for grace" (John, i. 16); so that "the life which they now live in the flesh, they live by the faith of the Son of God." (Gal. ii. 20.) And, therefore, if I am upheld, it is by the indwelling of the Spirit, who supplies from his infinite fountain of life all the strength and support I need throughout my dangerous way. By his Divine influence the dispensations of Providence also become the appointed means of drawing and keeping me near to my God. If, therefore, prosperity is endangering my soul, and strengthening my worldly bonds, may I not trust to the ever-watchful kindness of the Lord, to keep me low, and not to suffer me to be at ease in my forgetfulness? If the pleasures of sense, if the esteem of the world, or the good report of the church, are bringing a bewitching snare upon my soul, my God will lead me into the pathway of the cross—in the "valley of humiliation."

Here, then, is the secret of an unsteady walk—the neglect of leaning upon an Almighty arm! How fearfully is the danger of self-confidence unveiled! Standing by my own strength, very soon shall I be made to feel, that I cannot stand at all. No "mountain" seemed to "stand stronger" than Solomon's : yet when he became the very "fool" that he describes—" trusting in his own heart"— how quickly was it removed! (Comp. Ps. xxx. 6, 7. 1 Kings, xi. 1–10. Prov. xxviii. 26.)

Peter thought in the foolishness of his heart, that he could have walked upon the water unsupported by the arm of his Lord: but a moment's sense of weakness and danger brought him to his right mind : " and, *beginning to sink, he cried, saying—Lord ! save me !*" (Matt. xiv. 28–30.) Well would it have been for him, if his deliverance at that moment of peril had effectually rebuked his presumption. We should not then have heard from the same lips that language of most unwarranted self-confidence : " Although all shall be offended, yet will not I :—if I should die with thee, I will not deny thee in any wise." (Mark, xiv. 29, 31.) Poor deluded disciple ! thou art on the brink of a grievous fall ! (Prov. xvi. 18.) Yet was he *held up* from utterly sinking. "*I have prayed for thee*"—said the gracious Saviour —" *that thy faith fail not.*" (Luke, xxii. 31, 32.) And thus *held up* by the same faithful intercession of my powerful friend (whose prayers are not weak as mine, " nor will he fail or be discouraged" (Isa. xlii. 4) by my continual back-slidings), " *I*" too — though in the atmosphere of danger, in the slippery path of temptation, *shall be safe*—safe from an ensnaring world—safe from a treacherous heart—safe in life—safe in death—safe in eternity. Thus does an interest in the covenant encourage—not presumption— but faith, in all its exercises of humility, watchfulness, diligence, and prayer ; in this appointed way does the Lord securely " keep the feet of his saints."

Let me not, then, forget, either my continual liability to fall if left to myself, or the faithful engagements of my covenant God, to " keep me from falling." While I recollect for my comfort, that I " stand by faith," still is the exhortation most needful—" Be not high-minded, but fear." (Rom. xi. 20.) " By faith I stand," as it concerns God ; by fear as it regards myself. As light is composed of neither brilliant nor sombre rays, but of the combination of both in simultaneous action, so is every Christian grace combined with its opposite, " that it may be perfect and entire, wanting nothing." Hope, therefore, combined with fear, issues in that genuine, evangelical confidence, in which alone I can walk safely and closely with God. Let, then, the self-confident learn to distrust themselves, and the fearful be encouraged to trust their Saviour ; and in each let the recollection of grace and help vouchsafed " in time of need," lead to the stedfast resolution—*I will have respect unto thy statutes continually.* However self-denying they

may be in their requirements : however opposed in their
tendency to "the desires of the flesh and of the mind," I
take my God as the surety of my performance of them ;
and I desire to love them as the rule of my daily conduct,
and the very element of heavenly happiness to my soul.

118. *Thou hast trodden down all them that err from thy statutes : for their deceit is falsehood.* 119. *Thou puttest away
all the wicked of the earth like dross ; therefore I love thy
testimonies.*

The Psalmist's determination *to keep the statutes of God*
was strengthened by marking his judgments on those that
erred from them.   And thus the Lord expects us to learn
at their cost. (Ps. lviii. 10, 11. Isa. xxvi. 9. Zeph. iii. 6, 7.)
The cheerful, grateful *respect to his statutes* marks also a
difference of character indicative of a difference of state.
" His saints are in his hand, or sitting down at his feet"
(Deut. xxxiii. 3) ; his enemies are *trodden down* under his
feet in full conquest (Ps. cx. 1. Comp. Josh. x. 24), and
disgraceful punishment. (2 Kings, ix. 33. Mic. vii. 10.
Mal. iv. 3.)   His own people he has exalted to be " heirs
of God, and joint-heirs with Christ." (Rom. viii. 17.)
Even now " he hath made them to sit together in heavenly
places in Christ Jesus ;" and shortly will they " be a crown
of glory in the hand of the Lord, and a royal diadem in the
hand of their God" (Eph. ii. 6. Isa. lxii. 3. Comp. Matt.
xiii. 43) ; while the ungodly *are put away like dross* from
the precious gold. " Reprobate silver shall men call them,
because the Lord hath rejected them." (Jer. vi. 30.)   The
same difference he makes even in chastening — upholding
his own children under the scourging rod, lest they faint ;
but " breaking *the wicked* with a rod of iron, and dashing
them in pieces." (Isa. lvii. 16–18, with Ps. ii. 9.)
   This separation has been from the beginning ; in his

conduct to the first two children of men (Gen. iv. 4, 5.
Heb. xi. 4); and in his selection of Enoch (Gen. v. 22–24.
Heb. xi. 5), Noah (Gen. vii. 1), and Abraham (Gen. xii.
1–3), from the world of the ungodly, " as vessels of honour,
meet for the Master's use." (2 Tim. ii. 21.) In after ages,
he made Egypt " know, that he put a difference between
the Egyptians and Israel." (Exod. xi. 7.) They were his own
" people, that should dwell alone," and not " be reckoned
among the nations " (Numb. xxiii. 9)—a people, whom he
had " formed for himself, that they should show forth his
praise." (Isa. xliii. 21.) And the same difference he has
made ever since, between his people and the world—in
their character (1 John, v. 19)—their way (Prov. xv. 9)
—their exercises of mind (Rom. viii. 5)—their services
(Prov. xv. 8)—their privileges (Prov. iii. 32, 33)—and
their prospects. (Dan. xii. 2.) At the day of judgment, the
separation will be complete—final—everlasting. " When
the Son of Man shall come in his glory, and all the holy
angels with him, then shall he sit upon the throne of his
glory; and before him shall be gathered all nations; and
he shall separate them one from another, as a shepherd
divideth his sheep from the goats. And he shall set the
sheep on his right hand, but the goats on the left; and
these shall go away into everlasting punishment; but the
righteous into life eternal." (Matt. xxv. 31–33, 46. Comp.
iii. 12 ; xiii. 30. Mal. iii. 16–18.)

But mark the character—They *err from God's statutes*
—not in their minds, through ignorance ; but " in their
hearts" (Ps. xcv. 10. Comp. verse 21) through obstinacy.
They do not say, ' Lord, we *know not*,' but, " *We desire not
the knowledge of thy ways.*" (Job, xxi. 14.) It is not frailty,
but unbelief; not want of knowledge, but love of sin—
wilful, damnable. Justly, therefore, are they stamped as
the *wicked of the earth*, and marked out as objects of the

Lord's eternal frown—expectants of the "vengeance of eternal fire."

And is not this a solemn warning to those " that forget God"—that " they shall be turned into hell" (Ps. ix. 17); to " the proud"—that in " the day that shall burn as an oven, they shall be as stubble" (Mal. iv. 1);—to the worldly—that in some " night" of forgetfulness, their " souls will be required of them" (Luke, xii. 19, 20. Dan. v. 30);—to the "hypocrites in heart"—that they " are heaping up wrath?" (Job, xxxvi. 13.) Thus does the eye of faith discern through the apparent disorder of a world in ruins, the just, holy, and wise government of God. " Clouds and darkness are round about him; righteousness and judgment are the habitation of his throne." (Ps. xcvii. 2.) If *the wicked* seem to triumph, and the righteous to be trodden down under their feet, it shall not be always so. " The end" (Rom. vi. 21) and " wages of sin is death." (Ib. 23.) " The ungodly shall not stand in the judgment, nor sinners in the congregation of the righteous." (Ps. i. 5.)

How awful, then, and almost desperate their condition! *Their deceit is falsehood;* " deceiving and being deceived" (2 Tim. iii. 13)—perhaps given up to believe their own lie—perhaps one or another " blessing themselves in their own heart," saying, ' I shall have peace, though I walk in the imagination of my own heart, to add drunkenness to thirst.'" (Deut. xxix. 19.) What, then, is our duty? Carnal selfishness says, ' Be quiet—let them alone'—that is—" Destroy them by our" indolence and unfaithfulness, " for whom Christ died." (Comp. Rom. xiv. 15.) But what does Scripture, conscience, nay more,—what does common humanity say? " Cry aloud, spare not." (Isa. lviii. 1.) Awake the sleepers—sound the alarm, " Now is the accepted time—the day of salvation" (2 Cor. vi. 2)! the moment to lift up the prayer, and stretch forth the hand for plucking the brands out of the fire. (Zech. iii. 2. Jude, 23.) To-morrow, the door may be shut, never to be opened more. (Matt. xxv. 10.)

How awful the judgment of being *put away like dross!* Look at Saul (1 Sam. xxviii. 5–25), when *put away* — going out, to harden himself in the sullen pride of despondency. Hear the fearful doom of Israel—" Son of man, the house of Israel is to me *become dross;* all they are brass, and tin, and iron, and lead, in *the midst* of the furnace ; they are even the dross of silver. Therefore saith the Lord God — Because ye are all become *dross,* behold, therefore I will gather you into the midst of Jerusalem, as they gather silver, and brass, and iron, and lead, and tin into the midst of the furnaces to blow the fire upon it, to melt it ; so will I gather you in mine anger and in my fury ; and I will leave you there, and melt you." (Ezek. xxii. 18–20.) But how should this justice of the Lord's proceedings endear *his statutes* to us ! It is such a sensible demonstration of his truth, bringing with it such a close conviction of sovereign mercy to ourselves—not less guilty than they ! Add to this—If he were less observant of sin—less strict in its punishment as a transgression of his word—we should lose that awful display of the holiness of the word, which commends it supremely to our love—" Thy word is *very pure; therefore thy servant loveth it.*" (Verse 140.)

120. *My flesh trembleth for fear of thee; and I am afraid of thy judgments.*

The justice of God is a tremendously awful subject of contemplation, even to those who are safely shielded from its terrors. The believer, in the act of witnessing its righteous stroke upon *the wicked of the earth,* cannot forbear to cry out—*My flesh trembleth for fear of thee.** Thus

* ' A thrilling horror curdles my skin.' The thing cannot be poetically expressed without periphrasis.—Bishop HORSLEY.

did the holy men of old tremble, even with a frame approaching horror, in the presence of the Divine *judgments*. David trembled at the stroke of Uzzah, as if it came very near to himself (2 Sam. vi. 6–9). " *Destruction from God* " —saith holy Job—" *was a terror to me: and by reason of his highness I could not endure.*" (Job, xxxi. 23.) Such also was the Prophet's strong sensation—" *When I heard, my belly trembled; my lips quivered at thy voice: rottenness entered into my bones.*" (Hab. iii. 16. Comp. Jer. iv. 19. Dan. iv. 19.) And thus, when God comes to *tread down and put away* his enemies for the display of the holiness of his character, and to excite the *love* of his people—those that stand by, secure under the covert of *their hiding-place* (Verse 114)—cannot but " take up their parable and say —Alas! who shall live, when God doeth this!" (Numb. xxiv. 23.) The children of God reverence their Father's anger. They cannot see it (such is his " terrible Majesty!" Job, xxxvii. 22) without an awful fear ; and this *trembling* at his judgments upon the ungodly covers them from the heavy stroke. Those that refuse to tremble shall be made to feel, while those that are *afraid of his judgments* shall be secure. " Only with thine eyes shalt thou behold, and see the reward of the wicked." (Ps. xci. 8.) " I *trembled* in myself," said the prophet, " *that I might rest in the day of trouble.*" (Hab. iii. 16.) Even the manifestations of his coming " for the salvation of his people" are attended with all the marks of the most fearful terror—as if his voice would shake the earth to its very foundation—" Thou didst cause judgment to be heard from heaven—the earth feared and was still : *when* God arose to judgment, to *save all the meek of the earth.*" *

To mark this *trembling* as the character of the child of

* Ps. lxxvi. 7–9. See the effect of a manifestation of the glory of the Saviour to the Evangelist, for the purpose of special consolation and support. Rev. i. 17, 18. Comp. also Dan. x. 8–17.

God, we need only contrast it with the ungodly scoffing,
" Where is the God of judgment ? Where is the promise
of his coming ?   The Lord will not do good, neither will he
do evil." (Mal. ii. 17. 2 Pet. iii. 4. Zeph. i. 12.)   Thus
do men dare to " run upon the thick bosses of his bucklers "
(Job, xv. 26), instead of *trembling for fear of him!* This
" stoutness against the Lord" (Mal. iii. 13), excites the
astonishment of the hosts of heaven ; so discordant is it to
their notes of humble praise —" Who shall *not fear thee,* O
Lord, and glorify thy name ; for *thy judgments* are made
manifest !" (Rev. xv. 4.)   Such is the special acceptance
of this *trembling* spirit, that some shadow of it obtained a
respite even for wicked Ahab (1 Kings, xxi. 27–29), and a
pardon for the penitent Ninevites (Jonah, iii. 5–10) ; while
its genuine " tenderness of heart" screened Josiah from
the doom of his people (2 Chron. xxxiv. 27), and will ever
be regarded with the tokens of the favour of this terrible
God. " To this man," saith he, " will I look, even to him
that is poor, and of a contrite spirit, and that *trembleth at
my word."* (Isa. lxvi. 2, 5.)

Believers in Christ ! rejoice in your deliverance from
that " fear which hath torment." (1 John, iv. 18.)   Yet
cherish that holy reverential fear of the character and
judgments of God, which will form your most effectual
safeguard " from presumptuous sins." (Ps. xix. 13.)   The
very supposition, that, if God had not engaged himself to
you by an unchangeable covenant, his fearful *judgments*
would have been your eternal portion, is of itself sufficient
to mingle the wholesome ingredient of fear with the most
established assurance.   What ! can you look down into
the burning bottomless gulf beneath your feet, without the
recollection — If I were not immoveably fastened to the
" Rock of Ages" by the strong chain of everlasting love,
this must have been my abode through the countless ages
of eternity.   If I had not been thus upheld by the grace,

as well as by the providence, of God, I might have dropped out of his hand, as one and another not more rebellious than I have fallen, into this intolerable perdition ! O God ! *my flesh trembleth for fear of thee; and I am afraid of thy judgments.**

Thus the dread of *the judgments of God* is not necessarily of a slavish and tormenting character. " His saints" are called to "fear him" (Ps. xxxiv. 9) ; and their fear, so far from " gendering unto bondage," is consistent with the strongest assurance (Comp. Hab. iii. 16, with 17, 18) ; nay, even is its fruit and effect. (Heb. xii. 28.) It is at once the principle of present obedience (Ib. xi. 7), and of final perseverance. (Ib. iv. 1.) It is the confession of weakness, unworthiness, and sinfulness, laying us low before our God. It is our most valuable discipline. It is the " bit and bridle" that curbs the frowardness of the flesh, and enables us to " serve God acceptably," in the remembrance, that, though in love he is a reconciled Father, yet in holiness he is " a consuming fire." (Ib. xii. 29, with 28.)

Now, if we are under the influence of this reverential awe and seriousness of spirit, we shall learn to attach a supreme authority and consideration to the least of his commands. We shall dread the thought of wilfully offending him. The fear of grieving him will be far more operative now, than was the fear of hell in our unconverted state. Those who presume upon their *gospel* liberty, will

---

* How striking was H. Martyn's experimental apprehensions of this subject! 'In prayer in the evening I had such near and terrific views of *God's judgments* upon sinners in hell, that *my flesh trembled* for fear of them. The passages of God's holy word, that proved the certainty of hell-torments, were brought to me in such a way as I never before felt. I flew trembling to Jesus Christ, as if the flames were taking hold of me ! Oh! Christ will indeed save me, or else I perish.'— *Journals,* vol. i. 382.

not, probably, understand this language. But the humble believer well knows how intimately "the fear of the Lord" is connected with "the comfort of the Holy Ghost" (Acts, ix. 31. Comp. Matt. xxviii. 8), and with his own steady progress in holiness, and preparation for heaven.

PART XVI.

121. *I have done judgment and justice: leave me not to mine oppressors.* **122.** *Be surety for thy servant for good: let not the proud oppress me.*

THERE is something very solemn in the reflection, that God has set up a Vicegerent in the heart—an internal Judge, who takes cognizance of every thought, every emotion, every act—determining its character, and pronouncing its sentence. This tribunal tries every cause without respect to persons, time, place, or any circumstances, that might seem to separate it from other cases under the same jurisdiction. No criminal can escape detection from defect of evidence. No earthly power can hinder the immediate execution of the sentence. The sentence then, of this awful Judge, whether " accusing or excusing" (Rom. ii. 15), is of infinite moment. The ignorant expression—' Thank God, I have a clear conscience !' is used alike by the self-righteous and the careless. The awakened sinner, however, pleads guilty to its accusations, and knows not how to answer them. Blessed be God for the revelation of his gospel, which proclaims the blood of Jesus — sprinkling the conscience — silencing its charges — and setting before the sinner the way of peace ! And now *through Jesus*, " the new and living way" of access to God, conscience, sitting on the throne—speaks peace and acceptance ; and though sins of infirmity will remain, defiling every thought, desire, and act ; yet, like the motes on the face of the sun in the clearest day, they have little or no influence to obstruct the shining of the cheerful light upon the heart. (See Heb. x. 19–22.)

The clearing of conscience is however connected with Christian integrity. " *If our heart condemn us not, then have we confidence toward God.*" (1 John, iii. 21.)   This " testimony of conscience" has often been " the rejoicing" (2 Cor. i. 12) of the Lord's people, when suffering under unremitted reproach or *proud oppression.*   They have been enabled to plead it without offence in the presence of their holy, heart-searching God*—nay, even when in the near prospect of the great and final account, they might have been supposed to shrink from the strict and unerring scrutiny of their Omniscient Judge. (Isa. xxxviii. 1–3.)

But observe the influence of this testimony upon our spiritual comfort.   David was at this time under persecution—no new trial to a child of God (1 Pet. iv. 12. 2 Tim. iii. 12) and one that will never cease, so long as Satan has instruments at his command.   But see the blessing which conscious uprightness gave to his prayers : *I have done judgment and justice : leave me not to mine oppressors.*   Can my heart and conscience respond to this appeal ?   Then may I plead my cause before God, *Leave me not to my oppressors. Let not the proud oppress me.*   Plead my cause with them. Let my righteousness be made known.   Let it be seen, that thou " wilt not leave me in their hand, nor condemn me when I am judged.   Let integrity and uprightness preserve me : for I wait on thee." (Ps. xxxvii. 33 ; xxv. 21.) But if any deviation from the exact rule of righteousness between man and man (Matt. vii. 12) has been allowed— if the world charge me as ungodly, because they have proved me unrighteous—then let me not wonder, that " the con-

---

* SAMUEL—1 Sam. xii. 3–5.   NEHEMIAH—xiii. 14, 22.   JOB — x. 7.   DAVID—Ps. vii. 3–6 ; xviii. 20–24 ; xxvi. 1–6.   PAUL—Rom. ix. 1; and the APOSTLES—1 Thess. ii. 10.

solations of God shall be small with me" (Job, xv. 11.
Comp. Ps. lxvi. 18); nor let me expect a return of the Lord's
cheering manifestation, until the Achan has been removed
from the camp (Josh. vii. 10–15), and by confession to God
(Ib. 19), and reparation to man (Luke, xix. 8), I have "given
glory to the Lord God of Israel."

But let not this appeal be thought to savour of Pharisaical pride. He pleads not merit. He only asserts his
innocence—the righteousness of his cause—not of his
person. Though upright before man, he ever felt himself
a sinner before God. The highest tone of conscious integrity is therefore consistent with the deepest prostration of
evangelical humility. The difference is infinite between the
proud Pharisee and the upright believer. The Pharisee
makes the appeal with undisturbed self-complacency and
self-righteous pleading. The believer would ever accompany it with the Publican's prayer for mercy. (Luke, xviii.
9–13.) Instantly—in a deep conviction of need,—he
appends the supplication—*Be surety for thy servant for good.**
The keen eye of the world may possibly not be able to
affix any blot upon my outward profession ; but, " if
thou, Lord, shouldest mark iniquities, O Lord, who shall
stand?" (Ps. cxxx. 3.) The debt is continually accumu-
lating, and the prospect of payment as distant as ever. I
might well expect to be *left to my oppressors,* until I should
pay all that was due (Matt. xviii. 34) unto my Lord. But
behold! "Where is the fury of the oppressor?" (Isa. li.
13.) The surety is found—the debt is paid—the ransom
is accepted—the sinner is free! There was a voice heard
in heaven —" Deliver him from going down to the pit : I
have found a ransom." (Job, xxxiii. 24.) Yes, the Son of
God himself became " surety for a stranger," and " smarted

---

* Comp. Ps. xxvi. 11; Neh. xiii. 22; with 14—a bold testimony
of integrity presented in the character of a sinner.

for it." (Prov. xi. 15.) At an infinite cost—the cost of his own precious blood—he delivered me from *mine oppressors*—sin—Satan—the world—death—hell. " It was exacted : and he answered." (Isa. liii. 7. Bp. Lowth.) As Judah in the place of Benjamin, he was ready to stand in my stead before his Father—" I will be surety of him : of mine hand shalt thou require him." (Gen. xliii. 9.) As Paul in the stead of Onesimus, he was ready to plead, before the same tribunal—" If he hath wronged thee, or oweth thee aught, put that on mine account ; I will repay it." (Philem. 18, 19.)

Let this subject be ever present to my mind. Well indeed was it for me, that Jesus did not " hate suretyship." (See Prov. xi. 15, last clause.) Had he refused the vast undertaking, how could I have answered before the bar of God ? Or had he undertaken only for those who loved him, again should I have been left without a plea. But when as my *surety* he has brought me under his yoke, and made me his *servant*, I can plead with acceptance before his throne, *Be surety for thy servant for good,**—for the good, which thou knowest me to need—my present and eternal deliverance from my proud oppressors. And do not I need such a surety every moment ? And need I be told how fully he has performed the Surety's part ? So that I may boldly say—" Who is he that condemneth ? it is Christ that died. It is Christ that lives. There is therefore now no condemnation to them that are in Christ Jesus." (Rom. viii. 33, 34, 1.)

---

* Comp. Isa. xxxviii. 14, where the same words are used in the original. " *Be surety.*" " *Undertake for me.*" The same plea is urged—" *Let not the proud oppress me.*" " *O Lord, I am oppressed ; undertake.*" The same frame of conflict is marked—" *Mine eyes fail for thy salvation,*" verse 123, " *Mine eyes fail with looking upward.*"

123. *Mine eyes fail for thy salvation, and for the word of thy righteousness.*

And do thine *eyes*, tried believer, begin to *fail?* So did thy Redeemer's before thee. He, whom thou hast been recollecting as *thy Surety*, when he stood in thy place, burdened with the intolerable load of thy sin — bearing the weighty strokes of Infinite justice upon his soul — he too was constrained to cry out, " Mine eyes fail, while I wait for my God." (Ps. lxix. 3. Comp. xxii. 1–3.) Listen, then, to thy deserted Saviour counselling his deserted people ; " gifted with the tongue of the learned, that he should know how to speak a word in season to you that are weary"—" Who is among you that feareth the Lord, that obeyeth the voice of his servant ; that walketh in darkness, and hath no light ? Let him trust in the name of the Lord, and stay upon his God." (Isa. l. 4, 10.)

That *our Surety* will plead *for our good*, doubt not. Yet " the vision is for an appointed time." (Hab. ii. 3.) " But shall not God avenge his own elect, which cry day and night unto him, though he bear long with them ?" (Luke, xviii. 7, 8.) *Salvation*—a gift of such comprehensive and enduring blessing — is it not worth the waiting trial ? Wonderful is that arrangement, by which the word of grace is made *the word of righteousness!* God hath bound himself to us by his promises of grace, which are not, Yea and nay, but " Yea and amen" (2 Cor. i. 20)—under his own hand and seal. Who that has tried them, but will " set to his seal that God is true ?" (Josh. xxiii. 14, with John, iii. 33.) Cheering indeed is the thought, that, amidst the incessant changes in Christian experience, our hope is unchangeably fixed. We may not indeed always enjoy it ; but our salvation does not depend upon our present enjoyment of its consolation. Is not the blessing as certain—

yea—is not *our assurance of an interest in it as clear*, when
we are brought to the dust under a sense of sin, as if we
were " caught up into the third heaven" in a vision of
glory ?

In a season of desertion, therefore, while we maintain a
godly jealousy over our own hearts, let us beware of a mis-
trustful jealousy of God. Distrust will not cure our wound,
or quicken us to prayer, or recommend us to the favour of
God, or prepare us for the mercy of the Gospel. Complaining is not humility. Prayer without waiting is not
faith. The path is plain as noon-day. Continue to believe
as you can. Wait on the Lord. This is the act of faith,
depending on him — the act of hope, looking for him — the
act of patience, waiting his time — the act of submission,
resigned even if he should not come. Like thy Saviour, in
his " agony" of desertion, " pray more earnestly." (Luke,
xxii. 44.) Condemn thyself for the sins of which thou art
asking forgiveness. Bless him for his past mercy, even if
thou shouldest never taste it again. Can he frown thee
from his presence? Can he belie his promise to his waiting people? (Isa. xxx. 18 ; xlix. 23.) Impossible! Nay!
while he has taken away the sensible apprehensions of his
love, and in its room has kindled longing desires for the lost
blessing ; is not this to show himself — if he be " verily a
God that *hideth himself*"—yet still " *the God of Israel, the
Saviour?*" (Isa. xlv. 15.) Though he delays his promise,
and holds us as it were in suspense ; yet he would have us
know, that he has not forgotten *the word of his righteousness*.
But this is his wise and effectual mode of trying his own
gift of faith. And it is this " *trial of faith*"—*and not faith
untried*—that will be " found to praise, and honour, and
glory at the appearing of Jesus Christ." (1 Pet. i. 7.)

The full consolation of the Gospel is therefore the fruit
of patient, humble waiting for the Lord, and of earnest
desire, conflicting with impatience and unbelief, and at

length issuing in a state of child-like submission and dependence. The man who was here expressing his longing expectation for God's salvation, was evidently, though unconsciously, in possession of the promise. Nor would he at this moment have exchanged his hope, clouded as it was to his own view, for all " the pleasures of sin," or the riches of the world. Although at this moment he appeared to be under the partial hidings of his Father's countenance, yet it is important to observe, that he was not satisfied, as an indolent professor, to " lie upon his face" (Josh. vii. 10) in this sad condition. His " *eyes failed with looking upward* " —stretched up with earnest expectation to catch the first rising rays of the beaming Sun of Righteousness. He knew, what all Christians know, who walk closely with God, that his perseverance in waiting upon God, would issue in the eventual fulfilment of every desire of his heart.*

But can we assuredly plead *the word of his righteousness* for the anticipation of the object of our desire? Have we always an express promise answering to our expectations, " putting God in remembrance" (Isa. xliii. 26) of his word? Possibly we may have been asking not " according to his will" (1 John, v. 14. Jam. iv. 3), and therefore may have " charged God foolishly" (Job, i. 22), as if he had been unfaithful to his word, when no engagement had been

---

* Foxe tells us of Mr. Robert Glover, martyr at Coventry, two or three days before his death, overwhelmed with the prospect of martyrdom, and mentioning to a friend his earnest supplication for the light of God's countenance, yet without any sense of comfort. His darkness continued up to the period of his arriving within sight of the stake, when suddenly his whole soul was so filled with consolation, that he could not forbear clapping his hands, and crying out —' He is come!—he is come !' He appeared to go up to heaven in a chariot of fire, exhibiting little or no sensibility of his cruel death. Was not this the *word of his righteousness* to one, whose *eyes failed in looking for it.*—Foxe's *Acts and Monuments,* 1555.

pledged : when we had no warrant to build upon from *the word of his righteousness.* If, however, our petition should be found to be agreeable to his word of promise, and faith and patience hold on in submission to his will, we must not, we cannot, suppose, that one tittle that we have asked will fail. Whether the Lord deliver us or not, prayer and waiting will not be lost. It is a blessed posture for him to find us in, such as will not fail to ensure his acceptance, even though our request should be denied. An enlivening view of the Saviour is in reserve for us ; and *the word of righteousness* will yet speak—" This is the rest, wherewith ye may cause the weary to rest : and this is the refreshing." (Isa. xxviii. 12, also xxx. 15.) To every passing doubt and rising fear, oppose this *word of his righteousness.*

But let me bring my own heart to the test. Am I longing for the manifestation of God ? Surely if I am content with what I already know, I know but very little of the unsearchable depths of the love of Christ ; and I have abundant need to pray for more enlarged desires, and a more tender enjoyment of his Divine presence. If faith is not dead, yet it may have lost its conquering and quickening vigour. Let me then exercise my soul in diligent, careful, patient waiting upon God, equally removed from sloth and frowardness — and I shall yet find the truth of that consoling *word of his righteousness*—" Light is sown for the righteous, and gladness for the upright in heart."*

124. *Deal with thy servant according unto thy mercy, and teach me thy statutes.* 125. *I am thy servant; give me understanding, that I may know thy testimonies.*

A sense of *mercy*, and the privilege of Divine *teaching,*

* Ps. xcvii. 11. The same plea under similar circumstances of conflict is urged, Ps. cxliii. 1.

were the earnest of the Lord's *salvation*, for which *the eyes of his servant were failing*, and for which he was waiting in dependence upon the sure *word of his righteousness*. And indeed these two wants daily press upon every *servant* of God as matter for earnest supplication. Both are intimately connected. A deeper sense of *mercy* will bind us more strongly to his *statutes* (Ps. cxvi. 12–14); while a more spiritual *teaching in the statutes* will humble us in a sense of sin, and consequent need of *mercy*. (Jer. xxxi. 19.) As it respects the first—if there is a sinner upon the earth, who needs the special *mercy of God*, it is his own *servant*. For as the Lord sees abundantly more excellence in his feeblest desire, than in the professor's most splendid external duties ; so he sees far more sinfulness and provocation in the workings of his sin, than in the palpably defective services of professors, or in the open transgression of *the wicked of the earth*. Let him scrutinize his motives, thoughts, and affections, even in his moments of nearest and happiest approach unto his God ; and he will find such defilement cleaving to every offering, with all the aggravations of mercy, light, and knowledge, vouchsafed, that the confession of his soul, when comparing himself with his fellow-sinners, will be, " Of whom I am chief." (1 Tim. i. 15.) And therefore, as a *servant of God*, I can only come before him upon the ground of *mercy*. For my best performances I need an immeasurable world of mercy—pardoning—saving—everlasting mercy ; and yet by the blood of Jesus I dare to plead—*Deal with thy servant according unto thy mercy*.

But then I am ignorant as well as guilty ; and yet I dare not pray for *teaching*—much and hourly as I need it, until I have afresh obtained mercy. These two blessings lead me at once to the foundation of the gospel—in the work of Christ, and the work of the Spirit—*mercy* flowing from the blood of the Son (Eph. i. 7)—*teaching* from the

office of the Spirit. (John, xiv. 26 ; xvi. 13.) *Mercy* is the
first blessing, not only in point of importance, but in point
of order. I must know the Lord as a Saviour, before I can
go to him with any confidence to be my teacher. But
when once I have found acceptance for my petition—*Deal
with thy servant according unto thy mercy*—my way will be
opened to enlarge my petition—yea, once and again to
repeat it—*Teach me thy statutes. Give me understanding, that
I may know thy testimonies*—that I may know with intelligent conviction; walk, yea, " run in the way of thy commandments " (Verse 32) with " an enlarged heart." For
let me never forget, that I am " redeemed from the curse "
only—not from the service " of the law "—yea, redeemed
from its curse, that I may be bound to its service. (Gal.
ii. 19. Luke, i. 74, 75.) And does not my especial relation to my God as his *servant*, furnish me with a plea for
his acceptance? (Verse 94. Ps. cxliii. 12.) For when this
" earth is full of his mercy"—much more may I, as belonging to his house, plead for the special mercy of his
teaching (Verse 64)—his own covenant promise (Heb. viii.
10)—so needful for his *servant*, who desires to know, that
he may do, his will. (Verses 33, 34 ; lxxxvi. 11 ; cxliii.
8, 10.)

But if I am *the Lord's servant*, how did I become so?
Time was (let me be ashamed and confounded at the remembrance of it) when I was engaged for another master,
and in another service. (Rom. vi. 16, 20. Tit. iii. 3.) But
his sovereign grace called me from the dominion of sin—
from the chains of Satan—from the bondage of the world,
and drew me to himself. " His I am—and him I serve."
(Acts, xxvii. 23.) His service is my highest privilege : his
reward of grace is my glorious hope. " *If any man serve
me*," saith my Master, " *let him follow me: and where I am,
there shall also my servant be. If any man serve me, him will
my Father honour*." (John, xii. 26.) As his *servant*, there-

fore, I cast myself with confidence upon his *mercy*, and expect to be *dealt with according to that mercy.* Nay—I shall be denied nothing that I " ask according to his will." For he has condescended to call me—not *his servant*, but " his friend" (John, xv. 15)—yea more, to call himself " my brother." (John, xx. 17. Heb. ii. 11, 12.)

Lord ! thou hast showed me this great favour and grace, to make me *thy servant.* I would be thine for ever. I love thy service too well to wish to change it ; yet must I mourn over my dulness, my backwardness in doing thy will, and walking in thy way. Oh ! *teach me thy statutes* more clearly, more experimentally ! *Give me understanding* to discern their heavenly sweetness and their holy liberty, that I may live in a more simple and devoted obedience to them, until I come to see thy face, and to be *thy servant* in thy heavenly temple, " no more to go out."*

126. *It is time for thee, Lord, to work ; for they have made void thy law.*

If I desire a more spiritual *understanding* of the revelation of God, how can I but mourn to witness its awful neglect and contempt ? It seems as if the ungodly not only sin against it, but that they would drive it out of the world. (Exod. v. 2. Ps. xii. 4.) *They make it void*—denying its power to rule, to annul its power to punish. Oh ! let us

* Rev. vii. 15 ; iii. 12. The annals of the Reformation furnish a beautiful record of George of Anhalt—a godly young prince, of twelve years old. ' He put up constant and fervent prayer to God, beseeching him to bring his heart under the power of the truth ; and, often, in the privacy of his cabinet, he exclaimed with tears— *Deal with thy servant according to thy mercy, and teach me thy statutes.* His prayers were answered. Under strong conviction, and constrained to action on it, he fearlessly ranged himself on the side of the gospel.'—D'AUBIGNÉ's *History of the Reformation*, Book v. ch. vi.

cherish that distinguishing feature of the Lord's people,
" sighing and crying for all the abominations of the land"
(Ezek. ix. 4) ; so that we cannot hear or see the name of
God dishonoured, without feeling as for our Father's
wounded reputation.* Can we suffer the men of the world
quietly to go on their course ? Must we not throw in our
weight of influence, whatever it may be, to stem the flowing
torrent : and when (as, alas ! is too often the case) all
efforts are unavailing, carry the cause to the Lord—" It
is time *for thee*, Lord, to work ? " This pleading does not
contradict the law of love, which requires us to love, pray
for, and to bless our enemies (Matt. v. 44) ; for the Lord's
people are not angry for their own cause, but for his.
David had no regard to his own honour, but to God's law.
He had not injured his enemies. " He had laboured to
overcome their evil with good." (Ps. xxxv. 11–14.) He

* What a Christian ought to feel under these circumstances, let
us learn from the following extract of the diary of the saintly
Martyn. Upon hearing at Shiraz, in the course of his disputations,
some reproach of his Saviour's name, he writes thus —'I was cut
to the soul by this blasphemy. In prayer I could think of nothing
else but that great day, when the Son of God shall come in the
clouds of heaven "taking vengeance on them that know not God,"
and convince men of all their hard speeches which they have spoken
against him.' (We might also think that this verse was upon his
mind at this moment.) 'Mirza Seid Ali perceived that I was con-
siderably disordered, and was sorry for having repeated the verse,
but asked, what it was that was so offensive? I told him, that I
could not endure existence, if Jesus were not glorified; that it
would be hell to me, if he were to be always thus dishonoured. He
was astonished, and again asked the reason why. 'If any one pluck
out your eyes,' I replied, 'there is no saying why you feel pain. It
is feeling. It is because I am one with Christ, that I am thus
dreadfully wounded.' On his again apologizing, I told him, ' that
I rejoiced at what had happened, inasmuch as it made me feel
nearer the Lord than ever. *It is when the head or heart is struck,
that every member feels its membership.*'—MARTYN'S *Life*, p. 420, 8vo.
edition.

had often wept for their sins (Verses 136, 158), and prayed for their conversion. (Ps. lxxxiii. 16.) But all was in vain. ' Now, Lord, take the rod in thine own hand. " It is time *for thee*, Lord, to work."' This was true zeal—zeal of the Spirit, not of the flesh. How gracious is our God in permitting his servants thus to plead with him, and, as it were, to give him no rest, until (Isa. lxii. 7) " he shall arise, and *work*," and sit upon the throne of the kingdoms of the earth!

But why does he not break out with some overpowering manifestation of his power? They are " his sword and rod" for the chastening of his people (Ps. xvii. 13, 14. Isa. x. 5, 6), to discipline their watchfulness into constant exercise. (Ps. lix. 11.) They are the trial of their faith— believing the Lord's justice against apparent inconsistency (Ib. lxxiii. 16–18); and of their patience—" waiting the set time of deliverance." (Rev. xiii. 10.) Thus they become a profitable ministry for the church—and this valuable end accomplished, God works his work upon them (Isa. x. 12), and " will avenge his own elect speedily." (Luke, xviii. 8.)

Meanwhile—waiting for this " little while," let us " live by faith." Let us be found on the Lord's side — labouring for sinners—pleading with their hardness and rebellion in our Master's name, and for our Master's sake. Let all the weight of personal exertion and influence, consistent example, and wrestling supplication, be concentrated in " coming to the help of the Lord against the mighty." (Judg. v. 23.) Let us see to it, that if we cannot do what we would, we do what we can. (Mark, xiv. 8.) And if at last we be overborne by the torrent of ungodliness, we shall find our refuge and rest in pleading with our Lord for the honour of his name—*Remember this, that the enemy hath reproached, O Lord, and that the foolish people have blasphemed thy name.* (Ps. lxxiv. 18, also 10, 11, 22.) " His

Spirit shall not always strive with man." (Gen. vi. 3.)
Often, when he has seen *it time for him to work*, have
his judgments made the earth to tremble. " Sodom and
Gomorrah " have " known the power of his anger," and are
" set forth for an example, suffering the vengeance of eternal fire." (Jude, 7.) And when his *time to work* is fully
come, what is all the resistance of earth and hell, but as
" setting the briars and thorns against him in battle ? "
" *I would*"—saith he—" *go through them. I would burn them
together.*" (Isa. xxvii. 4.) A word — a frown — a look — is
destruction. " He is wise in heart, and mighty in strength.
Who hath hardened himself against him, and hath pros-
pered ? " (Job, ix. 4.) Or " who hath resisted his will ? "
(Rom. ix. 19.)

But what shall we say of that stupendous work of his
hand, by which — when men *had made void his law* — when
no restrictions could bind, no forbearance win them — when
he " saw that there was no man, and wondered that there
was no intercessor, *therefore his arm brought salvation unto
him, and his righteousness, it sustained him.*" (Isa. lix. 16.)
Surely, if we could conceive the hosts of heaven to have
taken up this expression of ardent concern for the glory of
God, *It is time for thee, Lord, to work* — they could little
have thought of such a *work* as this — they could never
have conceived to themselves such an unlooked-for, combined display of power, justice, and mercy. To set at
nought then this *work* — is it not to refuse all hope — all
remedy ? To persist in *making void the law* after so magnificent an exhibition of Almighty *working* — must it not
expose the transgressors to reap the fruit of their own
obstinacy, and to prepare to meet him as their Judge,
whom they refuse to receive as their Saviour ? Nor must
they wonder, if the Lord's people, with a holy indignation
against sin, and a fervent zeal for his glory, should appeal
to his faithfulness for the fulfilment of his judgments—*It is
time for thee, Lord, to work : for they have made void thy law.*

127. *Therefore I love thy commandments above gold; yea, above fine gold.*

Therefore I love thy commandments. Yes — shall they not have double valuation in mine eyes, for the scorn and reproach which the world cast upon them? They count them dross — *I love them above gold* — *yea, above fine gold.* This hope, confidence, and idol of the worldling (Job, xxxi. 24), the love of which has been the ruin of thousands (1 Tim. vi. 9, 10) — is not the *commandment* of God more to be desired than it? (Ps. xix. 10.) " The merchandize of it is better than the merchandize of silver, and the gain thereof than fine gold. It is more precious than rubies : and all the things thou canst desire are not to be compared unto it." (Prov. iii. 14, 15.) Here has the Lord unlocked to us his golden treasure, and enriched our souls with " the unsearchable riches of Christ."

This image brings the miser before us. His heart and treasure are in his gold. With what delight he counts it! with what watchfulness he keeps it! hiding it in safe custody, lest he should be despoiled of that which is dearer to him than life. Such should Christians be : spiritual misers : counting their treasure, which is *above fine gold;* and " hiding it in their heart,"* in safe keeping, where the great despoiler shall not be able to reach it. Oh, Christians! how much more is your portion to you than the miser's treasure! Hide it ; watch it ; retain it. You need

---

* Verse 11. Augustine tells us of himself, that while a Manichee, he slighted the Scripture for the plainness of its style, which appeared to him (from a false standard of criticism) not to be compared with the dignity of Ciceronian eloquence. (' Visa mihi est indigna scriptura quam Tullianæ dignitati compararem.'— Confess. lib. iii. cap. 5.) But after his blessed acquaintance with Christ, though Tully was still read with pleasure, yet this thing alone — said he — abated his former interest, *that the name of Christ was not there.* Lib. iii. cap. 4.

not be afraid of covetousness in spiritual things : rather
" covet earnestly" (1 Cor. xii. 31) to increase your store ;
and by living upon it, and living in it, it will grow richer
in extent, and more precious in value.

But have I through Divine grace been enabled to with-
draw my love from the unworthy objects which once possessed it : and to fix it on that which alone offers satisfaction ?   Let me attempt to give a reason to myself of the
high estimation in which I hold it, as infinitely transcend-
ing those things, which the world venture their all — even
their temporal happiness — to obtain.   *Therefore I love the*
commandments of God above gold: yea, above fine gold —
because, while the world and my own heart have only combined to flatter me, they have discovered to me my real
state, as a self-deceived (Rom. vii. 9), guilty (James, ii.
10), defiled (Rom. vii. 14) sinner before God : because they
have been as a " schoolmaster to bring me to Christ"(Gal.
iii. 24) — the only remedy for sin, the only rest for my
soul. *I love them;* because they have often supplied wholesome reproofs in my wanderings, and plain directions in my
perplexity. *I love them;* because they restrict me from
that which would prove my certain ruin ; and because in
the way of obedience to them the Lord has " accepted me
with my sweet savour." (Ezek. xx. 41. Comp. Isa. lxiv. 5.)
Should I not *love them?*   Can *gold, yea, fine gold,* offer to
me blessings such as these ?   Can it heal my broken heart ?
Can it give relief to my wounded spirit ?   Has it any peace
or prospect of comfort for me on my death-bed ?   And
what cannot — what has not — what will not — the precious
word of God do at that awful season of trial ?   O my God,
I would be deeply ashamed, that *I love thy commandments*
so coldly — that they are so little influential upon my conduct — that they so often give place to objects of comparative nothingness in thy sight.   O that my heart might be
wholly and habitually exercised in them, that I may find

the "work of righteousness to be peace, and the effect of righteousness, quietness, and assurance for ever!" (Isa. xxxii. 17.)

128. *Therefore I esteem all thy precepts concerning all things to be right: and I hate every false way.*

The general contempt of religion acts upon the Christian's judgment no less than upon his affections. Is wickedness breaking loose to *make void the law? Therefore he esteems it to be right.* His judgment—instead of being shaken—is more determined. How beautiful is it to see the leaven of grace pervading the whole man! In the fervour of his heart he *loves the commandments even above fine gold;* but yet his "love will abound yet more and more *in knowledge and in all judgment.*" (Philip. i. 9.) His is an intelligent and *universal* regard to them—*esteeming all the precepts concerning all things to be right.* This constitutes his separate and exclusive character. He is readily known from the thoughtless worldling. But his difference from the professor, though really as marked in the sight of God, is far less perceptible to general observation. Consisting more in the state of heart, than in any external mark of distinction, it is often only within the ken of that eye, whose sovereign prerogative it is to "search the heart" (Jer. xvii. 10), and to "weigh the spirits." (Prov. xvi. 2.)

Many profess to *esteem the precepts to be right,* so far as they inculcate the practice of those moral virtues, of which they may present some faint exhibition, and demand the abandonment of those sins, from the external influence of which they may have been delivered. But when they begin to observe the "exceeding breadth of the commandment" (Verse 96)—how it takes cognizance of the heart, and enforces the renunciation of the world, the crucifixion of sin, and the entire surrender of the heart unto God; this

searching touchstone separates them from the church, and
exposes to open day the brand of hypocrisy upon their
foreheads. " Herod did *many things.*" (Mark, vi. 20.)
And so the enemy still will allow a partial subjection to
the precepts. But—as he well knows—one sin holds us
his captive as well as a thousand. The wilful contempt of
one *precept* is the virtual rejection of all. *All*, therefore—
not *many*—is the Christian's word. He fails in some—
yea, in all—but all are the objects of his supreme regard
—every duty, and every circumstance and obligation of
duty (Luke, i. 6)—the evangelical as well as the moral
precepts—teaching him to renounce himself in every part
(his sins as a source of pleasure, and his duties as a ground
of dependence): and to believe in the Son of God as the
only ground of hope. (1 John, iii. 23 ; John, vi. 29.) He
never complains of the strictness of the *precepts!*—but he
is continually humbled in the recollection of his noncon-
formity to them. *Every way,* however pleasing to the
flesh, that is opposed to the revealed will of God, is *hated*,
as *false* in itself, and *false* to his God. This " godly sincerity " will apply to every part of the Christian Directory.
So that any plea for the indulgence of sin (as if it admitted of palliation, or was compensated by some surplus
duty, or allowed only for some temporary purpose) or any
wilful shrinking from the *universality* of obedience—blots
out all pretensions to uprightness of heart. If holiness be
really loved, it will be loved for its own sake ; and *equally
loved and followed in every part.* (2 Cor. vii. 1.) By this
entire " approval of things that are excellent," we shall
" be sincere and without offence unto the day of Christ."
(Philip. i. 10.)

O my soul, canst thou abide this close test ? Hast thou
as much regard to the precepts, as to the privileges, of the
Gospel ? Is no precept evaded, from repugnance to the
cross that is entailed to it ? Is no secret lust retained ?

Art thou content to let all go? If my hatred of sin is sincere, I shall hate it more in my own house than abroad; I shall hate it most of all in my own heart. Here lies the grand seat of hypocrisy. And therefore may the great Searcher of hearts enable me to search into its depths! May I take the lamp of the Lord to penetrate into its dark interior hiding-places of evil! May I often put the question to my conscience, 'What does the Omniscient Judge know of my heart?' Perhaps at the time that the Church holds my name in esteem, the voice of conscience, as the voice of God, may whisper to me—" That which is highly esteemed among men is an abomination in the sight of God." (Luke, xvi. 15.) Some *false way*, yet undetected within, may keep me lifeless and unfruitful in the midst of the quickening means of grace. Let me look into my house—my calling—my family—my soul; and in the course of this search how much matter will be found for prayer, contrition, renewed determination of heart, and dependence upon my God! " *O that my ways were directed to keep thy statutes! I will keep thy statutes; O forsake me not utterly.*" (Verses 5, 8.) And oh! let my spirit be wounded by every fresh discovery of sin. Let my soul bleed under it. But *specially and instantly* let me apply to the "fountain opened for sin and for uncleanness." Here let me wash my soul from the guilt of sin, and regain my peace with God. And to him, who opened this fountain, let me also repair for a large supply of spiritual strength. May his power and grace sharpen my weapons for the spiritual conflict, until every secret iniquity is overcome, and for ever dispossessed from my heart!

And just as sin, besides its guilt, brings its own misery; so does this whole-hearted purity carry with it its own happiness. Can I forget the time, when, under Divine grace and teaching, I made a full presentment of myself (See Rom. xii. 1), when I began to estimate myself as an

hallowed, devoted thing — sacred — set apart for God?
Was not this the first sunshine of my happiness? Nor
was this offering made with momentary excitement, notional
intelligence, forced acquiescence, or heartless assent. My
judgment accorded with the choice of my heart. All was
right in *his precepts*. All that was contrary to them was
abominable. And will not this form the essence of the
happiness of heaven, where every aspiration — every motion
— every pulse of the glorified soul — in the eternity of life
— will bear testimony to the holiness of the service of God?
(Rev. xv. 3, 4.)

PART XVII.

129. *Thy testimonies are wonderful: therefore doth my soul keep them.*

CAN the mere professor make this acknowledgment? He knows only the letter—the shell, which excites no interest. Yet hidden from his eye is an unsearchable depth, which will make the believer a learner to the end of his life. Even he, who "was caught up into paradise, and heard unspeakable words, which it is not lawful for a man to utter" (2 Cor. xii. 4), was brought to this adoring contemplation—"O the depths of the riches both of the wisdom and knowledge of God!" (Rom. xi. 33.) Every way indeed is this revelation worthy of him, the first letter of whose name is "Wonderful." (Isa. ix. 6.) It lays open to the heaven-taught soul what "eye hath not seen, nor ear heard, neither hath entered into the heart of man." (1 Cor. ii. 9.) Think of the Creator of the world becoming a creature—yea, "a curse for man." (John, i. 1–3, 14, with Gal. iii. 13; Philip. ii. 6–8.) Think of man—guilty and condemned—made just with God by a righteousness not his own. (Rom. iii. 19–22.) Think of God bringing out of the ruinous fall more glory to himself, and more happiness to man, than from his former innocence—in the display of his mercy—the glory of his justice, and the investment of sinners—not, as before, with a creature's righteousness, security, and reward, but with his own righteousness (Jer. xxiii. 6. 1 Cor. i. 30), guardianship

(John, vi. 39 ; x. 28. Col. iii. 3, 4), and glory. (John, xvii. 21–24. Rev. iii. 21.) Think how " the way into the holiest of all " is thus " made manifest." (Heb. ix. 8, with x. 19, 20.) Think how abounding grace is the death as well as the pardon of sin (Rom. v. 20, with vi. 1–6)—the present as well as the everlasting life of the soul. (John, iv. 14 ; vi. 57 ; xiv. 6, 19.) These are among the stupendous discoveries of the sacred book, that bow the humble and reflecting mind to the confession—*Thy testimonies are wonderful!* Let us therefore join with the Apostle, in " bowing our knees to the God and Father of our Lord Jesus Christ " —that we " might be able to comprehend *with all saints* " (for, blessed be God ! the privilege is common to all his people) " what is the breadth, and length, and depth, and height : and to know the " unsearchable " love of Christ " (Eph. iii. 14, 18, 19), " in whom are hid all the treasures of wisdom and knowledge." (Col. ii. 3.)

And how delightful is the recollection of these *testimonies* being our " *heritage for ever !* " (Verse 111.) For they are not less *wonderful* in their practical fulness, than in their deep unfathomable mysteries of love. Such is the infinite enlargement of this " heritage," that he who foreknew every thought that would find an entrance into the minds of his people, has here secretly laid up seasonable direction and encouragement for every, even the most minute occasion and circumstance of need. Here, again, is wrapped up, in words fitted by wisdom to receive the revelation, all that intercourse between God and man, throughout all ages of the Church, which is treasured up in the vast unsearchable depository of the Divine mind and purpose. Can we then forbear repeating the exclamation—*Thy testimonies are wonderful!*

But it is not enough to 'adore the fulness of Scripture :'*

* 'Adoro plenitudinem Scripturarum' was the exclamation of Tertullian—'in which posture of holy admiration,'—said the

we must seek to imbibe and exhibit its practical influence. Holy admiration of the *testimonies* will kindle spiritual devotedness to them—*Therefore doth my soul keep them.* The stamp of Divine authority upon them, while it deepens our reverence, commands our steady and cheerful obedience. To keep them is our privilege, no less than our obligation ; and in this path we shall delight to persevere to the end.

But how affecting is the thought of the mass, who look at these wonders with a careless or unmeaning eye, unconscious of their interesting import! They pass by the door of the treasury, hardly condescending to look aside into it : or only taking a transient glance, which comprehends nothing of its inexhaustible stores. " *I have written to them* "—saith the Lord—" *the great things of my law: but they are counted as a strange thing.*" (Hos. viii. 12.) But far more wonderful is it, that we, enlightened, in answer to

deeply-learned and pious Dr. Owen—'I desire my mind may be found while I am in this world.'

'What do I not owe to the Lord for permitting me to take a part in the translation of his word? Never did I see such wonders, and wisdom, and love, in the blessed book, as since I have been obliged to study every expression; and it is a delightful reflection, that death cannot deprive us of the pleasure of studying its mysteries.' —MARTYN's Life, p. 271. The same testimony was given by a kindred spirit employed in the same work. Shortly before his death, Dr. Buchanan, giving to a friend some details of his laborious revisions of his Syriac Testament, suddenly stopped, and burst into tears. On recovering himself—he said—'I am not ill, but I was completely overcome with the recollection of the delight which I have enjoyed in this exercise. At first I was disposed to shrink from the task as irksome, and apprehended that I should find even the Scriptures pall by the frequency of this critical examination. But so far from it, every fresh perusal seemed to throw fresh light on the word of God, and to convey additional joy and consolation to my mind.' 'How delightful'—observes his biographer—'is the contemplation of a servant of Christ thus devoutly engaged in his heavenly Master's work, almost to the very moment of his transition to the Divine source of light and truth itself!'

prayer (See verse 18), with "the Spirit of wisdom and revelation" (Eph. i. 17, 18)—should often be so indifferent to the mysteries of redeeming love here unfolded before us, and should experience so little of their practical influence! Oh! let the recollection of our indolence, and want of conformity to them, never cease to humble us. Let us not enter into *the testimonies*, as a dry task, or an ordinary study; but let us concentrate our minds, our faith, humility, and prayer, in a more devoted contemplation of them. Every such exercise will extend our view of those parts, with which we had conceived ourselves to be competently acquainted: opening a new field of wonders on every side, far beyond our present contracted apprehensions.*

And can any joy be imagined so sublime as the adoring contemplation of this revelation? It reflects even to angels a new and glorious manifestation of their God. (Eph. iii. 10.) It engages their every faculty with intense admiration and delight. (See 1 Pet. i. 12.) And while they behold and worship with self-abasement, their obedience is lively. "With twain he" (the seraph before the throne) "covered his face, and with twain he covered his feet, *and with twain he did fly.*" (Isa. vi. 2.) Thus may we study the same lessons, and with the same spirit. May our con-

---

* Augustine found this so experimentally true, that he tells us, 'that though he should with better capacity and greater diligence study all his lifetime, from the beginning of his childhood to decrepid age, nothing else but the Holy Scriptures; yet they are so compacted and thickly set with truths, that he might daily learn something which before he knew not.'—AUG. Epis. To this truth the late venerable Antistes Hess set his seal at the age of eighty-six, when he informed a young missionary to the Jews, that 'for seventy years the word of God had been the daily object of his unremitting researches: and that still he discovered in it new traces of the mysterious love and wisdom of God."—Jewish Expositor. Nov. 1825.

templation humble us in the dust, and animate us in the service of our God! *Thy testimonies are wonderful: therefore doth my soul keep them.*

130. *The entrance* of thy words giveth light: it giveth understanding to the simple.*

' So " *wonderful are thy testimonies*," gracious God,' that even by touching as it were only their threshold, *the entrance of thy words giveth light and understanding unto* my heart. The study commenced in simplicity and prayer, opens an *entrance* to the first dawning *light* of the word into the soul; often only sufficient to make darkness visible, but still " shining more and more unto the perfect day." (Prov. iv. 18.) Indeed all the spiritual light known in this dark world has flowed from the word, forcing its *entrance*, like the beams of the sun, upon the opening eyes of " a man that was born blind." It is a most striking instance of Divine condescension, that this word — so *wonderful* in its high and heavenly mysteries — should yet open a path so plain, that the most unlearned may find and walk in it. (Isa. xxxv. 8.) Indeed *the entrance of the word* into unintellectual and uncultivated minds, often gives an enlargement and elevation of thought, which is the earnest of the restoration of man to his original glory, when doubtless every mental as well as spiritual faculty was " filled with all the fulness of God." (Eph. iii. 19. Comp. Col. iii. 10.) So astonishing is the power of this heavenly light, that from any one page of this holy book, a child, or even an idiot, under heavenly teaching, may draw more instruction than the most acute philosopher could ever attain from any other fountain of light! Nay

* " Opening."—AINSWORTH.

—he may acquire a more intelligent perception of its contents, than the student, untaught by the Spirit of God, who may have devoted to its study the persevering industry of many successive years. For very possible is it to be possessed of all the treasures of literature, and yet to remain in total ignorance of everything that is most important for a sinner to know.* The Apostle's paradox unfolds the secret, " If any man among you seemeth to be wise in this world, let him become a fool, that he may be wise." (1 Cor. iii. 18.) We do not mean to disparage human wisdom ; but it is *the pride of wisdom*, so opposed to the simplicity of the gospel, which prevents us from " sitting at the feet of Jesus, and hearing his word." It makes the teacher instruct in " the words of man's wisdom," rather than in the knowledge of " Christ and him crucified" (Comp. 1 Cor. ii. 1–4), and hinders the learner from receiving Christ in the light and love of the truth.

It is painful to remember how much light may be shining around us on every side, without finding an *entrance* into the heart. " The light shineth in darkness ; and the darkness comprehended it not."† Not only the pride of human reason, but the love of sin, shuts out the light :

* ' A very extraordinary thing '—said one—' if I, who have read the Bible over and over in the original languages, have studied it day and night, and have written criticisms and comments on it—a very extraordinary thing, that I should not be able to understand that meaning in the Scripture, which is said to be so plain, that a " wayfaring man, though a fool, should not err " in the discovering of it.' And so it is extraordinary, till we open the Bible; and there we see the fact explained. The man who approaches the word of God in his own wisdom shall not find, what the " fool" will discover under the teaching of Divine wisdom. " For it is written, I will destroy the wisdom of the wise, and will bring to nothing the understanding of the prudent "—" God hath chosen the foolish things of the world to confound the wise."— CECIL'S Remains.

† John, i. 5, "Apprehended it not."— SCOTT. "Admitted it not."— CAMPBELL.

" Men *love darkness rather than light, because their deeds are evil.*" (John, iii. 19, 20.)   And thus because " the eye is evil, the whole body is full of darkness :" and " if the light that is in them is darkness, how great is that darkness !" (Matt. vi. 23.)   Most awful is the view given us of the conflict between the contending powers of light and darkness — " The god of this world blinding the eyes of them that believe not, *lest the light of the glorious gospel of Christ, who is the image of God, should shine unto them,*"— the Almighty God resisting his hateful influence, and " shining into the hearts" of his people, " *to give the light of the knowledge of the glory of God in the face of Jesus Christ.*" (Comp. 2 Cor. iv. 4–6.)   How necessary is it to watch vigilantly against the pride that " rebels against the light " (Job, xxiv. 13), and the indifference that neglects to cherish it ! How much more *entrance* would have been given to the word, and consequently how much clearer would have been the *diffusion* of light in the soul, were we as earnest and diligent in secret prayer for heavenly teaching, as we are accustomed to be in the public hearing of the word !

But the enthusiast is not satisfied with the light of the word.   The delusion of his own heart dreams of a light within — an immediate revelation of the Spirit, independent of the word.   It cannot however be safe to separate the light of the Spirit from the light of the word.   The word indeed moves in subserviency to the Spirit ; but the light of the Spirit is nowhere promised separate from the word. If it does not always guide directly by the word ; yet it is only manifested in the direction of the word.   The word is in the matter, if not in the mode ; and though the Spirit may by immediate light direct us to any path of duty, yet it is invariably to that path, which had been previously marked by the light of the word.   Thus the Spirit and the word conjointly become our guide — the Spirit enlightening and quickening the word — and the word evidencing the

light of the Spirit. Nor will their combined influence ever
leave the church of God, until she has joyfully and completely entered into Immanuel's land, where she shall need
no other light, than that of the glory of God, and of the
Lamb, which shall shine in her for ever. (See Rev. xxi. 23.)

But — Reader — rest not satisfied with whatever measure of light may have been hitherto vouchsafed. Seek
that the word may have " an entrance ministered unto you
abundantly." The most advanced believer is most ready to
acknowledge, how much of the word yet remains unexplored before him.* Cultivate the disposition of simplicity
— the spirit of a " little child " (Matt. xviii. 3) — willing
to receive, embrace, submit to, whatever the revelation of
God may produce before you. There will be many things
that we do not understand : but there is nothing that we
shall not believe. " Thus saith the Lord "— is sufficient
to satisfy reverential faith. To this spirit the promise of
heavenly light is exclusively made. " The testimony of the
Lord is sure, making wise the *simple*. The meek will he
guide in judgment ; *the meek* will he teach his way." (Ps.
xix. 7 ; xxv. 9.) It is beautiful to see a man like Solomon,
endued with enlarged powers of mind (1 Kings, iv. 29–34)
— acknowledging himself to be a little child (1 Kings,
iii. 7), afraid of trusting in his own light ; and seeking instruction from above. But never will an unhumbled mind
know the benefit of this Divine instruction. To such a
student, the Bible must ever be a dark book ; since its very
design is to destroy that disposition which he brings to
the inquiry. That knowledge, therefore, which is unable
to direct our way to heaven — nay, which by closing the
avenues of spiritual light, obstructs our entrance thither,
is far more a curse than a blessing. Far more glorious is
the simplicity of the word than the wisdom of the world.

* See the testimonies adduced in the notes on the preceding
verse.

" In that hour, Jesus rejoiced in spirit, and said, I thank thee, O Father, Lord of heaven and earth, because thou hast hid these things from the wise and prudent, and hast revealed them unto babes: even so, Father, for so it seemed good in thy sight." (Luke, x. 21.)

131. *I opened my mouth, and panted; for I longed for thy commandments.*

When the *" wonderful"* character of God's *" testimonies"* is apprehended; and when their *entrance has given light to the soul;* something far beyond ordinary affection and desire is excited. A thirsty man—burning with inward heat on a sultry day, *opening his mouth, and panting* for some alleviation of his thirst—is a fine image of the child of God intensely longing for the attainment of his object. Or, if we suppose before us the man nearly exhausted by the heat of his race, and *opening his mouth, and panting* to take in fresh breath to renew his course; so would the believer " rejoice," like the sun, to " run his" heavenward " race."* He cannot satisfy himself in his desires. The motions of his soul to his God are his life and his joy. It is a spring of perpetual motion beating within—perpetual, because natural—not a rapture, but a habit—a principle, having indeed its faintings, and its sickness, but still returning to its original spring of life and vigour. It seems as if the soul could never draw in enough of the influences of the spiritual life. Its longings are insatiable—as if the heart would " break with " (Verse 20) the overpowering strength of its own desires; until at length, wearied with the conflict, the believer *opens his mouth, and pants* to fetch in a fresh supply of invigorating grace. He enjoys " a little reviving " (Ezra, ix. 8) in his Lord's commandments;

* Ps. xix. 5.   For another illustration, see Job, xxix. 23.

enjoying the Lord himself as his well-spring of refreshment. (See on Verse 20.)

Hear the man of God elsewhere giving, or rather attempting to give, expression to his *pantings*—" As the hart panteth after the water-brooks, so panteth my soul after thee, O God.   My soul thirsteth for thee ; my flesh longeth for thee in a dry and thirsty land where no water is.   I stretch forth my hands unto thee ; my soul thirsteth after thee as a thirsty land." (Ps. xlii. 1 ; lxiii. 1 ; cxliii. 6.) Thus did Job *open his mouth, and pant.*   " O that I knew where I might find him ! that I might come even to his seat !" (Job, xxiii. 3.)   And the church—pouring out her heart before the Lord—" With my soul have I desired thee in the night ; yea, with my spirit within me will I seek thee early." (Isa. xxvi. 9.)   St. Paul also describes the same intenseness of his own desire—" Not as though I had already attained, either were already perfect ; but I follow after, if that I may apprehend that for which also I am apprehended of Christ Jesus.   Brethren, I count not myself to have apprehended ; but this one thing I do ; forgetting those things which are behind, and reaching forth unto those things which are before, I press towards the mark for the prize of the high calling of God in Christ Jesus." (Philip. iii. 12–14.)   But amidst all these examples, and *infinitely beyond them all*—behold the ardour of our blessed Master in his work.   Such was the *panting* of his heavenly desire, that, when " wearied with his journey," and " sitting at Jacob's well," he forgot even his natural want for his thirsty frame, in the joy of the conversion of a lost sinner to himself. (John, iv. 6, 31–34.)

And thus must our affections be fully engaged.*   The

* ' Be always displeased with what thou art, if thou desirest to attain to what thou art not: for where thou hast pleased thyself, there thou abidest.   But if thou sayest—' I have enough '—thou perishest.   Always add—always walk—always proceed.   Neither stand still, nor go back, nor deviate.'—AUGUSTINE.

soul must be kept open to heavenly influence; so that, when the Lord touches us with conviction, inclines our hearts to himself, and constrains us to his service, we may be ready to " exercise ourselves unto godliness " (1 Tim. iv. 7), in receiving, cherishing, and improving the heavenly *longing after his commandments;* and may *open our mouths, and pant* for more advanced progress in them. We look not so much to the quantity, as to the activity of faith ; always at work, stirring up a holy fire within, for the utmost stretch of human attainment : like men of large projects and high determinations, still aspiring to know more of God, both in the enjoyment of his love, and in conformity to his will. And shall we be ashamed of these feelings ? Shall we not rather be deeply humbled, that we know so little of them—encouraged, if we have any springing of them—alarmed, if we be utterly destitute of their influence ? Shall we not be *opening our mouth, and panting,* when any new path of service is opened before us ? For if we are content to be strangers to this *longing* after God— this readiness for duty ; what else can be expected, but " sliding back from the Lord by a perpetual backsliding ?" (Jer. viii. 5.) Growing in sin, declining in love, and gradually relinquishing the habit of prayer, we shall shortly find little attaching to us but the empty name— *Christianity without Christ.* The world will despise these exercises as enthusiasm, the distemper of a misguided imagination. But is it—can it be—otherwise than a " reasonable service" (Rom. xii. 1) as well as a bounden obligation, to give up our whole desires to him, who is alone worthy of them ? There can be no evidence of their sincerity, unless they are supreme.

But let union with Christ, and the life flowing from him, be the constant spring of this holy ardour. Thus shall I enjoy a more habitual influence of his love—that all-constraining principle, which overcomes all my complaints of coldness and deadness of heart, and fills me with *pantings and longing* in his service. But am I ready to shrink from this elevated standard? If my heart is drawing back, let me force it on. Let me lay my command, or rather God's command, upon it. Let conscience do its office, until my heart is brought into actual and close contact with this touchstone of my spiritual prosperity. What then—let me ask myself—is the pulse of my desires after spiritual things? What exercises of grace do I find in them? What improvement of grace do I derive from them? Do I *pant*, thirst, long, after the enjoyment of heavenly pleasure? Do I mourn over, and conflict with, that indolence and indifference, which so often hinders my race? Oh! let me be found a frequent suppliant at the throne of grace; bewailing my dulness, yet " stirring up" my faith " to lay hold on" (Isa. lxiv. 7) my God; seeking for larger views of the Gospel, a warmer experience of its promises, a more intense appetite for its enjoyments, and a more devoted attachment to its service. Surely such desires will issue in the confidence of faith. " *My soul shall be satisfied as with marrow and fatness.*" (Ps. lxiii. 5.)

132. *Look thou upon me, and be merciful unto me, as thou usest to do unto those that love thy name.*

The highest ardency of holy desire is no ground of satisfaction before God. Nor does the believer in his most elevated moments forget his proper character—always a sinner—needing mercy every moment—in every duty. His prayer for mercy therefore suitably follows his exalted expression of love—*Look thou upon me, and be merciful unto me.* Mercy is indeed secured to him beyond the power of earth and hell to despoil him of it; but the comfortable sense of this mercy is vouchsafed only according to the earnestness of his desires, and the simplicity of his faith. And this is indeed a blessing, with which no earthly source of satisfaction can compare. (Ps. iv. 6, 7.) What are all the riches of the world without it, but splendid poverty, as little able to supply the place of Jesus in the soul, as the magnificent array of the starry firmament is to compensate for the absence of the sun? It is night with the child of God — Egyptian night — " darkness which may be felt " (Exod. x. 21), until his Sun appear to chase away his gloom — until his Lord hear his cry — *Look thou upon me, and be merciful unto me!*

To have this portion of *those that love the name* of God, is, then, the grand object. To have our offering, as Abel's was (Gen. iv. 4), accepted with God — to walk as Enoch walked (Gen. v. 24), with God — to commune with him as Abraham (Gen. xviii. 17–33) and Moses (Exod. xxxiii. 11. Deut. xxxiv. 10) were privileged to do — to be conformed with the holy Apostle (Philip. iii. 10. Gal. ii. 20) to the death of Christ — in a word, to be interested in all the purchase of a Saviour's blood — " this is the heritage of the Lord's servants "— this is the " one thing that we have desired of the Lord, and are seeking after " (Ps. xxvii. 4),— " this," with the dying Psalmist, " is all our salvation, and all our desire." (2 Sam. xxiii. 5.) " Remember me then, O Lord, with the favour that thou bearest unto thy people ; O visit me with thy salvation ; that I may see the good of thy chosen : that I may rejoice in the gladness of thy nation ; that I may glory with thine inheritance." (Ps. cvi. 4, 5.)

And yet, alas ! how often has the power and deceitfulness of sin cast us into so lifeless a state, that we are not only living without the enjoyment of this portion, but at rest without it ; scarcely knowing or caring whether the Lord look on us or not ? Can we wonder, that our holy, jealous God, should " hide himself " (Isa. lvii. 17), and " go and return to his place ? " (Hos. v. 15.) His next manifestations will probably be in the way of sharp conviction, making us to feel our distance, our coldness, our barrenness : awakening us to search into the cause ; and, in the contrast of our sad condition with those who are walking in his favour, again bringing forth the cry — *Look thou upon me, and be merciful unto me, as thou usest to do unto those that love thy name.* The prayer of humility, earnestness, and perseverance, though it may be tried awhile, will surely never be forgotten. (Comp. Isa. xxx. 18; Hab. ii. 3.) If therefore we cannot yet "sing in the ways of the Lord" (Ps. cxxxviii. 5), yet let us not cease to mourn after him, till he *look upon us,* and " satisfy us with his mercy." (Ps. xc. 14.) And oh ! let us remember that there is but one way through which one gracious look, or one expression of tender mercy, can visit our souls. Let our eyes and heart then be ever fixed on Jesus. It is only in this his "beloved" Son that the Lord can *look upon us,* so as not to " behold iniquity in us." But we " are complete in him." (Comp. Num. xxiii. 21; Eph. i. 6; Col. ii. 10.) Here then let us wait ; and when this our prayer has received its answer in the Lord's best time—whether it be in " the goings of our God in the sanctuary" (Ps. lxviii. 24), or in the more secret manifestation (Matt. vi. 6. John, xiv. 21–23) of his love—Christians, " arise, and shine." (Isa. lx. 1.) Let it be known, that you have been on the mount with God, by the lustre of your face, the adorning of your profession, before the world.

Lord ! since our looks to thee are often so slight, so cold, so distant, that no impression is made upon our hearts ; do thou condescend continually to *look upon us* with mercy and with power. Vouchsafe us such a look, as may touch us with tenderness and contrition, in the remembrance of that sin, unbelief, and disobedience, which pierced the hands, the feet, the heart of our dearest Lord and Saviour. (Comp. Luke, xxii. 61.) Oh ! for that contrite

spirit, in which we shall enjoy the *look* of thy special favour!
(Isa. lxvi. 2.)   Oh! for a glimpse of thy love, that will put
our spiritual enemies to shame! (Ps. lxxxvi. 17.)   Oh! for
that sunshine of thy countenance, which brings present salvation to our souls! (Ps. lxxx. 19.)

133. *Order* my steps in thy word; and let not any iniquity
have dominion over me.*

To expect the favour of the Lord without an habitual
desire of conformity to his image, is one among the many
delusions of a self-deceiving heart.   It is the peculiar character of the Christian, that his desires are as earnest for
deliverance from the power as from the guilt of sin.   Having therefore prayed for acceptance, he now cries for holiness.   For even could we conceive the Lord *to look upon
him* with a sense of his favour, he would still feel himself
a miserable creature, until he has received an answer to his
prayer—*Let not any iniquity have dominion over me.*

But it is often difficult to distinguish the power of temptation from the prevalence of sin, and thus precisely to ascertain, when *iniquity* may be said to have *dominion over us.*
Is it not however the influence of temptation—not acting
upon the mind, but admitted with consent into the heart?
It is this actual consent of the will, obtained by the deceitfulness and solicitations of sin, that marks its real *dominion.*
Light, knowledge, and conscience, may open the path of
holiness ; but while the will—the sovereign power in the
soul—dissents, the reigning power of sin continues undisputed.   Much care, however, much singleness, and a most
jealous scrutiny of the springs of action, are required, accurately to determine the bias of the will, and consequently
the *dominion of iniquity.*   The perplexed, conflicting soul

---

* " Set straight my steps." LXX.   " Firmly direct."—AINSWORTH.

may mistake *the rebellion* for the *dominion of iniquity*—its
continued impression upon the heart for its ruling sway.
On the other hand, a constrained opposition of conviction
may present some hopeful symptoms of deliverance, while
the dominant principle is still unshaken.   The present resolution to any particular act of sin may be weakened,
while the love and habit of it remained unaffected.   Sin is
not always hated, when it is condemned, or even forsaken ;
nor are duties always loved in the act of their performance.
The opposition to sin, which the awakened superficial professor considers as his evidence of uprightness of heart, is
often only the unavailing resistance of a natural enlightened conscience to the ruling principle of the heart.   The
light and power of conscience may do much in condemning
every known sin, and in restraining from many ; in illus-
trating every known duty, and insisting upon the external
performance of many ; while yet the full *dominion of iniquity*
is undisturbed.   Were not Ahab and Judas as completely
under his *dominion* after their repentance as they were before ? (1 Kings, xxi. 27 ; xxii. Matt. xxvii. 3–5.)   Did
not Balaam, with all his knowledge—and the young ruler,
with all his natural loveliness and semblance of sincerity,
" lack that one thing"—a heart delivered from the *dominion of its own iniquity?* (2 Pet. ii. 15. Mark, x. 21, 22.)
Yet it is not occasional surprisals, resisted workings, abhorred lust, nor immediate injections of evil and blasphemous thoughts ; *but only the ascendancy of sin in the
affections*, that proves its reigning power.   The throne can
admit but of one ruler ; and therefore, though grace and
iniquity may and do co-exist within, they cannot be co-
partners in one sovereignty.   Yet forget not that every
sinful indulgence is *for the moment* putting the sceptre into
the hands of our worst enemies.   The setting up of an
usurper is the virtual dethronement of the rightful sove-

reign.   The subjection to sin is therefore the rejection of
Christ.

How inestimably precious is the thought, that deliverance from this cursed *dominion* is inseparably connected
with a state of acceptance with God !   The man who enjoys
the unspeakable blessing of pardoned iniquity, is he " in
whose spirit there is no guile." (Ps. xxxii. 1, 2.)   He has
a work done within him, as well as for him.   His Saviour
is a *whole* Christ—" made of God unto him Sanctification" and complete " Redemption" as well as " Righteousness." (1 Cor. i. 30.)   He comes to the cleansing fountain
(Zech. xiii. 1), as the double cure of his *iniquity*—equally
effectual to wash from its power, as from its guilt.

But let us duly estimate the value of David's preservation.   He had been used to " hide the word in his heart,"
as his safeguard against sin (Verse 11), and from his own
experience of its power he had recommended it to the especial attention of the young. (Verse 9.)   Yet the recollection of his continual forgetfulness and conscious weakness,
leads him to turn his rule into a matter of prayer—*Order
my steps in thy word;*—implying, that if his *steps* were not
ordered, from want of their keeping, *iniquity* would regain
its *dominion*.   And who of us have not daily need of this
ruling discipline?   Without it, all is disorder.   Our scattered affections need to be " united" in one central principle
(Ps. lxxxvi. 11), under the direction of *the word*.   The universal influence of this rule also is so important.   The word
not only cheers our path, but *orders our steps*. (Verse 105 ;
xvii. 4 ; xix. 11. Prov. vi. 23.)   Every act—every duty—
are as *steps* in the heavenward path—guarding us from the
devious paths on either side, beset with imperceptible danger, and spread with the fowler's snare.   And what a blessed
path would this be for us, if we had singleness and simplicity always to " look right on, and straight before us !"

(Prov. iv. 25.) But alas! we are often only half-roused from our security. The word is forgotten; or there is an unreadiness to receive its Divine impressions. Our own wisdom is consulted: and, " or ever we are aware," *iniquity* regains a temporary *dominion over us.*

Now I would ask myself—What do I know of this godly, careful walk? Am I frequently during the day looking upward to my heavenly guide; and then looking into his word as my direction in the way; and lastly considering my heart and conduct, whether it is *ordered in the word?* The man, who has " the law of God in his heart," alone possesses the security, " that none of his steps shall slide." (Ps. xxxvii. 31.) When I take therefore a step into the world, let me ask—Is it *ordered in God's word,* which exhibits Christ as my perfect example; so that, walking after him, and following in his steps, I may be able to frame my temper and habits according to this unsullied pattern?

But let us mark, how fully is this prayer warranted by the special promise of the Gospel—" *Sin shall not have dominion over you; for ye are not under the law, but under grace.*" (Rom. vi. 14, with 12.) The law stirred up sin, and gave it increased power; while it left us to our unassisted exertions to subdue it. We watch, pray, and strive against it; yet, alas! it mocks our efforts—rages, yea, tyrannizes more than ever. (Ib. vii. 8. 1 Cor. xv. 56.) But it is the cross of Calvary, that gave the child of God his first view of sin, that first made him loathe it, that first enabled him to contemplate a holy God without fear, and even with confidence. This— this alone—subdues his pride, rebellion, enmity, selfishness. In him that hung there we trust as an Almighty conqueror; and we are made ourselves " more than conquerors through him that loved us." (Rom. viii. 37.) His very name of Jesus (Matt. i. 21) marks his office, his crown, his glory. Here therefore—not in doubts and fears—not in indolent mourning for sin — here lies the appointed means of present relief — the only hope of final victory. *Iniquity*, even when subdued, will struggle to the last for *dominion:* but looking to and living on Jesus, we have the victory still. The more clear our view of Jesus, the more complete is our victory. Supplies of continual strength will ever be vouchsafed to restrain the *dominion of iniquity*, and even to "keep under" its daily risings; except as they may be needful for the exercise of our graces, and be eventually overruled for the glory and praise of our faithful God.

134. *Deliver me from the oppression of man: so will I keep thy precepts.*

"Many are the afflictions of the righteous" (Ps. xxxiv. 19), from external as well as from internal enemies — not only from their own *iniquity*, but *from the oppression of man.* Yet "man is only the Lord's hand and sword" (Ib. xvii. 13, 14), and he can only move under the overruling guidance of our Father's wisdom and love. Not indeed that the believer would (except in submission to the will of God)* desire his *deliverance* from this trouble on account of personal pain and distress: but he sometimes finds peculiar circumstances of trial an unavoidable hindrance in the service of his God. And his conviction sends him to the throne of grace: and there he never makes interest in vain. "*He cries unto the Lord because of the oppressors: and he sends a Saviour, and a great one: and he delivers him.*" (Isa. xix. 20.)

The power of faith is indeed Omnipotent. Mountains are removed from their place, or they become "plains before" it (Matt. xxi. 21, 22. Zech. iv. 7); or the "worm" is enabled to "thresh them, and beat them small, and make

---

* See the example of David. 2 Sam. xv. 25, 26; and of David's Lord, Luke, xxii. 42.

them as chaff." (Isa. xli. 14, 15.) Often is the Christian strengthened to overcome the most formidable opposition, and to " profess a good profession before many witnesses" (1 Tim. vi. 12), who are " watching for his halting." (Jer. xx. 10.) The grace of Christ will make the hardest duty easy; and the love of Christ will make the sharpest trials sweet : yet, where in the continued exercise of faith the obstacles to conscientious service remain unmoved (as, for instance, a child of God restrained in the fetters of a worldly family from a free and avowed obedience), we may lawfully pray that the providence of God would *deliver from the oppression of man, that we might keep his precepts.*

A time of *deliverance*, as well as a time of persecution, has proved a season of extraordinary prosperity in the church of God. When " the Churches *had rest* throughout all Judea and Galilee and Samaria," they " *were edified;* and walking in the fear of the Lord, and in the comfort of the Holy Ghost, *were multiplied.*" (Acts, ix. 31.) And thus in individual experience, whatever be the benefit of persecution, yet the weariness of a long-protracted conflict is often more than flesh and blood can bear ; and which he who " knoweth our frame" (Ps. ciii. 14), will not refuse to look upon, and remove, in answer to the prayers of his afflicted people. (Ps. cxxv. 3. 1 Cor. x. 13.) At the same time, our proneness, self-indulgence, and our natural inclination to shrink from discipline—as needful as our food—require this prayer to be presented with exceeding caution and self-jealousy. There is a great danger, lest, in our eagerness to escape from the difficulties of our path, we should lose the most important benefit intended by them. We must therefore accompany the petition for *deliverance* with a sincere purpose to *keep God's precepts.* (Luke, i. 74.) For how many have exposed the unsoundness of their own hearts, when the supplication has been heard, the *deliverance* granted, *and the promise of obedience been forgotten!*

Fellow-Christian! have your circumstances of trial ever dictated this prayer? How then have you improved your liberty, when the answer has been vouchsafed? Has the " way of escape made" for you been kept in grateful remembrance? (Comp. 2 Chron. xxxii. 22–25, with Ps. ix. 13, 14.) Has the effect of your *deliverance* been visible in an increasing love and devotedness to the Lord's service? Oh! let a special Ebenezer be set up to mark this special achievement of prayer. (1 Sam. vii. 12.) Let the mercy be connected with the sympathy of our " faithful and merciful High-Priest, who being himself touched with the feeling of your infirmities," has pleaded for your succour and release. (Heb. iv. 15 ; ii. 17, 18.) And be encouraged henceforth to tread the ways of God with more firmness and sensible stay, " having your feet shod with the preparation of the Gospel of peace." (Eph. vi. 15.) But remember— the blessing of the cross is lost, if it does not issue in a song of praise — if we have not taken it up as a token of fatherly love. At all times the safest and shortest way to peace, is to let God use his own methods with us ; to live the present moment to him in the situation he has placed us ; not dreaming of other circumstances more favourable to our spiritual prosperity ; but leaving ourselves, our difficulties, our discouragements, in his hands, who makes no mistakes in any of his dispensations — but who orders them all, that they " may turn to our salvation, through our prayer, and the supply of the Spirit of Jesus Christ." (Philip. i. 19.)

135. *Make thy face to shine upon thy servant; and teach me thy statutes.*

If the Lord *deliver us from the oppression of man*, and " make even our enemies to be at peace with us" (Prov. xvi. 7) ; still, if we are in spiritual health, we shall be restless and uneasy, until he *make his face to shine upon us.*

And in the Scripture revelation of God, " dwelling between the cherubims" (2 Kings, xix. 15. Ps. xcix. 1. Ezek. x. 1–5), and therefore on the mercy-seat (Exod. xxv. 17–22, with Rom. iii. 25)— with the " rainbow," the emblem of "the covenant of peace"—"*round about the throne*" (Rev. iv. 3), as if to invite the access of sinners from every quarter —have we not full warrant to plead—" *Thou that dwellest between the cherubims, shine forth;* stir up thy strength, and come and save us ?   Turn us again, O God ; and *cause thy face to shine*, and we shall be saved." (Ps. lxxx. 1–3.)   Others we see eagerly asking, " Who will show us any good ?" Alas ! they will discover in the end, that they have " spent their money for that which is not bread, and their labour for that which satisfieth not." (Isa. lv. 2, with Ps. iv. 6.) The believer's incessant cry is— Let me see " the King's face." (Comp. Prov. xvi. 15.)   This is a blessing worth praying for.   It is his heart's desire, his present privilege, and what is infinitely better—his sure and everlasting joy, " *They shall see his face.*" (Rev. xxii. 4.)

It is both important and interesting to mark the repetitions—always new—in this beautiful Psalm.   David had just before prayed, " *Look thou upon me, and be merciful unto me.*" (Verse 132.)   Perhaps another passing cloud had darkened his sky.   Again he darts up the same prayer, *Make thy face to shine upon thy servant.*   Such cries in the mouth of this holy servant of God, must have been most hopeless petitions—nay, the expression of the most daring presumption—had he not been acquainted with the only true way of access to God, joyfully led to renounce every other way, and enabled diligently to improve this acceptable approach to his God.   Indeed whatever obscurity may hang over the question relating to the faith of the Old Testament believers, their confidence at the throne of grace shows them to have attained a far more distinct perception of Christian privilege, through the shadowy

representations of their law, than is commonly imagined.
Else how could they have been so wrestling and persevering in their petitions; overcoming the spirit of bondage,
and breathing out the spirit of adoption in the expression
of their wants and desires before the Lord? The prayers
of the Old Testament church are not more distinguished
for their simplicity, spirituality, and earnestness, than for
their unfettered, evangelical confidence. When they ap-
proached the footstool of the Divine Majesty, with the
supplications—*Make thy face to shine upon thy servant,*—*Thou
that dwellest between the cherubims, shine forth*—it was as if
they had pleaded—'*Reconciled Father*—*thou that sittest upon
a throne of grace, look upon us*—*Abba, Father, be gracious
to us!*'

Many, however, seem to despise this child-like confidence. They go on in heartless complaining and uncertain
apprehensions of their state; as if *doubting* was their life,
and as if they might rest upon the presumption, that the
shining of God's face upon them is not indispensable to their
salvation. But will they then be content to " be saved,
yet so as by fire," instead of having an " entrance ministered
unto them *abundantly* into the everlasting kingdom of our
Lord and Saviour?" (Comp. 1 Cor. iii. 15 ; 2 Pet. i. 11.)
Is it enough for them to be *just alive,* when " the things
that remain," from want of being duly cherished, " are
ready to die?" If they can be safe without a conscious interest in the favour of God, can they be so without the
desire for it? Is not this assurance attainable? Is it not
commanded? (See 2 Cor. xiii. 5 ; Heb. vi. 11 ; 2 Pet. i. 10.)
Is it not most desirable? This cold contentment clouds the
integrity of their profession. For God's real people are
living habitually either in spiritual enjoyment, or in restless dissatisfaction. Their dark seasons are times of wrestling supplication (Ps. lxxxviii. 1–3 ; cxxx. 1, 2)—seasons
of deep humiliation (Lam: iii. 20–22. Mic. vii. 9), tender-

ness of spirit (Lam. iii. 31–40), and constant waiting upon God (Ps. xl. 1–3 ; cxxx. 5, 6. Isa. viii. 17 ; l. 10), until he *makes his face to shine upon his servants.* They can dispense with ordinary comforts. But it is death to be without him. " All their springs are in him." They estimate their happiness by the *shining*—and their misery by the clouding — *of his face.* This is the true principle of assurance, even if this most important blessing be not sensibly enjoyed.

How then stands the case between us and God ? From ourselves originates the mist, which darkens the *shining.* (Isa. lvii. 17.) His sovereign free grace blots the cloud away. (Isa. xliv. 22.) We raise the mountains of separation. (Isa. lix. 2.) The Almighty power of our great Zerubbabel removes them. (Zech. iv. 7.) To ourselves then be all the shame. To him be all the praise !

But how may we realize more constant sunshine ?— Apart from the hindrances just alluded to, others are mainly to be found in mistaken or contracted views of the Gospel. Hence, therefore, the value of enlarged apprehensions of the Gospel of the grace of God — of its fulness, satisfying every claim, and supplying every want — of its freeness, unencumbered with conditions, and holding forth encouragement to the most unworthy — of its holiness, restraining the sinful hindrances to enjoyment — and of its security, affording permanent rest in the foundations of the covenant of grace. The life of faith will thus be maintained in more full contemplation of Jesus, and renewed reliance upon him; and walking in closer communion with him, our hope will be enlivened with the constant sense of reconciliation and love.

We need not wonder at the Psalmist's persevering determination to seek *the shining of the Lord's face.* This high privilege is connected no less with the Christian's public usefulness than with his personal enjoyment. For who is most likely to win others to the love of the Saviour, and to the service of God—to enliven the drooping soul, or to recover the backslider? Is not he, who lives most in the sunshine of the Gospel, and who therefore has most to tell of its heavenly joy? But you say, ' My heart, alas! is so cold and barren, my affections so languid, my desires so faint, my sky so often clouded. I do not forget *that I am a child; but a child in disgrace* is too often my dishonourable character and wretched condition.' Then exercise your faith in going where David was wont to go. As a penitent child, " Arise and go to your Father"— " only acknowledge your iniquity" (Jer. iii. 13)—tell your complaint before him—resort much and often to him ; be importunate ; be patient ; plead the name (John, xiv. 13, 14) and merits of Jesus ; and you will not, you cannot plead in vain ; you will once more walk happily, holily, as well as confidently, in the light of your Father's countenance. And in marking more carefully his gracious dealings with your soul, you will be kept from formality, hardness, and despondency.

But we cannot expect this *shining*, save in the paths of God (John, xiv. 21–23. Isa. lxiv. 5. Gal. vi. 16) ; and he who looks for comfort, while careless of duty, is only the victim of his own delusions. Well, therefore, does the child of God—longing for higher enjoyment, and learning more of his own ignorance, add this petition—*Teach me thy statutes.* And he that taught us this petition, will himself, according to his promise, be our teacher in the way of holiness. (Ezek. xxxvi. 27.) And if, under his teaching, in the pathway to glory—our God *makes his face to shine upon us*, what more want we to beguile the toil and weariness of the way? And if one beam of his countenance, though but dimly seen through this sinful medium, exceeds the glories of ten thousand worlds—what will it be to live under the perpetual cloudless *shining of his face!*

Believer! does not this prospect invigorate every step of your journey? Your Lord is at hand. Soon will he appear to gladden with his inexpressible smile every soul that is in readiness for him. Oh! seek to realize his approach, and with holy aspirations and joyful expectancy respond to his welcome voice. *" He which testifieth these things saith, Surely I come quickly: Amen. Even so, come, Lord Jesus!"* (Rev. xxii. 20.)

136. *Rivers of waters run down mine eyes,* (Comp. Jer. ix. 1; xiv. 17; Lam. ii. 18) *because they keep not thy law.*

If the Lord *teaches us* the privileges of his *statutes,* he will teach us compassion for those who *keep them not.* This was the mind of Jesus. His life exhibited one, whose " heart was made of tenderness." But there were some occasions, when the display of his compassion was peculiarly striking. Near the close of his life, it is recorded, that, " when he was come near, and beheld the city"—" beautiful for situation, the joy of the whole earth" (Ps. xlviii. 2)— but now given up to its own ways, and " wrath coming upon it to the uttermost," he " wept over it." (Luke, xix. 41. Comp. Matt. xxiii. 37, also Mark, iii. 5.) It was then a moment of triumph. The air was rent with hosannahs. The road was strewed with branches from the trees, and all was joy and praise. (Comp. Luke, xix. 36–40.) Amid all this exultation, the Saviour alone seemed to have no voice for the triumph—no heart for joy. His omniscient mind embraced all the spiritual desolation of this sad case; and he could only weep in the midst of a solemn triumph. *Rivers of waters run down mine eyes, because they keep not thy law.*

Now a Christian, in this as in every other feature, will be conformed to the image of his Lord. His heart will therefore be touched with a tender concern for the honour of his God, and pitying concern for those wretched sinners, that *keep not his law*, and are perishing in their own transgressions. Thus was "*just Lot*" in Sodom "*vexed with the filthy conversation of the wicked.*" (2 Pet. ii. 7, 8.) Thus did Moses " fall down before the Lord, as at the first, forty days and forty nights ; *he did neither eat bread nor drink water; because of all their sins which they had sinned, in doing wickedly in the sight of the Lord to provoke him to anger.*" (Deut. ix. 18, 19.) Thus also Samuel, in the anticipation of the Lord's judgments upon Saul, " *grieved himself, and cried unto the Lord all night.*" (1 Sam. xv. 11, 35.) Ezra, on a similar occasion, in the deepest prostration of sorrow, "*rent his garment and his mantle, and plucked off the hair of his head and of his beard, and sat down astonied until the evening sacrifice.*" (Ezra, ix. 3, 4.) And if David was now suffering from *the oppression of man* (Verse 134), yet his own injuries never drew from him such expressions of overwhelming sorrow, as did the sight of the despised law of his God.

Need we advert to this tender spirit, as a special characteristic of " the ministers of the Lord ?" Can they fail in this day of abounding wickedness — even within the bounds of their own sphere — to hear the call to " weep between the porch and the altar ?" (Joel, ii. 17.) How instructive is the posture of the ancient prophet — first pleading openly with the rebellion of the people — then " his soul weeping in secret places for their pride !" (Jer. xiii. 17.) Not less instructive is the great apostle — his " conscience bearing witness in the Holy Ghost to his *great heaviness and continued sorrow in his heart for his brethren, his kinsmen according to the flesh.*" (Rom. ix. 1–3.) In reproving transgressors, he could only write to them, " *Out of much affliction and anguish of heart with many tears*" (2 Cor. ii. 4), and in speaking of them to others, with the same tenderness of spirit, he adds — "*Of whom I tell you even weep-*

ing." (Phil. iii. 18. Comp. Acts, xx. 19.) Tears were these of Christian eloquence no less than of Christian compassion.

Thus uniformly is the character of God's people represented—not merely as those that are *free from*, but as *" those that sigh and that cry for all the abominations that be done in the midst of the land."* They—they alone—are marked out for mercy in the midst of impending, universal ruin. (Ezek. ix. 4.) The want of this spirit is ever a feature of hardness and pride—a painful blot upon the profession of the gospel. (1 Cor. v. 2.) How wide the sphere presenting itself on every side for the unrestrained exercise of this yearning compassion! The appalling spectacle of a world apostatized from God, of multitudes sporting with everlasting destruction—as if the God of heaven were " a man that he should lie" (Num. xxiii. 19), is surely enough to force *rivers of waters* from the hearts of those who are concerned for his honour. What a mass of sin ascends as a cloud before the Lord, from a single heart! Add the aggregate of a village—a town—a country—a world! every day—every hour—every moment—well might the *rivers of waters* rise to an overflowing tide, ready to burst its barriers. We speak not of outward sensibility (in which some may be constitutionally deficient, and the exuberance of which may be no sign of real spiritual affection), but we ask—Do we lay to heart the perishing condition of our fellow-sinners? Could we witness a house on fire, without speedy and practical evidence of our compassion for the inhabitants? And yet, alas! how often do we witness souls on the brink of destruction—unconscious of danger, or bidding defiance to it—with comparative indifference! How are we Christians, if we believe not the Scripture warnings of their danger? or if, believing them, we do not bestir ourselves to their help? What hypocrisy is it to pray for their conversion, while we are making no effort to promote it! Oh! let it be our daily supplication, that this indifference concerning their everlasting state may give place to a spirit of weeping tenderness; that he may not be living as if this world were really, what it appears to be, a world without souls; that we may never see the sabbaths of God profaned, his laws trampled under foot, the ungodly "breaking their bands asunder, and casting away their cords from them" (Ps. ii. 3), without a more determined resolution ourselves to *keep these laws of our God*, and to plead for their honour with these obstinate transgressors. Have we no near and dear relatives, yet " lying in wickedness— dead in trespasses and sins?" To what blessed family, reader, do you belong, where there are no such objects of pity? Be it so—it is well. Yet are you silent? Have you no ungodly, ignorant neighbours around you? And are they unwarned, as well as unconverted? Do we visit them in the way of courtesy or kindness, yet give them no word of affectionate entreaty on the concerns of eternity? Let our families indeed possess, as they ought to possess, the first claim to our compassionate regard. Then let our parishes, our neighbourhood, our country, the world, find a place in our affectionate, prayerful, and earnest consideration.

Nor let it be supposed, that the doctrine of sovereign and effectual grace has any tendency to paralyze exertion. So far from it, the most powerful supports to perseverance are derived from this source. Left to himself—with only the invitations of the Gospel—not a sinner could ever have been saved. Added to these—there must be the Almighty energy of God—the seal of his secret purpose —working upon the sinner's will, and winning the heart to God. Not that this sovereign work prevents any from being saved. But it prevents the salvation from being in vain to all, by securing its application to some. The invitations manifest the pardoning love of God; but they change not the rebel heart of man. They show his enmity; yet they slay it not. They leave him without excuse; yet at the same time—they may be applied without salvation. The moment of life in the history of the saved sinner is, when he is "made willing in the day of the Lord's power" (Ps. cx. 3)—when he comes—he looks—he lives. It is this dispensation alone that gives the Christian labourer the spring of energy and hope. The palpable and awful proofs on every side, of the "enmity of the carnal mind against God," rejecting alike both his law and his Gospel, threaten to sink him in despondency. And nothing sustains his tender and compassionate interest, but the assurance of the power of God to remove the resisting medium, and of his purpose to accomplish the subjugation of natural corruption in a countless multitude of his redeemed people.

The same yearning sympathy forms the life, the pulse, and the strength of Missionary exertion, and has ever distinguished those honoured servants of God who have devoted their time, their health, their talent, their all, to the blessed work of " saving souls from death, and covering a multitude of sins." (Jam. v. 20.) Can we conceive a Missionary living in the spirit of his work—surrounded with thousands of mad idolaters, hearing their shouts, and witnessing their abominations, without a weeping spirit? Indignant grief for the dishonour done to God—amazement at the affecting spectacle of human blindness—detestation of human impiety—compassionate yearnings over human wretchedness and ruin—all combine to force tears of the deepest sorrow from a heart enlightened and constrained by the influence of a Saviour's love.* This, as

---

* ' My God! I feel the mournful scene;
  My bowels yearn o'er dying men;
  And fain my pity would reclaim,
  And snatch the fire-brands from the flame,

we have seen, was our Master's spirit. And let none presume themselves to be Christians, if they are destitute of "this mind that was in Christ Jesus" (See Philip. ii. 4–8); if they know nothing of his melting compassion for a lost world, or of his burning zeal for his heavenly Father's glory.

Oh, for that deep realizing sense of the preciousness of immortal souls, that would make us look at every sinner we meet as a soul to be "pulled out of the fire," and to be drawn to Christ;—which would render us willing to endure suffering, reproach, and the loss of all, so that we might win one soul to God, and raise one monument to his everlasting praise! Happy mourner in Zion! whose tears over the guilt and wretchedness of a perishing world are the outward indications of thy secret pleadings with God, and the effusion of a heart solemnly dedicated to the salvation of thy fellow-sinners!

> But feeble my compassion proves,
> And can but weep, where most it loves;
> Thine own all-saving arm employ,
> And turn these drops of grief to joy.'

PART XVIII.

137. *Righteous art thou, O Lord, and upright are thy judgments.* 138. *Thy testimonies that thou hast commanded, are righteous, and very faithful.*

THE advancing Christian learns to adore the awful perfections of his God, and to acknowledge his righteous character and government, even when "his ways are in the sea, and his paths in the great waters." (Ps. lxxvii. 19.) "Clouds and darkness are round about him; righteousness and judgment are the habitation of his throne." (Ps. xcvii. 2. Comp. Deut. xxxii. 4.) We have already brought out the unvarying testimony of his people to the righteous character of his afflictive dispensations. (Verse 75.) Even from haughty Pharaoh was a similar acknowledgment extorted. (Exod. ix. 27.) Adonibezek also, under the blow of his hand, cried out—"As I have done, so God hath requited me." (Judg. i. 7. Comp. 2 Chron. xii. 6.)

Yet in this path, "we walk by faith, not by sight." (2 Cor. v. 7.) *Often in Providence* "his footsteps are not known." (Ps. lxxvii. 19.) We cannot trace the reasons of the Divine mind. We must wait and see the "end of the Lord," when the disjointed pieces shall be compacted into one complete texture and frame-work. "At evening time there shall be light." (Zech. xiv. 7.) *Much more in the dispensation of grace* do we hear the voice,—"Be still, and know that I am God." (Ps. xlvi. 10.) Doubtless he could give his grace to all as well as to some. Yet none have a

364 EXPOSITION OF PSALM CXIX.

claim upon him. " Is it not his to do what he will with his own ? " " Nay, but, O man, who art thou that repliest against God ? " " Shall not the Judge of all the earth do right ? " (Matt. xx. 15. Rom. ix. 20. Gen. xviii. 25.) Thus much is plain — enough to silence cavil, and justify God — grace is freely offered to all. Man's own will rejects it, and leaves him without excuse. (Matt. xxiii. 37. John, v. 40.) Effectual grace is withheld from none, but those who deserve that it should be so. None are forced to sin. None are condemned without guilt. Therefore when we stand upon the ocean's brink, and cry — " Oh, the depth ! " (Rom. xi. 33) are we not constrained to the adoring acknowledgment — *Righteous art thou, O Lord, and upright are thy judgments?* And if this be our praise, even while " we see but as through a glass darkly, and know but in part," how much more, in the world of uncloudy day, when we shall see " face to face, and know even as we are known " (1 Cor. xiii. 12) — shall we sing with reverential joy " the song of the Lamb — Great and marvellous are thy works, Lord God Almighty ! *just and true are thy ways*, thou King of saints ! " (Rev. xv. 3.)

The young Christian, however, less able to grasp these deeper apprehensions, exercises himself chiefly in his more engaging perfections of long-suffering, goodness, and love. It is therefore a satisfactory evidence of growth in grace, when our habitual contemplation of God fixes upon our minds the more full and awful displays of his character ; and we gather from thence an increase of light, peace, humility, and consolation. But the cross of Calvary harmonizes to our view at once the most appalling and the most encouraging attributes. Though his own declaration —that " he will by no means clear the guilty" (Exod. xxxiv. 7) — seemed to present an insurmountable barrier to the purpose of mercy ; yet, rather than the glory of a God of love should be obscured, or his righteous law

should be mitigated, " he spared not his own Son" (Rom.
viii. 32) ; he "made him, who knew no sin, to be sin for
us." (2 Cor. v. 21.)

And do not we naturally argue from his nature to *his
testimonies?* If he be *righteous,* nothing unrighteous can
come from him. His *testimonies,* therefore, are his lively
image—like himself—*righteous and very faithful*—requiring nothing impossible—nothing unsuitable—perfect
love to God and man (Matt. xxii. 37–39)—" our reasonable service" (Rom. xii. 1), no less our privilege than our
duty to render. None that are blessed with a spiritual
apprehension of their nature, and are conformed and framed
to them, will hesitate in setting their seal to the inscription—" *The judgments of the Lord are true and righteous
altogether.*" " *The law is holy, and the commandment holy, and
just, and good.*" (Ps. xix. 9. Rom. vii. 12.)

But let us take care to exhibit the practical influence
of our contemplations of the character and government of
God. The unconverted—far from understanding or sub-
scribing to our acknowledgment—complain, " *The ways of
the Lord are not equal.*" " *My punishment is greater than I
can bear.*" (Ezek. xviii. 25. Gen. iv. 13.) And so opposed
are *the righteous judgments of God* to the perverseness of
corrupt nature, that even with the child of God there is
much murmuring within, that needs to be stilled—much
repining to be hushed—much impatience to be repressed—
many hard thoughts to be lamented, resisted, and banished.
Did we believe more simply, how much more joy would
there be in our faith, and readiness in our submission!
How clearly would our experience " show, that the Lord is
upright ; he is our rock, and there is no unrighteousness
in him!" (Ps. xcii. 15.) " In returning" then "and rest
shall we be saved ; in quietness and confidence shall be
our strength." (Isa. xxx. 15.) In the submissive acknowledgment of the Lord's dispensations, " our peace" will

flow as a river" (Isa. xlviii. 18); more deep and extensive
as it approaches the ocean, and fertilizing our souls with
abundant spiritual peace and enjoyment.

139. *My zeal hath consumed me; because mine enemies have
forgotten thy words.*

Such was David's high estimation of *the testimonies of
his God*, that his spirits were *consumed* with vehement
grief in witnessing their neglect. He could bear that *his
enemies* should *forget him*; but his *zeal* could not endure,
that they should *forget the words of his God*. Zeal is a
passion, whose real character must be determined by the
objects on which it is employed, and the principle by which
it is directed. There is a true and a false zeal, differing as
widely from each other, as an heavenly flame from the
infernal fire. The one is fervent, disinterested affection,
expanding the heart, and delighting to unite with the
whole empire of God in the pursuit of a good, which all
may enjoy without envious rivalry. The other is a selfish,
interested principle, contracting the heart, and ready to
sacrifice the good of mankind, and even the glory of God,
to its own individual advantage. (Matt. xxiii. 15. Gal. vi.
12, 13.) Were its power proportioned to its native tendency, or were it to operate extensively in an associated
body, it would end in detaching its several members each
from their proper centre; in disuniting them from each
other; and, as far as its influence could reach, crumbling
the moral system into discordant atoms. Too often does
this baneful principle exemplify itself in the Church —
either in an obstinate opposition to the truth of the gospel
(John, xvi. 2. Rom. x. 2, 3. Gal. i. 13, 14. Philip. iii. 6),
or in a self-willed contention for its own party. (Gal. iv.
17.) "This wisdom descendeth not from above: but it is
earthly, sensual, devilish." (Jam. iii. 15.) How much also

of that misguided heat, that spends itself upon the externals of religion (Matt. xv. 1, 2 ; xxiii. 25), or would " call fire down from heaven" in defence of fundamental truths, may be found among us, exposing its blind devotees to our Master's tender rebuke—"Ye know not what manner of spirit ye are of!" (Luke, ix. 54, 55.)

Often also do we see a distempered, counterfeit zeal, disproportioned in its exercise, wasting its strength upon the subordinate parts of the system, and comparatively feeble in its maintenance of the vital doctrines of Christ. (Rom. xiv. 1–6.) Thus it disunites the Church by adherence to points of difference, instead of compacting the Church together by strengthening the more important points of agreement. Often again, by the same process in practical religion, are the " mint, anise, and cummin," vehemently contended for ; " while the weightier matters of the law" (Matt. xxiii. 23) are little regarded.

Widely different from this fervour of selfishness is that genuine zeal, which marks the true disciple of our Lord. Enlightened by the word of God, and quickened into operation by the love of Christ, it both shines and warms at the same moment. It is indeed the kindled fire of heavenly love, exciting the most heavenly desires and constant efforts for the best interests of every child of man, so far as its sphere can reach ; and bounded only by a consistent regard to the general welfare of the whole. Thus earnest and compassionate in its influence, awakened to a sense of the preciousness of immortal souls, and the overwhelming importance of eternity, it is never at a loss to discover an extended sphere for its most vehement and constraining exercises. While it hates the sins that pass on every side before its view, it is all gentleness to the sinner ; and would gladly weep tears of blood over those who are deaf to the voice of persuasion, could such tears avail to turn them from their iniquity. But, knowing all human unassisted efforts to be insufficient, it gives to the world its protest against the abominations, which it is too feeble to prevent; and then hastens to the secret chamber to pour out its wrestling desires in the tenderness of our Master's intercession—" Father, forgive them! for they know not what they do." (Luke, xxiii. 34.)

Such was the zeal of the ancient Lawgiver, whose spirit, though, as it regarded his own cause, "*meek above all the men which were upon the face of the earth*" (Num. xii. 3, 13), "*waxed hot*" (Exod. xxxii. 19) on witnessing the grievous dishonour done to his God during his absence on the mount. At the same time (as if most clearly to distinguish the holy burning from the heat of his own spirit) how fervently did he plead his people's cause in secret before his God, as he had manifested his concern for the honour of his God before the congregation! (Exod. xxxii. 30–32.) Surely he could have taken up this language — *My zeal hath consumed me; because mine enemies have forgotten thy words.* Burning with the same holy flame, the great Old-Testament Reformer bore his testimony against the universal prevalence of idolatry; making use of the arm of temporal power (1 Kings, xviii. 17–40), and of the yet greater power of secret complaint (1 Kings, xix. 10), to stem the torrent of iniquity. The same impulse in later times marked the conduct of the Apostles: when, " rending their clothes, and running in among" a frantic multitude of idolaters, by all the power of their entreaties " *they were scarcely able to restrain the people, that they had not done sacrifice unto them.*" (Acts, xiv. 13–18.) On another occasion the great Apostle, forgetting " the goodly stones and buildings" that met his eye at Athens—found " *his spirit stirred in him, when he saw the city wholly given to idolatry.*" (Acts, xvii. 16.) In another city " was he pressed in spirit" (Acts, xviii. 5) by the intensity of his interest for the souls of his fellow-sinners and his Master's work.

Yet this is not a heat that wastes itself without a proportionate object. The truth of God is the grand object. Not one atom of its dust shall be lost. For its fundamentals all consequences must be hazarded (Gal. ii. 5) — yea, life itself — if need be — sacrificed. (Acts, xx. 24. Philip. ii. 17. Rev. xii. 11.) Nor does this fervour expend itself in strong impulses that wear out without fruit. It is a constant affection in " a good thing." (Gal. iv. 18.) Nor is it an undisciplined burst of warm feeling, but a sober controlled exercise of Christian judgment. The Apostle — with his inexpressible abhorrence of idolatry — yet remained in the midst of it for two, perhaps three, years, faithfully employed in his Master's work ; yet waiting for the fittest time of open protest against Diana's worship. (Acts, xix. 10 ; xx. 20, 21.) So admirably was " the spirit of power and love" disciplined by " the spirit of a sound mind." (2 Tim. i. 7.)

But, " compassed about, as we are, with so great a cloud of witnesses" (Heb. xii. 1), let us yet turn aside to look unto One greater than them all — to One, whose example in every temper of Christian conduct affords equal direction and encouragement. Jesus could testify to his Father — " *The zeal of thine house hath eaten me up.*" (Ps. lxix. 9, with John, ii. 17 ; Isa. lix. 17.) He was ever ready to put aside even lawful engagements and obligations, when they interfered with this paramount demand. (Luke, ii. 49.) Yet was his *zeal* tempered with a careful restraint from needless offence. Rather would he work a miracle (Matt. xvii. 24–27), and retreat from publicity (John, vi. 15), than seem to give occasion to those that might desire it. And if we bear the stamp of his disciples, without rushing into offence in the waywardness of our own spirits, and while rejoicing to have our own " names cast out as evil" (Luke, vi. 22. Acts, v. 41), we shall at the same time be tender of any reflection on the name of our God, as on our dearest friend and benefactor. We shall feel any slight of his honour as sensitively as a wound to our own reputation ; nor shall we hesitate to thrust ourselves between, to receive on ourselves any strokes that may be aimed at his cause. (Ps. lxix. 9. Rom. xv. 3. Comp. Ps. lxxxix. 50, 51.) This combined spirit of self-denial and self-devotedness kindles the flame, which " many waters cannot quench, neither can the floods drown." (Cant. viii. 7.) ' *I could bear*'—said holy Brainerd—' *any desertion or spiritual conflict, if I could but have my heart burning all the while within me with love to God, and desire for his glory.*'* It is indeed a delightful exercise to " spend and be spent" in the service of Him, who for our sakes was even consumed by the fire of his own zeal. (Luke, xii. 50.)

However, the surest evidence of Christian zeal is, when it begins at home, in a narrow scrutiny, and " vehement revenge" against the sins of our own hearts. (Comp. 2 Cor. vii. 11 ; Rev. iii. 19.) Do we mourn *over our own forgetfulness of God's words?* Are we zealous to redeem the loss to our Saviour's cause from this sinful neglect? And do we plainly show, that our opposition to sin in the ungodly is the opposition of love? And is this love manifested to the persons and souls of those, whose doctrines and practice we are constrained to resist, and in a careful restraint from the use of unhallowed " carnal weapons" in this spiritual " warfare?" (See 2 Cor. x. 4 ; Jam. i. 20.)

Perhaps the weak, timid child of God may be saying, ' I can do nothing for my God. I suffer his *words to be forgotten*, with little or no success in my efforts to prevent it.' Are you then making an effort? Every work done in faith bears fruit to God and to his church. You may not see it. But let your secret chamber witness to your zeal : and the Lord " will not be unrighteous to forget your

* BRAINERD'S Diary. EDWARDS' Works, iii. 107.

work and labour of love." (Heb. vi. 10.) He will even strengthen you for your dreaded conflict in the open confession of his cause—" *For he hath chosen the weak things of the world to confound the things that are mighty.*" (1 Cor. i. 27.) Or, should peculiar trials restrain the boldness of your profession, you may be found in the end to have made as effectual a resistance to the progress of sin by your intercession before God, as those who have shown a more open front in the face of the world.

140. *Thy word is very pure: therefore thy servant loveth it.*

The Psalmist's *love* for the law of his God may account for the *zeal* he felt on account of its general neglect. All other systems of religion (or rather of " philosophy falsely so called") allure their disciples by the indulgence of carnal lust or self-complacent pride. *The word of God* outweighs them all in its chief excellence—peculiar to itself—its purity. " Every word is *very pure* (Prov. xxx. 5. Ps. xix. 8)— tried to the uttermost" in the furnace, and found to be absolutely without dross.* Its promises are without a shadow of change or unfaithfulness. Its precepts reflect the holy image of their Divine Author. In a word, it contains ' truth without any mixture of error for its matter'†—*Therefore thy servant loveth it.*

' No one but a true servant of God can *therefore love it,* because it is *pure;* since he who loves it must desire to be like it, to feel its efficacy, to be reformed by it.'‡ The unlettered believer cannot well discern its *sublimity;* but he loves it for its *holiness.* The mere scholar, on the other hand, *admires* its sublimity—but the *secrets* which it reveals (such as the pride of the natural heart struggles to

---

* Prayer Book translation.— Comp. Ps. xii. 6.
† LOCKE.   ‡ Bishop HORNE *in loco.*

conceal) forbid him to love it. (See John, iii. 20.) Its
purity, which is the matter of love to the one, excites
enmity in the other. From "the glass" which shows him
"his natural face"—his neglected obligations—his fearfully self-deluded state—and his appalling prospects—he
turns away in disgust. The indulgence of sin effectually
precludes the benefit of the most industrious search into
the word of God. The heart must undergo an entire renewal—it must be sanctified and cleansed, yea, be "bap-
tized with the Holy Ghost" (Matt. iii. 11), before it can
discern, or—when it has discerned—can love, the purity
of the word of God.

Witness the breathings of Brainerd's soul in this holy
atmosphere—'*Oh, that my soul were holy, as he is holy!
Oh, that it were pure, even as Christ is pure; and perfect, as
my Father in heaven is perfect! These I feel are the sweetest
commands in God's book, comprising all others.*'* '*Oh, how
refreshing*'—exclaims the beloved Martyn—'*and supporting
to my soul was the holiness of the word of God! Sweeter
than the sweetest promise at this time, was the constant and
manifest tendency of the word, to lead men to holiness and the
deepest seriousness.*'†

The valuable end for which we "desire this word" is,
"that we may grow thereby" (1 Pet. ii. 2)—grow in purity
of heart and conduct; learning to shrink from the touch
of sin; "cleansing ourselves from all filthiness of flesh and
spirit, and perfecting holiness in the fear of God." (2 Cor.
vii. 1.) Our "esteem" for it—"*more than our necessary
food*" (Job, xxiii. 12)—will be in proportion to our growth
in grace, an evidence of this growth, and a constant spring
of holy enjoyment.

An additional excitement to *love its purity* is the exhibition of *that purity* embodied in our perfect pattern, in

---

* EDWARDS' Works, iii. 171.   † MARTYN's Life, pp. 206, 207.

Him, *who was* " *holy, harmless, undefiled, and separate from sinners.*" (Heb. vii. 26.) For the habit of " beholding the Saviour" with the eye of faith " in the glass of the word," conforms us to his image. (Comp. 2 Cor. iii. 18.) But be it ever remembered, that its holiness can have no fellowship, and communicate no life, except in its own atmosphere. Oh, for a larger influence of the Spirit of God upon our souls, that we may enjoy the purifying delights of the word of God; that we may live in it, live by it to the glory of our dear Redeemer, and to the edification of his Church!

141. *I am small and despised; yet do not I forget thy precepts.*

Evidently David did not *love the word* for selfish gain. *Small and despised* was his condition, when the Lord first looked on him. (1 Sam. xvi. 11.) It was also the reproach, which in the height of his glory he endured for the name of his God. (2 Sam. vi. 20.) *Yet* — stripped and destitute as he might be — *did he not forget his precepts.* The remembrance of his God was a cheering encouragement to his faith in his lowly condition (1 Sam. xvii. 34–36); and no less his support in the far greater trials of his prosperity. Thus habitually did he realize the unspeakable privilege of an ever-present God!

The objects of the Lord's sovereign choice (Exod. xix. 5), whom he has stamped as a " peculiar treasure unto him above all people," and whom at the day of his appearing he will bring forth as the " jewels" (Mal. iii. 17) of his crown — are most frequently in their worldly condition (1 Cor. i. 27–29. Jam. ii. 5) — always in the eyes of the world (1 Cor. iv. 9–13), and in their own estimation (Ps. xl. 17. 1 Cor. xv. 9. Eph. iii. 8) — *small and despised.* And yet pride and hypocrisy in the natural heart will sometimes assume this character for selfish ends. **This** language of humility is not unfrequently in the mouth of the professor, to enable him to maintain " a name to live" in the church of God. But are those who call themselves *small and despised* willing to be taken at their word? Are they content to be *despised* by those, whose esteem this " voluntary" spurious " humility" was meant to secure? Do they really believe themselves to be what they profess —false, vile, mean, deceitful creatures? Have they any experimental knowledge of the depth of inner wickedness, that God could open door after door in " the chamber of imagery" to confound them with the sight of greater, and yet " greater abominations !" (Ezek. viii. 5–15.) When, therefore, they " take the lowest place," do they feel it to be *their own place?* Or does not the language of self-abasement mean in the eyes of God—' *Come, see how humble I am?*'*

Christian! think not these self-inquiries unnecessary for the cautious scrutiny of thine own heart. A self-annihilating spirit *before men*, as well as before God ;—to

---

* ' Many hypocrites make great pretences to humility as well as other graces. But they cannot find out what a humble speech and behaviour is, or how to speak and act, so that there may be indeed a savour of Christian humility in what they say or do. That sweet humble air and mien is beyond their art, being not " led by the Spirit," or naturally guided to a behaviour becoming holy humility by the vigour of a lowly spirit within them. And therefore they have no other way, but to be much in declaring that they are humble, and telling how they were humbled to the dust at such and such times, and abounding in very bad expressions about themselves,—such as—' I have a dreadful wicked heart,'—' Oh ! this cursed heart of mine,' &c. Such expressions are very often used— not with a heart broken—not with the tears of her that ." washed Jesus's feet with her tears,"—not as " remembering and being confounded, and never opening their mouth because of their shame when God is pacified " (Ezek. xvi. 63); but with a light air, or with pharisaical affectation.'— EDWARDS *on Affections*, part iii. sect. vi.

feel *small and despised*, when we have a reputable name in
the Church—is a rare attainment—a glorious triumph
of victorious grace—usually the fruit of sharp affliction.
This was the spirit of Brainerd—that meek and lowly
disciple of his Master, who would express his astonishment
that any one above the rank of "the beasts that perish"
could condescend to notice him.*   But if we are *small and
despised*, in the estimation of men, let us think of "Him,
whom man despiseth—Him whom the nation abhorreth."
(Isa. xlix. 7. Comp. Ps. xxii. 6.)   Never was such an instance of magnanimity displayed, as when Pilate brought
out the blessed Jesus, arrayed in the mockery of royalty,
and with the blood streaming from his temples : and said,
" Behold the man !" (John, xix. 5.)   Then was there a
human being, sustaining himself in the simple exclusive
consciousness of the favour of God, against the universal
scorn of every face.   This was independence—this was
greatness indeed.   With such a pattern before our eyes,
and such a motive touching our hearts, we may well account it " *a very small thing*, that we should be judged of
man's judgment." (1 Cor. iv. 3.)   What upheld " the man
Christ Jesus," will uphold his servants also.   " He committed himself to him that judgeth righteously." (1 Pet.
ii. 23.)   Must we not desire to "know the fellowship of
his sufferings"—yea, to rejoice in the participation of
them ? (Philip. iii. 10. 1 Pet. iv. 13.)

Christian ! dost thou love to be low, and still desire to
be lower than ever ? *Small and despised* as thou art in thine

* ' God feeds me with crumbs. Blessed be his name for anything ! I felt a great desire, that all God's people should know how
mean, and little, and vile I am, that they might see I am nothing,
that so they might pray for me aright, and not have the least
dependence upon me. I could not bear to think of Christians
showing me any respect. I saw myself exceedingly vile and unworthy ; so that I was ashamed that any one should bestow any
favour upon me, or show me any respect.'—BRAINERD's *Diary.*

own eyes, and in the eyes of the world, " thou art precious in the eyes of Him," who gave a price " for thy ransom" —infinitely more precious than " Egypt, Ethiopia, and Seba" (Comp. Isa. xliii. 3, 4, with Acts, xx. 28), and who will suffer " none to pluck thee out of his hands." (John, x. 28.) Many may rebuke thee ; many may scorn thee ; even thy brethren may treat thee with contempt ; yet thy God, thy Redeemer, will not depart from thee, will not suffer thee to depart from him ; but will put his Spirit within thee, and bring forth his precepts to thy remembrance, that thou mayest keep them, and many a sweet supporting promise for thy consolation. Therefore " fear not, *thou worm Jacob;* I will help thee, saith the Lord, and thy Redeemer, the Holy One of Israel." (Isa. xli. 14.)

142. *Thy righteousness is an everlasting righteousness, and thy law is the truth.*

The Psalmist in the midst of his trials could not *forget the precepts,* while he maintained so just a perception of their exalted character. His mind at this time seems to have been filled with the contemplation of the righteous government of God. He therefore repeats his adoration (Comp. Verse 137), not as applied to any particular instance, but as distinguishing the general character of his administration from *everlasting.*

But on whom is this government appointed to rest? Think of our Immanuel—the human brow encircled with Divine glory—the crucified hands wielding the sceptre of the universe—Him, whom they mocked as the King of the Jews, seated on his own exalted throne—" King of kings, and Lord of lords !" " *The government is upon his shoulder: and of the increase of his government and peace there shall be no end.*" (Isa. ix. 6, 7.) How delightful to join Jehovah himself in the ascription of praise—" *Thy throne, O God, is for ever and ever; a sceptre of righteousness is the sceptre of thy kingdom!"* (Ps. xlv. 6. Heb. i. 8.) How glorious also to praise that *everlasting righteousness* — the ground on which the administration of his church is framed — which Jesus " brought in," and " which is unto all them that believe" (Dan. ix. 24. Rom. iii. 22); which, when once clothed with it, is our infinite glory and reward!

" Every ordinance of man" is connected only with time. The Divine government has a constant reference to eternity, past and to come. "*And I heard*"— said the enraptured disciple —"*the angel of the waters say; Thou art righteous, which art, and wast, and shalt be; because thou hast judged thus."* (Rev. xvi. 5.) Every instance, therefore, of his righteous administration, is that display of the Divine character which constrains the adoration of heaven. " One cried to another, and said, *Holy, holy, holy, is the Lord of hosts: the whole earth is full of his glory."* (Isa. vi. 3.) His *law* —"the manifestation of his righteousness"—*is the truth. " Thy word is true from the beginning! and every one of thy righteous judgments endureth for ever."* (Verse 160.)

This *truth is the law of righteousness,* which Jesus bound himself to " fulfil" (Matt. iii. 15)—to which he " came to bear witness" (John, xviii. 37), and for which he commended his people to his Father as the means of their sanctification (John, xvii. 17); for what else is holiness, but the influence of *truth,* digested and practically embodied in the life and conduct? There may be fragments of truth elsewhere found — the scattered remnants of the fall. There may be systems imbued with large portions of *truth* deduced from this *law.* But here alone is it found perfect — unsullied. How carefully, therefore, should we test, by this standard, every doctrine — every revelation (1 Thess. v. 21. 1 John, iv. 1); receiving with implicit subjection all that is conformed to it (Acts, xvii. 11, 12); rejecting with uncompromising decision whatever will not

abide the fiery trial. (Isa. viii. 20. Gal. i. 8, 9.) Most
careful also should we be to preserve its unadulterated
simplicity. (2 Cor. ii. 17 ; iv. 2.) Even the most seemingly trifling infusion of fundamental error is the grain
of poison cast into the food, and making it " a savour of
death unto death." Such was the error of the Galatian
Church — " another gospel, yet not another" (Gal. i. 6, 7)
— not deserving the name — *not putting ordinances in the
stead of Christ* (an error too gross to beguile a Christian
profession), but what is far more subtle, and equally
destructive, *mixing them with Christ;* thus impairing the
integrity of the foundation, paralyzing the springs, poison-
ing the sources of life, yea, converting life itself into death.
(Gal. iv. 9–11 ; v. 1–4.) Let this church stand out as a
beacon to our own — as a much-needed warning to each of
her members.

But in a more general view, let us adore the Divine revelation, as bearing so full an impress of a " God that cannot lie" — of a " covenant ordered in all things" beyond
human contrivance, " and sure" beyond the possibility of a
change. (Tit. i. 2. 2 Sam. xxiii. 5.) How many dying testimonies have sealed the truth of the precious promises!
Joshua (Josh. xxiii. 14), Simeon (Luke, ii. 25–29), and a
" cloud of witnesses with which we are compassed about"
(Heb. xii. 1), have " set to their seals that God is true"
(John, iii. 33) — that " all the promises of God are in Christ
Jesus yea and amen" (2 Cor. i. 20) — that " all are come to
pass unto them, and not one thing has failed thereof."
Equally manifest is the truth of his threatenings. Hell is
truth seen too late. Those on the right hand and those
on the left, at the great day of God, will combine their
testimony to the declaration of the " Faithful and True
Witness" (Rev. iii. 14) — " Heaven and earth shall pass
away, but my words shall not pass away." (Matt. xxiv. 35.)

143. *Trouble and anguish have taken hold on me: yet thy commandments are my delights.*

Christian! expect not unmixed sorrow or uninterrupted joy as your present portion. Heaven will be joy without sorrow. Hell will be sorrow without joy. Earth presents to you every joy mingled with grief—every grief tempered with joy. To be accounted *small and despised* does not comprise the whole of your trials. Like the great apostle, you must expect not only *trouble* without, but *anguish* within. (2 Cor. vii. 5 ; i. 8.) Others may not have it. (Ps. lv. 19; lxxiii. 3–5.) But your Saviour engages—" *You shall.*" (John, xvi. 33. Comp. Acts, xiv. 22; 1 Thess. iii. 3 ; 2 Tim. iii. 12 ; Rev. vii. 14.) To all his people he has not meted out the same measure. Some have rebuke. Some have a scourge. But all have the cross, and this a daily cross (Luke, ix. 23)—not a single or an occasional trial—but a life of trial—constant contradiction to the will—constant mortification of the flesh. And this *takes hold of us.* We cannot escape from it. Should we wish to escape it? This discipline, as Luther observes in his own way (and who was a better calculator in this school?), ' is more necessary for us, than all the riches and dignities of the whole world.' And the exercise of faith and patience in the endurance will bring more honour to God and profit to ourselves than a life of ease and indulgence. The instruction of the rod delivers us from its curse, and brings a substantial and enriching blessing. (Ps. xciv. 12.)

But how precious is the sympathy of Jesus—"in all things made like unto his brethren"—enduring *trouble and anguish* inconceivable to human apprehension, " that he might be a merciful and faithful High Priest to succour his tempted people!" (Heb. ii. 17, 18.) How does it lift up our head amid the billows, when in communion with our

Lord we can call to mind, that his sorrow was for the sake of his dear purchased people ; that they might drink their lighter cup bereft of its bitter ingredients !

The Psalmist did not find that the Lord afflicted him to leave him in misery, but rather to increase his happiness. *The precepts which he had not forgotten* (Verse 141), were now *his delights.* The scriptural records of the trials of the Lord's people bear similar abundant testimony to the inexhaustible resources of support in the Book of God : and they are written for our learning, " that we through patience and comfort of the Scriptures might have hope." (Rom. xv. 4.) The child of God, whose thoughts are habitually occupied in the word, will always find it to be his food and light, his joy and strength ; witnessing within, the presence and power of God, even where its sensible comfort may not be enjoyed.

But specially is affliction the time, that unfolds the *delights of the word* (Verse 92), such as more than counterbalances the painful *trouble and anguish* of the flesh. Such cheering prospects of hope and deliverance does it set forth ! Such mighty supports in the endurance of trial does it realize ! Truly the experimental power of the word in keeping the soul alive—much more than this—cheerful—sustained—established (Deut. viii. 3. Matt. iv. 4)—is there any blessing like this—the fruit of the cross ? Can we mourn over that cross, that brings so gainful a harvest ? The bitterness of the cross then best realizes the *delights of the commandments.* But never does the believer more " rejoice in tribulation," than when the *trouble and anguish which take hold of him*, is for the love he bears to the name of his dear Lord. (Acts, v. 41.) Persecution for his sake, far from appalling him, only endears his service to his heart. It is in his eyes — *" not a penalty endured, but a privilege conferred," " to suffer for his name's sake."**

* Phil. i. 29. One of the witnesses for the truth, when impri-

But contrast the condition of the child of God and the follower of the world, in the hour of affliction. The one in the midst of his troubles drinks of the fountain of all-sufficiency ; and such is his peace and security, that, " in the floods of great waters they shall not come nigh unto him." (Ps. xxxii. 6.) The other, " in the fulness of his sufficiency, is in straits." (Job, xx. 22.) David could look upward, and find the way of escape in the midst of his trouble : but for Saul, when *trouble and anguish took hold of him*, no source of comfort opened to his view. " God was departed from him, and was become his enemy." (1 Sam. xxviii. 15, 16.) It was therefore *trouble* without support, *anguish* without relief—*trouble and anguish;* such as will at length *take hold of* them that forget God, when nothing will be left, but the unavailing " cry to the mountains and the hills to fall upon them, and cover them." (Rev. vi. 16.) Thanks be to God for deliverance from this fearful prospect ! Thanks for the hope of unfading *delights*, when earthly pleasures shall have passed away ! The first sheaf of the heavenly harvest will blot out the painful remembrance of the weeping seed-time which preceded it. (Ps. cxxvi. 5, 6.) The first moment of heaven will compensate for all the *troubles and anguish* of earth ; and these moments will last throughout eternity. " Say *ye to the righteous, it shall be well with him*" (Isa. iii. 10)—*eternally well.*

soned for conscience' sake in Queen Mary's persecution of the Church, is said to have thus written to a friend—'A prisoner for Christ! What is this for a poor worm ? " Such honour have" not " all his saints." Both the degrees which I took in the University have not set me so high, as the honour of becoming a prisoner of the Lord.' Philpot, again, could say of his prison—'In the judgment of the world we are in hell; but I find in it the sweet consolations of heaven.' So holy Bradford—'My prison is sweeter to me than any parlour, than any pleasure I have had in all my life.'

144. *The righteousness of thy testimonies is everlasting : give me understanding, and I shall live.* (Comp. verses 137, 138.)

What deep — weighty — impressive thoughts were exercising the Psalmist's mind! He had just marked the happy influence of *the testimonies* upon the believer's heart. Now he again recurs to their *righteousness* — as the Divine administration — not subject to the incessant variations of the human standard — but *everlasting* — of unalterable obligation — binding us unchangeably to God, and God to us. His creatures can virtually "*make them void*" by their rebellion (Verse 126); but they cannot change their character, or shake their foundation. Nay — themselves shall be the instruments of their fulfilment. Every word shall be established either by them as his obedient servants, or in and upon them as rebel transgressors. What solemn weight therefore is due to this Divine standard! It seems now to be trampled under foot; but its *righteousness*, inflexible in its demands, and unalterable in its obligations — will ere long assert its sovereignty over the world, when every other standard shall have passed away. It will be the rule of the Divine procedure at the great day of decision. When the "great white throne" is set up — when "the dead, small and great, stand before God, and the books are opened, and another book is opened, which is the book of life;" and the dead are judged out of those things which were written in the books, "*according to their works*" (Rev. xx. 11, 12) — the acknowledgment will be made throughout the universe of God — *The righteousness of thy testimonies is everlasting.* How glorious is the confidence of being dealt with in that great day upon an *everlasting* foundation of *righteousness!* (Acts, xvii. 31.)

But this view of the Divine *righteousness* and *everlasting* obligation *of the testimonies*, naturally suggests the prayer for a more spiritual, enlightened, and experimental acquaintance with them. Often before had the petition been sent up. (Verses 33, 34, 73.) But who can cry too often or too earnestly? One ray of this *understanding* is of far higher value than all the intellectual or speculative knowledge in the world. (Jer. ix. 23, 24.) If its first dawn exhibits the infinite difference between light and darkness—if prayer for it implies a measure already received, still—*Give me understanding*—will be the cry—not of the "little child" whose spiritual perception is just opening—but of the "father who has known Him that is from the beginning." (1 John, ii. 13, 14.) Let me know the holiness of thy *testimonies*—their extent—their perfection—their intimate connexion with every part of my daily walk—with the restraint of my inclination, the regulation of my temper, the direction of every step of my path. And indeed the more devoutly we study them, the more shall we feel our need of supplication for Divine teaching, to give us more adoring and thankful views of the government of God, and to subjugate our cavilling disposition to the humbling influence of faith.

The principle of spiritual and eternal life flows from the enlightened perception of the testimonies of God. *Give me understanding, and I shall live.* For "*this is life eternal, that we might know thee, the only true God, and Jesus Christ whom thou hast sent.*" (John, xvii. 3.) His *testimonies* are the revelation of himself. If then we "have an unction from the Holy One, and know all things" (1 John, ii. 20), our knowledge of them will become more spiritual in its character, more experimental in its comforts, and more practical in its fruits. And thus, 'the life of God in the soul' will invigorate us for higher attainments in evangelical knowledge, and more steady advancement in Christian holiness. But how infinitely do we live below the full privilege of knowing God in his *testimonies!* Christians of a Scriptural

standard are "forgetting those things which are behind, and
reaching forth unto those things which are before. Let us
therefore, as many as be perfect, be thus minded." (Philip.
iii. 13, 15.)

And then — what will it be at the great consummation ;
when our God of love will have put his last hand to his
glorious work ; when the mark of all our aims — the term
of all our hopes and desires — all that we' have so long
laboured for — so earnestly panted after — so restlessly pursued — when all shall be attained ? Then indeed we shall
live a life worthy of the name — not as now under the sha-
dowed glimmerings — but under the immediate full-eyed
glory of his light and love ; having escaped for ever the
deadliest of all dangers — sin — the very deadliness of death
itself.

PART XIX.

145. I cried with my whole heart; hear me, O Lord, I will keep thy statutes. 146. I cried unto thee; save me and I shall keep thy testimonies.

THIS is indeed the "pouring out of the soul before the Lord" (1 Sam. i. 15), a beautiful and encouraging picture of a soul wrestling with God, in a few short sentences, with as much power and success as in the most continued length of supplication. Brief as are the petitions, the whole compass of language could not make them more comprehensive. *Hear me. The whole heart* is engaged in the *cry. Save me*—includes a sinner's whole need—pardon, acceptance, access, holiness, strength, comfort, heaven, all in one word—Christ. *Save me*—from myself, from Satan, from the world, from the curse of sin, from the wrath of God. This is the need of every moment to the end. *I cried unto thee.*—What a mercy to know where to go! The way of access must have been implied, though *not mentioned*, in these short ejaculations. *Hear me*—must have been in the name of the all-prevailing Advocate. *Save me*— through Him, whose name is, Jesus the Saviour. A moment's interruption of our view of Jesus casts *for the time* an impenetrable cloud over our way to God, and paralyzes the spirit of prayer. Prayer is not only the sense of guilt, and the cry of mercy, but the exercise of faith. When I come to God, I would always bring with me the blood of Christ—my price—my plea in my hand. He cannot cast it out.   Thus am I " a prince, that hath power with God, and prevail." (Gen. xxxii. 28.)   Here is the warrant to believe, that my God does, and will *hear me*.   Here is my encouragement to " look up" (Ps. v. 3)—to be " watching at his gate" (Prov. viii. 34)—like the cripple at the " beautiful gate of the temple (Acts, iii. 2–5), expecting to receive somewhat of him." Not a word of *such* prayer is lost. It is as seed —not cast into the earth, exposed to hazard and loss (Matt. xiii. 3–7)—but cast into the bosom of God—and here—as in the natural harvest, " *he which soweth bountifully, shall reap also bountifully*." (2 Cor. ix. 6.) The most frequent comers are the largest receivers—always wanting—always asking—living upon what they have, but still hungering for more.

With many, however, the ceremony of prayer is everything, without any thought, desire, anxiety, or waiting for an answer.   These slight dealings prove low thoughts of God, and deep and guilty insensibility ;—that the sense of pressing need is not sharp enough to put an edge upon the affections.   But are none of God's dear children, too, who in days past never missed the presence of God, but they " sought it carefully with tears"—now too easily satisfied with the act of prayer, without this " great object of it— *the enjoyment of God?*"*   Perhaps you lament your de-

---

* ' *The great object in prayer should constantly be the enjoyment of God;* and however inadequate the believer's conceptions may be, yet he has a distinct idea of his object; so distinct, that you can never impose upon a real saint, by offering him something else in the room of it. He knows what he wants; and he knows that this or that is not the thing which he wants.'—AUGUSTINE, Epistle 121.

In the same epistle he very judiciously recommends the use of short and quick ejaculations (like these under consideration), rather than long protracted supplications. unless the mind be in a fervent frame; in which case the petitions, as he justly observes, may be indefinitely prolonged, without incurring the censure implied in Matt. vi. 7.

ficiencies, your weakness in the hour of temptation, your indulgence of ease, your unfaithfulness of heart. But is your *cry* continually ascending *with your whole heart?* Your soul would not be so empty of comfort, if your mouth were not so empty of prayer. The Lord never *charges presumption* upon the frequency or extent of your supplications; but he is often ready to " *upbraid you with your unbelief* " (Mark, xvi. 14), that you are so reluctant in your approach, and so straitened in your desires — that you are so unready to receive what he is so ready to give — that your vessels are too narrow to take in his full blessing — that you are content with drops, when he has promised " floods,"—yea " rivers of living water " (Isa. xliv. 3. John, vii. 38),—and above all, that you are so negligent in praising him for what you have already received.

We must not lightly give up our suit. We must not be content with keeping up the duty, without keeping up " continued instancy in prayer " (Rom. xii. 12) in our duty. This alone preserves in temptation. Satan strikes at all of God in the soul. Unbelief readily yields to his suggestions. This is the element in which we live — the warfare of every moment. Will then the customary devotion of morning and evening (*even supposing it to be sincere*) suffice for such an emergency ? No. The Christian must " *put on the whole armour of God;* " and buckle on his panoply with unceasing " prayer and watchfulness in the Spirit." * If his heart be dead and cold, let him rather cry and wait (as Luther was used to do , till it be warm and enlivened. The hypocrite, indeed, would be satisfied with the barren performance of the duty. But the child

---

* Eph. vi. 13–18. ' The violence of temptation stupifies,'—said Luther on one occasion, speaking of his own experience,—' that I cannot open my mouth. *As soon as ever it pleases God that I can lift up my heart in prayer, and make use of Scriptural expressions, it ceases to prevail.*'— Milner, vol. v. p. 484.

of God, while he mourns in the dust —" Behold I am vile !"
(Job, xl. 4 ; also xlii. 5, 6)—still holds on, though sometimes with *a cry*, that probably finds no utterance with his
lips (Exod. xiv. 15. 1 Sam. i. 13. Neh. ii. 5), that vents
itself only with tears, or " groanings that cannot be
uttered." (Rom. viii. 26.)   And shall such *a cry* fail to
enter into the ears of the Lord of Sabaoth ?   *The Lord
hath heard the voice of my weeping.   Lord, all my desire is
before thee ; and my groaning is not hid from thee.* (Ps. vi. 8 ;
xxxviii. 9.)

But why is the believer so earnest for an audience ?—
why so restless in his cries for salvation ?   Is it not, that
he loves *the statutes* of his God ; that he is grieved on
account of his inability to keep them ; and that he longs
for mercy, as the spring of his obedience ?   *Hear me ; I
will keep thy statutes.   Save me : and I shall keep thy testimonies*—a most satisfactory evidence of an upright heart.
Sin can have no fellowship with *the statutes*.   As saved
sinners, they are *our delight*.

Lord ! thou knowest how our hearts draw back from
the spiritual work of prayer : and how we nourish our unbelief by our distance from thee.   Oh, " pour upon us this
Spirit of grace and supplication."   " Teach us to pray"
(Luke, xi. 1)—even our hearts—*our whole hearts*—to
cry unto thee.   Give us the privilege of real communion
with thee—the only satisfying joy of earth or heaven.
Then shall we " run the way of thy commandments, when
thou shalt enlarge our hearts." (Verse 32.)

147. *I prevented the dawning of the morning, and cried: I
hoped in thy word.*   148. *Mine eyes prevent the night-
watches, that I might meditate in thy word.*

The Psalmist here brings before us not only the fervency, but the seasons, of his supplication.   Like Daniel,

he had set times of prayer—" three times a-day." (Ps. lv. 17, with Dan. vi. 10.) Yet did not this frequent exercise satisfy him, without an habitual " waiting all the day upon his God." (Ps. xxv. 5.) Prayer was indeed his meat, and drink, and breath. " *I give myself unto prayer.*"* His sketch of the " blessed man delighting in the law of his God, and"—as an evidence of this delight—" meditating therein day and night" (Ps. i. 2)—unconsciously furnished an accurate picture of himself. For early and late was he found in the work of God ; *preventing the dawning of the morning* for prayer, and again *the night-watches, that he might meditate in the word.* But to look above the example of David to David's Lord—surely " it was written" most peculiarly " for our learning," that Jesus—after a laborious Sabbath—every moment of which appears to have been spent for the benefit of sinners ; and when his body, subject to the same infirmities, and therefore needing the same refreshment with our own, seemed to require repose—" *in the morning, rising up a great while before day, went out and departed into a solitary place, and there prayed.*" (Mark, i. 21–35.) On another occasion, when intensely engaged in the service of his church, and about to lay her foundation in the choice of her first ministers, *did his eyes prevent the night-watches.* " *He continued all night in prayer to God.*" (Luke, vi. 12–16.)

So long as *the duty only* of prayer is known, we shall be content with our set seasons. But when *the privilege* is felt, we shall be early at work, following it closely morning and night. (Ps. v. 3 ; lxxxviii. 13. Isa. xxvi. 9.) While, however, family and social exercises are refreshing—while

---

* Ps. cix. 4. 'But I prayer,' Heb.—all over prayer—always ready for prayer—at all seasons, besides the frequency of set times of communion—one, whose life is a continual prayer—"prayer without ceasing."—1 Thess. v. 17.

" the tabernacles of the Lord are amiable" in our view, and we delight to " wait at the posts of his doors" (Ps. lxxxiv. 1. Prov. viii. 34) ; yet it is the lonely, confidential intercourse with our God—" the door shut "—the Church as well as the world excluded—that makes our closest walk with God. (Matt. vi. 6.) *Secret prayer is most likely to be true prayer. At least there is no true prayer without it.* It was the " garden" prayer—separate even from his own disciples— that brought special support to the fainting humanity of Jesus. (Luke, xxii. 41–43.) And if he needed this perfect retirement, whose affections were always fixed upon their centre, what must be our own need, whose desires are so unstable and languishing! And how cheering is his suc-couring sympathy, knowing as he does experimentally the heart of a secret, earnest pleader! Such, doubtless, were David's *cries*—penetrating no ear, but his Father's—yet delightful incense there. (Ps. lvi. 8. Prov. xv. 8. Ps. cxli. 2. Cant. ii. 14.)

But to see the King of Israel, with all his urgent re-sponsibilities, " sanctifying" such frequent daily seasons " with the word of God and prayer"—how does it expose the insincerity of the worldling's excuse, that the pressing avocations of the day afford no time for the service of God! It is not, that such men are busy, and have no time for prayer ; but that they are worldly, and have no heart to pray. The consecrated heart will always find time for secret duties, and will rather, as David, redeem it from sleep, than lose it from prayer.*

* Most instructive is the example of Mr. Cadogan, as recorded by his admirable biographer : ' Feeling strongly that he must walk with God in secret at any rate; when he had company, he would often retire from them into his study, rather than omit his accus-tomed waiting upon his God. Often has be been found there, when most of the family were gone to rest, surprised on his knees by the

And does not the uniform experience of the Lord's people warrant the remark — how much our vital spirituality depends upon the daily consecration of *the first-fruits of our time* to the Lord? How often are opportunities for heavenly communion during the day unavoidably straitened! But *the night watches* and *the dawning of the morning* afford seasons free from interruption, when our God expects to hear from us, and when " the joy" of " fellowship with him" will be " our strength" (Neh. viii. 10) for active service, and our preservation from many a worldly snare. What a standard of enjoyment would it be, with our last thoughts in *the night watches*, to leave as it were our hearts with him, and to find them with him in the morning, awaking as with our hearts in heaven! Surely the refreshments of our visits to him, and his abidance with us, will often constrain us to acknowledge — " *Truly our fellowship is with the Father, and with his Son Jesus Christ.*" (1 John, i. 3.) The thoughts of God were clearly the first visitors to David's waking mind (See Ps. cxxxix. 17, 18); and to this may be ascribed his habitual success in realizing his presence throughout the day. The lukewarmness and our want of spiritual enjoyment may often be traced to that morning indolence (which the zeal of the ungodly (Exod. xxxii. 6. Isa. v. 11. Mic. ii. 1) might put to shame), which not only throws the business of the day into confusion, but also consumes the time in self-indulgence or trifling, which should have been given to sacred intercourse. For — not to speak of the seasonableness of the early hours for devotion — the very exertion made to overcome " this lust of

domestic who usually took care of the house.'— CECIL's *Life of Cadogan.*

Perhaps in an observation once made to an excellent minister the importance of the truth may furnish an apology for the quaintness of the dress —' If you did not plough in your closet, you would not reap in the pulpit.'

the flesh," and to steal a march upon the demands of the world, is an exercise of self-denial, honourable to God, "that shall in no wise lose its reward." No remembrance of the past will be so refreshing at a dying hour, as the time redeemed for communion with God.

And, even should there be no actual enjoyment, at least let us honour God by expectancy. *I hoped in thy word.** There can be no exercise of faith in the neglect of prayer; but the ground of faith, and that which gives to it life, hope, and joy, is the view of God in his word *as a promising God.* Therefore when his Providence opens no present encouragement, let us seek it in his covenant. To *hope in his word* is to build up ourselves upon "our most holy faith" (Jude, 20), and to lay all our desires, all our cares,

---

* One of Melancthon's correspondents describes Luther thus— 'I cannot enough admire the extraordinary cheerfulness, constancy, faith, and hope of the man in these trying and vexatious times. He constantly feeds these gracious affections by a very diligent study of the word of God. *Then not a day passes, in which he does not employ in prayer at least three of his very best hours.* Once I happened to hear him at prayer. Gracious God! what spirit and what faith is there in his expressions! He petitions God with as much reverence, as if he was in the Divine presence; and yet with as firm a hope and confidence, as he would address a father or a friend. 'I know'—said he—'thou art our Father and our God; and therefore I am sure thou wilt bring to nought the persecutors of thy children. For shouldest thou fail to do this, thine own cause, being connected with ours, would be endangered. It is entirely thine own concern. We, by thy providence, have been compelled to take a part. Thou therefore wilt be our defence.' Whilst I was listening to Luther praying in this manner at a distance, my soul seemed on fire within me, to hear the man address God so like a friend, and yet with so much gravity and reverence; and also to hear him, in the course of his prayer, insisting upon the promises contained in the Psalms, as if he was sure his petitions would be granted.'—MILNER's *History*, vol. v. p. 565. Again referred to in SCOTT's Continuation, vol. i. p. 77. Was not this an illustration of David's confidence—*I hoped in thy word?*

all our weights, and burdens, upon a solid, unsinking foundation.

Well, therefore, were David's *night-watches* employed in *meditation in the word.* For, in order to stay ourselves upon it in time of need, it must occupy our whole study, thought, and desire. Instability of faith arises from a want of fixed recollection of the promises of God. This superficial habit may suffice for times of quietness; but amid the billows of temptation we can only cast "anchor sure and stedfast" in an habitual and intelligent confidence upon the full, free, firm promise of the word. Let it therefore be the food of our meditation, and the ground of our support, when our suit seems to hang at the throne of grace without any tokens of present acceptance. Often will it lift up our fainting hands, and supply strength for fresh conflict, and the earnest of blessed victory. The ground is always sure for faith. May the Lord ever furnish us with faith enough for our daily work, conflict, consolation, and establishment!

149. *Hear my voice according to thy loving-kindness: O Lord, quicken me according to thy judgment.*

In the eyes of the world, David appeared "in all his glory," when seated on his throne, and surrounded with the magnificence of his kingdom. But never did he appear so glorious in the sight of God, as when presenting himself as a suppliant before the mercy-seat, seeking an audience of the King of kings, only to send up reiterated cries for quickening grace. And do I not need the same grace every moment, in every duty? Does not "the gift of God within me" need to be daily "stirred up?" (2 Tim. i. 6.) Are not the "things that remain" often "ready to die?" (Rev. iii. 2.) Then *hear my voice, O Lord; quicken me.*

But to urge my suit successfully, I must "order my cause before God;" I must "fill my mouth with arguments." (Job, xxiii. 4.) And if I can draw a favourable plea from the character of my Judge—if I can prove that promises have been made in my behalf, these will be most encouraging earnests of a successful issue. Now David had been so used to plead in cases of extremity, that arguments suited to his present distress were always ready at hand. He now pleads with God for *quickening* grace, on the ground of his own *loving-kindness and judgment*. Can he " deny himself ? "

And with what " full assurance of faith" (Heb. x. 22), may I ask to be *heard* on account of that transcendant proof of *loving-kindness* manifested in the gift of God's dear Son—(John, iii. 16)—not only as his chiefest mercy, but as the pledge of every other mercy—(See Rom. viii. 32)—and manifested too at the fittest time—(See Gal. iv. 4)—*according to his judgment*,—after the inefficiency of the power of reason (Comp. 1 Cor. i. 21), and the sanctions of the law (Comp. Jer. xxxi. 31–33), to influence the heart, had been most clearly displayed! And what a plea is it to ask for *quickening* influences, that this is the very end for which this gift of *loving-kindness* was vouchsafed (John, x. 10. 1 John, iv. 9), and that the gift itself is the channel, through which the quickening life of the Godhead is imparted! (1 John, v. 11.) Could I ask for this grace on any other ground than *loving-kindness?* All ground of fitness or merit is swept away. (Ezek. xxxvi. 32.) On the footing of mercy alone, can I stand before him. (Eph. ii. 7. Tit. iii. 4.) And how is my faith enlivened in retracing the records of my soul from the beginning—how he " betrothed"—(Hos. ii. 19)—how he " drew—me with *loving-kindness!*" (Jer. xxxi. 3.) May I not then cry—" Oh! continue thy *loving-kindness?*" (Ps. xxxvi. 10.) And not less full is my conviction of his *judgment*, in dealing wisely and tenderly with me, according to his infallible perception of my need. Left to my own judgment—often should I have prayed myself into evil, and asked what it would have been my curse to have received. (Ps. cvi. 15.) But I have learned, that the child must not be guided by his own will, but by his father's better mind — not the patient by his own humour, but by the physician's skill. Truly, even the Lord's corrections have been in *judgment!* (Jer. x. 24.) And in the thankful remembrance of them my confidence for the time to come is established! Gladly will I " set to my seal," that " *the Lord is a God of judgment;*" and that " *blessed are all they that wait for him.*" (Isa. xxx. 18.) He knows not only what grace is needed, but at what time. Not a moment sooner will it come ; not a moment later will it be delayed. " As thou wilt, what thou wilt, when thou wilt"*— is the expression of faith and resignation, with which all must be committed to the Lord, waiting for the end in humility, desire, expectation. And if in pleading my suit for a hearing *according to his loving-kindness,* my poor, polluted, lifeless petitions should find no liberty of approach ; may I be but enabled to direct one believing look to " the Lamb that is in the midst of the throne !" (Rev. v. 6), and I will not doubt that my feeblest offering shall come up as a memorial before God.

150. *They draw nigh that follow after mischief: they are far from thy law.* 151. *Thou art near, O Lord: and all thy commandments are truth.*

The imminent danger in which David was living (Ps. lvii. 4) quickened his cries to his God. Often does the Lord permit this pressing trial ! Seldom, but in extremity, are our graces brought to their full exercise. Confidence is then shaken from man, and established in God. (2 Cor. i. 9.) For now it is that we enjoy our God as

* Thomas à Kempis.

" a very present help in trouble" (Ps. xlvi. 1), and that our dependence on his *commandment* is a *true* and solid foundation of comfort to our soul.   An awful character is indeed drawn of the ungodly — *They are far from God's law* — and that not from ignorance, but from wilful enmity.   This is God's witness against them (Ps. l. 17. Comp. Prov. i. 22, 25, 29); and they are not ashamed to consent, that this " witness is true."   No wonder, therefore, that those, that are *far from God's law*, should *draw nigh to follow after mischief.**   But if *they draw nigh*, the Lord is nearer still. " I *am thy shield*" (Gen. xv. 1) — saith he to his distressed child — who echoes back the promise in the cheerfulness of faith — " *Thou art my hiding-place, and my shield: I hope in thy word.*" (Verse 114.)   Elisha knew the power of this shield, when he quelled the alarm of his terrified servant.   He beheld them *draw nigh that follow after mischief.*   But the eye of faith assured his heart ; and when " the Lord opened the eyes of the young man," he too was enabled to testify — *Thou art near, O Lord !* (Comp. 2 Kings, vi. 14–17.)

---

* ' He cannot brook the child, that hateth the father ; he cannot mind the servant, that careth not for the master.   If ye were of the world, the world would love you ; ye should dwell quietly. There would be no griefs, no molestation, if the devil dwelt in you (which God forbid).   He would not stir up his knights to besiege your house. . . . . But because Christ dwelleth in you (as he does by faith) ; therefore stirreth he up his first-begotten son, the world, to seek how to disquiet you, to rob you, to spoil you, to destroy ; and perchance your dear Father, to try to make known to you and the world, that ye are destinate to another dwelling than here on earth, to another city than man's eyes have seen at any time, hath given, or will give power to Satan or to the world to take from you the things which he hath lent you ; and by taking away, to try your fidelity, obedience, and love towards him (for ye may not love them above him) as by giving that ye have, and keeping it, he hath declared his love towards you.'— BRADFORD'S *Epistles — Fathers of the English Church*, vol. vi. pp. 58, 59.

But near as the Lord is to his people as their outward shield, is he not yet nearer still, as dwelling in their hearts? Here is "his temple" (2 Cor. vi. 16), his desired habitation—like Zion of old, of which he said—"This is my rest for ever; here will I dwell, for I have desired it." (Ps. cxxxii. 13, 14, with Eph. ii. 22.) This is the dwelling, which, once possessed of its Divine Inhabitant, will never be left desolate.

Our spiritual enemies, like David's persecutors, are ever present and active. The devouring "lion" (1 Pet. v. 8), or the insinuating "serpent" (Rev. xii. 9), is *nigh to follow after mischief;* and so much the more dangerous, as his approaches are invisible. Nigh also is a tempting, ensnaring world: and nearer still a lurking world within, separating us from communion with our God. But in turning habitually and immediately to our stronghold, we can enjoy the confidence—*Thou art near, O Lord.* Though "the High and Lofty One, whose name is Holy" (Isa. lvii. 15); though the just and terrible God, yet art thou made nigh to thy people (Col. i. 20), and they to thee (Eph. ii. 13), "by the blood of the cross." And thou dost manifest thy presence to them in "the Son of thy love."

Indeed to the Son himself, the nearness of his Father's presence was a source of consolation and support, when *they drew nigh, that followed after mischief. "He is near"—* said he—"*which justifieth me: who will contend with me? let us stand together. Who is mine adversary? Let him come near to me. Behold! the Lord God will help me: who is he that shall condemn me? Lo they all shall wax old as doth a garment: the moth shall eat them up.*" (Isa. l. 8, 9.) "*Behold,*" said he to his affrighted disciples, as his hour drew near—"*the hour cometh, yea is now come, that ye shall be scattered every one to his own, and shall leave me alone: and yet I am not alone, because the Father is with me.*" (John, xvi. 32.) And thus his people in earthly desolation flee to the promises of their God ; and in the recollection of his faithful, ever-present help, " set to their seal," that *all his commandments are truth.* The mischief intended for them only proves, that " Thou, Lord, wilt bless the righteous ; with favour wilt thou compass him as with a shield." (Ps. v. 12.)

But may the Lord not only be brought *near* in our interest in him, but may we be kept *near* in communion with him ! Let our hearts be sacred to him. Let us be most careful to watch against any strangeness with this beloved Friend, and to cultivate a growing cordiality and closeness in our walk with him. If our character is formed by the society in which we live, what " treasures of wisdom and knowledge" should we find, what a spirit of unbounded love should we imbibe — by a nearer and more constant intercourse with him ; willing as he is to impart himself freely, inexhaustibly unto us ! In a backsliding state, we must expect to lose this heavenly *nearness.* (Cant. v. 2–6.) In a state of darkness, it is the exercise of faith, to believe that unseen he is *near ;* and the practical influence of faith will lead us to speak, and pray, and think, and praise, " as seeing him who is invisible." (Heb. xi. 27.) In a state of enjoyment, let us anticipate the time when he will be ever *near* to us.

" And I heard a great voice out of heaven, saying, Behold ! the tabernacle of God is with men, and he will dwell with them, and they shall be his people, and God himself shall be with them, and be their God." (Rev. xxi. 3.)

152. *Concerning thy testimonies, I have known of old, that thou hast founded them for ever.*

The " *truth of the commandments*," which the Psalmist had just asserted, was an *everlasting foundation.* He stated it not upon slight conviction. But he *knew it*—and that not recently—but as the result of early consideration—he *had known it of old.* It is most important to have a full certainty of the ground of our faith. How else can we have that " good thing—a heart established with grace?" (Heb. xiii. 9)—how " continue in the faith grounded and settled?"—how be kept from being " moved away from the hope of the gospel?" (Col. i. 23.) Praised be God! We feel our ground to be firm. As God is the same, so must *his testimonies* be. (Ps. lxxxix. 34; cxi. 7–9.) We cannot conceive of his promising without performance, or threatening without effect. (Num. xxiii. 19.) They are therefore expressly revealed as a firm foundation, in express contrast with this world's fairest promise. (Isa. xl. 1–8.)

But let us mark this eternal basis of *the testimonies.* The whole plan of redemption was emphatically *founded for ever.* The Saviour " was *foreordained before the foundation of the world.*" (1 Pet. i. 20. Comp. Rev. xiii. 8.) The people of God are " *chosen in Christ before the world began!*" (Eph. i. 4. 2 Tim. i. 9.) The great Author " *declares the end from the beginning*" (Isa. xlvi. 9, 10), and thus clears his dispensations from any charge of mutability or contingency. Every event in the church is fixed, permitted, and provided for—not in the passing moment of time, but in the counsels of eternity. All God's faithful engagements with his people of old are *founded for ever* upon the oath and promise of God—the two " immutable things, in which it is impossible for God to lie." (Heb. vi. 16–18.) May we not then " have strong consolation" in venturing every hope for eternity upon this rock? nor need we be dismayed to see all our earthly stays, " the world, and the lust, and the fashion of it—passing away" before us. (1 John, ii. 17; 1 Cor. vii. 31.) Yet we are most of us strangely attached to this fleeting scene, even when experience and Divine teaching have instructed us in its vanity: and it is not until repeated proofs of this truth have touched us very closely in the destruction of our dearest consolations, that we take the full comfort of the enduring foundation of God's *testimonies*, and of the imperishable character of their treasure.

Now let me realize the special support of this view in a dying hour : ' I am on the borders of an unknown world ; but " my hope maketh not ashamed" (Rom. v. 5) at the moment of peril it is as " an anchor of the soul, sure and stedfast ;" and in the strength of it I do not fear to plunge into eternity. " I know whom I have believed, and am persuaded that he is able to keep that which I have committed to him against that day." (2 Tim. i. 12.) I know—not his sufficiency merely, but his *All-sufficiency*. I know his conquering power over the great enemies of my soul. I know that he has " spoiled the principalities and powers" (Col. ii. 15) of hell, of the strength to triumph over his ransomed people. I know also, that he is " the Lord ; he changeth not" (Mal. iii. 6) ; his word changeth not ; his testimonies abide the same : *I have known of old, that he has founded them for ever.*' Thus we look for the removing of those " things which are shaken, as of things that are made, that those things which cannot be shaken may remain." (Heb. xii. 27.) The scoffer may say,—" If the foundations be destroyed, what can the righteous do ?" (Ps. xi. 3.) Let God himself give the answer—" *Lift up your eyes to the heavens, and look upon the earth beneath: for the heavens shall vanish away like smoke, and the earth shall wax old like a garment, and they that dwell therein shall die in like manner; but my salvation shall be for ever, and my righteousness shall not be abolished.*" (Isa. li. 6.)

PART XX.

153. *Consider mine affliction, and deliver me: for I do not forget thy law.*

ANOTHER note of the child of sorrow! Hated by the world (John, xv. 19)—vexed by his restless enemy (Job, i. 7. Luke, xxii. 31. 1 Pet. v. 8)—chastened by his God (1 Cor. xi. 32. Heb. xii. 10, 11)—burdened with his "body of death" (Rom. vii. 24 ; viii. 23)—what else can he do but cry—*Consider mine affliction!* How manifestly is this world, not our rest, but our exercise for rest! Well is it that our "days are few," when they are so "evil." (Gen. xlvii. 9.) But how could we hold on as we do, had we not our Saviour's pitying heart and Almighty help? The want of this sympathy was the overwhelming sorrow, that well-nigh "broke his" sorrowing "heart"—" *I looked for some to take pity, but there was none; and for comforters, but I found none.*" (Ps. lxix. 20. Comp. xxii. 11.) This depth of trial combined with every other part of his unknown sufferings to make him " *such an High Priest as became us*" (Heb. vii. 26), " *touched with the feeling of our infirmities*" (Heb. iv. 15) ; *considering our afflictions:* and, " *in that he himself hath suffered being tempted, able to succour them that are tempted.*" (Heb. ii. 18.) With what sympathy did he *consider the affliction* of his people in Egypt!—"*I have surely seen the affliction of my people which are in Egypt, and I know their sorrows.*" (Exod. iii. 7, also ii. 25.) At a subsequent period—"*his soul was grieved for the misery of Israel*" (Judg. x.

16)—a cheering example of that compassionate interest, with which " *in all his people's afflictions he is afflicted.*" (Isa. lxiii. 9.) Well may his people take encouragement to pray, *Consider mine affliction.* " Now, therefore, let not all the trouble *seem little before thee, that hath come upon us.*" (Neh. ix. 32. Comp. Ps. cxxxii. 1.)

Yet is he not only sympathizing to *consider*, but mighty to *deliver.* " Who is this glorious" conqueror with his " dyed garments" of victory—" travelling in the greatness of his strength ? I that speak in righteousness—*mighty to save.*" (Isa. lxiii. 1.) Such did the noble confessors in Babylon (Dan. iii. 17, 25–28)—such did Daniel in the den of lions (Dan. vi. 23, 27)—find him, fully justifying their unwavering confidence in his love and power. And what age of the Church has been wanting in testimony, that " the Lord knoweth how to *deliver* the godly out of temptations" (2 Pet. ii. 9), and that " he that hath delivered, doth deliver, and will even to the end deliver?" (2 Cor. i. 10.) The consciousness that *we do not forget his law*, is our plea, that he would *consider our affliction, and deliver* us ;* and is of itself an evidence, that the affliction has performed its appointed work. Let me then expect in mine affliction the fulfilment of his gracious promise —" Because he hath set his love upon me, therefore *will I deliver* him ; I will set him on high, because he hath known my name. He shall call upon me, and " *I will deliver him: I will be with him in trouble; I will deliver him, and honour him.*" (Ps. xci. 14, 15.) In the midst of my trials I would prepare my hymn of praise for his kind *consideration* and faithful *deliverance*—" I will be glad and rejoice in thy mercy : for thou hast *considered my trouble;* thou hast known my soul in adversities, and hast not shut me up into the hand of the enemy ; thou hast set my feet in a large room !" (Ps. xxxi. 7, 8.) Let me then

* The same plea is often urged in this Psalm, verses 94, 173, 176.

remember my *affliction*, only as it may be the means of increasing my acquaintance with my tender and Almighty friend. Poor and afflicted as I may be, let me be more poor and afflicted still, if I may but have fresh evidence that he " thinketh upon me " (Ps. xl. 17) — that he *considers my affliction*, and in his own gracious time and way will *deliver me*.

154. *Plead my cause, and deliver me; quicken me according to thy word.*

Oppressed as the Psalmist appeared to be by the weight of his *affliction*, he is at no loss where to apply for help. He carries his righteous cause to him, who " stilleth the enemy and the avenger " (Ps. viii. 2) — " Plead my cause, O Lord, with them that strive with me : fight against them that fight against me. Take hold of shield and buckler, and stand up for my help. Draw out also the spear, and stop the way against them that persecute me ; say unto my soul, I am thy salvation." (Ps. xxxv. 1–3.) Thus must we throughout our warfare maintain " the patience of hope " (1 Thess. i. 3), waiting for the Lord, " until he plead our cause, and execute judgment for us." (Mic. vii. 9.) If there is an accuser to resist (Zech. iii. 1. Rev. xii. 10), " *we have* an advocate " to *plead* (1 John, ii. 1), who could testify of his prevailing acceptance in the court of heaven, " Father, I thank thee, that thou hast heard me. And I knew that thou hearest me always." (John, xi. 41, 42.) Our Redeemer does indeed *plead our cause* successfully for our *deliverance ;* when but for his powerful advocacy we must have stood speechless in the judgment — helpless, without any prospect of acceptance. Awful indeed was the cause which he had to manage. Our adversary had the law on his side. We could not deny the charge, or offer satisfaction. We could neither " stand in the judgment," nor flee from the impending wrath.   But at that moment of infinite peril, our cause was pleaded by a " Counsellor " (Isa. ix. 6), who never was nonsuited in court, who brought irresistible pleas, and produced satisfaction that could not be denied.   The voice of *deliverance* was heard in heaven — " *Deliver them from going down to the pit : I have found a ransom.*" (Job, xxxiii. 24.)   This ransom is no less than the price of his own " precious blood," " shed for many for the remission of sins " (1 Pet. i. 19. Matt. xxvi. 28), a ransom, which has merited and obtained eternal *deliverance* (Heb. ix. 12) for his people, and which still pleads for the expiation of the guilt, which attaches to their holiest services, and defiles their happiest approaches to their God. When therefore Satan accuses me : yea, when my own heart condemns me, I may look upward to my heavenly Advocate — *Plead my cause, and deliver me.** " O Lord, I am oppressed ; undertake for me.   Thou wilt answer, O Lord, my God."†

Poor trembling sinner ! take courage.   " Your Redeemer is strong — he will thoroughly plead your cause " (Jer. l. 34), and leave no charge unanswered.   But you say — ' How know I that he speaks for me ? '   Yet if not for you, for whom does he speak ?   Who needs an advocate more than you ?   He pleads indeed nothing favourable *of*

---

* ' The word translated " *deliver me*," is taken from the office of a redeemer or next of kin amongst the Israelites, to whom it belonged to redeem the inheritance, or ransom the person of his impoverished or enslaved relative : and also to be his patron and defender against injustice and oppression, and the avenger of his blood, if he was slain.'—Scott.   The use therefore of this word in the original in this verse, naturally points the believer's attention to him, who indeed is near of kin to him, and has combined all the offices of the ancient redeemer in his one beloved person; and therefore at once illustrates and warrants the view that is here given of the passage.

† Isa. xxxviii. 14. Ps. xxxviii. 15. Margin and P. T.

you; but much, very much *for you.* For he pleads the merit of his own blood, " that taketh away the sin of the world " (John, i. 29)—even that great sin of " unbelief," of which his Spirit is now " convincing " you (John, xvi. 8, 9. M. R.) ; and which you are now made to feel, lament, and resist, as the bitterest foe to your peace. And does he not " ever live to make intercession for you?" Why then hesitate to apply the certain and consoling inference, that " he is able to save *to the uttermost?*" (Heb. vii. 25.) Why discouraged by the sight of sin, temptation, backsliding, difficulty, and fear, arising before you on every side ; when after you have taken the most extended view of the prospect of sorrow, this one word " *uttermost*" goes beyond it ? If you feel it hard to believe, send up your cry—" Help thou mine unbelief." (Mark, ix. 24.) Only do not dishonour him by wilful despondency ; and do not add the sin of disobedience, in delaying this moment to come to him.

After all, however, even while exercising faith in our heavenly Advocate, we must mourn over our sluggishness in his service. Well, therefore, do we accompany our pleading for *deliverance* with the supplication— *Quicken me!* Every moment's perseverance depends upon this Divine supply. Blessed be God for the sure warrant of expectation—*According to thy word!* Here we shall receive not only the living principle, but its lively operation ; not only the fire to kindle the lamp, but the oil to feed the flame. For he that is our Advocate to *plead* for us, and our Saviour to *deliver* us, is also our *quickening* Head, filled with " the residue of the Spirit" to " revive his work." " *Thou hast ascended on high, and hast received gifts for men: yea, for the rebellious also, that the Lord God might dwell among them.*" (Ps. lxviii. 18.) Do we therefore want a heart to pray, to praise, to believe, to love ? Let us only look to an ascended Saviour, sending down the life-giving influence from above, as the purchase of his blood, and the fruit of his intercession. Thus will our hope be enlivened, our faith established, and the graces of the Spirit will abound to the glory of our God.

155. *Salvation is far from the wicked; for they seek not thy statutes.*

How striking the contrast!—how awfully destitute the condition! They have no one to *consider their affliction* —no one to *deliver them*—no one to *plead their cause.* Indeed, all the misery that an immortal soul is capable of enduring throughout eternity is included in this sentence —*Salvation is far from the wicked.* The full picture of it is drawn by our Lord himself, "The rich man died, and was buried; and *in hell he lifted up his eyes, being in torments, and seeth Abraham afar off, and Lazarus in his bosom.*" (Luke, xvi. 22–24.) The present enjoyment of *salvation is far from the wicked.* "There is no peace, saith my God, to the wicked." (Isa. lvii. 21.) Their common employments are "sin." (Prov. xxi. 4.) Their "sacrifice is an abomination." (Prov. xv. 8.) Their life is "without Christ, having no hope, and without God in the world." (Eph. ii. 12.) But who can tell the curse of eternity, with this *salvation far from them?* To be eternally shut out from God—from heaven! To be eternally shut in with the enemies of God, and the heirs of hell! Fellow-Christians—look from what ye have escaped—what ye were, when "ye were sometimes afar off,"—what ye would have been now and for ever, had ye not "in Christ Jesus been made nigh by the blood of Christ" (Eph. ii. 13): and then "if you hold your peace, the stones will immediately cry out" against you. (Luke, xix. 40.)

But whence this inexpressibly awful condition of *the wicked?* Is not *salvation* offered to them? Are they shut out from hope, and sternly refused an interest in the cove-

nant? Oh! no; it is their own doing, or rather their own
undoing. Would they but *seek* the ways of God, they might
plead for *deliverance;* yea, they might have a prevailing
Advocate to *plead their cause, and deliver them.* But now
salvation is far from them, because " *they are far from God's
law.*" (Ps. lxxiii. 27.) It does not fly from them ; " but
they fly from it. Every act is a stride of mind, more or
less vigorous in departure from God. Nay — such is their
pride, that " they will *not even seek his statutes.*" (Ib. x. 4.)
They " desire not the knowledge of his ways." They say
to God —" Depart from us" (Job, xxi. 14); God, therefore,
will say to them, " Depart from me." (Matt. vii. 23 ; xxv.
41.) They say to Christ, " We will not have this man to
reign over us ;" He will say of them, " Those mine enemies, that would not I should reign over them, bring
hither, and slay them before me." (Luke, xix. 14, 27.) It
is not then so much God that punishes them, as they that
punish themselves. Their own sin — the necessity of the
case — punishes them. They " will not come to Christ,
that they might have life" (John, v. 40) : " so that they
are without excuse"—die they must. (Matt. xxiii. 37, 38.)

   But who are *the wicked?* Alas ! this is a melancholy
question, as involving within its sphere so much that passes
for amiable, virtuous, and lovely, in the estimation of the
world. Not to speak of those, whose name is broadly
written upon their foreheads ; it includes " all that forget
God" (Ps. ix. 17), however blameless their moral character, or their external Christian profession. It is determined upon immutable authority — it is the decree of our
eternal Judge—" If any man have not the Spirit of Christ,
he is none of his" (Rom. viii. 9) ; and if none of his, then
it follows in unavoidable consequence, that *salvation is far
from him.*

   Oh ! could we but persuade such of their awful state.
Oh ! could we awake them from their death-like, deadly

sleep — slumbering on the brink of ruin! on the borders
of hell! But they are closed up in their own self-esteem,
or in the favourable comparison drawn between themselves
and many around them ; forgetting that the rule, by which
they will be judged, is not the world's standard of moral
rectitude, but the statutes of a holy, heart-searching God ;
forgetting too, that all may be decency without, while all
is corruption within. Let them test their hearts by an
honest and prayerful scrutiny of *the statutes ;* and while
they must confess themselves guilty before God, a sense of
danger would awaken the hearty cry for salvation (Acts,
xvi. 30) which would not *then be far from them.* (See Ps.
lxxxv. 9.) For " the Lord is nigh unto all them that call
upon him, to all that call upon him in truth. He will
fulfil the desire of them that fear him ; he also will hear
their cry, and *will save them.*" (Ps. cxlv. 18, 19.)

O thou Almighty Spirit, whose power is alone able to
" turn the hearts of the disobedient to the wisdom of the
just" (Luke, i. 17), " raise up thy power, and come among
us ;" " rend the heavens, and come down" (Isa. lxiv. 1) ;
rend the hearts of sinners, of the ungodly, the moral, the
naturally amiable, the self-righteous. " Fill their faces
with shame, that they may seek thy name, O Lord." (Ps.
lxxxiii. 16.)

156. *Great are thy tender mercies, O Lord; quicken me ac-*
cording to thy judgments.

It is most cheering to pass from judgment to mercy —
from the awful state of *the wicked,* to adore *the mercies of*
God to his own people. We were naturally no better than
they. The most eminent saved sinner looks on himself
with wonder — " Is not this a brand plucked out of the
fire ?" (Zech. iii. 2.) Never will he lose the remembrance
— " Who maketh thee to differ ?" (1 Cor. iv. 7.) To mercy

— rich mercy alone—we trace the distinction between those that are " quickened," and those that remain " dead in trespasses and sins." (Eph. ii. 1, 4, 5.)

But let us mark the features of this *mercy.* *How great* in extent ! Estimate its *greatness* by the infinite debt which it blots out (Isa. xliii. 22–25 ; i. 18)—the eternal ruin from which it saves (Ps. lxxxvi. 13)—the heavenly crown to which it raises. (Rev. i. 5, 6.) Trace it to the mind of God—that first eternal purpose of mercy, which set us apart for his glory. (Eph. i. 4–6.) Mark it in that " time of love," when *his mercy* rescued us from Satan, sin, death, and hell, and drew us to himself. (Ezek. xvi. 6–8.) As soon might we span the arch of heaven, as fully grasp the *greatness of his mercy.* (Ps. ciii. 11. Isa. lv. 8, 9.) And then how *tender* is it in its exercise ! Such was the first beam of mercy that " visited us." (Luke, i. 78.) Such has been the continued display. So natural, as from a Father. (2 Cor. i. 3. Ps. ciii. 13.) So yearning, " as one whom his mother comforteth !" (Is. lxvi. 13.) Such a multitude of those *tender mercies!* The overflowing stream follows us through every step of our wilderness-journey. The blessing " compasses us about," abounds towards us, keeps us stedfast, or restores us when wandering, and will preserve us to the end. Happy are we—not in the general perception —not in the hearsay report (John, iv. 42)—but in the experimental enjoyment of it. " Bless the Lord, O my soul, and all that is within me, bless his holy name." (Ps. ciii. 1–3.) But what poor returns have we made for this infinite love ! Surely the petition for *quickening* grace suits us well. This was the constant burden of David's prayer. For he was not like many professors, who can maintain their assurance in a lower and careless walk. No, he was a believer of a very high standard ; desirous not only of proving his title to the blessing, but of living in its habitual and active enjoyment.

Often as this petition has been brought before us, in the course of this Psalm, it is too important ever to be passed over. Let us at this time use it for the purpose of individual self-inquiry. In what respects do I need *quickening* grace? Are my views of sin, and especially of the sin of my own heart, slight and superficial? Do they fail in producing humility, abasement, tenderness of conscience, circumspection of conduct? If it be so — *Quicken me, O my God!* Does my apprehension of a Saviour's love serve to embitter sin to me? to crucify sin in me, to warm and enliven my heart with love to him, and zeal in his service? If I am convicted of coldness to such a Saviour, and sluggishness in such a service, I need to pray — *O Lord, quicken me!* And how do I find it with regard to prayer itself? Are not my prayers general — unfrequent — wandering? Is not my service too often constrained, a forced duty, rather than a privilege and delight? *O Lord, quicken me!*

Yet many Christians, through a mistaken perception, know not when they have received the blessing. They have looked for it in strong and sensible excitement; and in defect of this they sink into despondency. Whereas the solid influence is independent of sensations, and consists in a tender sensibility of sin, a spiritual appetite for the gospel, active energy in Christian duties, and continual progress in heavenly exercises. But under no circumstances must the evil of a dead and drooping state be lightly thought of; obscuring as it does the difference between the believer and the worldling, or rather between the believer and the formalist. O believer, you have great need to carry your complaint again and again unto the Lord! ' *Quicken me — quicken me — according to thy judgments* — according to those gracious promises, which are the method of thy proceedings, and the rule of thy dispensations of grace.' You cannot be too earnest to welcome the breathings of the Spirit, or too cautious, that your indolence resists not his Divine impression. When he quickens you with his influence, do you quicken him with your supplications—"*Awake, O north wind; and come, thou south: blow upon my garden, that the spices thereof may flow out.*" (Cant. iv. 16.) Persuade—entreat—constrain his stay. Enlivened by his energy, how happy, and in your own sphere how useful, a member of the Church of Christ you may be found! Your soul will be invigorated—your graces strengthened—and your affections elevated—in humble, cheerful, steady dependence upon the Saviour, and in daily renewed devotedness to his service. The more the spiritual life is thus " exercised unto godliness, the more delightfully will you realise the active service and everlasting praise, which will constitute the perfection of heavenly enjoyment." (Rev. xxii. 3, 4; iv. 8.)

157. *Many are my persecutors and mine enemies; yet do I not decline from thy testimonies.*

David's experience is common to us all. *Many*, indeed, *are our persecutors and enemies.* This is a solemn cost. Let those who are setting out in the Christian course count it well. From neglect of our Lord's rule of Scriptural calculation (Luke, xiv. 28–33), many seem to begin well; but they have been " hindered" (Gal. v. 7 ; iii. 3)—they turn back ; they are zealous but inconsiderate ; warm-hearted, but ignorant of themselves, their work, and their resources. They were allured at first, perhaps, by an interest in the Gospel—some delusive excitement of love to the Saviour—the picture of the paths of " pleasantness and peace" (Prov. iii. 17), or the joys of heaven. The cross was out of sight, and out of mind. But this promise of ease and happiness was no less foolish and unwarrantable, than that of a soldier, utterly forgetful of his profession, and who should promise himself peace at the very time that he was called out to the wars. Surely, if like God's ancient people, we begin our road in sunshine, it is well to be provided against the storms, which will soon overtake us. (Exod. xv. 1 ; xvi. 1–3.) We would say therefore to all — specially to sanguine beginners — Let your course be commenced with serious consideration, and zealous self-scrutiny. Beware of hasty determinations. See to it, that your resources are drawn, not from your own resolutions, or from the sincerity and ardour of your love ; but from the fulness that is treasured up in Jesus for your present distress. Feel every step of your way by the light of the sacred word. If you expect Christian consistency to command the esteem of an ungodly world, you have forgotten both your Master's word and example (John, xv. 20) ; and you will soon be ready to exclaim—*Many are my persecutors, and mine enemies.* For if their hostility is not always active, the enmity " is not dead, but sleepeth." If, however, their unexpected surprisals and inveteracy should daunt you in the conflict, you are again forgetting the word of cheering support in the most awful crisis—" *My grace is sufficient for thee; for my strength is made perfect in weakness.*" (2 Cor. xii. 9.) Thus the word of God will be " the armour of righteousness on the right hand and on the left." (2 Cor. vi. 7.) Presumption is cast down, self-confidence is humbled, and the trembling simplicity of dependence upon an Almighty arm is upheld and honoured.

Count then upon the difficulties that beset the heavenly path. You will never pluck the Rose of Sharon, if you are afraid of being pricked by the thorns which surround it. You will never reach the crown, if you flinch from the cross in the way to it. Oh ! think of the honour of bearing this cross. It is conformity to the Son of God. Let the mind be deeply imbued with the remembrance of his

daily cross of suffering and reproach ; and we shall gladly
"*go forth without the camp, bearing his reproach,*" yea—*even
"rejoicing, if we are counted worthy to suffer shame*" (Heb.
xiii. 13. Acts, v. 41) with him and for him. Indeed, what
is our love, if we will not take up a cross for him? How
can we be his followers, without his cross? (See Matt. xvi.
24.) How can we be Christians, if we are not confessors
of Christ before a world that despises his Gospel?

But a steady, consistent profession is no matter of
course. The crown is not easily won. *Many are our persecutors, and our enemies.* Persecution, to the false professor, is an occasion of apostasy (Matt. xiii. 20, 21) ; to the
faithful servant of Christ, it is the trial of his faith (1 Pet.
i. 6, 7), the source of his richest consolations (Matt. v. 10–
12. Acts, xiii. 50–52. 1 Pet. iv. 12–16), the guard of his
profession (Matt. x. 16. Phil. ii. 14–16), and the strength
of his perseverance. (Acts, xx. 22–24.) It drives him to
his God. He casts himself upon his Saviour for immediate
refuge and support ; and the *quickening* influence, which he
had just been seeking, enables him to say—*Yet do I not
decline from thy testimonies.* Thus did the great Apostle, at
the time, when his *persecutors were many,* and human help
even from his friends had failed him, maintain an unshaken
confidence in the service of his God—"At my first answer"
—he tells us—" no man stood with me, but all men forsook me. Notwithstanding, the Lord *stood with me, and
strengthened me.*" (2 Tim. iv. 16, 17.) David himself often
acknowledged the same principle of perseverance under
similar trials—" Lord, how are they increased that trouble
me ! Many are they that rise up against me. Many
there be, which say of my soul, There is no help for him in
God. But *Thou, O Lord, art a shield for me ; my glory, and
the lifter-up of my head. O God the Lord, the strength of my
salvation, thou hast covered my head in the day of battle.*"
(Ps. iii. 1–3 ; cxl. 7.)

EXPOSITION OF PSALM CXIX.

EXPOSITION OF PSALM CXIX.

But have we never taken a devious path in *declining from the Lord's testimonies*, to escape the appointed cross? Do we never shrink from "the voice of him that reproacheth" and blasphemeth, by reason of the enemy and the avenger? Can we always in the integrity of our heart appeal to an Omniscient God—"*All this is come upon us; yet have we not forgotten thee, neither have we dealt falsely in thy covenant; our heart is not turned back, neither have our steps declined from thy way: though thou hast sore broken us in the place of dragons, and covered us with the shadow of death?*" (Ps. xliv. 16–19.) This profession is not the foolish confidence of boasting; but the fulfilment of the covenant promise—"I will put my fear in their hearts, that they shall not depart from me." (Jer. xxxii. 40.) So beautifully does the promise of perseverance connect itself with the duty of persevering! And so clearly in this, as in every other way, does the "wrath of man" ("howbeit he meaneth not so, neither doth his heart think so") "praise God." (Comp. Isa. x. 7, with Ps. lxxvi. 10.) How glorious is the display of the power of his grace in the constancy of his people! like the rocks in the ocean, immoveable amidst the fury of the waves; like the trees of the forest, "rooted and stablished" by every shaking of the tempest! Must not the world, in witnessing the total defeat of their enmity against the Lord's people (or rather its eventual results in their increased prosperity), be constrained to confess to the honour of God, "*Surely there is no enchantment against Jacob, neither is there any divination against Israel: according to this time it shall be said of Jacob and of Israel—What hath God wrought!*" (Num. xxiii. 23.)

158. *I beheld the transgressors, and was grieved; because they kept not thy word.*

We shall not tire in listening to this repeated expres-

sion (Comp. Verses 53, 136) of the Psalmist's tenderness
for the honour of God. No trouble from his *many persecutors and enemies* came so near to his heart, as the sight
of the dishonour and contempt of God's word. The glory
of God was dearer to him than life. O that every recollection of this tried servant of God might deepen the special
mark of acceptance (See Ezek. ix. 4–6) upon our too cold
and indifferent hearts ! Our joys and sorrows are the pulse
of the soul. A fellowship with the joys of angels over re-
penting sinners (Luke, xv. 10) will be accompanied with
bitterness of godly sorrow over the hardness and impeni-
tency of those, who *keep not the word of God.*

But even here we need much and earnest prayer, in order
to obtain a clear perception of our real principles. Sin is so
subtle in its nature and workings, that it insinuates itself
into our holiest desires, and often so far interweaves itself
into the graces of the Spirit, as greatly to mar their beauty,
and obstruct their operations. How often is zeal for the
honour of God mingled with the unhallowed fire of our own
spirit! (See Luke, ix. 54, 55.) True zeal is indeed a precious fruit of the Spirit. Its other name is love — active,
self-denying, compassionate love for sinners. ' *Let me never
fancy I have zeal* ' — said a Christian of a very high order —
' *till my heart overflows with love to every man living.*' * If then
we are really under its holy influence, we shall lose no opportunity of active exertions on behalf of wretched *transgressors:*
and the limits of our zeal will be only the limits of a fallen
world. Especially within our own sphere shall we employ
all our labours and pains to stem the tide of unrighteousness — " saying unto the fools — deal not foolishly — How
long, ye simple ones, will ye love simplicity? Turn ye,
turn ye, why will ye die ?" (Ps. lxxv. 4. Prov. i. 22. Ezek.
xxxiii. 11.)

* MARTYN's Life, p. 192.

But the fervency of zeal will express itself in something more difficult than personal service. We can often warn and plead with transgressors, when we are sinfully backward in sending up sighs and cries on their behalf; and in presenting these poor lepers by faith to that great and good Physician, whose "power present to heal" (Luke, v. 17) has been so abundantly manifested. This is indeed zeal of rare attainment through our own unbelief. But it brings its own rich blessing to the soul; because it is the zeal of the compassionate Jesus; who, though he looked round on sinners with anger, " being *grieved* for the hardness of their hearts " (Mark, iii. 5), did not forget to plead on their behalf—" *Father, forgive them; for they know not what they do.*" (Luke, xxiii. 34.) It was the zeal and love of him, who so identified his Father's interest with his own, that he endured the reproaches cast upon him in his bosom. (Ps. lxix. 9, 20, with Rom. xv. 3.) And should not the members feel, when the Head is wounded? Should not we consider every dishonour done to Jesus as a shaft piercing our own breast? Can we bear to *behold* all around us united in a conspiracy against the honour, and—if it were possible—against the life, of our dearest friend and benefactor, and not be painfully *grieved?* * Yet genuine *grief* must begin with our own heart—" all of us mourning, every one for his iniquity." (Ezek. vii. 16.) The wickedness of others will stir up the conviction within our own conscience—" I do remember my faults this day." (Gen. xli. 9.) And when once we begin the enumeration, where shall we end? *Who can understand his errors? Cleanse thou me from secret faults.*

---

* Celerinus, in Cyprian's Epistles, acquaints a friend with his great grief for the apostasy of a woman through fear of persecution, which afflicted him so much, that at the feast of Easter (the queen of feasts in the Primitive Church) he wept night and day, and resolved never to know a moment's delight, till, through the mercy of God, she should be recovered.

Enter not into judgment with thy servant." (Ps. xix. 12 ; cxliii. 2.)

159. *Consider how I love thy precepts ; quicken me, O Lord, according to thy loving-kindness.*

Love for the precepts, such as this Psalm describes, is a distinguishing characteristic of a child of God. *The transgressors* neither *love the precepts,* nor desire *quickening* grace to keep them. For though " not grievous " (1 John, v. 3) in themselves, they are too strict, too humbling for the unrenewed, proud, worldly heart. (Comp. Jer. vi. 10.) *Love* therefore to them—not being the growth of the natural man — must be " a plant which our heavenly Father hath planted," a witness of the Spirit of adoption, and the principle of Christian devotedness. And how encouraging is the recollection of the Lord's readiness to *consider how we love his precepts!* " *I know Abraham,* that he will command his children and his household after him, and they shall keep the way of the Lord, that the Lord may bring upon Abraham that which he hath spoken of him." (Gen. xviii. 19.) Thus also did he challenge "the accuser of the brethren," to "*consider* his servant Job, that there is none like him in the earth, a perfect and an upright man, one that feareth God, and escheweth evil." (Job, i. 8.)

But while *love of the precepts* realizes the full confidence of the Lord's *consideration,* the consciousness of its imperfection and scanty measure will always prevent us from urging it as the ground of acceptance. Christian! you know not — or at least you allow not — the proud boast — " God, I thank thee, that I am not as other men are." (Luke, xviii. 11.) No, rather—your constant cry to the end is — *Quicken me.* Your plea is not merit, but mercy. Not that you deserve to be helped—*because you love the precepts :* but you desire and trust to be helped—*according to thy loving-kindness.* And what must be *the loving-kindness* of a God of infinite love! Only do not sit still, and wait for the breezes of his love. Rather call to the " north wind to awake, and to the south wind to blow " (Cant. iv. 16), to fill your sails, and urge you on. God—his word, his works, his perfections, his holiness; Jesus—his pity, his love, his grace —is your delight, your chief delight; yet how infinitely is it below the scriptural standard of privilege, attainment, and expectation!

Under the painful influence of straitened desires and heartless affections, how refreshing is it to mark the springs of life flowing from *the loving-kindness of the Lord!* Yes, indeed—he is the overflowing spring of his church. Every mercy is his grace. Every holy suggestion is his influence. Even the passing thought that our Christian progress proceeds from our own resources, opens the door of fearful departure from God. And yet such is the self-deceitfulness of the heart, that, in the very act of professing to " rejoice in Christ Jesus," the Omniscient eye traces a " confidence in the flesh." (Philip. iii. 3.) The *real* dependence is on the " mountain that stands strong," not on " the favour that makes " it so. (Ps. xxx. 7.) Even our first father, in his original unimpaired strength, could " not *quicken* his own soul." (Ps. xxii. 29.) Can we wonder that the fallen nature, even though partially upheld by Divine power, is changeable and unstable? The most advanced Christian needs the supply to the end, as much as he did in his first stage of infantine weakness. And will he not continue to need it throughout eternity, in every exercise of adoring service, as well as for his active existence?

But when we ask for this *quickening*, are we expecting, as we ought to be, a large answer to our prayer? (Ps. lxxxi. 10.) Or are we " limiting " our God (Ib. lxxviii. 41), by the scanty apprehensions of our poor faith? Remember he is glorified—not in possessing, but in dispensing his gifts.

(John, xvi. 13.) If we really expect his blessing, can we be satisfied without it? It is not our unworthiness, but our unbelief, that stops the current. (Matt. xiii. 58. Mark, vi. 5.) Would that we gave him full credit for his exuberant flow of free, rich, ceaseless mercy!

Blessed Jesus! we plead thy promise to *be filled*. (Matt. v. 6.) We have life from thee; but give it us "*more abundantly*" (John, x. 10)—as much as these houses of clay—as much as these earthen vessels—can contain. Our taste of thy love, and our knowledge of its unbounded fulness, encourage our plea to ask thee still for more—*Quicken us according to thy loving-kindness.* Often as the Psalmist had repeated this prayer for quickening grace,* it was not a "*vain repetition.*" (Comp. Matt. vi. 7.) Each time was it enlivened with faith, feeling of necessity, and ardent affection: and should we, in the consciousness of our weakness and coldness, offer it a hundred times a-day, it would never fail of acceptance.

160. *Thy word is true from the beginning: and every one of thy righteous judgments endureth for ever.*

The "*loving-kindness and the truth of God*" were two heavenly notes, on which "the sweet Psalmist of Israel" loved to dwell†—his "*loving-kindness*" in giving, and his "*truth*" in fulfilling—his gracious promises. Indeed the displays of his truth—whether to his Church collectively,

---

* Nine times is this petition urged, verses 25, 37, 40, 88, 107, 149, 154, 156, 159.

† See his character described—"*Good and upright* is the Lord," Ps. xxv. 8—and mark these perfections pleaded in their combined connexion with his purposes of grace—"Thou wilt perform *the truth to Jacob, and the mercy to Abraham*"—"*mercy*" in the original grant—"*truth*" in the subsequent ratification and performance. Mic. vii. 20. Comp. Luke, i. 72, 73.

or to his people individually—have always been every way
worthy of himself. Often has his word seemed on the eve
of being falsified, clearly with the design of a brighter and
more striking display of its faithfulness. The very night
previous to the close of the four hundred and thirty years,
Israel was, to all human appearances, as far from deliverance as at any former period. But " the vision was for an
appointed time" (Hab. ii. 3) : nothing could hasten, nothing
could delay it; for *" it came to pass at the end of the four hundred and thirty years, even the self-same day it came to pass,*
that all the hosts of the Lord went out from the land of
Egypt." (Exod. xii. 41.) At a subsequent period, the family
of David appeared upon the point of extinction; and it
seemed as if the promise of God would fall to the ground.
But to exhibit *the word of God* (Comp. 2 Sam. vii. 16), *as
true from the beginning,* a providential, and almost a miracu-
lous, interference was manifested. When Athaliah destroyed
all the seed-royal of the house of Judah, Joash was stolen
away, put under a nurse, hid in the house of the Lord six
years, and in God's appointed time brought forth to the
people *as the fulfilment of the express promise of God*—" *Behold! the king's son shall reign, as the Lord had said of the
sons of David.*" (2 Chron. xxii. 10–12; xxiii. 3.) " Whoso
is wise, and will observe these things, even they shall understand the loving-kindness of the Lord." (Ps. cvii. 43.)

And thus have many of his own people been tempted in
seasons of despondency to " charge God foolishly." (Job,
i. 22.) But who of them has not afterwards, in some unexpected deliverance, " set to his seal"—*Thy word is true
from the beginning?* (Gen. xlii. 36, with xlviii. 15, 16.)
" The Lord shall judge his people, and repent himself for
his servants, *when he seeth that their power is gone, and there
is none shut up or left.*" (Deut. xxxii. 36. Comp. 2 Kings,
xiv. 26, 27.) And how do these recollections put to shame
the suggestions of unbelief, and strengthen our confidence

in the prospect, or even in the present endurance, of " manifold temptations!"

The full acknowledgment of the truths of God's word is
the ground of all our peace and comfort. The believing
reception of the testimony opens to us a free access to God.
(Eph. iii. 12.) We stand before him self-condemned, and yet
we believe that " there is no condemnation." (Rom. iii. 19;
viii. 1.) " The Spirit beareth witness" to and " with our
spirits," that " this God is our God for ever and ever "—
" unto death" (Rom. viii. 16. Ps. xlviii. 14), in death (Ps.
lxxiii. 26), and through eternity. (Rev. xxi. 3.) In this
simplicity of rest upon the testimony, we go to our God, like
Abraham, in sensible helplessness, but in assured confidence,
" strong in faith, giving glory to God." (Rom. iv. 19, 20.)

Many, however, have been so used to indulge the pride
of their own reasonings, that they scarcely know how to read
the Book of God without cavilling. If they believe while it
is in their hands, they are not prepared to give a reason of
their faith. They have ventured into conflict with the
enemy with unproved armour, and so have been shaken and
troubled. *Or perhaps their faith does not reach the whole testimony :* and therefore, being partial only it is not genuine.
For if we do not give full credence to all, we do not give
true credence to any. We do not receive it on the authority
of God, but only so far as our reasoning can explain it, or
our will may approve it. What need then have we to pray
for a teachable simplicity of faith—not asking—' What
thinkest thou?' but—" *How readest thou?*" In this spirit
we shall hold our anchor on solid ground; and should we
again be " tossed with the tempest," we shall look to him,
who stilleth the storm, and there shall be " *a great calm.*"
(Mark, iv. 39.) Confidence simply built upon the word of
God, will endure the storms of earth and hell.

Yet we may loosely believe all, while we practically be-

lieve none. The generalities of truth have no influence
without an individual application. The summary look of
acquiescence will miss all the solid blessings of a reverential
and experimental faith. But to find — as the woman of
Samaria found — that ' it is all true,' — because it answers
to our convictions, our wants, and our feelings (John, iv. 29)
to know that the promises are true, because they have been
fulfilled in us — this is tasting, feeling, handling — this is
indeed blessedness — this makes the word unspeakably precious to us — " a treasure to be desired." (Prov. xxi. 20.)
To have the witness in ourselves that " we have not followed
cunningly devised fables," but that it is " a faithful saying,
and worthy of all acceptation, that Christ Jesus came into
the world to save sinners " (1 Tim. i. 15) — this is indeed
" life from the dead." Oh! how should we seek thus to
receive the word " with much assurance!" (1 Thess. i. 5.)
The Israelites were not satisfied with inquiring respecting
the manna — " What is this ? " (Exod. xvi. 15, margin), or
with discovering that it had descended from heaven; but
they gathered it each for himself, and fed upon it as their
daily bread. Nor will it be of any avail to us to prove beyond contradiction, and to acknowledge with the fullest
assurance, the truth of God's word, unless we thus embrace
it, and live upon it as our heavenly portion. Faith alone
can give this spiritual apprehension — " *He that believeth,
hath the witness in himself.*" (1 John, v. 10.) But if the word
be the truth of God *from the beginning*, it must be eternal
truth in its character and its results; like its Great Author
in every particular — *enduring for ever.* " *For ever, O Lord,
Thy word is settled in heaven ; thy faithfulness is unto all generations.*" (Verses 89, 90.) Here is the rock of my confidence.
How could I rest my hope on any salvation, that did not
proceed from the primary, unchangeable, eternal mind ?
What assurance could I have elsewhere, that the grand plan

might not be defeated by some unexpected combination ? Whereas every act of reliance in his faithfulness establishes more firmly his title to my confidence, and strengthens the soul into a habit of intelligent, vigorous faith.

Lord! give unto us that " precious faith," which makes the acknowledgment of the *truth of thy word from the beginning*, and its *endurance for ever*, the spring of continual life and consolation to our souls.

PART XXI.

161. *Princes have persecuted me without a cause : but my heart standeth in awe of thy word.*

So contrary are the principles of God and the world ! God chastens his people for their sin (Isa. xxvii. 9) ; the world persecutes them for their godliness. (John, xv. 19.) So it has been from the beginning (Gal. iv. 29), and will continue to the end. (2 Tim. iii. 12.) David had before mentioned his *persecutors* as *many*. (Verse 157.) Now he tells us, that they were, like those of David's Lord, the *princes* of the earth. (Verse 23. 1 Sam. xviii. 8, 28, 29, with Ps. ii. 2. 1 Cor. ii. 8.) In both cases, however, was it confessedly without cause. (1 Sam. xxiv. 17; xxvi. 21. John, xv. 25. Matt. xxvi. 59, 60. Comp. Dan. vi. 4, 5.) Had it been *with cause*, it would have been his shame. (Verse 39. 1 Pet. ii. 20; iii. 17; iv. 15.) Now it was his glory. (Verse 46. 2 Sam. vi. 22. Matt. v. 10–12. 1 Pet. iv. 14.) In the former case it would have been his own—here it was his Master's — cross.

His *awe of God's word* was the gracious restraint to his own spirit. (1 Sam. xxiv. 6.) And this godly fear has always marked the people of God. Witness Joseph (Gen. xxxix. 9), Moses (Heb. xi. 27), Nehemiah (Neh. v. 15), and the Jews (Ezra, ix. 4 ; x. 3), and the three Babylonish captives. (Dan. iii. 16–18.) Josiah also obtained a special mark of acceptance. (2 Chron. xxxiv. 26, 27.) For the man " *that trembleth at God's word,*" whether he be found on the throne or on the dunghill, is the man, " to whom the Lord will look." (Isa. lxvi. 2.) And certainly where, as with David, the wrath of *princes* and the wrath of God are weighed against each other; who can doubt, but that it is better to incur the persecution of men by a decided adherence to the word of God, than the wrath of God by declining from it?

Our Saviour, " knowing what was in man," had clearly fore-warned and fore-armed his disciples against these difficulties. (Luke, xii. 11, 12.) The trial at the first onset proved too hard for them; Peter's *heart stood in awe* of the *persecuting princes,* and in a moment of temptation he disowned his Master (Matt. xxvi. 69–75): but when " the Spirit of power" (2 Tim. i. 7) was poured from on high, such was the *holy awe,* in which himself and his brethren *stood of God's word,* that they declared, in the face of the whole council—" Whether it be right in the sight of God to hearken unto you more than unto God, judge ye. We ought to obey God rather than men." (Acts, iv. 19, 20 ; v. 39.) ' I fear God,'—Colonel Gardiner used to say— ' and I have nothing else to fear.'

Indeed the spirit of adoption—the Christian's distinguishing character and privilege—produces an *awe* of God; a dread of sinning against the tenderest Father, of grieving the dearest Friend. And this *awe* of God will naturally extend *to his word;* so that we shall be more tenderly afraid of disregarding its dictates, than the most faithful subject of breaking the law of his beloved Sovereign. There is nothing slavish or legal in this fear. It is the freedom and the holiness of the Gospel, the very soul of religion ; the best preservative of our joys and privileges ; and the best evidence of their scriptural character. We shall find, with David, this principle a valuable safeguard against the richest allurements, or the more powerful reproach of men, to go " beyond the word of the Lord to do less or more." (Numb. xxii. 18.)

But what must be the state of that heart, where the word of the great God—the Creator and Judge of the earth—commands no reverence! Could the sinner hear a voice from heaven, addressed distinctly to himself, would he dare to reject it? Yet "we have a more sure word, whereunto we do well that we take heed" (2 Pet. i. 19); that we receive it with silent *awe*, bow before it with the most unlimited subjection, and yield ourselves entirely to its holy influence. But if it does not stand infinitely higher in our estimation than all—*even the best*—books of man, we have no just perception of its value, nor can we expect any communication of its treasures to our hearts. The holiness of God is stamped upon its every sentence.* Let us then cherish an *awe of his word*—" receiving it"—not as a common book, " not as the word of men, but as it is in truth, the word of God " (1 Thess. ii. 13), in the true spirit of Cornelius and his company—" Now therefore are we all here present before God, to hear all things that are commanded thee of God."†

---

* The Jews' frontispiece to their great Bible is Jacob's expression of fear and astonishment upon his vision of God at Bethel—" How dreadful is this place! This is none other but the house of God, and this is the gate of heaven!" ' So ought we,'—as Dr. Owen remarks upon this—' to look upon the word with a holy awe and reverence of the presence of God in it.'

' I would advise you all, that come to the reading or hearing of this book, which is the word of God, the most precious jewel, and most holy relic that remained upon earth, that ye bring with you the fear of God, and that ye do it with all due reverence, and use your knowledge thereof, not to vain glory of frivolous disputation, but to the honour of God, increase of virtue, and edification both of yourselves and others.'—CRANMER's *Judgment of Scripture*, p. 20.

† Acts, x. 33. On this particular, a hint from a heathen may not be unworthy of our remark. "Ehud said to Eglon, I have a message from God unto thee. And *he arose out of his seat.*" Judg. iii. 20.

162. *I rejoice at thy word, as one that findeth great spoil.*

The *awe* in which we should *stand of God's word*, so far from hindering our delight in it, is, as we have just hinted, the most suitable preparation for its most happy enjoyment. (Ps. cxii. 1. Acts, ix. 31.) In receiving every word of it as the condescending message from him, before whom angels veil their faces, we shall *rejoice at it, as one that findeth great spoil.* Often had David found *great spoil* in his many wars;* but never had his greatest victories brought him such rich *spoil*, as he had now discovered in the word of God. The *joy* in this treasure (like that of the church at the advent of Christ (Isa. ix. 3), described by this figure) evidently implied no common delight. If then the saints of old could so largely enrich their souls from their scanty portion of the word; must not we, who are favoured with the entire revelation of God, acknowledge — " The lines are fallen unto us in pleasant places ; yea, we have a goodly heritage ? " (Ps. xvi. 6.)

This expressive image may remind us, that the *spoils of this precious word* are not to be gained without conflict : Here " the kingdom of heaven suffereth violence." Our natural taste and temper revolt from *the word.* Our indolence indisposes for the necessary habitual effort of prayer, self-denial, and faith. But still " the violent *do take* the kingdom by force." (Matt. xi. 12.) No pains are lost — no struggle is ineffectual. What *great spoil* is divided as the fruit of the conflict ! What abundant recompense is in reserve for the " good soldier of Jesus Christ," who is determined, in Divine strength, to " endure hardness" (2 Tim. ii. 3), until he overcomes the reluctance of his heart for the

* At Ziklag—1 Sam. xxx. 19, 26–31. From the children of Ammon—2 Sam. xii. 30.

spiritual duty? It is not a sudden flash, or impression upon the imagination; but the conqueror's joy in spoiling the field of conflict—solid and enriching. Sometimes indeed (as in the Syrian camp, 2 Kings, vii. 8), we *find the spoil* unexpectedly. Sometimes we see the treasure long before we can make it our own. And when we gird ourselves to the conflict, paralyzed by the weakness of our spiritual perceptions and the power of unbelief; many a prayer, and many a sigh, is sent up for Divine aid, before we are crowned with victory, and as the fruit of our conquest, joyfully appropriate the word to our present distress.

But from a cursory, superficial reading of the word of God, no such fruit can be anticipated. When therefore the flesh or the world have deadened our delight, and taken from us this *great spoil*, should we not arm ourselves for repossession of it? Should we be unaffected by our loss? Oh, then, since there are such treasures found and enjoyed in this field of conflict, let us not lose our interest in them by the indulgence of presumption, heartlessness, or despondency. Before we attempt to read, let us cry to the Lord, under the sense of utter helplessness to perform one spiritual act, for his powerful help and Almighty teaching. Then we shall persevere with unconquerable and unwearied vigour, and not fail to share in the blessed spoil of victory, views of a Saviour's dying love—an interest in the precious blessings of the cross—*great spoil*—" unsearchable riches." (Eph. iii. 8.)

163. *I hate and abhor lying : but thy law do I love.*

We can neither *stand in awe of God's word*, nor *rejoice at it*, unless we *abhor* all contrary ways. And here lies the spiritual conflict. For so opposed are our natural affections to the character and will of God, that we love what God hates, and we hate what God loves. Our new principle and bias, however, as directly falls in with the dictates of God's law, as before we have revolted from it. *Lying* is now *hated and abhorred* as contrary to " a God of truth ;" and the *law* is now *loved*, as the reflexion of his image, and the manifestation of his will. David had before prayed to have " *lying ways removed from him*," and a love for the law of God imparted. (See Verse 29.) His utter detestation shows, that these *ways had been removed*, and a renewed *inclination to the law granted to him*.

To have *avoided lying*, and to have *practised the law*, might have been sufficient for the regulation of his outward conduct. But *his* was the religion of the heart— not meant only to control his actions ; but to renew his habits, motions, tempers, and taste. He would not therefore only *refrain* from lying, or manifest a *disinclination to it* — he must *hate and abhor** it as hell itself. Nor was *external conformity*, or approval of the law, his standard : he must *love* it. If sin was counted common, fashionable, venial, profitable, or pleasant ; if contempt was cast upon the law of God — this stopped him not. Every sin, though only a hair's breadth deviation from the rule, was in his eyes hateful, defiling, damning. He would " *resist unto blood*, striving against it." (Heb. xii. 4.) Every act, desire, and habit of conformity, with whatever shame it might be attended, was his delight. Such, Christian, should be our standard. Lord! humble us in the daily sense of deviation and defect. Vouchsafe to us larger desires, growing conformity to thy perfect rule.

Well had it been for Eve and for her children, had she

---

* Under this *hated and abhorred lying* he intended to include —not only those more or less deviations from truth, of which he had himself been guilty (with Ahimelech, 1 Sam. xxi. 2—twice with Achish, 1 Sam. xxi. 13 ; xxvii. 10), but as before remarked, whatever in any shape, or degree, is inconsistent with the truth of God. Comp. on verse 29.

turned from the tempter's lie with this strong determination. (Gen. iii. 4–6.) But—" *Ye shall not surely die*"—
has from that fatal moment been a most effectual instrument in captivating unwary souls. So plausible is it in
itself, so agreeable to our natural inclinations, that it is
readily cherished, even where the first contact with temptation assures the wretched victims, that its " *deceit is falsehood.*" But they do not *hate and abhor it :* they do not flee
from it, as a concern for the honour of God and their own
safety would lead them ; and therefore justly are they
" given up to believe it " (2 Thess. ii. 11) as the fruit of
their delusion, and the punishment of their unfaithfulness.
Oh ! if we are ever tempted by the flattery and allurements
of the world, let us only mark the opposition of their
standard, taste, maxims, and pursuits to the truth of God,
and we shall turn away with *hatred and abhorrence.*

The " overseers of the purchased flock" (Acts, xx. 28)
of Christ—yea, all " who earnestly contend for the faith
which was once delivered unto the saints" (Jude, 3) will
anxiously watch any deterioration of doctrine or principle
— any deviation from the simplicity of the Gospel, and
brand it as a lie. " I have not written unto you"—said
the venerable Apostle, " *because ye know not the truth ; but
because ye know it, and that no lie is of the truth.* Who is
a liar, but he that denieth that Jesus is the Christ ?"
(1 John, ii. 21, 22.) How does the great Apostle teach
us to look at the *adulteration of the doctrine of grace* before
referred to (Page 367)—a system not of faith, but of fear
—not of joy, but of slavish awe — not of confidence, but of
doubt—palsying the springs of life : withering, blighting,
chilling the glow of love ; " entangling again the free-born
children of God in a yoke of bondage !" (Gal. iv. 31 ; v. 1.)
The champion of the faith would not tolerate it for a
moment. (Gal. ii. 4, 5.) And he bids his people *hate and
abhor* it, even though from an angel's mouth, as the be-

guiling *lie* of the great "corrupter" of the church. (Gal. i.
8, 9, with 2 Cor. xi. 2–4.) Equally would he have us
abhor the licentious abuse of the gospel flowing from the same
source—" Shall *we continue in sin, that grace may abound?
God forbid!*" (Rom. vi. 1, 2.)

After all, however, this verse must include an *abhorrence* of the literal sin of *lying* in all its forms. A lie is so
gross a sin, that we might be disposed to spiritualize this
expression, rather than to analyse some of the plausible
shapes, in which the sin may be detected in our own profession. Exaggeration, a false gloss, a slight deviation
(hardly perceptible) from the straight line, excuses made
to one another, which we durst not make to God, want
of accuracy in relating what we hear—all these are
forms of *lying* to be shunned, *hated and abhorred* by the
man, who is really "walking in the light, and having fellowship with God" (1 John, i. 5–7), as much as the more
palpable falsehoods, with which the world abounds, which
it excuses, and even boasts of.

Believer! would you have your *hatred and abhorrence
of* every kind of *lying* yet further deepened? Would you
summon every passion of the soul—" indignation, vehement desire, zeal, revenge" (2 Cor. vii. 11)—against it?
Then learn to *abhor* it, not only as *your* enemy, but as
God's. (Comp. Ps. cxxxix. 21, 22.) Pray that the arrow
of conviction may be dipped in the blood of Christ; and
then, however deep and painful be the wound, it cannot
be mortal. Mortal indeed it will be to the sin, but healing
to the soul. Pray that your *hatred* of sin may flow from a
sense of reconciliation; for never will it be so perfect, as
when you feel yourself sheltered from its everlasting curse.
(Compare Ezek. xvi. 63; xx. 43.) To lie before your
Saviour as his redeemed sinner, and to wash his feet with
your tears of contrition, will be your highest and happiest
privilege on this side heaven. In this spirit and daily

posture you will most clearly manifest the inseparable connexion of *hatred of lying ways* with *a love for the law of
God.*

164. *Seven times a-day do I praise thee, because of thy righteous judgments.*

David had just spoken of his *fear, joy, hatred, and love.*
He now expresses his love in praise.   And indeed it is the
mixture of praise with prayer, that makes this Psalm so
complete an exhibition of Christian experience.   Early and
late, and habitually throughout the day, have we seen this
man of God " *give himself to prayer.*"*   But his " spirit of
supplication," in strict conformity with the Apostolical
rule, was ever mingled " *with thanksgiving.*"†   Indeed, self-
love—the sense of want—may prompt us to pray.   But
love to God is the spirit of praise.   The neglect, therefore,
of this service is robbing God, no less than ourselves.   Not
that he needs it, but that he deserves and desires it.   Not
that it brings any merit to us, but that it strengthens our
dependence, and elevates our love.   If then we feel it to
be " good (Ps. xcii. 1), comely (Ps. xxxiii. 1), and pleasant "
(Ps. cxxxv. 3; cxlvii. 1), it will be as needless to define its
frequency, as to prescribe the limit of our service to a beloved friend, to whom our obligations were daily increasing.
The casuistry of love would answer all the entangling
scruples of a bondage system.   We should aim at living
in praise (Ps. xxxiv. 1; lxxi. 8, 14. Luke, xxiv. 53), as the
element of our souls, the atmosphere of our enjoyment, our
reward more than our duty—that which identifies our
interest with heaven, and forms our meetness for it.

Young Christians indeed sometimes unwarily bring

* See on Verses 147, 148.
† Philip. iv. 6. *Seven times.* Comp. Prov. xxiv. 16.

themselves into "bondage," in forcing their consciences to a frequency of set times for duty, interfering with present obligations, or pressing unduly upon the weakness of the flesh. Our rule of service, though not measured by our indolence, yet should be accommodated to those legitimate daily engagements, which, when " *done as to the Lord*" (Col. iii. 23 ; Eph. vi. 7 ; v. 20. Heb. xiii. 15), form as real and necessary a part of our religion, as the more spiritual sacrifices of prayer and praise. To observe any particular time (beyond the Sabbath, and the " morning and evening sacrifice") *because it is the time — however wearied our spirits may be, or however immediate obligations may interfere* — is to forget the weighty instruction of one well qualified to speak, — " *Bodily exercise profiteth little* " (1 Tim. iv. 8). Rather let us " go, and learn what that meaneth — *I will have mercy, and not sacrifice.*" (Hos. vi. 6, with Matt. ix. 13 ; xii. 7.) Growth in grace will, however, gradually mould our profession into habitual intercourse with God. As our views become more solid and settled, each duty of the day will find its proper place, our services will become more free, and our obedience more evangelical.

But the formalist considers *seven times a-day* — to be an infringement of the sacred canon — " *Be not righteous overmuch.*" (Eccles. vii. 16.) He pays his customary service twice a-day ; he says his prayers and his praises too ; and his conscience slumbers again. And alas ! there are times of slumber, when we little differ from him. Oh ! let us be alarmed at every symptom of such a state, and " find no rest to our spirit," until we have regained some measure of this frame of hearty and overflowing praise. If there be a heavenly nature, there must be a heavenly work. Tongue and heart should be set on fire by love. Thus we will go to our work, whatever it may be, and sing at it.

But the Christian sometimes feels, that he has no heart, and — he almost fears — no right to praise. Having no sensible token of love to call him forth, his harp "hangs upon the willows;" nor does he care to take it down, even to "sing one of the Lord's songs in this strange land." (Ps. cxxxvii. 2, 4.) But how many have found with Bunyan —'When I believe and sing, my doubting ceases!' "Meat cometh out of the eater,"—cheering rays out of the darkest cloud. Endeavour therefore to bring to mind some spiritual, or even temporal, mercies. Or, if recollection fails you, open your Bible; turn to some subject of praise, such as the song of the Angels at the birth of our Saviour (Luke, ii. 13, 14), or the song of the Redeemed to the honour of the Lamb. (Rev. v. 12.) Have you no part or interest in it? Do you not need the Saviour? Can you be happy without Him? Then inquire, and feel, and try, whether you cannot give "thanks unto God for his unspeakable gift." (2 Cor. ix. 15.) Peradventure, your notes may rise into praise, and in the excitement of praise, prayer will again mingle itself with its wonted enjoyment. It is your sinful folly to yield to that continual depression, which unfits you for the exercise of your duties and your privileges. How fully do our Liturgical services elevate and sustain the ascent of the soul heavenward! Language better adapted for strengthening its feeble aspiration will not readily be found; consecrated as it is in the remembrance of its acceptable use by a throng of the Lord's favoured people during successive generations, now united to the general assembly above, and worshipping with everlasting acceptance "before the throne of God and the Lamb."

The Lord's *righteous judgments* in his word are a constant matter for praise. Such light, food, and comfort! Such a stronghold of God! Such a firm hope to anchor on! Such a clear rule to walk by! Truly the distinguishing favour of this gracious gift stirs up the song— "*Praise ye the Lord.*" (Ps. cxlvii. 19, 20; lvi. 10.) Add to which—*the righteous judgments*—his decrees and declarations respecting his Church — occupied the Psalmist's "midnight" (Verse 62), as well as his daily, song. " *O Lord, thou art my God*"—said the enraptured prophet in the name of the Church—" *I will exalt thee, I will praise thy name; for thou hast done wonderful things; thy counsels of old are faithfulness and truth.*" (Isa. xxv. 1.) Inscrutable indeed they may sometimes appear ; and opposed to our best prospects of happiness ; yet the language of faith in the darkest hour will be—" We know that all things work together for good to them that love God, to them who are the called according to his purpose." (Rom. viii. 28.) But neither *seven times a-day*, nor " seventy times seven," will satisfy us in heaven. Then our song—even " the song of Moses and the Lamb"—will still be " the Lord's *righteous judgments*" (Rev. xv. 3, 4 ; xvi. 7) ; and for this ever " new song" the harps of God will never be unstrung, and never out of tune, throughout an eternity of praise. (Rev. iv. 8.) But a moment, and we shall be engaged in this heavenly employ—no reluctancy of the spirit—no weariness of the flesh. Every moment is hastening on this near, this cheering, this overwhelming glorious—prospect. Blessed be God !

165. *Great peace have they which love thy law, and nothing shall offend them.*

Here is the happiness of a child of God summed up in one word—*peace*. Looked at with an eye of sense, slighted by the world, and often chastened with " the rod of affliction," he is an object of pity. But look at him with the eye of faith—he *loves the law of his God*, and his heritage is *peace*. Every feature of the covenant bears some resemblance to its nature ; full of grace, peace, and love. Two of the agents are fitly represented by the lamb and the dove —emblems of peace. The tendency of its principles " is

first pure, " *then peaceable*." (Jam. iii. 17.)   Its present enjoyment and privilege is *peace—great peace*. (Isa. xi. 6–9.
Comp. ii. 4.)   Its end will be universal, eternal peace. (Ps.
xxxvii. 37. Rom. ii. 10.)

Christian! have you not discovered the connexion of
peace with love for the law—the whole revealed will of God ?
Looking at it as *the law of truth*—was not its disturbance
of your peace of self-satisfaction and self-delusion the first
step to the attainment of solid *peace ?*   You learned to see
yourself as God sees you.   Every fresh view humbled you
more deeply.   Your dissatisfaction exercised you in an anxious and diligent search for true *peace*.   And then, looking
at it again as the " *law of faith* "—here is your ground of
peace laid open.   Your way to God is clear—your acceptance free—your   confidence   assured — your   communion
heavenly.   " Being justified by faith, you have peace with
God through our Lord Jesus Christ ;" yea—you are "filled
with peace, all *peace in believing*." (Rom. v. 1, 10, 11 ; xv. 13.)
And have you not equal reason to *love this law*, as a *law
of obedience ?*   Here is your question answered —" Lord !
what wilt thou have me to do ?" (Acts, ix. 6.)   Let " this
word dwell in you richly in all wisdom ;" and it will be your
daily directory of life and conduct.   You will " delight in it
after the inner man." (Rom. vii. 22.)   Walking in the light
of it, you will go on to the full enjoyment of *peace*.   " Taking " cheerfully your Saviour's " yoke upon you, and learning of him, you will " ever " find rest unto your soul."   " All
his paths are peace." (Matt. xi. 29. Prov. iii. 17.)

Professor! what do you lose by your indulged indifference
to *the law of God ?*   Conscience tells you, that you are a
stranger to this peace—this *great peace*.   A secret root
of idolatry cankers the principles of peace.   Notions will
not bring it.   Nothing but vital godliness—the *love for
God's law*—" the truth received in the love of it"—will
realize the blessing.

Young Christian! be not disheartened, though your *love to the law* be so weak, interrupted, clouded, that sometimes you fear that you have no love at all. Do you not mourn over its coldness? Do you not desire to love? Seek to know more of the constraining influence of the love of Christ. If your chariot-wheels now, like those of the Egyptians, drive heavily, you will then move, like the chariots in the prophet's vision, " upon wheels and upon wings." (Comp. Ex. xiv. 25, with Ezek. i. 15, 23.) At least you are on the way to peace. Stir up the habit of diligent faith; be active—be more earnest in dependence on the Lord. Soon will he visit you with his cheering sunshine (Mal. iv. 2), and bless you with his heavenly *peace.* " The Lord is your shepherd :" and dwelling near the shepherd's tent, " you shall not want." (Ps. xxix. 11; lxxxv. 8 ; xxiii. 1.) Nothing comes to you without his appointment ; and whatever he takes away was only what he had first given, and leaves you nothing but to say—" Blessed be the name of the Lord !" (Job, i. 21.) Whatever he lays upon you is infinitely less than you deserve, and with the fatherly design " to do you good at the latter end." (Deut. viii. 16.) Whatever he gives you is peace, *great peace*—" *perfect peace*" (Isa. xxvi. 3): and though at best, *as to its actual enjoyment*, it is only a chequered gift, linked with " this world's tribulation " (John, xvi. 33) ; yet, as the earnest of that " peace into which the righteous shall enter, when taken away from the evil to come " (Isa. lvii. 1, 2), it is an incalculable blessing.

The stedfastness of our profession is a most important fruit of this blessing—*Nothing shall offend them.** The daily cross (Mark, x. 21, 22), the humbling doctrine (John, vi. 60, 65, 66), the fiery trial (Matt. xiii. 21)—which, by *offending the professor*, detect the unsoundness of his heart—

---

* ' To them is no stumbling-block.'—AINSWORTH.

these are the principles of strength and consolation to the faithful *lover of God's law.* Those " had no root in themselves," who were stumbled by " tribulation or persecution." (Mark, vi. 17.) Hence there was no *love* in their hearts ; consequently no *peace* in their experience, and no stability in their course. The frequency of such cases in a day of profession is a most painful subject of observation. A course of religion, commenced under the impulse of momentary excitement, is like a " reed shaken by the wind." The first breath of the storm beats down all resolutions, that were not formed upon the conviction of utter helplessness, and in entire dependence upon Divine grace. (Comp. John, xv. 5 ; 2 Cor. xii. 9.) Light without *love* ends in fearful ruin. (2 Thess. ii. 10–12.) Genuine *love to the law* alone keeps the soul—a love of no common character—a devoted, persevering attachment. The claim of the law is above every other. Every thing—even life itself—if need be—must be sacrificed for it. (Rev. xii. 11.) And when it has been thus embraced on a fair calculation of its cost, from a deep sense of its value, and with a spiritual perception of its character and application to our necessities—*there will be no stumbling-block.*

Indeed genuine love will prove our safeguard *against all grounds of offence.* The doctrine of the total depravity of man is objected to : but *love to the law of God,* moulding our minds into its heavenly impression—will remove all ground of offence. The pride of man's wisdom revolts from the doctrine of the cross, and the freeness of the grace of God. But we *love* it as a part of the *law* of faith. It suits our case. It answers our need, and therefore here also *nothing offends us.* Thus, whatever be the hindrance— whether from Satan or himself—whether from the enmity of the world, or the inconsistencies of the church—the believer, while he mourns over these things, is *not offended at* them, or at the Gospel through them. He has learned a more Scriptural standard, and to exercise a more discriminating judgment. *Love to the law of God* enables him, instead of being " tossed to and fro" in doubtful perplexity, to "make straight paths for his feet." (Heb. xii. 13, with Prov. iv. 25–27.) If his cross be grievous, he seeks from the Lord a quiet spirit ; and thus, " in patience possessing his soul," he finds " the yoke easy, and the burden light." (Luke, xxi. 19. Matt. xi. 30.) His difficulties exercise and strengthen his faith, and add fresh testimony to the faithfulness of the promise. Whether therefore his way be dark or light, his soul is at peace. In the enjoyment of his Saviour's love, he has the witness in his own heart, that " the work of righteousness"—of *love to the law of his God*— " shall be peace ; and the effect of righteousness quietness and assurance for ever." (Isa. xxxii. 17.)

166. *Lord, I have hoped for thy salvation, and done thy commandments.*

The *great peace* connected with *the love of God's law*, is at once the fruit of faith, and the motive of obedience. And the enjoyment of it leads the man of God to give renewed expression to his faith and devotedness. " Faith, which worketh by love" (Gal. v. 6), is no less the characteristic of the Old, than of the New Testament, Church. For mark here the principle and the object of faith—*I have hoped for thy salvation*—and the practical influence of faith —I have *done thy commandments.* " Walked not believers always in the same spirit ? Walked they not in the same steps ? "

Faith is the exercise of the soul in a sense of need, in desire, and in trust. Faith goes to God on the ground of the promise ; *hope* in the expectation of the thing promised. Thus *hope* implies the operation of faith. It appropriates to itself the object of faith. The power to take hold of the promises of faith, and to stay our souls upon their "ever-lasting consolation," is the energy of " a good hope through grace"—such as "maketh not ashamed." (2 Thess. ii. 16. Rom. v. 5.) Conscious unworthiness may give a trembling feebleness to the hand of faith ; but the feeblest apprehension of one of the least of the promises of the gospel assures us of our interest in them all. Why may we not set all the fulness of the covenant before the weakest as well as before the strongest believer, and proclaim to both with equal freedom the triumphant challenge—" *Who shall lay anything to the charge of God's elect?   Who is he that condemneth?*" (Rom. viii. 33, 34.)   Every believer is alike interested in the gospel of grace.   " There is no difference" *in the righteousness* of the gospel, which is " the righteousness of God"—nor in *the imputation* of it, which is " *unto all and upon all,*" nor *in the subjects*—which is *them that believe*—nor *in the means of its application*, which in all cases is " *by faith of Jesus Christ,*"—*nor in the need of the blessing*— "*All have sinned*" without difference.   All therefore are justified without difference. (Rom. iii. 22, 23.)   The only difference regards *the strength or weakness* of the faith, by which the righteousness is more or less distinctly appropriated, and its consequent blessings enjoyed.   No soul, however, can sink into perdition, that grasps the promise of Christ with the hand of faith, be that hand ever so weak and trembling ; though if the promise did not hold us more firmly by its unchangeableness, than we hold it by our faith, who could ever attain the blessing?

Not that our interest in the Gospel is transient or uncertain.   For though the perception of it may be often interrupted, yet is it not still in the Bible, in the covenant of God, in the heart of God?   And is it not constantly renewed in the exercise of faith?   The repetition of the same act of faith is therefore equally necessary every successive moment, as at the first moment of our spiritual life.   What-

ever be our standing in the Gospel, faith will always realize
to the end the same *hope for God's salvation.* Indeed the
neglect of the cultivation of its habitual exercise materially
weakens its operation in great emergencies. Let it then
be regarded as the breathing of the soul. Let it be constantly exercised in the daily occasions of need ; and we
shall enjoy its clear light and active influence upon occasions, where its special energy is required.

Now is not this sometimes your experience? You are
distressed by an unsuccessful struggle with wandering, defiling imaginations. You know the promise, and the remedy. But " the shield of faith" has been laid by. You
have therefore to seek it, when you want it at hand for the
present moment ; and thus you lie powerless, at a distance
from the cure, instead of being able to bring your sin at
once to Jesus—' Lord, this is my trouble ; this is the
" plague of my heart ;" " but speak the word only, and thy
servant shall be healed."' (Matt. viii. 8.)   Thus the indolent neglect of the quickening principle greatly impairs its
powerful energy, and the " confidence and rejoicing of hope"
(Heb. iii. 6, 14) flowing from it.   If " the life in the flesh
is" not " a life of faith on the Son of God," no solid rest or
acceptance can be known.

But on what ground is this *hope for the Lord's salvation*
built ?   On his faithfulness, not on our sincerity ; on his
promises, not on our frames ; on his unchangeableness, not
on our constancy. (Heb. vi. 17, 18.)   It is built, not on
the work of grace in us, but on the work of Christ for us ;
a work which has satisfied every claim, provided every security, and pledged all the Divine perfections on our behalf ;
a work so finished and complete, that all the difficulties of
salvation on the part of God are removed ; and the sinner,
finding no hindrance in the way *but himself,* is warranted,
though covered with guilt and defilement, to apply for full,

immediate, and unconditional forgiveness. What then hinders the instant reception of the privilege, but disbelief of the record? It is this which dares to "make God a liar" (1 John, v. 10); which therefore must not, as is too often the case, be lamented as an infirmity (except indeed in cases of constitutional weakness); but watched, prayed against, and resisted, as a deep and aggravated sin. The present enjoyment of the blessing is indeed often marred by looking at *the fruits of faith* (contrition, love, diligence, &c.) as prerequisites for believing, instead of looking *to the object of faith*, to put away our sin, and to produce these fruits in us. *This* not only binds our sin upon us, but robs God of his honour; and, whilst it restrains his blessing on our souls, reflects upon his wisdom and grace, who has laid the foundation of a sinner's hope on his own dear Son (Isa. xxviii. 16), irrespective of any warrant of faith in himself. We want to be enlivened with sensible comfort, *as a ground for our believing in Christ;* or, if we look for it from faith, it is from faith *as an act* (in which respect it is no more a proper ground for comfort than any other grace,) instead of looking for it *from the object of faith.* Thus we not only lose the peace and joy we are seeking, but we lose it by our mistaken way of seeking it.

The fulness of Christ, and the promises of God in him, are the only basis of a full assurance of salvation : and *this* basis is equally firm at all times, and under all circumstances. *"Ye are complete in him."* (Col. ii. 10.) Your title at this moment is as perfect, your interest as secure, as ever it will be at the day of *" the redemption of the purchased possession."* (Eph. i. 14.) Awakened sinner! let not then a sense of unworthiness paralyze your faith. As a guilty sinner, you are invited. As a willing sinner, you are welcome. As a believing sinner, you are assured. Why hesitate then to " lay hold on eternal life?" Is it presumption in

the drowning man to attempt to swim to the rock of safety?
Why then should not the sinking soul cast itself upon the
" Rock of Ages?" *Lord, I have hoped for thy salvation.*
Believer! " Behold!" saith your Lord, " I come quickly;
hold that fast which thou hast, that no man take thy crown."
" Hold fast your confidence and the rejoicing of your hope."
(Rev. iii. 11. Heb. iii. 6.) This is of no trifling importance.
An established confidence ought to result from, and to witness to, your interest in the Lord's salvation.* For without it, you have no relief from the spirit of bondage; no
enlargement in duties; no enjoyment of privileges; no
" growth in grace, and in the knowledge of the Saviour;"
no honoured usefulness in the Church of God. " The things
which remain will be ready to die." (Rev. iii. 2.) Rest not,
then, satisfied with an occasional gleam of light and joy,
while your horizon is overcast with doubts and fears.
Waste not time in heartless complaints, that would be far
better employed in a vigorous habit of faith. Live above
frames and feelings, upon this glorious truth—' *Christ has
undertaken for me.*' He lives, and reigns, and pleads for
every sinner that trusts in him. Exercise your dependence
upon him in importunate and persevering supplication.
" Give all diligence"—at all times—in all ways, private
and public—" instant in season and out of season." Thus
" an entrance into" the joy, peace, and glory of " the everlasting kingdom of our Lord and Saviour, will be richly
ministered unto you." (2 Pet. i. 5–11.) You shall be re-
leased from the prison-house of despondency, and shall
breathe the free atmosphere of adoption and heavenly
love.

But remember, that this " assurance of hope," even in
its weakest and lowest influence, is a practical principle—
I have done thy commandments. Every man that hath this

* See Heb. iii. 6. Whose house are we—*if we,* &c. ib. 14.

hope in him purifieth himself, even as he is pure." (1 John, iii. 3.) All obedience that springs not from this source is of a low and legal character; the fruit of self-will, self-righteousness, self-sufficiency. Evangelical obedience can only flow from Evangelical faith and hope. Love to Christ catches fire from the perception of his love to us. Without this perception, all is weariness, toil, and travail of soul in his service; duty, not privilege; constraint, not delight; conscience, not love. Hence the most assured believers will be the most devoted servants of their Master. "The joy of the Lord"—"the joy of faith," of acceptance, of communion—"is their strength." (Neh. viii. 10.) They live by faith; and as they believe, they love; they deny themselves; they lay themselves out for their Master's work; they conquer all that opposes their progress.

We cannot, therefore, *do his commandments* without *a hope for his salvation.* For only in proportion as we have assured our title to the promises of the Gospel, can we take hold of them, plead them, or experience their support. When therefore our hope is indistinct, we are almost left to our own unassisted resources; and our course will probably end in "perpetual backsliding." *Active devotedness flows from assured acceptance.* (See 1 Cor. xv. 58.) Where there is no certainty, there can be little love, little delight, little diligence. Let us walk in sunshine, and we shall work cheerfully and honourably for God. (Comp. Isa. vi. 6–8.)

Keep then the eye fixed on Christ as *the ground*, and on obedience as *the evidence*, of our *hope*. Thus will our own confidence be more established; and others, beholding in us the power of our Christian hope, will be led to say —"We will go with you, for we have heard that God is with you."*

* Zech. viii. 23. We conclude with giving a full and Scriptural view of the principles and character of Christian assurance. *That*

167. *My soul hath kept thy testimonies; and I love them exceedingly.* 168. *I have kept thy precepts and thy testimonies: for all my ways are before thee.*

Those only who have *hoped in the Lord's salvation* can express this joyful delight in his *precepts.* The Christian

a full sense of acceptance with God grounded upon the Divine testimonies is attainable—there can be no doubt. The "covenant ordered in all things and sure"—(2 Sam. xxiii. 5) offers ample warrant for the most assured confidence. The promises of this covenant are full, free, multiplied; adapted to all possible diversity of cases; attested by the oath and seal of God for this declared end—"the full assurance of hope," and the "strong consolation" of his people. (Heb. vi. 11–18.) The instructions of our Lord and his Apostles had the same blessed purpose in view. (John, xv. 11; xvi. 33. 1 John, v. 13.) The design and efficacy of his atonement, as contrasted with the weakness of legal services, was, to make his people "perfect *as pertaining to the conscience.*" (Heb. ix. 9; with x. 14.) Under both dispensations has this sense of appropriation and conscious security been maintained. (Job, xix. 25. Ps. xviii. 1. Cant. ii. 16; vii. 10; with 2 Tim. i. 12. 1 John, iv. 16; v. 19, 20.) Its basis is ground common to all. (Rom. viii. 35, 38, 39; with 31–34.) The want of it is evidently reproved. (2 Cor. xiii. 5.) Exhortations are given to press forward to it. (Heb. vi. 11. 2 Pet. i. 10.) *Faith* (Eph. i. 13. Heb. vi. 17, 18), *Obedience* (Isa. xxxii. 17; xlviii. 17, 18; lxiv. 5. John, xiv. 21–23. 1 John, ii. 3–5; iii. 24), *The fear of God* (Ps. xxv. 14), *Love* (1 John, iii. 14, 18–21; iv. 12), *Diligence* (Heb. vi. 11. 2 Pet. i. 5–11), *Perseverance* (Hos. vi. 3), *on our part, Affliction* (Zech. xiii. 9), *The gift of the Spirit* (Rom. viii. 16. 1 John, iii. 24; iv. 13) *on God's part*—are the means of its attainment. *Active devotedness* (Isa. vi. 1–8), *Support in temptation* (Job, xix. 21–25), *in suffering* (2 Tim. i. 12), and *in the prospect of eternity* (2 Cor. v. 1. 2 Tim. iv. 6–8), are its blessed results.

It is evidently, therefore, our Father's will, that his children's complete acceptance should not be with them a matter of present uncertainty. He intends, not only that they should reach heaven at last, but that heaven should commence on earth in a state of conscious security and peace; not only that *they should have eternal life, but that they should know that they have it.* (1 John, v. 13.) The does not acknowledge the popular separation of duty and privilege, according as it may be constraint or indulgence to his inclination.   Every part of his walk identifies these

gospel, instead of forbidding this privilege, warrants, produces, and establishes it; for the conviction of the professor, the excitement of the slumbering, and the encouragement of the weak.

Yet we must not so identify assurance with faith, as to conclude all that are destitute of it to be unbelievers. It springs indeed from faith, and can grow upon no other root. All the practical principles connected with it are the fruits of faith. "The promise of the Spirit," by whom the privilege is applied, "is received by faith." (Gal. iii. 14.)   The want of assurance also is, in fact, a want of faith.   It is the soul seeking "confidence in the flesh," instead of "rejoicing in Christ Jesus."   The revolting view of its own sin, *unconnected with the covering of the atonement*, produces despondency instead of assurance.   Whereas, on the other hand, a clear apprehension of the doctrines of the Gospel is always a ground for the exercise of faith, and a means of establishing Christian confidence.

And yet, unless we separate between *the principle* and *the conscious interest in the objects* of faith, we shall, in a spirit of evangelical self-righteousness, rest our salvation, not upon faith as a means of laying hold of Christ, but upon some feeling or sensation of our own mind.   Besides, the Old Testament saints occasionally lost their *consciousness of the Divine favour*—that is, *their assurance* (Job, xiii. 24; xix. 11. Ps. xiii. 1; xxxi. 22; lxxvii. 7–9; lxxxviii. 7, 14–16): while "the root of the matter,"—*the root of faith*—was still "in them."   With the disciples, while they were engrafted *by faith*, as living branches of the true vine, *the privilege of assurance was prospective*. (John, xv. 1–5; with xiv. 20.)   Faith, as a means of salvation, does not seem *necessarily* to imply an *appropriating interest in the Gospel*. (John, i. 49, 50. Acts, viii. 37. Rom. x. 9. 1 John, v. 1.)   The Apostles exhort *to assurance* those "who had obtained like precious faith with them." (2 Pet. i. 1–10.)   They write to *sincere believers, that they might be assured believers;* plainly distinguishing between *believing unto life* and "*knowing that we have life;*" and defining assurance to be rather the *strengthened exercise, than the essential principle, of faith*. (1 John, v. 13.)   They separate again between faith as *the result of hearing*, and the sealing of the Spirit, i. e. *assurance—as the consequence of faith* (Eph. i. 13); as also between "*the things that are freely given to us of God*," and *our knowledge or perception of them by the Spirit of God*. (1 Cor. ii. 12.)

terms of distinction. If it is his *duty*, it is no less his *privilege*, to *love the precepts*. Nothing holds him to them —nothing enables him thoroughly *to keep them*, but love.

And is our knowledge of these free gifts always distinct? Have we no part in them, till we have fully cleared up our interest in them? And does the right of the heir depend upon his consciousness of the validity of his title? The "command" *instantly* to "believe on the name of Jesus Christ," is indeed as binding upon us all, as any part of the Decalogue. (John, vi. 28, 29. 1 John, iii. 23.) But as faith is the means *of obtaining forgiveness* (Acts, x. 43; xiii. 38, 39; xxvi. 18) —if it be supposed to imply a *persuasion of forgiveness*, it would involve the absurdity of believing *that we are accepted, that we may be accepted*. Thus forgiveness would be made to precede faith, instead of being the result of it. Again—as faith is the instrument by which we are engrafted into Christ (John, xv. 4), and brought into this state of acceptance, we must have faith, before we can be in this state—consequently before we can *have assurance that we are in it.* Faith therefore must be supposed separable from, and antecedent to, assurance. Thus also—if assurance be correctly defined—"*knowing whom we have believed*" (2 Tim. i. 12)—consciousness supposes the previous exercise of faith on its object—that is—faith preceding assurance.

Nor do many of the exercises of faith recorded in the Gospels exhibit distinct marks of assurance. Sense of need, desire, use of the appointed means, and a spirit of dependence, mainly characterized the applicants for the Saviour's mercy. Doubts of his willingness (Matt. viii. 2, 3) or his ability (Mark, ix. 22) often mingled themselves with the sincere workings of faith. Our Lord himself seemed to consider the centurion's case as an exception. (Matt. viii. 8–10.) Seldom did dependence amount to *certainty;* and *appropriation* was generally rather the result than the principle of the application.

"The assurance of faith"—as it properly respects a *dependence upon the record*—is indeed the essential principle of Christian life. But "the assurance of hope"—*a conscious interest in the record—the real privilege of assurance*—seems to be a distinct and separable idea. The truth of the record—"*Him that cometh unto me* I will in no wise cast out"—may be implicitly received; yet a consciousness of coming or having come, may be much obscured by negligence, self-righteousness, indistinct perception of the acts of faith, or the power of unbelief in some of its various forms. Consequently, there will

All resolutions, vows, covenants, would be as ineffectual to bind him, as the green withs to fasten the giant. (Judg. xvi. 7–9.) David had not *done the commandments* from

be doubt of an interest in the record—*a want of assurance.* For the Bible is not the "Lamb's book of life," the register of the elect of God. No man can, therefore, bring from thence a direct testimony for his personal salvation. His character, not his name, is in the record. The declaration is—" He *that believeth*" not *any particular individual mentioned by name*—" shall be saved." No man is commanded in the first instance to believe that Christ died for him *individually*, but for such as he is—for the unworthy, the guilty, the condemned, the perishing. This is the warrant of his own application, the event of which will—*ultimately, if not immediately*—be appropriation and assurance.

We are deeply convinced, that a lowered exhibition of this precious doctrine and inestimable privilege has greatly deteriorated the standard of Evangelical religion. The objections against it are founded in ignorance or misconception. Instead of *savouring of presumption*, it is the very principle of humility. It is the reception of the Divine testimony without *reasoning or disputation*. Whereas doubting may be justly considered (to use an anomalous term) *proud humility.* For does not the doubt on account of our unworthiness, imply a secret dependence on worthiness as a ground of acceptance? Nor again does assurance militate against the influence of godly fear, which was never meant to impair the certainty of our faith, but to guard us against carnal security and self-confidence. We work out our salvation " with *fear and trembling*," *upon the ground of assurance*—that is—upon the appropriating confidence in God " *working all our works in us.*" (Phil. ii. 12, 13. Isa. xxvi. 12.) The assured hope of the gospel is the *principle*, not the hindrance, of godly fear. (Heb. xii. 28.) Indeed we must consider this doctrine, scripturally stated, to be the life of present privilege, and the spring of practical devotedness. Where, therefore, it is defectively set forth, or scarcely set forth at all, or guarded with an over-anxious care against abuse; the privilege is but little known, and the springs of active love are weak and uncertain. And thus believers too often, in a languid and highly sinful state of unbelief, acquiesce in a feeble exercise of this vital principle, indolently yielding up all effort for a vigorous and healthy habit of faith. They go about their duties, like an expiring person about his work; agitated about the business of the moment; while the desirableness of health and strength, the Physician and constraint ; but *his soul kept them;* yea, he *loved them exceedingly.* (Verses 48, 97, 127.) Indeed, the bias of the new nature to *keep the precepts* is as prevalent, as that of

the remedy, are given up in despondency. Their case is perfectly recoverable by due attention to the appointed means, and to the real nature and symptoms of their disease. Yet they sit down to the miserable and degrading conclusion, that their powers are paralyzed; and though they may preserve the notion of spiritual life, and the hope of salvation at last; yet they think they must be content to be feeble, comfortless, and unprofitable.

Much injury has also arisen from restricting this privilege to a higher order of Christians, or to a more full maturity of Christian experience. Many defraud themselves of the sure and warranted comfort of the gospel, by not aiming at a more simple dependence upon the record. They acknowledge confidence to be their duty, and they look forward to some indefinitely future day, when they shall enjoy it as their happiness. But does not the apostle place this privilege at the very threshold of the gospel, when he wrote to " little children—because their sins were forgiven them for Christ's name's sake?" (1 John, ii. 12.) And ought we not, after the inspired pattern, to " desire every one to give diligence," in pressing towards this mark? (Heb. vi. 11, 12.) It is undoubtedly the equal and common right of every member of the family—the youngest as well as the oldest—according to the terms of the covenant of grace. Unbelief, sloth, or backsliding, may for a while preclude the enjoyment of it. But our gracious Lord has linked it to the first, no less than to the latter, exercises of faith; to its most trembling, as well as its most collected, act. (Acts, xiii. 38, 39.) Indeed the first genuine act of faith is at least as strenuous as any subsequent act; and perseverance in this act, where the hand is trembling, is often the characteristic of the greatest decision, courage, and maturity. Nothing therefore stands in the way of our consolation, if we do not " beguile" ourselves " of our reward by a voluntary humility." Nothing shall exclude us, if we do not exclude ourselves.

Serious errors, however, prevail as to the nature and ground of this privilege. Not unfrequently is it identified with warm and sensible excitement, connected at least as much with the bodily as the spiritual temperament, and of course subject to all the variations of this temperament. Now this is the assurance of feeling. The true blessing is the assurance of faith, often without, and even in despite of, feeling. (Job, xiii. 15. Isa. l. 10.) The Christian confidence is—

the old nature to break them. Once the believer would have wished the law of God blotted out of the universe, or at least exchanged for a more indulgent dispensation. But

" I know"—not what I feel—or what I have felt, but—" whom I have believed." (2 Tim. i. 12.) It is grounded, not upon spiritual sensation within, but upon the person, work, and office of the Saviour set out in the testimony. (Heb. x. 19–22.) Grounded upon this rock—unlike its counterfeit, its influence is steady and powerfully effective. We would not indeed have a religion without feelings. The glow of the affections is the choicest joy of life. But a religion grounded upon feeling, is a religion of delusion. And the intelligent, self-observant Christian learns to distrust his feelings, the more they are excited. Else will they " corrupt" him insensibly "from the simplicity that is in Christ" into a subtle spiritual self-righteousness.

Perhaps also another mistake in the nature of assurance may sometimes obscure the apprehension. The sincere Christian, intent solely on " working out his salvation," feels a repugnance to any doctrine, which, but in appearance, seems contradictory to this unquestionable and constant duty. He does not clearly apprehend the distinct views, which we ought always to maintain, of the Saviour and of ourselves in the great business. Hence he feels an inconsistency between a due and abiding sense of his utter weakness and unworthiness, and between being " strong in the Lord," and accepted in his love. He does not realize the connexion between self-distrust and rejoicing confidence in the Lord. But he who was most bold in the expression of his own personal assurance, was not less clear in the acknowledgment of his weakness and liability to fall, except as the Lord kept him humble, diligent, and persevering. (2 Tim. i. 12 ; with 1 Cor. ix. 27.)

Upon the whole then it appears, that all should be exhorted to assurance ; nor should the youngest be satisfied without the attainment of it. Many realize it at a very early stage of experience. And where they fall short of it, it is not from defect in the object, or in the warrant, but in the mean. It is offered to all. All are invited to it. And were it not for the obstacles I have mentioned, most would attain it in greater degree, and at an earlier period. But too often the testimony—*which is the sole ground of the privilege*—is not received and appropriated with that simplicity, which brings with it "joy and peace in believing." (See Acts, viii. 5, 8, 39; xvi. 31–34; 1 Thess. i. 6.)

now that it is written in his heart, even its restraint is delightful to him ; and as he gains a closer intimacy with it, and a clearer discernment of its spirituality, he *loves it*

We cannot, however, absolutely identify faith and assurance. Adoption into the family of God " by faith" (Gal. iii. 26) does not, as we conceive, depend upon, nor is it in all cases connected with, consciousness of this relation. A child may be fully assured of his interest in the family, and title to the patrimony. But while an infant—when his relation and interest were as complete as at any subsequent period—he had no such consciousness. And thus many of the dear children of God have no consciousness that they are so; yet they cry, they long, they walk, or they try to walk, as children; and so they evince that they are children. Or, (to use another illustration) we may have light sufficient to distinguish objects, and to guide us on our way: while yet we do not see clearly, and therefore cannot possibly be conscious that we see clearly. What judgment, we may also ask, must we form of those distressing cases of constitutional infirmity, the characteristic of which is, not so much positive unbelief, (though the symptoms may present a mixture of this principle) as a want of mental power (often sudden and unaccountable), to apprehend the objects of faith in any distinct gospel relation? They cannot be seen in their true light and bearing. The spiritual optics, though not destroyed, are greatly obscured; so that the eye of sense and natural conscience fills the retina of contemplation with its own false views. This is a very different case from spiritual indolence, or want of laboriously distinct statement— that is—where the view of the elementary materials is clear, and wants only the exercise of industry in the arrangements of them. This is the state of a person in a swoon, not of a corpse. The principle of life is not extinct, though the consciousness of it is wholly wanting, and may continue so for some time.

If, again, assurance be the essential principle of faith, then faith can never be conceived in an imperfect state, or connected with any variation of growth or declension, or of spiritual intelligence. All that are destitute of it, must also be in a state of unbelief. We have therefore to account for the strange anomaly of unbelievers, " knowing the plague of their own hearts," hating sin, separate from the world, and renewed in heart, temper, life, and conduct. For such unquestionably, are many, who, though kept in bondage by their doubts and fears, and far from having attained a conscious interest in Christ, are yet (upon this supposition) bringing forth the fruits of faith upon the root of unbelief! Is not this a stumbling to the *exceedingly.* Not one, indeed, of the *precepts or testimonies* does he *keep* as he ought, and as he desires ; but there is not one of them that he does not delight in, and most anxiously desire to fulfil. Thus every feature of the Divine image is inwrought in the soul, beautiful in its place and proportion ; and all other graces grow in connexion with *love to the testimonies.*

Nor let our consciousness of daily failures restrain this strong expression of confidence. The most humble believer need not hesitate to adopt it ' as an evidence of grace, not as a claim of merit.'* This frequent repetition† marks the godly jealousy of the man of God, mindful of his own self-deceitfulness and manifold infirmi-

unconverted? Is it not rather "despising" than cherishing "the day of small things?" Is it not breaking rather than binding up the "bruised reed?" Let us pray for faith to receive and to exhibit "the fulness of the blessing," "the high calling," and consequent responsibilities ; but let us not shut the "little ones" out of the camp. Like Jacob of old, and after the pattern of a more wise and tender shepherd than he, we must "gently lead those that are with young." (Gen. xxxiii. 13, 14. Isa. xl. 11.)

The Scripture seems therefore fully to warrant the distinction prevalent among the Puritan divines—that assurance is ' necessary to the Christian—for his well-being, not for his being;' for his consolation and establishment, not for his salvation. For our own part—though we would not scruple to say—" He that believeth not shall be damned" (Mark, xvi. 16), we dare not say,—' He that is not assured shall be damned.' There can indeed be no peace without some conscious liberty to call God our own. And to be satisfied without the exercise of freedom, is alike to rob God and ourselves.

Yet let not the trembling believer conclude too hastily against himself from the want of this assurance. Diligence and dependence will ensure the blessing. Let him remember, when he prays for stronger faith, to act the faith that is given, and expect the strength to be vouchsafed, not in yielding to the natural impossibility, but in the endeavour to believe. (See Mark, iii. 1–5.) In this practical "obedience of faith," ere long will he record his profession of confidence—" I know whom I have believed." (2 Tim. i. 12.)

* Bishop Horne.
† Thrice in these three successive verses.

ties, and "giving" careful "diligence to make his calling and election sure." (2 Pet. i. 5–10.) David knew himself to be a poor sinner ; but he was conscious of spirituality of obedience, *exceeding love* to the word, and an habitual walk under the eye of his God — the evidences of a heart (often mentioned in the Old Testament*) "perfect with him." ' Christ alone kept the old law, and he enables us to observe the new.'†

The active love to the word should be cultivated on the principle of our public walk before God. We must not study the Scripture merely for our present gratification, or to furnish materials for our Christian intercourse. We ought rather, from every step in the history of Christ, as well as from the more finished course of instruction in the Epistles, to be gathering some help to " set the Lord always before us" (Ps. xvi. 8)—realizing the interest that he takes in us, and his presence with us as our Father, Governor, Teacher, Comforter, Friend.

Now, let us ask — Do our *souls* thus *keep the Lord's testimonies* habitually, perseveringly? Does conscience testify that, with all our defects and sinful mixture, they are uppermost in our minds ; that our love rises above the worldly rules of expediency, prudence, or the example of those around us (the too common measurement of scanty obedience)—as if it could never burn with sufficient fervour in his service, " who loved us, and gave himself for us?" (Gal. ii. 20.) Why, then, should we shrink from

---

* Compare verse 1. Margin; 2 Chron. xv. 17; xvi. 9; 2 Kings, xx. 3. The import of the term is limited and explained by the word "upright" united with it. (Job, i. 8. Ps. xxxvii. 37.) The Scripture use of the word perhaps refers rather to our desires than our attainments (Comp. Phil. iii. 13–15), and in general seems to mark Christian maturity, as contrasted with the weakness of the babe, and the inexperience of the young man in Christ. (Comp. the use of the same word τελειος in 1 Cor. ii. 6; xiv. 20. Heb. v. 14.)

† Bishop Horne.

this acknowledgment of " simplicity and godly sincerity?"
If we are ready to own, that " without Christ we can do
nothing ;" that his Spirit " has wrought all our works in
us" (Isa. xxvi. 12, with John, xv. 5) ; that " by the grace of
God we are what we are" (1 Cor. xv. 10) ; that our hope of
acceptance is *grounded only* upon the finished work on the
cross—why should we refuse to confess the grace of God
in us ?   Yet we must not forget, that allowed unfaithfulness, neglect of secret prayer, impurity of motive, or any
" iniquity regarded in the heart"—though they will not
loosen the ground of our hope—will obscure the comfort
of our Christian confidence.   How beautiful is that princely
spirit, which will not serve the Lord " of that which doth
cost us nothing" (2 Sam. xxiv. 24) ; that not only longs
for holiness as the way to heaven, but loves heaven the
better for the holy way that leads to it, and for the perfect
holiness that reigns there eternally !

But never let us lose sight of the recollection, that *all
our ways are before God!* that every act, every thought,
every desire, every word, is registered by conscience as his
viceregent, and laid up in his book of remembrance !   Well
would it be for us, if we walked less before men, and more
before God; if in secret, in business, at home and abroad,
we heard the solemn voice—"*I am the Almighty God:
walk before me, and be thou perfect.*" (Gen. xvii. 1.)   We
may be unreproveable in the sight of men, while it is a
mere artificial walk, grounded upon base external principles—a " walking after the flesh"—not *before God.*
Even the engagements of active duty may be the subtle
snare of the great enemy to divert us from intense personal religion, and to spoil the hidden walk of communion
with God, by concentrating the mind upon a more public,
and, apparently, a more useful walk.   Thus too often the
vital principle of religion sinks into a stated formal habit.
" Walking with God" (Gen. v. 24 ; vi. 9) is the secret

spring of the Christian. "Walking before God" is the manifestation and the exercise of the hidden principle. For in all things, private as well as public, the most trivial as well as the most weighty, to have our eye fixed in dutiful reverence upon the Omniscient, Omnipresent eye of Jehovah—what solemnity would it give to our whole behaviour! what influence would it have upon our public professions, our general conversation, our secret duties! We should be energetic in "serving our own generation by the will of God" (Acts, xiii. 36); and yet, while walking before men, should be truly "walking before God"— *all our ways before him,* "done" in his sight, "as to him" (Eph. vi. 7), and accepted in his favour.

When, therefore, I am about to venture upon any line of conduct, let me consider the watchful eye, that pierces into the deepest recesses of my thoughts, and brings, as it were, to daylight, my principles, my motives, and my ends. Above all, let me ever recollect, that he, *before whom are all my ways,* is he that hung upon the cross for my sins. Let me then walk, as if he were standing before me in all the endearing obligations of his love. Oh, do not I owe him sacrifice for sacrifice, heart for heart, life for life? Then surely I cannot be dead, insensible, sluggish in *keeping his precepts.* I cannot forbear to show this practical proof of my love to him. (John, xiv. 15.) Let not, then, the fear of legality make me neglect this privilege of "keeping the commandments" of my beloved Master and Lord. Let me live under the solemn recollection— "Thou, God, seest me" (Gen. xvi. 13, with John, i. 48); and in the joyful assurance—"Thou, God, lovest me" (Jer. xxxi. 3, with John, xiii. 1); and his ways will be to me holiness, happiness, heaven.

PART XXII.

169. *Let my cry come near before thee, O Lord; give me
understanding, according to thy word.* 170. *Let my
supplication come before thee: deliver me according to
thy word.*

WE mark David here, where he always loved to be, a sup-
plicant at the throne of grace. Many had been his *cries
and. supplications.* His petition now is—that they may
come near before his Lord. Oh, that our wants of every
moment were felt with the same pressure, and carried to
the Lord with the same faith, earnestness, humility, and
perseverance! Richness of expression, and fluency of
utterance, are the mere shell and shadow of prayer. The
life of prayer is the *cry* of the heart to God. The eloquence of prayer is its earnestness. The power of prayer
is that, which cometh not from education, or from the
natural desire of the man ; but that " which is from above"
—" the spirit of supplication"—" the spirit of adoption."
The urgency of present need calls for instant prayer. The
soul is at stake ; the enemy is within the walls, perhaps
within the citadel. Oh, what a privilege to know, that we
have a " strong habitation, whereunto we may continually
resort ;" to be able to remind the Lord—" *Thou hast given
commandment to save me : for thou art my rock and my for-
tress !*" (Ps. lxxi. 3.)

But then we must see that our *cry comes before*—*comes
near before*—*the Lord;* that nothing blocks up the way, or
interrupts the communication. If we are believers, the

way is open : " the middle wall of partition is broken
down." Oh, let us be excited to greater nearness of communion — " Having boldness to enter into the holiest by
the blood of Jesus, by a new and living way, which he hath
consecrated for us, through the veil, that is to say, his
flesh." (Heb. x. 19, 20), why should we be backward to
come? Had we not seen the way marked by this blood of
sprinkling, we should (if we have had any sight into our own
hearts) no more have dared to take one step into the awful
presence of God, than to rush into the devouring flame.
If in a moment of extremity, we had felt that we must
pray or perish, we should have had no boldness to open our
mouth before God, much less to expect that our *supplication would come near before him*, had we not been " made
nigh by the blood of Christ." (Eph. ii. 13.) But what an
amount of privilege is it, that this way to God is always
open ; that, as members of Christ, we stand in the sight
of God as pure as Christ is pure ; that we have not only
" access," but " *access with confidence ;*" * — yea, with the
same confidence as the Son of God himself! For the
Father is never weary of delighting in his dear Son, or in
those who are one with him. If he, therefore, takes our
names into the holy place ; if he offer sacrifice and incense
for us, and sprinkle us with his blood, we " are complete in
him" (Col. ii. 10)—" in him," therefore, let us " glory."
(Isa. xlv. 25.) " Having an High-priest over the house
of God ; let us draw near with a true heart, in full assurance of faith." (Heb. x. 21, 22.)

But where we feel as if we did not, could not, reach the
throne of grace, " is there not a cause?" Our distance
from God must be traced to a deeper origin than the
dulness and insensibility of our hearts. The real difficulty
of prayer, and indeed the actual inability to pray, arises in

---

* Eph. iii. 12. Esther had " access" to the King—but not
" with confidence."—iv. 16.

many, and probably in most, cases, from an indistinct perception of the way of access. We must admit this, not only in those who are totally ignorant of Christ, but also in the cases of weak, unestablished, or negligent Christians. Through ignorance of the fulness and freeness of the gospel in the one, and indulgence of sin or secret unwatchfulness in the other, the way of access (only perceptible by the eye of faith) becomes obscured, the desire faint, the spiritual strength weakened. And instead of the acknowledgment —" The Lord hath heard the voice of my supplications" (Ps. vi. 9), we have the mournful complaints—" My soul cleaveth to the dust—oh, that I were as in months past!" (Verse 25. Job, xxix. 2.) It must be so ; for prayer without faith is a heartless ceremony in the spirit of bondage. That which gives to it life and acceptance is the believing apprehension of Christ. (Heb. iv. 14–16 ; x. 19–22.) The ignorant and self-righteous may find it a matter of course (as easy as it is fruitless) to bow their knee in the form of prayer. But the light that darts in upon the awakened conscience reveals something hitherto unknown of God and of themselves, and shows the ground of confidence, for a self-condemned sinner, to be a matter of the deepest mystery, and most amazing difficulty. Such a confidence, however, God has laid open to us. We cannot honour him more than by making use of it. All that come in the name of Jesus are welcome. Why, then, penitent sinner, should not you be welcome ? The throne of grace was raised for sinners such as you. You cannot want larger promises or a better plea. You come, not because you are worthy, but because you are bid, to come. Take the command and lay it upon your conscience. Christ is your only way to God. Faith is the act and exercise of coming to Christ. Faith, therefore, will bring you to God, if you have not hitherto come ; or restore you to God, if you have wandered from him.

But there may be a secret departure from God even in
the engagement of active service, or in the exercises of
social religion. For if these duties are substituted for
secret communion with God, " the things that remain in
us will be ready to die" (Rev. iii. 2) ; ordinances will fail
to enrich ; Christian fellowship will bring no refreshment ;
and the soul, while blessed with the abundance of means
of grace, " in the fulness of its sufficiency will be in straits."
(Job, xx. 22.) Indeed, if our affections and feelings are
moved in social exercises, and are cold and insensible when
we are alone with God, it is a bad symptom of our state.
What, then, do we know of the comforts of the closet?
Do we pray, because we love to pray, or only because our
consciences constrain us to the duty?   Does the Lord
mark those secret transactions with himself, that manifest
our hearts to be really drawn to him ?   Is it any pressing
business of our soul's salvation that brings us to God?
Are our services enlivened with spiritual manifestations of
Christ? It is possible long to continue in the outward
course of duty : and yet not one of *our* prayers to *come near
before the Lord*.   We have not come in the appointed way ;
and, therefore, we have not really come at all.   Or if the
name of Christ has been affixed to our prayers, it has been
as a component part of a formal system, not as an exercise
of dependence in seeking acceptance with God.

But it may be, that we have backslidden from God, in
a habit of indulged coldness or wilful iniquity.   Now if
we would expect " the candle of the Lord again to shine
upon our heads, and his secret to be upon our tabernacle"
(Job, xxix. 3, 4), we must rest satisfied with nothing short
of the full restoration of our privileges.   We must return
to the Lord with deepened contrition in his appointed way,
and wait for him to look upon us, and once more to *let our
supplication come near before him*.   He had " gone, and returned to his place, till we acknowledged our offence, and

sought his face" (Hos. v. 15); and he is now sitting on a "throne of grace, waiting that he may be gracious." (Isa. xxx. 18.) Again and again, therefore, let us fall down at his feet, and never cease to pray, until we feel that our *cry and supplication come near before him*, and spiritual *understanding of our case, and deliverance* from our danger, are vouchsafed. As a God of wisdom and yearning mercy, we may trust him to "perform all things for us." (Ps. lvii. 2.) Let him then judge for the time and means of our *deliverance*. Only let it be *according to his own word* of faithfulness, and we "shall yet praise him." (Ps. xlii. 11.)

It is beautiful to observe the oil of the Psalmist's faith feeding the flame of his supplication. Every petition is urged upon the warrant of a promise—*according to thy word.* The promises were the very breath of his supplication; exciting his expectation for a favourable answer, and exercising his patience, until the answer should come. Though in possession of so comparatively small a portion of the blessed book, he seemed always to find a word for the present occasion; always able to show to his God his own hand and seal. Alas! sometimes, with the whole word of God before us, we are at a loss to appropriate one of its innumerable promises to the present emergency. Yet with all our contracted views of the covenant, still our interest in it is not denied. Such is the condescension of our tender Father, that he accepts even the stammering language of faith in his children! The cry "Abba, Father"—'though' (as Luther sweetly expresses it) 'it is but a cry; yet it doth so pierce the clouds, that there is nothing else heard in heaven of God and his angels.'* And how delightful is

* Luther on Gal. iv. 6. And again—'This little word, Father, conceived effectually in the heart, passeth all the eloquence of Demosthenes, Cicero, and of the most eloquent rhetoricians that ever were in the world. This matter is not expressed with words, but with groanings; which groanings cannot be uttered with any words of eloquence, for no tongue can express them.'

the thought that God's elect—as they will shortly be
gathered a countless multitude around the heavenly throne
(Rev. vii. 9)—so do they now hold spiritual communion
with each other, while " they cry day and night" (Luke,
xviii. 7) before their Father's throne of grace! True it is
—we understand not one another's tongues. Yet does our
loving Father understand us all. Nor do our different
dialects cause any confusion in heaven—rather do they
unite, and form one cloud of incense, ascending with continual acceptance and delight in his presence. Ineffable is
the delight, with which our Beloved enjoys that communion
with his people, " which he purchased with his own blood"
—" O my dove, that art in the clefts of the rocks, in the
secret places of the stairs, *let me see thy countenance, let me
hear thy voice; for sweet is thy voice, and thy countenance is
comely.*" (Cant. ii. 14, also iv. 11.)

171. *My lips shall utter praise, when thou hast taught me thy
statutes.*

How happy is it to bring to God a heart as large in
praise as in prayer! The answer of the supplication for
spiritual understanding and deliverance naturally issues in
the sacrifice of praise. Guilt had sealed David's lips;
while living in sin, and restrained alike the utterance of
praise and prayer. But when awakened to a sense of his
sin, how earnest were his cries!—" Restore unto me the
joy of thy salvation. O Lord, open thou my lips; and
my mouth shall show forth thy praise." (Ps. li. 12, 15.)
And if guilt or unbelief has made us dumb, his petitions
will tune our hearts to the " songs of Zion." When *the
Lord has taught us in his statutes* the revelation of himself,
as having given his dear Son for us and to us, " the tongue
of the dumb is made to sing." (Isa. xxxv. 6.) " Thanks
be to God for his unspeakable gift!" (2 Cor. ix. 15.)

And do I not remember " the time of love," when I first
knew myself to be " a brand plucked out of the fire"— a
redeemed sinner — a pardoned rebel — destined for a seat on
the throne of God — indulged with a taste, and assured of
the completion, of heavenly bliss ? This was a work worthy
of God — a work, which none but God could have wrought.
What *mercy* is this! Everlasting! Unchangeable! Let me
cast myself daily upon it ; yea, let me bury myself in it!
What gratitude is demanded! *My lips shall utter praise,*
now that he has taught me his statutes. " O Lord, I will praise
thee ; though thou wast angry with me, thine anger is
turned away, and thou comfortedst me." (Isa. xii. 1.)

Again — I seemed to have sunk beyond all help. No
means, no ministers, no providences, could reach my extremity. All were " physicians of no value" (Job, xiii. 4),
tried and tried again : but tried in vain. But " in weakness" thoroughly felt, " strength was made perfect." (2
Cor. xii. 9:) The threatening clouds were dispersed ; the
breaches were healed ; the veil of unbelief was rent. " The
right hand of the Lord hath brought mighty things to
pass." (Ps. cxviii. 16. Prayer-book version) — " He hath
both spoken unto me, and himself hath done it " (Isa.
xxxviii. 15), and it is " marvellous in our eyes." (Ps. cxviii.
23.) Let my stammering *lips utter praise.* What a display of *power !* It is the spark preserved in the ocean
unquenched, the drop in the flames unconsumed ; the
feather in the storm unshaken. " Who is a God like unto
thee ? Not unto us, O Lord, not unto us ; but unto thy
name give glory." (Mic. vii. 18. Ps. cxv. 1.)

And again — I was perplexed in a dark and bewildered
path. Every dispensation appeared to frown upon me.
One dark hour had blotted out all the recollections of my
former comforts ; and it was as if I never could, never
should, rejoice again. But little did I think how the Lord
was " abounding towards me in all wisdom and prudence "

(Eph. i. 8)—how his arrows were sharpened with love—
how he was " humbling me, and proving me, to know what
was in my heart" (Deut. viii. 2) and in the moment of
chastening was speaking to me—" I know the thoughts
that I think towards you, thoughts of peace, and not of
evil, *to give you an expected end.*" (Jer. xxix. 11.)   What a
display of " *wisdom !*"   *My lips shall utter praise ;* for if I
" should hold my peace, the stones would immediately cry
out." (Luke, xix. 40.)

The thought of what I was before my conversion—
what I have been since—what I am now, overwhelms me
with shame and with praise.   " Lord, how is it that thou
shouldst have manifested thyself to me, as thou hast not
unto the world?"   " Who am I, O Lord God, that thou
hast brought me hitherto?"   And how much more " that
thou hast spoken of thy servant for a great while to come !"
(2 Sam. vii. 18, 19.)   For thou hast prepared for me a
happy eternity in thy unclouded presence.   Should not
then my praise be bubbling up, as from a fountain (Ps. xlv.
1. M. R.)—pouring forth, as from a rich treasure-house?
(Matt. xii. 34.)   Should not my instrument, if not always
employed, be always kept in tune? (Ps. lvii. 7 ; cviii. 1.)
Forward we may be in prayer.   But how backward we are
in praise !   Self-love may constrain the one.   Only the
love of God will quicken the other.   And yet ought we not
to be more touched in receiving mercies, than we were in
asking for them?   In the one case we only knew them by
testimony or report.   In the other we know them by our
own experience.   We hear of one, who had much forgiven,
and who " loved much." (Luke, vii. 47.)   And surely the
more sin pardoned—the more mercies received—does not
God justly expect of us more love in the heart—more
utterance of praise from the lips?

And yet who of us are fit to *praise,* except those whom
God has taught?   The " new song" ill accords with the old

heart.   God vouchsafes his grace for the praise of his grace. (Eph. i. 12. 1 Pet. ii. 9.)   Ought not we then to glory in our Saviour—a privilege as high as to enjoy him—nay—the very means of increasing our enjoyment of him, in the active excitement of our love, and every grace for his sake?   Let not the enemy rob me, as too often he has done, of my high privilege.   Let me prize secret prayer.   Let me be separated from an ensnaring world.   Let me dread separation from my God ; and if ever estranged from him, let me never rest, until, by " receiving the atonement," always presented and accepted on my behalf, I once more walk in the light of his countenance.   Let me then fix the eye of my faith, weak and dim as it may be, constantly upon Jesus.   He must do all for me, in me, by me ; he must *teach* me more and more of the *statutes* of my God, that my heart may be delightfully engaged with *my lips in uttering his praise.*

172. *My tongue shall speak of thy word; for all thy commandments are righteousness.*

To speak of God and for him, will be the desire and delight of him, whose heart and lips have been taught to *utter praise.*   Yet alas ! how seldom is " our conversation seasoned with grace !" (Col. iv. 6.)   So much of this poor world's nothing !   So little of Jesus !   ' If only five minutes can be redeemed for prayer, for Scripture, or for thought ; let it be seized as an inestimable jewel.   If we can pass five minutes less in foolish or ensnaring company, secure the advantage.'*   If vain words are flowing up from the bottom, look on the restraint that represses them from our lips as a triumphant mercy.   This active energy of Christian discipline will communicate a fragrance to our conversation, most acceptable to our beloved Lord (Cant. iv. 11) ; and

* Nottidge's Correspondence, p. 350.

will make our "lips" enriching (Prov. x. 20), feeding (Prov. x. 21), and instructive (Prov. xv. 7) to his church. And truly when we see how hardly men judge of him, how they count his "commandments grievous," and his ways "unequal" (Ezek. xviii. 25), it will be delightful to bear our testimony, that *all his commandments are righteousness;* restraining the power of sin, and conforming the soul to his image.

"Lord, open thou my lips, that my *tongue may speak of thy word.*" Honour me, O my God, by helping me to show, that *all thy commandments are righteousness.* In our own atmosphere, and our own spirit, how often do we pour out our words without waiting on the Lord for unction and power; speaking of the things of God without his presence and blessing! Were we living fully in the atmosphere and breathing of prayer, enriched with habitual meditation in the word; how much more fluent would our tongue be to *speak of his word* "to the use of edifying!" (Eph. iv. 29, with Col. iii. 16.) It would be made really our own, known experimentally; and then how cheering, how enlivening the conversation of the man of God! His "light so shines before men, that" they are constrained to "glorify his Father which is in heaven." (Matt. v. 16.)

Perhaps, Believer, *supposed* inability, natural bashfulness, or want of seasonable opportunity, may restrain your lips. But under the most unfavourable circumstances something may generally be said or done in the service of God. And whilst it is well carefully to watch against the "talk of the lips, which tendeth only to penury" (Prov. xiv. 23); beware, lest, through the scrupulous tenderness of conscience, "Satan get advantage" to shut the mouth of the faithful witnesses of God, and thus to weaken that cause, which it is your first desire to support.* Guard then

---

* It was an excellent saying of Archbishop Usher, when in the society of his friends—' A word of Christ before we part.'

against the influence of unbelief. Bring your weakness and inability daily to the Lord. Let any dreaded inconsistency of profession be searched out, examined, and lamented before him, and opposed in dependence on his grace ; but never let it be made a covering for indolence, or supply fuel for despondency. Consider how your interest in a Divine Saviour makes your way open to bring all your wants to him. Be encouraged therefore to ask for the Spirit of God to guide your lips : that a poor weak sinner may be permitted to " show forth the praises of Him," who is surrounded with all the Hosts of Heaven.

When however our silence has arisen from the too feeble resistance of our natural carelessness and indolence, the recollection of many important opportunities of glorifying our Saviour, lost beyond recall, may well excite the prayer, " Deliver me from blood-guiltiness, O God ; and my tongue shall sing aloud of thy righteousness." (Ps. li. 14.) Oh ! to have the preciousness of souls deeply impressed upon our hearts ! Oh ! for that compassionate love, that would never suffer us to meet a fellow-sinner without lifting up our hearts to God on his behalf : without making an effort to win his soul to Christ, and manifesting an earnest desire for his salvation ! What loss is there to our own souls in these neglected opportunities of blessing the souls of others ! For never do we receive richer fruit to ourselves, than in the act or endeavour to communicate to others. The heart becomes enlarged by every practical exercise of Christian love. Yet much simplicity, much unction from above, much tenderness of heart, much wisdom combined with boldness — is needed in our daily conversation, that we may " make manifest the savour of the knowledge of Christ in every place" (2 Cor. ii. 14) ; and especially, that our very desires to bring sinners to the Gospel may proceed, not from a goading conscience, much less from pride and vainglory ; but from the pure source of love to Christ and to

our fellow-sinners. For even if we are as " full of matter"
as Elihu (Comp. Job, xxxii. 18–20) was, nothing will be
said for God—nothing, that will "minister grace to the
hearers," unless the influence of the Divine Spirit fills our
hearts (Comp. Eph. v. 18, 19), as " a well of water, springing up into everlasting life" (John, iv. 14)—a blessing to
all around us.

173. *Let thy hand help me: for I have chosen thy precepts.*

David, having engaged himself to a bold profession of
his God, now comes to seek his needful supply of *help. Let
thine hand help me.* And if we may " come to the throne of
grace," that we may find " grace to help *in time of need*"
(Heb. iv. 16), when should we not come ? For is not every
moment a " time of need," such as may quicken us to flee
to the " strong tower," whither " the righteous runneth,
and is safe?" (Prov. xviii. 10.) Besieged without ; be-
trayed within ; " wrestling against flesh and blood," and yet
" not against flesh and blood" only (Eph. vi. 12) : disput-
ing every inch of ground, yet often discouraged by the
little ground we seem to gain ; surely we need all the help
of Omnipotence to sustain us in the tremendous conflict.
We may plead our *choice of his precepts*, in looking for his
help. (Verse 94.) David had before " taken the *testimonies*
of God as his heritage" (Verse 111) — including all the precious promises of the Gospel, extending to every necessity
of time, and to every prospect of eternity. He now con-
fesses his obligation, *in choosing the precepts*—a happy
choice, the influence of the Spirit upon his heart. (See
Ezek. xi. 19, 20.)
This choice is the distinctive mark of the Lord's people
(Isa. lvi. 4) — the exercise of a well-instructed and deliberate judgment ; prompt obedience in the simplicity of faith.
It is *the choice of all the precepts*—no other than the volun-

tary acknowledgment of our Baptismal obligations. Many
carnal suggestions offer themselves the moment that the
purpose is forming into the choice. " The things that were
gain to us," and which now must be " counted loss for
Christ" (Philip. iii. 7), (should we allow their weight in the
balance at this crisis) will bring much hesitation and perplexity. Conferences "with flesh and blood" are most
subtle hindrances to Christian determination. (Comp.
Gal. i. 16.) 'What will the world say? If I go too far,
I shall give offence; I shall lose all my influence, and blast
all my prospects of eventual benefit to those around me.'
The apprehension also of losing the affection and of incurring the displeasure of those whom my heart holds dear,
is most fearful. And then this sacrifice is too costly to
make; that pleasure too hard to resign. Such thoughts—
the injections of the tempter—are ever at the door; and
even when effectual resistance is offered, the struggle is
most severe. But it is such a mighty help in this conflict,
when one desire has taken sole possession of the heart—
" Lord, what wilt thou have me to do?" (Acts, ix. 6)—
when we are so crucified to worldly influence, whether of
pleasure, profit, fear, or esteem, as to be ready to act upon
the resolution—" Wherefore henceforth know we no man
after the flesh." (2 Cor. v. 16.) *Now* the heavenly beauty
of the religion of the gospel breaks in upon us.

Experience of our own weakness, and of the great power
of the world, is gradually preparing us for victory over it.
We shall then most specially find our happiness in losing
our own will; and our Master's cross will be a delightful
burden; like wings to a bird, or sails to a ship; assisting,
instead of retarding, our course. The more we trust to his
help and guidance in everything, the more we shall be able
to do, and the more delightful will his service be to us.

The want of a determined choice is the secret of the
halting profession that prevails among us. A compromise

is attempted with the world. " The offence of the cross" begins to " cease." A middle path of serious religion is marked out, divested of what is called *needless offensiveness*. But the religion that pleases the world will never be acceptable with God ; nor can the religion that pleases God, be ever accommodated to the inclination of the world. Oh ! we shall do well to consider, whether the way of *the Lord's precepts* may not be found too hard, too strait, too unfrequented ; whether we are prepared to brave the pointed finger and whispered scoff of the ungodly, and perhaps the mistaken opposition of beloved friends. (Comp. Luke, xiv. 26.) Often has the profession of Christ been hastily taken up and relinquished. (Comp. Matt. viii. 19, 20.) He that wishes to abide by it, must daily learn this lesson—" *Without me ye can do nothing*" (John, xv. 5) : and in conscious helplessness, he will often breathe the cry — *Let thine hand help me.*

Nor is this petition needful only in the first determination of this choice. In the growing and more decided conviction of its superior happiness, and in the daily endeavour to live in it, we shall find increasing need for the same acknowledgment of helplessness, and the same cry for support. Dependence is a principle of deep humility and mighty energy. The thought that we are entering upon the work in the Lord's strength is a great stay. Blessed indeed is that helplessness, that makes us lie in the bosom of our Saviour, supported and cherished ! Blessed be God for the " help laid" for us " upon one that is mighty" (Ps. lxxxix. 19) ; so that our insufficiency and all-sufficiency are visible at one glance : and " when we are" most " weak, then are we" most " strong !" (2 Cor. xii. 10.) " They that war against thee shall be as nothing, and as a thing of nought. For I the Lord thy God will hold thy right hand, saying unto thee, *Fear not, I will help thee.*"*

* Isa. xli. 12, 13. Comp. the whole passage, verses 10–16.

174. *I have longed for thy salvation, O Lord; and thy law is my delight.*

Before we close this Psalm, let us dwell once more upon this word—*salvation*. Common as is its use, to the believer it has a constant freshness and an infinite meaning. Do we wonder at his *longing for it? Look at its fulness*— including all the mercy of the everlasting covenant. *Look at its ground*—that work of Calvary's cross once "finished" (John, xix. 30), and leaving nothing to be filled up or improved; standing out in all its glorious completeness; constraining the admiration, and encouraging the confidence, of the chief of sinners; but wholly disclaiming all assistance from the most eminent saint. *Look at its simplicity* —not keeping the sinner aloof from the Saviour, not hedging up or bewildering the open freeness of his path, but bringing to him immediate peace and joy in resting upon the great atonement of the gospel. (See Acts, ii. 37–47 ; viii. 5–8, 39 ; xvi. 31–34. 1 Thess. i. 6.) *Mark its unchangeableness*—independent of and above all frames and feelings, so that, while "walking in darkness" we can " stay upon our God" (Isa. l. 10), expecting salvation even from the hand that seems ready for our destruction (Job, xiii. 15) ; leaving it to our heavenly Father to frown or to smile, to change as he pleaseth from the one to the other ; and looking at every aspect of his countenance, as only a different arrangement of the same features of ineffable paternity ; and the different, suitable, and seasonable expression of unchangeable covenant love.

Is not this an object for the *longing* of the soul, that feels its own pressing wants, and sees in this *salvation* an instant and full supply ? This *longing* marks the character of evangelical religion —*not merely duty, but delight.* The mind wearies in the continued exertion *for duty;* but it readily falls in with *delight*. Duties become privileges, when Christ is their source and life. Thus every step of progress is progress in happiness. The world's all to the believer is really nothing. It presents nothing to feed the appetite, or quench the thirst, of an immortal soul. Indeed the creatures were commissioned to withhold consolation, until every desire was concentrated in the single object. " Thou, O God, art the thing that I long for" (Ps. lxxi. 4, P. T.) ; until the sinner has found rest in the answer to his prayer—" *Say unto my soul, I am thy salvation.*" (Ps. xxxv. 3.) And now he enjoys his earthly comforts, " as not abusing them" (1 Cor. vii. 31), because he loves them as God would have them loved, *and longs for his salvation* above them all. This is true religion ; when the Lord of all occupies that place in the heart, which he fills in the universe—*There* he is " All in all." *Here* the believer cries—" *Whom have I in heaven but thee? and there is none upon earth that I desire beside thee.*" (Ps. lxxiii. 25.) Oh, what a privilege is it to have him in heart, in thought, and in view ; to be rejoicing in his presence ; and to be *longing* for a more full conformity to his image, and for a more lively enjoyment of his love ! If this be but earth, what must heaven be ! This *longing* is a satisfactory evidence of the work of God. (See Neh. i. 11.) It exercises the soul in habitual contemplation of the Saviour, in nearer communion with him, and supreme *delight in his law.* Such desires will be unutterably increased, and infinitely satisfied in the ' fruition of his glorious Godhead.'*

But the Lord often brings this charge against his professing people—" *Thou hast left thy first love.*" (Rev. ii. 4.) The principle is not dead, but the energy is decayed. Human nature is prone to apostasy. Slumber unconsciously steals upon the soul. Faith is not in *habitual* exercise. The attraction of the Saviour is not felt. His

* Collect for Epiphany.

love is not meditated upon. The soul is satisfied with former affections to him. There is little heart to labour for him. The means of communion with him are slighted. The heart naturally becomes cold in spiritual desires, and warm in worldly pursuits; and too often without any smitings of conscience for divided love.

Some professors indeed consider this declension of affections to be a matter of course. The young convert is supposed to abound most in love, and, as he advances, his fervour gradually subsides into matured judgment. Those indeed, who "have no root in themselves," lose their lively affections, and their religion with them. (See Matt. xiii. 20, 21.) But surely the *real* principle of love cannot decay; that is, our esteem of God cannot be lowered: our *longing for his salvation* cannot languish; our delight in its enjoyment cannot diminish, without guilt and loss to our souls. He claims our love (See Prov. xxiii. 26), and it is most unreasonable to deny him his own. He is the same, as when we first loved him. Then we thought him worthy of our highest love. Do we now repent of having loved him so much? Have we found him less than our expectations? Can we bestow our heart elsewhere with stricter justice, or to better advantage? Do not all the grounds of our love to him continue in full force? Have they not rather increased every day and hour? What would an indulgent husband think of incessant and increasing attentions repaid with diminished affection? Oh! let us be ashamed of our indolence, and " remember" the times when our *longings for his salvation* were more intense; when our communion with him was more heavenly; when we were ready to labour and suffer for him, and even to die to go home to his presence. Let us "repent" with deeper contrition, and " do our first works" (See Rev. ii. 5): never resting till we can take up afresh the language of delight — *I have longed for thy salvation, O Lord.*

Some, however, of the Lord's dear children are distressed
in the conscious coldness of their spiritual affections. But
if it be a mark of the decay of grace to " lose our first love,"
it is at least a mark of the truth of grace to mourn over
this loss.   There is always a blessing for those " that hunger and thirst after righteousness." (Matt. v. 6.)   These
restless desires are the beating pulse of the hidden life ;
and if there be not always a sensible growth of desire and
enjoyment, there may be (as with the trees in winter)
growth at the root, in a more fixed habit of grace and love,
in a deeper spirit of humility, and in a more established
self-knowledge and simplicity.   Yet the shortest way of
peace will be to look off from our *longing for this salvation*,
to the salvation itself. (See Heb. xii. 2, Gr.)   For nothing
is more desecrating to this great work — nothing is more
paralyzing to its saving power, than the incorporating with
it the admixture of our own experience as the ground of
hope.   The most Christian feelings must find no place at
the foundation.   Indeed their continual variation renders
them, especially in the hour of temptation, very uncertain.
Yet amid all these fluctuations, Christ may always be safely
trusted.   While therefore our coldness humbles us before
him, let not brooding despondency cover his precious cross
from view.   Let not our eyes be so filled with tears of contrition, as to obscure the sight of his free and full salvation.   " Looking" singly " unto Jesus " as our peace and
our life, is at once our duty, our safety, and the secret principle of our daily progress heavenward.   We shall but
realize the perception of our own emptiness in the contemplation of his unbounded fulness.

But the connexion between *longing for salvation*, and
delight in the law, is at least an incidental evidence, that
right apprehensions of *salvation* must be grounded upon
the word or *law of God;* and that a religion of feeling is
self-delusion.   Our *delight* is not only *in his love*, but *in*

his law. And so practical is Christian privilege, that *longing for salvation* will always expand itself in habitual *delight in the law:* which in its turn will enlarge the desire for the full enjoyment of *salvation.* All spiritual desire therefore, that is not practical in its exercise, is impulse, excitement ; not, as in this man of God, the religion of the heart ; holiness, *delight.*

Would that this beautiful Psalm might quicken us to be followers of him, who evidently knew so much of the heavenly joys of religion ! Why should we not, why do we not determine to know as much of God as we can ? Why are our *longings for his salvation* so transient and so few ? The religion of thousands who bear the name is of a very different stamp ; empty instead of solid ; withering instead of profitable ; insipid instead of delightful. If there be any exercise, it is only " the door turning upon hinges " (Prov. xxvi. 14), movement without progress. The head is stored with knowledge, but there is no unction in the heart, " ever learning, and never able to come to the knowledge of the truth." (2 Tim. iii. 7.)

But the soul that really *longs* shall " not be ashamed of its hope." Even to taste the present fruits (though it be but a taste) in a sense of reconciliation, liberty of access, a beam of the love of Jesus in the heart, is unutterable enjoyment. It strengthens the soul for endurance of trials, and for a devoted, self-denying, obedient service. But there are heights and depths of Divine love yet unexplored. (Eph. iii. 18, 19.) He who has vouchsafed large apprehensions of them to others, " is rich in mercy to *all that call upon him.*" (Rom. x. 12.) The fountain of everlasting love is ever flowing, ever full ; and he who commands us to " open our mouths wide," has promised—" I will fill them." (Ps. lxxxi. 10.) After all, however, the grand consummation is the object, to which these *longings for salvation* stretch with full expansion. The fulness (Eph. iii. 19) and likeness of

God (Ps. xvii. 15 ; Phil. iii. 20, 21) ; the complete and
everlasting deliverance from sin (Rom. viii. 23 ; 2 Cor. v.
1–8) ; the glorious "manifestation of the sons of God"
(Rom. viii. 19–21) ; the coming of the Lord. (Rev. xxii.
20.) Then—not till then—will they be fully and eternally satisfied. Praised be God! "Now is our salvation
nearer than when we believed."*

Lord of all power and might! create in our souls a
more intense *longing for thy salvation*, and a more fervent
delight in thy law. And as our *longings for thy salvation*
increase, oh ! nail us to the door-posts of thy house, that we
may be thy happy servants for ever !

175. *Let my soul live, and it shall praise thee ; and let thy
judgments help me.*

There must be *life*, in order to *praise.* For how can
the dead speak ? Yet is it as natural for the *living* soul
to *praise*, as for the living man to speak. And is not *thé
life* that the Psalmist is now praying for, the *salvation* for
which he was *longing?* The taste that he has received
makes him hunger for a higher and continued enjoyment ;
not for any selfish gratification, but that he might employ
himself in *the praise of his God.* Indeed, the close of this
Psalm exhibits that pervading character of praise which
has been generally remarked in the concluding Psalms of
this sacred book.† Yet he alone is fitted for this heavenly

* Rom. xiii. 11. 'This salvation has been the object of the
hopes, the desires, and *longing* expectation of the faithful, from
Adam to this hour; and will continue so to be, until he, who hath
already visited us in great humility, shall come again in glorious
majesty, to complete our redemption, and take us to himself.'—
BISHOP HORNE. Comp. also SCOTT *in loco.*

† Verses 164, 171, 172. The last six Psalms are for the most
part throughout the breathings of praise. They were probably
written at the close of life, and may be considered as striking in-

exercise, of whom it has been said—" This my son was dead, and is alive again." (Luke, xv. 24.) And how will he, who has " looked to the hole of the pit whence he was digged" (Isa. li. 1), who has been awakened to a sight of that tremendous gulf, from which he is but "scarcely saved" (1 Pet. iv. 18), long to give utterance to the effusions of a praising heart! How will he cry for the quickening influence of " the Lord and Giver of life," to stir him up to this delightful privilege! Praise springs from prayer—*Let my soul live, and it shall praise thee.* When the breathing of *life into our souls* enlivens our services, we become, in the noblest sense, " living souls." (Gen. ii. 7.)

Too often, however, the consciousness of inconsistency, carelessness, and unspirituality, damps our song. But let every recollection of our sin be accompanied with an humble yet assured confidence in the Lord's pardoning grace. The abominations of a desperately wicked and unsearchably deceitful heart may well lead us to " abhor ourselves in dust and ashes." (Job, xlii. 6.) Yet in the lowest depths of abasement, the Saviour's blood, applied to the conscience, " cleanseth from all sin." (1 John, i. 7.) He who once " passed by us, and saw us polluted in our blood, and said unto us, when we were in our blood, Live" (Ezek. xvi. 6) —still " holdeth our souls in life" (Ps. lxvi. 9) ; covering our daily infirmities, and maintaining our everlasting acceptance before God.

But while the song of *praise* dwells on our lips for life thus freely given, let us guard against all hindrance to its growth and influence. For if the life within waxes low, praise will be dull and heartless. But when the assured

dications of a soul ripening for glory. As the perfumes of Arabia Felix are said to exhale their odours in the neighbouring provinces ; so it is no marvel, if, as " the sweet Psalmist of Israel" drew near to the happy country, he should have inhaled its atmosphere of praise.

believer cries with acceptance—*Let my soul live, and it shall praise thee*—see how his spirit kindles with holy fire —" Blessed be the God and Father of our Lord Jesus Christ, which according to his abundant mercy hath begotten us again unto a lively hope by the resurrection of Jesus Christ from the dead!"* The work of praise is now his nature, his element, his delight. No wonder, then, that he continues his cry for the daily renewal of his spiritual life, that he may return to this sweet antepast of heaven — *Let my soul live.* And, indeed, this *life*—the more it is known, the more will it form the constant matter for prayer. For what besides makes existence tolerable to a child of God? The mere actings of a sickly pulsation can never satisfy him. Considering how much nearer he might live to God than he has yet known, he longs for more vigorous influence of the Divine principle. In his most active enjoyments, his insufficiency for this sacred work presses upon him, and stirs up petition for help— *Let thy judgments help me.* Give me such an enlightened apprehension of thy word, of thy character, and of thy perfections as the God of my salvation, as may furnish abundant matter of unceasing praise; so that my daily exercise may be—" Giving thanks always for all things unto God and the Father, in the name of our Lord Jesus Christ." (Eph. v. 20.)

176. *I have gone astray like a lost sheep: seek thy servant; for I do not forget thy commandments.*

The natural disposition to wander from the fold is con-

---

* 1 Pet. i. 3. ' It is sufficient for me'—said Luther—triumphing in the very heat of conflict —' that I have a precious Redeemer —a powerful High Priest—my Lord Jesus Christ. I will praise him as long as I have breath. If another will not join me in praising with me, what is that to me?'—D'AUBIGNÉ's History of the Reformation, Book iv. ch. i.

stant ground for prayer for the *help of the Lord's judgments*,
to give us clearer light and preserving principles. Yet our
need of this safeguard opens to us a most humbling truth.
Who can gainsay the testimony from the mouth of God—
that " all *we like sheep have gone astray?*" (Isa. liii. 6.) But
how afflicting is the thought, that this should not only be
the description of a world living without God, but the confession even of God's own people! And yet where is the
child of God that does not set his own seal with shame to
the confession—*I have gone astray like a lost sheep?* " Who
can understand his errors?" If he be not found, like
Peter, in the open path of wandering ; yet has he not need
to cry—" Cleanse thou me from secret faults?" (Ps. xix.
12.)   Is he never led away by sense, fancy, appetite? If
the will be sincere, how far is it from being perfect! And
only a little yielding, a little bending to the flesh, giving
way to evil—who knoweth what may be the end of this
crooked path? Who knoweth what pride, waywardness,
earthliness, may be working within, even while the gracious
Lord is strengthening, guiding, comforting his poor *stray-
ing sheep?* That they should ever wander from privileges
so great, from a God so good, from a Shepherd so kind!
What can induce them to turn their backs upon their best
Friend, and sin against the most precious love that was
ever known, but something that must, upon reflection, fill
them with shame! The blame is readily cast upon the
temptations of Satan, the seductive witcheries of the world,
or some untoward circumstances. But whoever deals with
himself must trace the backsliding to his own heart—
" This is *my* infirmity." (Ps. lxxvii. 10.) And have we
replaced what we have wilfully yielded up, with anything
of equal or superior value? May it not be asked of us—
" What fruit had ye in those things, whereof ye are
now ashamed ; for the end of those things is death."
(Rom. vi. 21.)

But there is no enjoyment while distant from the be-

loved fold. It is as impossible for the child of God to be
happy, when separated from his God, as if he were in the
regions of eternal despair. He has not lost — he cannot
wholly lose — his recollection of the forsaken blessing. In
struggling, weeping faith, he cries — *Seek thy servant.* ' I
cannot find my way back : * the good Shepherd must *seek*
me. Once I knew the path : but now that I have wandered into bye-paths, I am no more able to return, than I
was to come at first. I have no guide but the Shepherd
whom I have left.' How cheering, then, is his office character! — " Behold I, even I, will both search my sheep,
and seek them out : as a shepherd seeketh out his flock in
the day that he is among his sheep that are scattered ; so
will I seek out my sheep, and will deliver them out of all
places where they have been scattered in the cloudy and
dark day" (Ezek. xxxiv. 11, 12.) Cannot I set my seal
to his faithful discharge of his office — " He restoreth my
soul?" (Ps. xxiii. 3.)

If I want further encouragement to guide my steps
homeward, let me think of his own description of tender
faithfulness, and compassionate yearnings over his lost
sheep ; not showing it the way back to the fold, and
leaving it to come after him : but " laying it upon his
own shoulders, and bringing it home :" all upbraidings
forgotten ; all recollection of his own pains swallowed up
in the joy, that he hath " found the sheep which was lost."
(Luke, xv. 4–6.) Let me remember the express commission, that brought the Shepherd from heaven to earth,
from the throne of God to the manger, and thence to the
garden and cross, " to seek and to save that which was
lost." (Luke, xix. 10.) Let me see upon him the especial
mark of " the Good Shepherd, giving his life for the sheep."
(John, x. 11.) Let me observe this sacrifice, as covering

* ' Domine, errare potui ; redire non potui'—was Augustine's
true and humbling confession.

the guilt of my wanderings, and opening my way to return
—yea, drawing me into the way. (Isa. liii. 5, 6.) Surely then,
I may add to my contrite confession the prayer of confidence
— *seek thy servant.* I cannot forbear to plead, that though
a rebellious prodigal, I am still *thy servant,* thy child : I
still bear the child's mark of an interest in thy covenant.
Though a wanderer from the fold, *I do not forget thy commandments.* Nothing can erase thy law, which was " written
in my mind and inward parts" (Jer. xxxi. 33) by the finger
and Spirit of God, as an earnest of my adoption, as the
pledge of my restoration. What man writes is easily
blotted out ; what God writes is indelible. Let me then
lie humbled and self-abased. But let me not forget my
claim — what has been done for me. Thus, again, I hope
to be received as a " dear" and " pleasant child" (Ib. verse
20) ; again to be clothed with " the best robe," to be wel-
comed with fresh tokens of my Father's everlasting love
(Luke, xv. 22, 23), and to be assured with the precious
promise — " My sheep shall never perish, and none shall
pluck them out of my hand." (John, x. 28.)

Such, Christian reader, would be the application we
should make of this verse to ourselves ; and such a penitent confession of our backslidings, united with a believing
dependence on the long-tried grace and faithfulness of our
God, would form a suitable conclusion to our meditations
on this most interesting Psalm. We would unite the publican's prayer with the great Apostle's confidence ; and, while
in holy brokenness of heart we would wish to live and die,
smiting upon our breast, and saying, " God be merciful to
me a sinner" (Luke, xviii. 13): the remembrance of our
adoption warrants the expression of assurance — " I know
whom I have believed, and am persuaded that he is able
to keep that which I have committed to him against that
day." (2 Tim. i. 12.) Yet, as it regards the experience of
David, is there not something striking, and we had almost

said, unexpected, in the conclusion of this Psalm? To
hear one, who has throughout been expressing such holy
and joyful aspirations for the salvation of his God, such
fervent praises of his love, that we seem to shrink back
from the comparison with him, as if considering him
almost on the verge of heaven—to hear this "man after
God's own heart," sinking himself to the lowest dust,
under the sense of the evil of his heart, and his perpetual
tendency to wander from his God, is indeed a most instructive lesson. It marks the believer's conflict sustained
to the end : the humility, and yet the strength, of his confidence ; the highest notes of praise combining with the
deepest expressions of abasement—forming that harmony
of acceptable service, which ascends "like pillars of
smoke" (Cant. iii. 6) before God. And thus will our
Christian progress be chequered, until we reach the regions of unmixed praise, where we shall no longer mourn
over our wanderings, no longer feel any inclination to err
from him, or the difficulty of returning to him—where we
shall be eternally safe in the heavenly fold, to "go no
more out." (Rev. iii. 12.) For " HE THAT SITTETH ON THE
THRONE SHALL DWELL AMONG THEM : THEY SHALL HUNGER
NO MORE, NEITHER THIRST ANY MORE : NEITHER SHALL THE
SUN LIGHT ON THEM, NOR ANY HEAT. FOR THE LAMB WHICH
IS IN THE MIDST OF THE THRONE SHALL FEED THEM, AND
SHALL LEAD THEM UNTO LIVING FOUNTAINS OF WATERS : AND
GOD SHALL WIPE AWAY ALL TEARS FROM THEIR EYES."
(Rev. vii. 15–17.)

INDEX.

484 INDEX.

Undefiled way, 1
———— privileges of, 2
Understanding, spiritual, 186, 250, 257, 353, 383
Unenlightened conscience. See Conscience.
Ungodly, duty to, 416
Upholding grace, 298
Usher, Archbishop, quoted, 465 n.

Vain thoughts, 285
———— distress of, 286
———— encouragement under, 288
Vanity of the world, 89, 187
—— resistance to, 91
Venn, Rev. H., quoted, Preface xiii. n.
Vows, religious, 266
—— advantages of, 267
—— evangelical character of, 269

Waiting faith. See Trials of Faith.
Walking before God. See Believer.
Watchfulness, importance of, 89
Ways of God, liberty of. See Liberty.
———— pleasures of, 117
—— of lying. See False Ways and Lying.
Weariness and duties consistent with grace, 99
Wholeness of heart, 4, 20, 144, 179. See Integrity.
Wicked, character of, 369, 407
———— compassion due to. See Compassion.
———— condition of, 304, 406, 408
Wisdom, spiritual. See Understanding.
Word of God, its application to our need, 30, 125 n.

Word of God, authority of, 249, 420, 421
———— cleansing power of, 18, 372
Word, delight of believer. See Believer.
—— foundation of, 230, 396
—— fulness of, 62, 81, 334
—— harmony of, 8
—— hid in the heart, 22
—— holiness of, 252, 255, 372, 377
—— hope of believer. See Hope.
—— light of. See Light.
—— names of, Preface xii.
—— quickening power. See Quickening.
—— reverence of, 227, 424
—— riches of, 326
—— support of, 122, 220, 234, 378, 380
—— sweetness of, 249
—— truth of, 398, 418, 420
—— wonders of, 38, 334, 335 n.
Works of creation. See Creation.
———— new creation, 5, 189
———— redemption. See Redemption.
World, awful state of, 132, 359
—— compassion due to, 306, 360
—— emptiness of, 187, 243, 321
Worldly conformity. See Conformity.
———— sorrow. See Affliction.

Young Christian encouraged, 437
———— warned, 412, 432
—— persons addressed, 115
Youth, corruption of heart from. See Corruption.

Zeal, Christian, 324, 366, 389, 416
—— false, 366